ST(P) MATHEMATICS 5A

ST(P) MATHEMATICS series

ST(P) 1A
ST(P) 1B
ST(P) 1A Teacher's Notes and Answers
ST(P) 1B Teacher's Notes and Answers

ST(P) 2A
ST(P) 2B
ST(P) 2A Teacher's Notes and Answers
ST(P) 2B Teacher's Notes and Answers

ST(P) 3A
ST(P) 3B
ST(P) 3A Teacher's Notes and Answers
ST(P) 3B Teacher's Notes and Answers

ST(P) 4A
ST(P) 4B
ST(P) 4A Teacher's Notes and Answers
ST(P) 4B Teacher's Notes and Answers

ST(P) 5A (with answers)
ST(P) 5B (with answers)

ST(P) 5C
ST(P) 5C Copy Masters
ST(P) 5C Teacher's Notes and Answers

ST(P) Resource Book

ST(P)
MATHEMATICS 5A

L. Bostock, B.Sc.

S. Chandler, B.Sc.

A. Shepherd, B.Sc.

E. Smith, M.Sc.

Second Edition

Stanley Thornes (Publishers) Ltd

First Published 1987 by
Stanley Thornes (Publishers) Ltd,
Ellenborough House
Wellington Street
CHELTENHAM GL50 1YD

Reprinted 1988
Reprinted 1989
Reprinted 1990
Reprinted 1991
Second edition 1993
Reprinted 1993

A catalogue record for this book is available from the British Library.

ISBN 0 7487 1601 7

Typeset by Tech-Set, Gateshead, Tyne & Wear
Printed in Great Britain by BPCC Wheatons Ltd, Exeter

CONTENTS

INTRODUCTION

This book completes the work necessary for the written papers in mathematics at the higher tier of most GCSE syllabuses. The contents complete coverage of Level 10 of the National Curriculum.

There is a good deal of material for revision and consolidation. The last chapter contains revision exercises covering Levels 7 to 10 for Attainment Targets 2, 3, 4 and 5. There are also exercises of problems, investigations and practical work that are suitable for practising assessment on Attainment Target 1. Some questions in the main body of the book are suitable for this purpose and these have been marked with an asterisk.

There are a great many straightforward questions and a few that are a little more demanding. The types of question are identified clearly in the exercises.

The first type, indicated by plain numbers, e.g. **8,** are considered to be necessary for consolidation.

The second type, identified by a double underline, e.g. **8,** are more demanding questions.

ACKNOWLEDGEMENTS

The authors and publishers would like to thank the following for permission to include material.

Esso, France: for the French map on page 112

Ordnance Survey: for the English map on page 112

Barclays Bank, for part of a questionnaire on pp. 311–12

Mrs Laura Huxley for the extract from a short story by Aldous Huxley entitled 'Green Tunnel' taken from *Mortal Coil,* published by Chatto and Windus Ltd, on page 422, extract (i)

David Higham Associates for the extract from Graham Greene's novel *It is a Battlefield*, published by Heinemann Ltd, © 1934 Verdant SA, on page 422, extract (ii)

ACKNOWLEDGEMENTS

1 THE LANGUAGE OF MATHEMATICS

The further anyone progresses in mathematics, the more vital it becomes to express ideas precisely and accurately. You may so far have taken the view that if *you* know what you mean, and your answer is correct, then that is all that matters. Sooner or later, however, some of you will need to communicate more advanced ideas to other people so that *they* know *exactly* what you mean.

The ability to use clear, correct, unambiguous mathematical language cannot be acquired overnight. It depends, first of all, on a frame of mind which sees the necessity for meticulous care in expression, and then it must be developed steadily and consistently until it becomes second nature.

For those who are thinking of taking mathematics further, now is the time to begin to develop the skill of using mathematical language correctly. Because this is done by starting at the beginning, inevitably we shall initially be looking at examples that seem almost too trivial to bother with. This should not deter a student with real mathematical potential, for the introduction to rigour which these simple cases give can create the attitude of mind required to use the language fully.

The language of mathematics is a combination of words and symbols, each symbol being the shorthand form for a word or phrase. When the words and symbols are correctly used a piece of mathematical reasoning can be read, as prose can, in properly constructed sentences.

You have already used a fair number of symbols but not, perhaps, always with enough care for their precise meaning. As we now take a look at some familiar symbols we find that some can be translated correctly in more than one way.

THE USE AND MISUSE OF SYMBOLS AND WORDS

First consider the elementary symbol $+$.
This can be read as 'plus' or 'and' or 'together with' or 'positive'.

e.g. $3 + 2$ means   3 plus 2   or   3 and 2

$\mathbf{a} + \mathbf{b}$ means   vector $\mathbf{a}$ together with vector $\mathbf{b}$

1

The symbol $-$ has a similar variety of translations.

e.g. $5-4$ means   5 minus 4

$5-(-4)$ means   5 minus 'negative 4'

Now consider $\times$ which can be read as 'multiplied by' or 'times' or 'of'.

e.g. 7×5 means   7 multiplied by 5   or   7 times 5

$\frac{1}{100} \times x$ means   one hundredth of x

Note. When 'times' is used for $\times$, it really means 'lots of', e.g. 3×8 means 3 lots of 8. It is quite incorrect, therefore, to say, 'times 3 by 8' a phrase which teachers often hear, because clearly it is nonsense to write 'lots of 3 by 8'. (This emphasises that 'times' is not a verb.) If we want to use $\times$ as an instruction, the corresponding word must be 'multiply', i.e. '3×8' can read 'multiply 3 by 8'.

The next sign we consider is $=$ which means 'is equal to'. This symbol should be used *only* to link two quantities that are equal in value. Used in this way a short complete sentence is formed, e.g.

$x = 3$ is read as   'x is equal to 3'.

It is very easy to slip into the habit of saying 'equals' or 'equal' instead of 'is equal to'. For instance it is not good English to write 'Let $x = 3$' because this really translates to 'Let x is equal to 3'. While this sort of misuse may seem (and, up to this level, is) trivial it can be serious at a more advanced level and is better avoided altogether.

It is also bad practice to use $=$ in place of the word 'is'. For instance, when defining a symbol such as the radius of a circle we should say 'the radius of the given circle is r cm' and *not* 'the radius of the given circle $= r$ cm', because r cm and the radius are not two separate quantities of equal value; r cm *stands for* the radius.

Of course, if the radius is later found to be 4 cm, it is then correct to say '$r = 4$'.

EXERCISE 1a

In this exercise we give some problems followed by solutions which, although ending with the correct answer, contain nonsense on the way. These solutions have been taken from actual students' work and are examples of very common misuses of language.

In each case criticise the solution, and write a correct version.

1. Simplify $2\frac{1}{2} + 1\frac{1}{4} - 2\frac{1}{3}$.

$$2\frac{1}{2} + 1\frac{1}{4} = 3\frac{3}{4} - 2\frac{1}{3}$$
$$= 1\frac{5}{12}$$

2. Solve the equation $6x + 5 = 3x + 11$.

$$6x + 5 = 3x + 11$$
$$= 3x + 5 = 11$$
$$= \quad 3x = 6$$
$$= \quad x = 2$$

3. Find $\widehat{A}$ when $\sin A = 0.5$

$$\sin A = 0.5$$
$$= 30°$$

4. Write down the formula for the circumference of a circle.

The formula for the circumference of a circle is $2\pi r$.

5. Two angles of an isosceles triangle each measure $70°$. Find the size of the third angle.

$$\text{Third angle} = 70° + 70°$$
$$= 180° - 140°$$
$$= 40°$$

6. Three buns and two cakes cost 54p and five buns and one cake cost 62p. Find the cost of one bun and of one cake.

$$\text{Buns} = x\,\text{p} \qquad \text{Cakes} = y\,\text{p}$$
$$3x + 2y = 54\,\text{p}$$
$$5x + y = 62\,\text{p}$$
$$10x + 2y = 124\,\text{p}$$
$$7x = 70\,\text{p}$$
$$x = 10\,\text{p} \quad \text{and} \quad y = 12\,\text{p}$$

7. $A = \begin{pmatrix} 1 & 2 \\ 3 & 4 \end{pmatrix}$, $B = \begin{pmatrix} 4 & -3 \\ 2 & 1 \end{pmatrix}$.   Find $A + B$.

$$A = \begin{pmatrix} 1 & 2 \\ 3 & 4 \end{pmatrix} + B = \begin{pmatrix} 4 & -3 \\ 2 & 1 \end{pmatrix}$$
$$= \begin{pmatrix} 5 & -1 \\ 5 & 5 \end{pmatrix}$$

SYMBOLS THAT CONNECT STATEMENTS

The symbol $\therefore$, meaning 'therefore', introduces a fact, complete in itself, which follows from a previous complete fact. It is correct to write

$$x^2 = 9$$

$$\therefore \qquad x = \pm 3$$

It is not correct, however, to use $\therefore$ to link the next two lines

$$3x - 4y - 2x + y$$

$$x - 3y$$

Each of these lines is simply an expression, not a complete fact, and in this case we link the lines by the symbol $\Rightarrow$. This means 'giving' or 'which gives', i.e.

$$3x - 4y - 2x + y$$

$$\Rightarrow \qquad x - 3y$$

Note that $\Rightarrow$ can correctly be used as an alternative to $\therefore$, e.g. $\qquad x^2 = 9 \quad \Rightarrow \quad x = \pm 3$

The converse is not always true.

Note also that in the context of Mathematical Logic, the symbol $\Rightarrow$ means 'implies that'.

There are occasions when none of these symbols is absolutely correct, a very simple example being

$$3 = x$$

$$x = 3$$

These two statements give exactly the same information, so neither $\therefore$ nor $\Rightarrow$ is quite right. In this situation it is best to use 'i.e.' ('that is'):

$$3 = x$$

i.e. $\qquad x = 3$

It is quite common to see the word 'or' where we have used 'i.e.'. Although this is not actually wrong it should be treated with caution because 'or' strongly suggests that an *alternative result* is being given, and not just the same result rearranged.

A similar criticism of bad practice can be levelled at the way some people try to give their reasons for steps in a solution. In the solution of a pair of simultaneous equations, for example, we sometimes see

$$3x - 4y = 5 \qquad \times 2$$
$$2x + 7y = 13 \qquad \times 3$$

$$6x - 8y = 10$$
$$6x + 21y = 39$$

These four lines are disjointed, do not really explain what is happening and cannot be read sensibly in words. It is much better to present this piece of work in one of the following ways:

a)
$$3x - 4y = 5 \qquad [1]$$
$$2x + 7y = 13 \qquad [2]$$

$$2 \times [1] \quad \Rightarrow \quad 6x - 8y = 10$$
$$3 \times [2] \quad \Rightarrow \quad 6x + 21y = 39$$

After the initial definition of equations [1] and [2] this now reads '2 times equation [1] gives $6x - 8y = 10$' and '3 times equation [2] gives $6x + 21y = 39$'.

b)
$$3x - 4y = 5 \qquad [1]$$
$$2x + 7y = 13 \qquad [2]$$

$$6x - 8y = 10 \qquad (\text{multiplying } [1] \text{ by } 2)$$
$$6x + 21y = 39 \qquad (\text{multiplying } [2] \text{ by } 3)$$

This version too can be read:
$6x - 8y = 10$; multiplying equation [1] by 2, etc.

Note. In (a) an instruction was given first, describing the operation to be carried out and leading to an equation, whereas in (b) the operation was carried out and then explained.

Either of these approaches can be extended satisfactorily to more advanced mathematics.

MORE USEFUL LINK WORDS

The words and symbols mentioned so far do, in fact, provide sufficient vocabulary to write and read most mathematics at this level, and will continue to be used as the work develops, supplemented by the extra symbols needed for each new area of study.

Even at present, however, variety can be added by a few more words that link or introduce facts.

A traditional, but still useful, one is 'hence' which means 'from this'. It fits nicely into the following type of situation:

Circle A has a radius of 4 cm and circle B has a radius of 2 cm.

Hence the area of circle A is four times that of circle B.

It sometimes happens that, in a solution, one line of thought is pursued for a few steps and then a new idea is introduced. This situation is clearly expressed by the word 'now', as in the following example:

$$2x + 3y = 7 \qquad [1]$$
$$8x - 5y = 11 \qquad [2]$$
$$4 \times [1] \quad \Rightarrow \qquad 8x + 12y = 28 \qquad [3]$$
$$[3] - [2] \quad \Rightarrow \qquad 17y = 17$$
$$\therefore \qquad y = 1$$
$$\text{In } [1], y = 1 \quad \Rightarrow \qquad 2x + 3 = 7$$
$$\Rightarrow \qquad x = 2$$

$\therefore$ the solution of the equations is $x = 2, y = 1$.

Now we know that if two lines, whose equations are given, are plotted on the same axes, the coordinates of their point of intersection satisfy both equations.

Hence the lines with equations $2x + 3y = 7$ and $8x - 5y = 11$, meet at the point $(2, 1)$.

Here is an example showing the use of some of the words and symbols discussed in this chapter.

In the diagram opposite the area of $\triangle PQS$ is 16 cm^2 and the area of $\triangle QRS$ is 9 cm^2. Find the ratio of PQ to QR. Find also the value of PR : PS, using the ratio of the areas of triangles PQS and PSR.

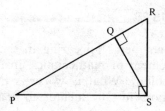

The area of $\triangle PQS$ is given by $\frac{1}{2}PQ \times QS$

$\therefore$ $\qquad\qquad\qquad\qquad$ $\frac{1}{2}PQ \times QS = 16$ $\qquad$ [1]

The area of $\triangle QRS$ is given by $\frac{1}{2}QR \times QS$

$\therefore$ $\qquad\qquad\qquad\qquad$ $\frac{1}{2}QR \times QS = 9$ $\qquad$ [2]

$[1] \div [2]$ $\quad\Rightarrow$ $\qquad\qquad$ $\dfrac{\frac{1}{2}PQ \times QS}{\frac{1}{2}QR \times QS} = \dfrac{16}{9}$

i.e. $\qquad\qquad\qquad\qquad$ $PQ : QR = 16 : 9$

In triangles PQS and PSR

$\qquad\qquad\qquad\qquad$ $P\widehat{Q}S = P\widehat{S}R$ $\qquad$ (both 90°)

$\qquad\qquad\qquad\qquad$ $Q\widehat{P}S$ is common

$\qquad\qquad\qquad\qquad$ $P\widehat{S}Q = P\widehat{R}S$ $\qquad$ (third angles equal)

Hence $\qquad\qquad\qquad\qquad$ $\triangle s \dfrac{PQS}{PSR}$ are similar. $\quad$ (3 pairs of equal angles)

Now the ratio of the areas of similar figures is equal to the ratio of the squares of corresponding sides.

$\therefore$ $\qquad\qquad\qquad\qquad$ $\dfrac{\text{Area } \triangle PSR}{\text{Area } \triangle PQS} = \dfrac{(PR)^2}{(PS)^2}$

$\Rightarrow$ $\qquad\qquad$ $\left(\dfrac{PR}{PS}\right)^2 = \dfrac{\text{Area } \triangle PQS + \text{Area } \triangle QRS}{\text{Area } \triangle PQS}$

$\qquad\qquad\qquad\qquad\qquad\qquad = \dfrac{16 + 9}{16}$

Hence $\qquad\qquad\qquad\qquad$ $\dfrac{PR}{PS} = \sqrt{\dfrac{25}{16}}$

i.e. $\qquad\qquad\qquad\qquad$ $PR : PS = 5 : 4.$

(Where reasons are given in brackets you will need to interpret the first bracket as 'because'...)

SOME MEDIA MISUSES

Sometimes when items appearing in the press or on radio or television contain an element of mathematics, insufficient care is taken to use the correct terminology. What is worse is that there are cases of deliberate misrepresentation in an attempt to make an argument appear to be stronger. It is therefore vital that we do not accept everything we read or hear without carefully considering its true meaning and implications, its accuracy and its honesty.

Here are two examples of careless terminology:

a) In mathematics the word 'plus' is used only when collecting two quantities together, one on either side of 'plus'. However, advertisements often include phrases such as 'Send in your order today and you will have the chance to win £1000. PLUS Steve Stardust will present the cheque to the women.' (To express this correctly, although in a less eye-catching way, we could say 'Send in your order today and you will have the chance to win £1000 plus the chance to have it presented by Steve Stardust'.)

This particular misuse is both grammatically and mathematically wrong. Grammar, however, does tend to change with time and no doubt 'plus' will continue to be used in this way. This does *not* mean, though, that the mathematical definition of 'plus' can be changed, so take care.

b) We often hear a news item saying, for instance, that 'the rate of inflation has fallen by one percentage point'. What is meant is that 'the rate of inflation has fallen by one per cent'. The misuse of 'percentage point' can be very confusing, especially when a decimal point is involved, e.g. if the fall in the rate of inflation is from 4.7% to 3.7%. In fact 'one percentage point' has been understood by at least one person to mean 0.1%.

Keep your eyes and ears open, and see if you can spot more examples of misuse — there are a good many.

EXERCISE 1b

The examples in this exercise are based on actual items culled from radio or television or newspapers. The numbers and names involved may have been changed.

Comment on the use or misuse of mathematical language and, where possible, write a better version.

1. A puzzle in a local evening paper.

   Mrs Antrobus picked up a small rubber ball and said to Mr Baxter, 'Test your powers of deduction on this. If I were to place this ball on a flat surface how many balls of equal size can be placed around it so that they all touch the original ball?'

   Can you deduce the answer?

2. On the 'Today' Programme.

   A Member of Parliament was heard to say that the average profit made by a group of four Public Service Companies was 190%. When queried about this he said that the profits of the four companies were 600%, 50%, 50% and 60%.

3. From an advertisement.

   Pay five times less for your POGO STICK!

4. From a radio broadcast.

   I am determined to raise reading standards so that at least three-quarters of the children are above average standard.

5. From a test for seven year olds.

   Add $4 + 3$, $5 + 5$ and $6 + 2$.

6. From the financial columns of a leading national newspaper.

The 'Wretchedness Index'

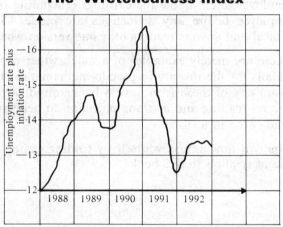

Up and down the Wretchedness Index

The 'Wretchedness Index', which combines the inflation rate with the unemployment rate, expressed in percentage terms, fell last year because of the drop in inflation from 9 per cent to 4.5 per cent. The higher rate of unemployment this year has resulted in a rise in the index from 9.2 per cent to 9.9 per cent between January and August. The fall in the inflation rate since May has helped to keep it down in recent months.

MISCONCEPTIONS

The wrong interpretation of information given in the media can often arise, either from misleading presentation or from misuse of words or from lack of care in reading and considering the information.

The problem of misleading presentation usually occurs when graphs or charts are used to illustrate a situation. Enough has been written already in this series about misleading graphs, so we will not labour that point here. The misuse of words has just been discussed so this too we need take no further.

Therefore we will now consider the importance of careful reading and thoughtful weighing up of news items with a mathematical content.

Take, for example, the statement 'the rate of inflation is falling'. Some people think that this means that prices are coming down, but it doesn't. Inflation means rising prices; the rate of inflation measures how fast they are rising. If the *rate* goes down it simply means that prices do not rise so quickly – but they still keep on rising.

There are areas where conflicting figures are given to represent what is apparently the same thing. In wage negotiations, for example, the pay of a 'typical employee' might vary considerably; a union official might choose the basic wage of the lowest-paid after all possible deductions whereas the employer might quote the earnings (including overtime) of a higher-paid employee before any deductions are made. Clearly neither of these is typical and anyone reading only one version would be misled.

These are merely examples of a much wider problem and there are many pitfalls for the unwary in pseudo-mathematical reporting. The best way to avoid any of these is to have a background of precise language, cautious, careful reading and a strong objection to believing everything you hear or read – even in textbooks.

You can now amuse yourself by finding examples of 'bad practice' in the use of symbols in this book!

2 THE BASIC ARITHMETIC PROCESSES

This chapter is in sections. Each section starts with a set of diagnostic tests, followed by revision material and further practice exercises.

The tests will help you to decide whether revision of a topic is necessary (you should get all the answers correct). It is sometimes difficult to know whether mistakes indicate carelessness or lack of understanding. Remember that accuracy matters, so do not rush these tests, and check your answers for reasonableness and for accuracy.

The chapter ends with a set of mixed exercises. These use the basic processes in a variety of problems and should not be omitted.

WHOLE NUMBERS

Do not use a calculator in these tests.

Test 2A   The Four Rules

Calculate

1. $36 + 27 + 19$	**4.** 215×3	**7.** 199×9
2. $32 - 18$	**5.** $1279 + 398$	**8.** $36 - 51 + 81$
3. $29 - 4 + 7$	**6.** $301 \div 7$	**9.** $2 \times 4 \times 6$

Test 2B   Directed Numbers and Order of Operations

Calculate

1. $7 - 12$	**7.** $4 \div (-2)$	**13.** $(3 - 2)(5 + 1)$
2. -3×4	**8.** $4 - (-5)$	**14.** $6 - 3 \times 4 + 2$
3. -5×-2	**9.** $-4 - 6$	**15.** $4 - 3(2 + 1)$
4. $-2 - 4 + 3$	**10.** $1 + 3 \times 2$	**16.** $-2(76 + 5) \div 9$
5. 6×-2	**11.** $8 \times 3 - 2$	**17.** $3 \times 2 + 7 \times (3 - 5)$
6. $-8 \div 4$	**12.** $4 - 2(1 - 2)$	**18.** $4 + 15 \div 3 + 2$

11

Test 2C   Factors and Multiples

Find the highest number that is a common factor of

1. 4 and 6   **3.** 14 and 21   **5.** 70 and 84

2. 8 and 20   **4.** 35 and 56   **6.** 16, 24 and 40

Find the lowest number that is a common multiple of

7. 2 and 3   **9.** 6 and 5   **11.** 25 and 20

8. 4 and 6   **10.** 12 and 15   **12.** 8, 6 and 15

Express the following numbers as products of their prime factors.

13. 30   **14.** 108   **15.** 3150

THE FOUR RULES

Addition and Subtraction   This is a case in which practice makes perfect. Both speed and accuracy are improved with practice. Check additions by adding in reverse order, i.e. up a column and then down the column, or left to right and then right to left. One way to speed up the addition of a string of numbers is to look for pairs of digits that add up to ten — but be careful that you don't count them in twice.

There are quick ways of adding and subtracting numbers that are close to 100, 200, ..., etc. For example to add 197, you could add 200 and then take 3 away. To subtract 197 you could subtract 200 and then add on 3.

When a calculation involves both addition and subtraction, remember that the additions can be done first. For example, $5 - 6 + 2$ can be done in the order $5 + 2 - 6$.

Multiplication and Division   For speed and accuracy you need to know the multiplication tables.

Remember that multiplication is repeated addition,

e.g. 199×8 means 199 lots of 8.

Hence 199×8 can be calculated by finding 200×8 and subtracting 8, i.e. $199 \times 8 = 1600 - 8 = 1592$.

EXERCISE 2a

Find, without using a calculator

1. $25 + 14 + 72$	**5.** $89 - 17$	**9.** $86 - 21 + 15$
2. $36 + 56 + 125$	**6.** $31 - 19$	**10.** $72 - 95 + 26$
3. $253 + 891$	**7.** $127 - 59$	**11.** $18 + 3 - 15$
4. $1993 + 827$	**8.** $2561 - 290$	**12.** $42 + 15 - 26 - 18$
13. 94×8	**17.** $152 \div 8$	**21.** $2 \times 5 \times 3$
14. 3×506	**18.** $186 \div 6$	**22.** $9 \times 8 \times 7$
15. 297×6	**19.** $135 \div 5$	**23.** $4 \times 3 \times 2 \times 5$
16. 1009×51	**20.** $882 \div 7$	**24.** $3 \times 2 \times 2 \times 5$

DIRECTED NUMBERS AND ORDER OF OPERATIONS

Remember that

negative multiplied by negative
or positive multiplied by positive $\Big\}$ gives a positive result;

negative multiplied by positive
or positive multiplied by negative $\Big\}$ gives a negative result.

The same rules apply to division.

Calculations involving mixed operations must be done in the following order: calculations inside brackets first, multiplication and division next and finally addition and subtraction. Remember that the positive sign at the start of a calculation is often omitted. Also remember that it is the sign before the number that tells you what to do with that number, i.e. $6 \div 2 \times 4$ means $(6 \div 2) \times 4$. It does not mean $6 \div (2 \times 4)$.

EXERCISE 2b

Find, without using a calculator

1. $3 - (-2)$	**5.** $4 - 2(1 - 3)$	**9.** $-2 + 4 - 6$
2. $5 + (-4)$	**6.** $-6 \div -2$	**10.** $-2 \times 4 \times (-6)$
3. $5 \times (-2)$	**7.** $-8 \div 4$	**11.** $(-4)^2$
4. -5×-3	**8.** $-5 - 2$	**12.** $(-1)^2 + (1)^2$

13. $3 + 2 \times 6$ **17.** $(3 + 2) \times 5 - 6$ **21.** $\dfrac{-12}{-3}$

14. $(3 + 2) \times 6$ **18.** $3 - 2 \times 4 - 6 \div 2$ **22.** $-2 \times -3 \times -2$

15. $8 - 5 \times 2$ **19.** $3 \times 2 - 4$ **23.** $5 + 3 - 2 \times 4$

16. $(8 - 5) \times 2$ **20.** $3 - 2 + 4$ **24.** $4 \times (-2)^2$

FACTORS AND MULTIPLES

A *factor* of a number divides exactly into the number. For example, 2, 3, 4 and 6 are factors of 12.

A common factor of two (or more) numbers is a factor of each number. For example, 2, 3 and 6 are common factors of 12 and 18. Further, 6 is the *highest common factor* (HCF) of 12 and 18.

To express a number as the product of its *prime factors,* start by trying to divide by 2 and continue to divide the result by 2 until you no longer can exactly. Then try 3 in the same way, then 5 and so on until you are left with 1.

For example, to express 276 as a product of its prime factors, we test the prime numbers in order:

$$
\begin{array}{r}
2\,\underline{)\,276} \\
2\,\underline{)\,138} \\
3\,\underline{)\ \,69} \\
23\,\underline{)\ \,23} \\
1
\end{array}
$$

therefore $276 = 2 \times 2 \times 3 \times 23$
$= 2^2 \times 3 \times 23.$

A *multiple* of a number has the number as a factor. For example, 6, 9, 12, ... are multiples of 3.

A common multiple of two (or more) numbers has each of these numbers as a factor. For example, 24, 48, ... are common multiples of 6 and 8.

The number used as the common denominator when adding or subtracting fractions should be the lowest common multiple (LCM) of the denominators.

EXERCISE 2c

Find the highest number that is a common factor of

1. 18 and 12   **3.** 15 and 20   **5.** 72 and 18

2. 4 and 8   **4.** 36 and 24   **6.** 36 and 48

Find the lowest number that is a multiple of both

7. 3 and 5   **9.** 6 and 15   **11.** 8 and 12

8. 3 and 6   **10.** 4 and 10   **12.** 14 and 21

In each question from 13 to 16, find (a) the highest common factor, (b) the lowest common multiple, of the given set of numbers.

13. 54, 36 and 24   **15.** 28, 35 and 20

14. 144, 108 and 96   **16.** 63, 18 and 45

Express 1764 as a product of its prime factors and hence find $\sqrt{1764}$ without using a calculator.

```
2)1764
2) 882        ∴     1764 = 2 × 2 × 3 × 3 × 7 × 7
3) 441
3) 147              = (2 × 3 × 7) × (2 × 3 × 7)
7)  49
7)   7        ∴  √1764 = 2 × 3 × 7
     1               = 42
```

Express 600 as a product of its prime factors and hence find the lowest number by which 600 can be multiplied to make a perfect square.

```
2)600
2)300        ∴   600 = 2 × 2 × 2 × 3 × 5 × 5
2)150        Multiplying by 2 × 3 gives an even number of
3) 75        2s and 3s and 5s as factors.
5) 25        600 × 2 × 3 = 2 × 2 × 2 × 2 × 3 × 3 × 5 × 5
5)  5                    = (2 × 2 × 3 × 5) × (2 × 2 × 3 × 5)
    1
```

∴   multiplying 600 by 6 makes a perfect square.

Express as a product of prime factors

17. 24   **19.** 588   **21.** 132   **23.** 234

18. 72   **20.** 300   **22.** 78   **24.** 1800

Express each of the following numbers as a product of its prime factors and hence find its square root.

25. 900   **26.** 196   **27.** 3136   **28.** 1521

Express each of the following numbers as a product of its prime factors and hence find the lowest number by which it can be multiplied to give a perfect square.

29. 75   **30.** 162   **31.** 60   **32.** 11 088

33. a) Cyclist A rides round a circular track taking 12 min to complete each lap. Cyclist B takes 15 mins. If they start together how long will it be before they are together again?

  b) Repeat part (a) if A takes 756 s and B takes 1092 s.

34. Two pieces of tape, of lengths 864 cm and 600 cm, are both to be cut into a number of shorter pieces of equal length.

  a) What is the greatest possible length for each shorter piece if there is to be no tape left over?

  b) How many pieces of tape will there be?

35. Find, without using a calculator, the side of a square field of area 15 876 m^2.

FRACTIONS

Do not use a calculator.

Test 2D   The Four Rules

1. $\frac{1}{3} + \frac{3}{4}$ **6.** $1\frac{2}{7} \times \frac{1}{5}$ **11.** $\frac{2}{3}$ of $1\frac{1}{5}$

2. $\frac{1}{3} \times \frac{3}{4}$ **7.** $\frac{3}{4} \times 5$ **12.** $\frac{1}{2} \div \frac{5}{8} + 1\frac{1}{4}$

3. $\frac{3}{4} - \frac{2}{5}$ **8.** $3\frac{1}{8} - 1\frac{3}{5}$ **13.** $\left(\frac{1}{4} + \frac{2}{5}\right) \times \frac{10}{11}$

4. $\frac{3}{4} \div \frac{2}{5}$ **9.** $\frac{5}{12} + \frac{2}{9} \times \frac{5}{6}$ **14.** $\dfrac{\frac{1}{2} + \frac{1}{3}}{\frac{1}{4} - \frac{1}{5}}$

5. $1\frac{2}{7} + \frac{1}{5}$ **10.** $1\frac{1}{3} \div 3\frac{1}{4}$ **15.** $\left(3 - 1\frac{1}{8}\right) \times \left(\frac{1}{2} + 1\frac{1}{3}\right)$

Addition and subtraction   Before fractions can be added or subtracted, they must be expressed with the *same* denominator. When mixed numbers are involved, the whole numbers can be dealt with first, e.g.

$$2\tfrac{1}{2} - 1\tfrac{2}{3} = 1\tfrac{1}{2} - \tfrac{2}{3} = \tfrac{9}{6} - \tfrac{4}{6} = \tfrac{5}{6}$$

Alternatively, all mixed fractions can be changed to improper fractions, but this has the disadvantage that the numerators can get rather large.

Multiplication and Division   All mixed numbers must be changed to improper fractions for multiplication and division.

Fractions are multiplied by taking the product of the numerators and the product of the denominators.

Whole numbers can be written as fractions, e.g. $5 = \tfrac{5}{1}$.

To divide by a fraction, we multiply by its reciprocal.

For example
$$\tfrac{1}{2} \div \tfrac{2}{5} = \tfrac{1}{2} \times \tfrac{5}{2}$$
$$= \tfrac{5}{4}$$

Remember to cancel any common factors of numerators and denominators.

For mixed operations, remember that calculations inside brackets must be done first. Sometimes brackets are not present but are implied by the way the calculation is written.

For example, to find $\dfrac{\frac{3}{4} + \frac{1}{9}}{\frac{2}{3}}$, the sum in the numerator must be found first

i.e.
$$\frac{\frac{3}{4} + \frac{1}{9}}{\frac{2}{3}} = \left(\tfrac{3}{4} + \tfrac{1}{9}\right) \div \tfrac{2}{3}$$
$$= \left(\tfrac{27 + 4}{36}\right) \times \tfrac{3}{2}$$
$$= \tfrac{31}{36} \times \tfrac{3}{2}$$
$$= \tfrac{31}{24} = 1\tfrac{7}{24}$$

EXERCISE 2d

Find

1. $\tfrac{5}{8} + \tfrac{7}{12}$ **3.** $\tfrac{2}{5} - \tfrac{1}{4}$ **5.** $\tfrac{2}{3} \times \tfrac{9}{10}$

2. $1\tfrac{3}{5} + 3\tfrac{1}{7}$ **4.** $2\tfrac{1}{3} - 1\tfrac{1}{6}$ **6.** $1\tfrac{1}{2} \times 3\tfrac{1}{3}$

7. $2\frac{5}{11} \div 21$

8. $\frac{5}{8} \div 1\frac{1}{5}$

9. $\frac{2}{9} - \frac{5}{6} + \frac{3}{4}$

10. $\frac{2}{5} \times \frac{3}{4} \times 1\frac{1}{2}$

11. $\left(\frac{3}{4} \div \frac{1}{2}\right) \times 1\frac{1}{5}$

12. $1\frac{1}{2} + \frac{2}{5} - 1\frac{1}{3}$

13. $\frac{2}{3} \times \left(-\frac{1}{4}\right)$

14. $\frac{2}{5} \div \frac{10}{11} + \frac{4}{25}$

15. $\frac{1}{2} + \frac{3}{4} \times \frac{1}{5}$

16. $\frac{3}{8}$ of $2\frac{1}{2}$

17. $18 \times 3\frac{2}{9} + 4$

18. $27 \div 2\frac{2}{11}$

19. $\dfrac{\frac{3}{4} - \frac{1}{3}}{\frac{1}{2} \times \frac{1}{4}}$

20. $\dfrac{\frac{1}{4} \times \frac{3}{8}}{\frac{3}{4} \times \frac{1}{12}}$

21. $\dfrac{1\frac{1}{2} + \frac{3}{5}}{\frac{4}{9} - \frac{5}{12}}$

22. $\dfrac{2\frac{1}{2} + \frac{4}{5}}{5\frac{1}{2}}$

23. $\dfrac{\frac{1}{2}}{\frac{3}{4} + \frac{1}{3}} \times \dfrac{\frac{2}{5}}{\frac{1}{3} - \frac{1}{4}}$

24. $\dfrac{1\frac{1}{2} + \frac{1}{8}}{13} \div \dfrac{26}{2\frac{1}{6} \times \frac{3}{4}}$

DECIMALS

Test 2E   The Four Rules

Find, without using a calculator

1. $1.2 - 0.9$

2. $0.03 + 1.2$

3. $5 - 0.79$

4. $1.3 - 2.9 + 0.21$

5. 1.2×0.6

6. 0.01×1.7

7. 15×0.03

8. 0.02×0.8

9. $15 \div 0.3$

10. $2.7 \div 9$

11. $3.2 \div 0.8$

12. $1.2 \div 0.03$

Test 2F   Calculator Work

Use a calculator and give the answer correct to the number of significant figures given in brackets. Use a rough estimate to check your answers.

1. 1.275×0.37 (2)

2. 25.9×362 (2)

3. 589×1902 (3)

4. $270 \div 15.2$ (3)

5. $0.098 \div 1.39$ (3)

6. $\dfrac{0.25 + 1.092}{0.36 \times 1.33}$ (2)

7. 0.1291×1.992 (4)

8. $3.8752 \div 0.77$ (4)

9. $\dfrac{1.37 - 0.0025}{5.89}$ (3)

The four rules without a calculator When adding or subtracting decimals, make sure that tenths are added to tenths etc.

To multiply decimals, first ignore the decimal point and multiply the numbers. Then the number of decimal places in the answer is the sum of the number of decimal places in the original numbers.

To divide by a decimal, that decimal and the number it is being divided into must both be multiplied by the power of the ten that makes the divisor into a whole number. For example $8.1 \div 0.09 = 810 \div 9 = 90$.

EXERCISE 2e

Find, without using a calculator

1.	$1.8 \div 0.03$	**5.**	$0.15 + 1.273$	**9.**	$12 + 0.58$
2.	0.27×0.02	**6.**	$16 \div 0.02$	**10.**	$(0.5)^3$
3.	0.8×0.08	**7.**	$(1.2)^2$	**11.**	$1.72 - 2.45$
4.	$3.7 - 2.91$	**8.**	$9 - 12.4$	**12.**	$0.53 - 0.072$

13. $\dfrac{2.5 \times 0.3}{0.15 \times 5}$ **15.** $\dfrac{2.7 - 1.9}{4 \times 0.2}$ **17.** $(1.8 + 3.6) \div 80$

14. $\dfrac{1.9 + 0.1}{4.1 - 3.6}$ **16.** $\dfrac{5.3 + 0.7}{0.3 \times 0.4}$ **18.** $(6.9 \div 115) \times 15$

Significant figures and decimal places   Many calculations do not have exact answers, and even if they do it is not always necessary to give the exact value. It is usually sufficient to give values correct to the nearest tenth, hundredth, or whatever is required by the context of a problem.

Most problems specify the degree of accuracy required, as, for example, correct to 3 significant figures or correct to 1 decimal place.

Decimal places are easy to identify; the first decimal place is the first digit to the right of the point, and so on. The first significant figure in a number is the first *non-zero* digit reading from left to right.

For example, in both 26.4 and 0.0264 the first significant figure is 2.

The second significant figure is the digit (including zero this time) on the right of the first, and so on for the third and fourth significant figures etc.

For example, 0 is the second significant figure in 2.05 and the third significant figure is 5.

To correct a number to a given number of figures, look at the next figure: if this is 5 or more, add 1 to the previous figure (i.e. round up); if this is less than 5, leave the previous figure alone (i.e. round down).

For example,   3.897 is 3.90 correct to 3 s.f.
and   3.894 is 3.89 correct to 3 s.f.

Rough estimates It is important to have a rough idea of the size of an answer before using a calculator. This can be found by approximating each number in the calculation to one significant figure,

e.g. $$\frac{1.802 + 9.75}{22.3} \approx \frac{2 + 10}{20} \approx \frac{10}{20} = 0.5$$

Remember that it is not necessary to write down all the figures in the display. If an answer is required *correct* to three significant figures, then five significant figures can be written down for any intermediate steps and four significant figures only need be written down before rounding up or down.

EXERCISE 2f

Correct each number to 1 s.f. and hence give a rough answer for

a) $\dfrac{6.623 \times 18.7}{93.4}$ b) $\dfrac{0.534}{6.242 \times 0.819}$ c) $\dfrac{3.72^2 + 8.64^2}{3.72 \times 8.64}$

a) $\dfrac{6.623 \times 18.7}{93.4} \approx \dfrac{7 \times 20}{90} = \dfrac{140}{90} \approx 1.5$

b) $\dfrac{0.534}{6.242 \times 0.819} \approx \dfrac{0.5}{6 \times 0.8} = \dfrac{5}{6 \times 8} = \dfrac{5}{48} \approx \dfrac{5}{50} = 0.1$

c) $\dfrac{3.72^2 + 8.64^2}{3.72 \times 8.64} \approx \dfrac{4^2 + 9^2}{4 \times 9} = \dfrac{16 + 81}{36} = \dfrac{97}{36} \approx \dfrac{100}{40} = 2.5$

Correct each number to 1 s.f. and hence give a rough answer to each of the following calculations.

1. 16.21×0.937

2. $40.34 \div 7.626$

3. $\dfrac{86.05 \times 0.078\,24}{5.95}$

4. $\left(\dfrac{0.7921}{0.4105}\right)^2$

5. $\sqrt{\dfrac{44.75}{14.78}}$

6. $\dfrac{9.26^2 + 2.964^2}{9.26 \times 2.964}$

7. $\sqrt{\dfrac{17.26^2 - 9.64^2}{2 \times 17.26^2 + 4 \times 9.64^2}}$

9. $\sqrt{\dfrac{0.7842}{0.0517}}$

8. $\dfrac{1}{84} + \dfrac{1}{38}$

10. $\dfrac{5.2^2 - 0.98 \times 7.47}{3.14 \times 3.97 - 5.2 \times 1.24}$

The value of T is given by the formula

$$T = 2\pi \sqrt{\dfrac{h^2 + k^2}{hg}}$$

Without using a calculator estimate the value for T when $h = 8.92$, $k = 3.22$, $g = 9.81$ and $\pi = 3.14$. Show clearly the approximations made at each stage of your working.

Writing each value correct to 1 significant figure, $h \approx 9$, $k \approx 3$, $g \approx 10$ and $\pi \approx 3$.

$$\therefore \qquad T \approx 2 \times 3 \sqrt{\dfrac{9^2 + 3^2}{9 \times 10}}$$

$$= 6 \times \sqrt{\dfrac{81 + 9}{90}}$$

$$= 6 \times \sqrt{\dfrac{90}{90}}$$

$$= 6 \times \sqrt{1}$$

$$= 6$$

Therefore the approximate value of T is 6.
(The calculator value is 6.370 correct to 4 s.f.)

In questions 11 to 15 do not use a calculator.

11. The value of E is given by the formula $E = \frac{1}{2}mu^2$.
Estimate E when $m = 12.6$ and $u = 9.21$

12. The value of I is given by the formula $I = \dfrac{m(a^2 + b^2)}{3}$.
Estimate I when $m = 5.92$, $a = 21.4$ and $b = 9.72$

13. The value of T is given by the formula $T = 2\pi \sqrt{\dfrac{l}{g}}$.
Estimate T when $l = 41.3$, $g = 9.81$ and $\pi = 3.142$

14. The value of V is given by the formula $V = (u^2 + v^2)^{1/2}$
Estimate V when $u = 8.24$ and $v = 5.72$

15. Estimate the value of $\sin^2 \alpha + \cos^2 \alpha$ when $\sin \alpha = 0.3907$ and
$\cos \alpha = 0.9205$ [$\sin^2 \alpha$ means $(\sin \alpha) \times (\sin \alpha)$].

USE OF CALCULATORS

Calculators vary so the labels on the buttons on your calculator may be
different from the ones used here. For instance, the button to enter a
number in the memory may be labelled $\boxed{\text{STO}}$ or $\boxed{\text{Min}}$. The button to
retrieve the number in the memory may be labelled $\boxed{\text{RCL}}$ or $\boxed{\text{MR}}$. There
may also be buttons to add or subtract a number to that already stored in
the memory; these are typically labelled $\boxed{\text{M}+}$ and $\boxed{\text{M}-}$.

**If your calculator does not have the keys listed here, or gives different
results, consult your manual.**

If you are asked to find, say, $\dfrac{3+4}{5+1}$ by using a calculator, there are several

different key sequences that can be used.

A. If you think of the expression as $(3+4) \div (5+1)$ then you
might use the keying

$$\boxed{(}\boxed{3}\boxed{+}\boxed{4}\boxed{)}\boxed{\div}\boxed{(}\boxed{5}\boxed{+}\boxed{1}\boxed{)}\boxed{=}$$

B. If you just start at the beginning without thinking of the
calculation as a whole you might key

$$\boxed{3}\boxed{+}\boxed{4}\boxed{=}\boxed{\text{Min}}\boxed{5}\boxed{+}\boxed{1}\boxed{=}\boxed{1/x}\boxed{\times}\boxed{\text{MR}}\boxed{=}$$

realising in the middle that you need to divide by $(5+1)$
and retrieving the situation by using the reciprocal key.

C. If you had thought about the division, then the following
keying might be used:

$$\boxed{5}\boxed{+}\boxed{1}\boxed{=}\boxed{\text{Min}}\boxed{3}\boxed{+}\boxed{4}\boxed{=}\boxed{\div}\boxed{\text{MR}}\boxed{=}$$

D. In an emergency, you might find yourself writing down the
results of calculating $3+4$ and $5+1$ and then start afresh
to do the division. This should be avoided however, as it can
lead to copying mistakes, apart from adding to the amount
of work to be done.

A and C are the methods to consider. Be prepared to use either, depending on the circumstances.

Remember that the key $\boxed{+/-}$ can be used to change the sign of a number so that, for example, $(-6)^3$ can be found by keying

$$\boxed{6}\boxed{+/-}\boxed{x^y}\boxed{3}\boxed{=}$$

EXERCISE 2g

Calculators should be used in this exercise and answers given correct to 3 significant figures where necessary. Use rough estimates where possible to check your answers.

Find

1. $(-2.7)^5$

2. 4.78^{-4}

3. $\sqrt{4.2} + \sqrt{2.1}$

4. $\sqrt{4.2 + 2.1}$

5. $3.8^2 + 16.2^3$

6. $\dfrac{1}{4.678}$

7. a) Give a rough estimate of the value of $\dfrac{4.6 + 3.1}{7.8 + 3.4}$

   b) Use your calculator to find the value of the expression using
      i) brackets but not the memory
      ii) memory but not brackets.

   c) Which method do you think is neatest in this case and why ?

   d) Repeat (a) and (b) for

   i) $\dfrac{4.5}{2.4 + 8.5 - 4}$ ii) $\dfrac{\sqrt{4.6 + 3.9}}{6.73 - 5.8}$

8. a) Rewrite $\dfrac{(-3) \times (-4)^2}{(-5)^3}$ so that it contains at most one minus sign.
   Calculate the value of the expression.

   b) Calculate the value of the original expression using the $\boxed{+/-}$ key. Write down your keying.

9. a) Find $1 \div 9$. To how many decimal places is this given on your calculator ? To how many places could you give it ?

   b) Write down $1 \div 9$ as a recurring decimal.

   c) Without further working, write down the value of $\frac{5}{9}$ as a recurring decimal.

10. Give the following fractions as recurring decimals.
   a) $\frac{1}{7}$ b) $\frac{2}{11}$ c) $\frac{5}{6}$ d) $\frac{7}{30}$

Sometimes these questions are reversed, i.e. find two whole numbers which, when divided, give a particular display. These can often be recognised but if they cannot, the worked example suggests a method that might find them.

Find a fraction which when converted to a decimal gives the display 0.363 6363.

Enter 0.363 6363

Press $\boxed{\frac{1}{x}}$: This gives 2.750 000 5

i.e.
$$\frac{1}{0.363\,6363} \approx 2.75$$

$$= 2\tfrac{3}{4}$$

$$= \tfrac{11}{4}$$

$\therefore$ 0.363 6363 is given by $\tfrac{4}{11}$

Alternatively, $0.363\,6363 = 36 \times 0.010\,1010$

Now 0.010 1010 could be recognised as $\tfrac{1}{99}$

$\therefore$ $0.363\,6363 = \dfrac{\overset{4}{\cancel{36}}}{1} \times \dfrac{1}{\underset{11}{\cancel{99}}}$

$$= \tfrac{4}{11}$$

Write down the fraction which when converted to decimal form gives the following display.

11. 0.222 222

12. 0.333 333 3

13. 3.333 333 3

14. 0.011 111 1

15. 0.033 333 3

16. 1.111 111 1

17. 0.010 101 0

18. 0.030 303 0

19. 0.101 010 1

20. a) Find $\tfrac{1}{13}$ as a decimal and write down the figures on the display. How many decimal places are shown ?

b) Give the answer in (a) correct to as many decimal places as the display allows.

c) Is the last figure in the display rounded or not ?
Describe a method for checking this.

d) When a calculator is used to express $\tfrac{25}{143}$ as a decimal, the display shows 0.174 825 1. Explain how, *without using a calculator*, it can be shown whether this number is exact or if it has been rounded up or down.

Arrange the following numbers in order of size with the smallest first.

$$0.57, \quad \tfrac{5}{11}, \quad 0.643, \quad 0.555\,555$$

$$\tfrac{5}{11} = 0.454\,545$$

In order of size: $\tfrac{5}{11}$, $0.555\,555$, 0.57, 0.643

Write each set of numbers in order of size, with the smallest first.

21. 0.25,   0.026,   2.07,   0.52,   0.053

22. $\tfrac{1}{2}$,   0.67, $\tfrac{2}{3}$,   0.555

23. 0.037,   0.295 $\tfrac{4}{15}$,   0.542, $\tfrac{1}{20}$

24. $\tfrac{3}{8}$, -3,   3.8,   2.7

25. -1.63, $1\tfrac{2}{3}$,   2.25, $-2\tfrac{2}{3}$

26. Consider $8 \div 9 \times 9$

Press $\boxed{8}\,\boxed{\div}\,\boxed{9}\,\boxed{\times}\,\boxed{9}\,\boxed{=}$ or $\boxed{8}\,\boxed{\div}\,\boxed{9}\,\boxed{=}\,\boxed{\times}\,\boxed{9}\,\boxed{=}$ and you should get $\boxed{8}$
on a scientific calculator.

Try it on a simple non-scientific calculator and you may get 7.999 999. Explain why this might happen.

STANDARD FORM

A number such as 32 400 000 can be written in standard form as 3.24×10^7, i.e. a number between 1 and 10 multiplied by the appropriate power of 10. In the same way 0.000 006 28 can be written 6.28×10^{-6}.

On a calculator display, this will appear as 6.28 $^{-06}$.

To enter a number in the calculator in standard form, e.g. 2×10^6, press

$\boxed{2}\,\boxed{\text{EXP}}\,\boxed{6}$ and to enter 3×10^{-3} press $\boxed{3}\,\boxed{\text{EXP}}\,\boxed{3}\,\boxed{+/-}$.

When multiplying and dividing numbers in standard form without a calculator leave the numbers in that form. If adding or subtracting write the numbers out in full.

$$(8 \times 10^4) \div (2 \times 10^2) = (8 \div 2) \times (10^4 \div 10^2) = 4 \times 10^2$$

but

$$(8 \times 10^4) + (2 \times 10^2) = 80\,000 + 200 = 80\,200 = 8.02 \times 10^4$$

MIXED CALCULATIONS ━━━━━━━━━━━━━━━━━━━━━━━━━━━━━━

EXERCISE 2h

Do not use a calculator for questions 1 to 6.

If $a = 4 \times 10^4$, $b = 5 \times 10^6$ and $c = 2 \times 10^{-2}$, find

1. ab **3.** $a \div c$ **5.** $\dfrac{a}{b} + c$

2. bc **4.** $a + b$ **6.** $b - ac$

For question 7 onwards, use a calculator, in as neat a way as possible.

7. $\pi \times \sqrt{4.2^2 + 3.2^2}$ **11.** $7.2 \times 10^3 \times 8.1 \times 10^{-1}$

8. $\sqrt[3]{\dfrac{4.2 + 6.9}{3.7 + 8.6}}$ **12.** $\dfrac{4\pi}{3} \times 2.6^3$

9. $\dfrac{1}{4.8} + \dfrac{1}{7.9}$ **13.** $\left(\dfrac{0.0426}{16.3}\right)^4$

10. $7.2 \times 10^3 + 8.1 \times 10^{-1}$ **14.** $\dfrac{7.922 + 13.072}{\sqrt{24.9 - 13.6}}$

15. Use your calculator for questions 1 to 10 in Exercise 2f, giving your answers correct to 3 significant figures; make sure that your answers agree with the rough estimates.

16. The special theory of relativity states that a mass m is equivalent to a quantity of energy, E, where $E = mc^2$.

c m/s is the speed of light and $c = 2.998 \times 10^8$.

Find E when $m = 1.66 \times 10^{-27}$.

17. The quantity of nitrate in one bottle of mineral water is 1.5×10^{-3} g. The quantity of nitrate in another bottle of mineral water is 7.3×10^{-4} g.

The two bottles are emptied into the same jug. How much nitrate is there in the water in the jug?

18. The planet Xeron is 5.87×10^7 km from its sun. The planet Alpha is 2.71×10^8 km from the same sun.

a) Light travels at 3.0×10^5 km/s. Find, to the nearest minute, the time that light takes to travel to Alpha from its sun.

b) Find the difference between the distances of Xeron and Alpha from their sun.

PERCENTAGES

Test 2G   Percentages, Fractions and Decimals

1. Express as percentages

    a) $\frac{6}{25}$ b) 0.29   c) $1\frac{3}{4}$ d) 0.015

2. Express as fractions

    a) 42%   b) 0.28   c) $2\frac{1}{2}$%   d) 1.2

3. Express as decimals

    a) 12%   b) 115%   c) $6\frac{2}{5}$ d) $\frac{9}{20}$

4. Find 15% of £380.

5. Find $\frac{2}{9}$ of 153 m³.

6. In a school with 640 pupils, $\frac{3}{8}$ are boys. How many girls are there ?

7. When discs are cut from a sheet of card, 28% of the card is wasted. What area is used from a sheet of 400 cm² ?

8. A boy ate 8 sweets from a bag of 20 sweets. What fraction of the sweets did he leave ?

9. A girl gets 26 out of 40 in a test. What is her percentage mark ?

Test 2H   Increase and Decrease

1. A standard pack of detergent holds 250 g. A promotional pack contains an extra 20% by weight. What is the weight in the promotional pack ?

2. An uncooked chicken weighs 5 lb. It loses 12% of its weight during cooking. How much does it weigh when cooked ?

3. A curtain was 3.5 m long when new. After washing it was 2.8 m long. Find the percentage change in length.

4. After a price increase of 20%, a unit of electricity costs 6 p. Find the cost before the increase.

5. After public examinations in June, the number of pupils attending a school falls by 20% to 640. How many pupils attend before the examinations ?

FRACTIONS, DECIMALS AND PERCENTAGES ━━━━━━━━

To express a fraction as a decimal, divide the denominator into the numerator,

e.g. $\frac{7}{8} = 7 \div 8 = 0.875$

'Per cent' means 'per hundred', so 12% means 12 per 100. Hence to express a percentage as a fraction or a decimal, divide the percentage by 100,

e.g. $12\% = \dfrac{12}{100}$

$= 0.12$

To express a fraction or a decimal as a percentage, the operation is reversed, i.e. multiply by 100,

e.g. $\frac{2}{9} = \frac{2}{9} \times 100\% = \dfrac{200}{9}\% = 22\frac{2}{9}\%$

and $0.136 = 0.136 \times 100\% = 13.6\%$

Finding a percentage of a given quantity is therefore the same as finding the equivalent fraction of that quantity,

e.g. 12% of £40 $= \dfrac{12}{100}$ of £40

$= £\dfrac{12 \times 40}{100} = £4.80$

or 12% of £40 $= 0.12 \times £40 = £4.80$

EXERCISE 2i

Give all answers that are not exact correct to 3 s.f.

1. Express the following as fractions.

    a) 30%   b) 0.82   c) 130%   d) 1.25

2. Express the following as percentages.

    a) 0.93   b) 0.095   c) $\frac{3}{8}$ d) $\frac{7}{15}$

3. Express the following as decimals.

    a) 54%   b) $2\frac{3}{5}$ c) 138%   d) $\frac{4}{11}$

4. Arrange the following in order of size with the smallest first.

    $\frac{2}{7}$,   28%,   0.3, $\frac{1}{3}$

5. Arrange the following in order of size with the largest first.

$$\frac{5}{11}, \quad 55\%, \quad \frac{4}{7}, \quad 0.48$$

6. Find   a) 22 % of £ 10   b) 140 % of 500 g.

7. Find   a) $\frac{3}{8}$ of £ 24   b) $\frac{5}{9}$ of 63 miles.

8. Find   a) $12\frac{1}{2}$ % of 65 m   b) 105 % of £ 52.

9. Find   a) $\frac{4}{11}$ of 132 litres   b) $\frac{5}{8}$ of 0.96 m.

10. Express 20 out of 65 as   a) a fraction   b) a percentage.

11. Ten of a box of 25 oranges were bad. What percentage of the oranges were bad ?

12. In a class of 40 children, 5 % were away from school. How many were at school ?

13. Peter got 15 out of 26 for a test. What percentage did he get ?

14. For a particular football match, 23 % of the available 3700 tickets were unsold. How many tickets were sold ?

15. A public library lost 260 books from a total of 6500 books. What percentage of the books were lost ?

PERCENTAGE CHANGE

When a quantity is increased or decreased by a given percentage, the change is always calculated as a percentage of the original quantity (i.e. the quantity before the increase or decrease).

Thus, if £ 20 is increased by 2 %

then   the increase is 2 % of £ 20

and   the increased sum is (100 % + 2 %) of £ 20

$$= 102 \% \text{ of } £ 20$$

If 20 m is increased to 25 m,

then   the change is an increase of 5 m

and   the percentage increase is 5 m as a percentage of 20 m,

i.e. $\frac{5}{20} \times 100 \% = 25 \%$

Similarly if £ 450 is decreased by 15 %

then   the decrease is 15 % of £ 450

and   the decreased quantity is $(100\% - 15\%)$ of £ 450

$$= 85\% \text{ of } £450$$

When a quantity is known after a percentage change has taken place, then

the changed quantity $= (100\% \pm \%$ change $)$ of the original

Thus if a sum of money is increased by 15 % to £ 260

then   £ 260 = 115 % of sum before the increase

i.e. $£260 = \dfrac{115}{100} \times (\text{original sum})$

Similarly if a marked price is decreased by 25 % to £ 60

then   £ 60 = 75 % of marked price

i.e. $£60 = \dfrac{75}{100} \times (\text{marked price})$

EXERCISE 2j

The bus fare from Petts Corner to the Old Oak was increased by 5 % to 42 p. Find the fare before the increase.

Let the original fare be x pence,

then   42 p = 105 % of x pence

i.e. $42 = \dfrac{105}{100} \times x$

giving $\dfrac{\overset{2}{\cancel{42}} \times \overset{20}{\cancel{100}}}{\cancel{105}_{21}} = x$

$$40 = x$$

The fare before the increase was 40 p.

1. Increase £80 by   a) 10%   b) 15%   c) $7\frac{1}{2}$%.

2. Decrease £150 by   a) 7%   b) 30%   c) $12\frac{1}{2}$%.

3. Find the percentage change when
   a) £80 increases to £100
   b) 20 m decreases to 16 m
   c) 5 m increases to 5.5 m
   d) 16 litres decreases to 14 litres.

4. After an increase of 8%, a car costs £12096. Find the cost before the increase.

5. A builders' merchant marks prices net of VAT. Find the price to be paid for an item marked at £36 if VAT is charged at $17\frac{1}{2}$%.

6. A DIY shop marks prices inclusive of VAT at $17\frac{1}{2}$%. Find the price, exclusive of VAT, of a tin of paint marked at £5.05.

7. The label on a roll of fabric says "allow for 5% shrinkage". A dress pattern requires 2.5 m of fabric. How much should be bought to allow for shrinkage?

8. A chicken weighs $4\frac{1}{2}$ lb before cooking and 4 lbs after cooking. Find the percentage change in its weight.

The questions in the remainder of this exercise are mixed percentage problems.

9. A house bought for £87000 is sold at a profit of 15%. Find the selling price of the house.

10. In a box containing two dozen eggs, it is found that nine are broken. What percentage of the eggs are broken?

11. A girl is 8% taller this year than she was last year. Her height is now 175 cm. How tall was she last year?

12. In a sale a jacket was marked down from £58.00 to £43.50. What percentage reduction was this?

13. In an examination a boy got a mark of 49 and was told this was 70%. What was the maximum possible mark?

14. Mr Evans paid £448 income tax in one year. The tax was charged at a standard rate of 32%. Find Mr Evans' taxable income for that year.

15. If bread dough loses 8% of its weight when baked, find the weight of a baked loaf made from 500 g of dough.

16. It is found that 12% of the wheat crop from a field is not saleable. How much is saleable from a crop of 750 tons?

17. After a wage increase of $6\frac{1}{2}$%, Brenda Adstore's weekly pay was £159.75. What was her weekly pay before the increase ?

18. Maya Jacobs invested £750 in a deposit account which paid interest at 6.5% p.a. She did not withdraw the interest. How much was in the account after two years ?

19. A machine automatically cuts rolls of paper into short lengths. One day it is incorrectly set so that it cuts pieces 31.5 cm long instead of 30 cm long. What is the percentage error on

a) one piece of paper,   b) 1000 pieces of paper ?

20. The total cost of a coat was given in an advertisement as £59.47. This included VAT at $17\frac{1}{2}$% and £2.50 for postage and packing. What was the basic price of the coat before VAT and postage were added ?

INSURANCE

Although all property and people are at risk, relatively few suffer loss. Insurance works by spreading the cost of loss among all who are insured.

Some forms of insurance are legal requirements. For example, any driver using a car or motor cycle on a public road must, by law, be insured for third party risks. Third party risk covers damage caused to other people or their property. Other forms of insurance are sensible precautions against possible loss or damage.

The payment for insurance is called the *premium*. The premium may be given in a form such as £2 per £100 insured value, or the premium may be quoted as a total amount for a particular insurance. Premiums are usually payable yearly.

Some insurances give a discount if the insured person bears part of the risk. For example a householder may agree to pay the first £50 of any loss. This has the misleading name of 'an *excess*'.

Car insurances usually offer discounts for several consecutive years in which no claims have been made. This form of discount is called a *no claims bonus*.

EXERCISE 2k

> The premium for insuring a building worth £86000 is £4.30 per £1000 value. Find the premium to be paid.
>
> $$\text{Premium} = £4.30 \times 86$$
> $$= £369.80$$

The table gives the premiums for insuring buildings and contents as quoted by Northern Star Insurance Co.

	Buildings/£1000	Contents/£1000
Area A	£1.80	£ 6.50
Area B	£2.10	£ 8.00
Area C	£2.20	£10.80
Area D	£2.80	£12.90

Use this table to answer questions 1 to 5.

1. Find the premium for insuring a house worth £150000 (building only) in area D.

2. Find the premium for insuring a house worth £80000 and its contents worth £9000 in area B.

3. Mr and Mrs Hadinsky live in Area A and value the contents of their house at £12000. This includes a piano worth £850, a ring worth £700 and a watch worth £350. One condition of the insurance cover is that all items whose value is greater than 5% of the total insured must be listed.

   a) Find the premium to be paid.

   b) State the items that have to be listed.

4. a) The insurance premium for comprehensive cover on a small family car in Liverpool is £350. Daniel Kirby wants to insure himself to drive such a car but finds that because he is under 25 years of age, there is a 50% surcharge on the premium. What premium does he have to pay?

   b) Three years later, when Daniel is over 25 years old, he no longer has to pay the surcharge and because he has made no claims on his insurance, finds that he is entitled to a 40% no claims bonus. However, the basic premium has increased to £420. Find the premium he has to pay now.

5. A householder living in area C has a house valued at £75 000 with contents worth £8000. The discount on the buildings premium is 2% for an excess of £500 and on the contents the discount is 5% for an excess of £200. Find the premium for insuring house and contents if

a) no excess is agreed   b) both excesses are agreed.

Insurance is only one part of the cost of running a car. In addition there are the annual road fund licence, repairs and maintenance, petrol and, lastly, payment for the vehicle itself. Some people also add in the depreciation of the value of the car.

6. Maya Liang wants to take out a loan to buy herself a second-hand car and decides to estimate what it will cost her for a year. The repayments on the loan are £94 a calender month. Maya has been quoted £250 premium for insurance. The road tax is £125 and she estimates that she will do 10 000 miles at an average of 40 m.p.g. Petrol is £2.00 a gallon. Maya also estimates that she will need one service costing about £120.

How much does her estimate for 1 year's motoring come to ?

How much is this a week ?

7. Derek James buys a new car costing £10 000 and decides to work out the cost of running the car for its first year. He includes repayments of £350 per month, depreciation of 25% of the purchase price, £500 for insurance, £125 road tax, a service charge of £200 and £14 a week for petrol.

How much does it cost him each week to run his car ?

RATIO

Test 2I

1. One square has sides of length 5 metres and a second square has sides of length 7.5 metres. What is the ratio of these lengths ?

2. Express the ratio $2 : 7$ in the form $1 : n$.

3. A map ratio is $1 : 100 000$. How long is a road which on the map measures 2.5 cm ?

4. Simplify the ratio $50 : 125$.

5. Divide £36 into two parts in the ratio $7 : 2$.

6. Divide a length of 48 m into three parts in the ratio $1 : 3 : 4$.

7. The lengths of two lines are in the ratio $3 : 5$. The shorter line is 18 cm long. How long is the other line ?

WORKING WITH RATIO

Ratio is a way of comparing sizes.

For example, if one line is 8 cm long and another line is 12 cm long, then

the length of the shorter line compared with the length of the longer line is 8 : 12

8 cm $= 2 \times 4$ cm and 12 cm $= 3 \times 4$ cm

i.e.   for every 2 units of length in the shorter line, there are 3 units of length in the longer line.

Thus a ratio can be simplified (by dividing or by multiplying both parts of the ratio by the same number) and 8 : 12 can be written as 2 : 3.

Ratios can also be expressed in the form 1 : n by performing the appropriate divisions,

i.e. $2 : 3 = 1 : \frac{3}{2} = 1 : 1.5$

Map ratios are usually given in this form, i.e. 1 : n.

If the ratio of two quantities is known and the size of one quantity is known, the size of the other can be found.

For example, if two sums of money are in the ratio 3 : 5 and the smaller sum is £ 1.80, then for every 3 portions in the smaller sum there are 5 portions in the larger sum.

i.e.   the larger sum $= £\dfrac{1.80 \times 5}{3} = £3.00$

Similarly, if we have a total sum of money, say £ 10, and need to divide it into three amounts in the ratio 2 : 7 : 11 then for every 2 portions in the smallest sum there are 7 portions in the middle sum and 11 portions in the larger sum.

Hence we divide £ 10 into (2 + 7 + 11) portions.

Each portion is $£10 \times \frac{1}{20}$ therefore the three sums are

$£10 \times \frac{2}{20}$, $£10 \times \frac{7}{20}$, $£10 \times \frac{11}{20}$ i.e. £ 1, £ 3.50, £ 5.50

EXERCISE 2I

Simplify

1. 400 : 75   **2.** $5 : \frac{2}{3}$ **3.** 14 : 28 : 49

Find in the form 1 : n

4. 4 : 7   **5.** 8 : 25   **6.** 3 : 12 000

Find the ratio of the two given quantities

7. £2, £3.50   **8.** 2 cm, 1 m   **9.** 1 cm², 1 m²

Find, in the form $1:n$, the ratio of the given quantities

10. 1 cm, 2 km   **11.** 2 mm, 5 m   **12.** 3 inches, 2 yards

13. Give $3.2 \times 10^4 : 1.6 \times 10^7$ in the form $1:n$

14. Two lines have lengths in the ratio 2 : 5. If the longer line is 15 cm long, find the length of the other line.

15. A road on a map measures 2.5 cm. The actual road is 1 km long. Find the map ratio in the form $1:n$.

16. A map ratio is 1 : 100 000. Find the length of a road which on the map measures 2.6 cm.

17. Divide £45 into 2 parts in the ratio 4 : 5.

18. Divide £56 into 3 parts in the ratio 2 : 3 : 3.

19. A design team makes a model of a table, using a scale of 1 : 20. The actual table is intended to be 1 metre long. How long is the model ?

20. A school decides to give 20 % of the proceeds of a jumble sale to charity and the rest to the school fund. In what ratio are the proceeds to be divided ?

EQUIVALENCE BETWEEN METRIC AND IMPERIAL UNITS ─────

In supermarkets it is not unusual to find apples, say, in priced prepacked bags of 500 g or 1 kg but to find loose apples sold by the pound.

This mixture of Imperial and metric units in everyday use means that we should all know rough equivalents for corresponding units.

Length: 8 km ≈ 5 miles

                   1 metre ≈ 39 inches   (1 m is roughly 1 yd)

                   10 cm ≈ 4 inches

Area: 1 hectare ≈ 2.5 acres

Weight: 1 tonne ≈ 1 ton   (1 tonne is slightly less than 1 ton)

                   1 kg ≈ 2.2 lb

                   100 g ≈ 3.5 oz   (100 g is roughly a quarter of a lb)

Capacity: 1 litre ≈ 1.75 pints

                   1 gallon ≈ 4.5 litres

RATES OF CONSUMPTION

The rate at which quantities are consumed is usually expressed as an amount of one quantity with respect to one unit of another.

Speed is the rate at which a moving object covers distance and it is given as the distance covered in one unit of time.

The common units for speed are kilometres per hour (km/h), miles per hour (m.p.h.) and metres per second (m/s).

Fuel consumption is the rate at which fuel is used. For cars etc. it is usually expressed as distance covered on one unit quantity of fuel, e.g. miles per gallon (m.p.g.), kilometres per litre (km/l). It is also often given as litres per 100 km.

When vast quantities of fuel are used, it is given as the fuel used in covering a unit of distance or time, e.g. gallons per mile or litres per second.

Coverage of paint, fertilizer, spray etc. is the rate at which it covers (or should cover) area, so it is expressed as a quantity of liquid per unit of area; for example, litres per square metre (l/m^2).

EXERCISE 2m

1. The petrol tank on my car holds 12 gallons. How many litres is this ?

2. An old dressmaking pattern states that the seam allowance is $\frac{5}{8}$ inch. How many millimetres is this ?

3. Sarat knows that he is 5 ft 10 in tall, but he has to give his height in metres on his application form for a passport. What should he say his height is ?

4. Apples are sold in 1 kg bags at 98 p per bag, or loose at 42 p a pound. Which is the cheaper way to buy the apples ?

5. A particular brand of carpet is priced at £8.75 per square yard in a local shop and at £9.60 per square metre in a department store. Where is the carpet cheaper ?

6. The area of a garden is given as 0.8 hectares.
a) How many acres is this ?
b) If the adjacent plot, of area 1.8 acres, is added to the garden, what is the total area in hectares ?

Express a speed of 60 m.p.h. in m/s using $8 \text{ km} \approx 5 \text{ miles}$.

$$60 \text{ m.p.h.} \approx \frac{60 \times 8}{5} \text{ km/h}$$

$$= \frac{60 \times 8 \times 1000}{5} \text{ m/h}$$

$$= \frac{60 \times 8 \times 1000}{8 \times 60 \times 60} \text{ m/s}$$

$$= \frac{80}{3} \text{ m/s} = 26.7 \text{ m/s} \quad (\text{correct to 3 s.f.})$$

i.e. $60 \text{ m.p.h.} \approx 27 \text{ m/s}$.

7. Express (a) 80 km/h in m/s   (b) 8 m/s in km/h.

8. Express (a) 40 km/h in m.p.h.   (b) 70 m.p.h. in km/h.

9. Express $50 \text{ m}^2/\text{litre}$ in sq ft/gallon.

10. The average petrol consumption of a car is 35 m.p.g. The driver puts 25 litres of petrol into the tank. How far can the car be expected to travel ?

11. A bottle of liquid insecticide contains 500 ml. The instructions state that it should be diluted in the ratio 2.5 ml of insecticide to 2 litres of water and the diluted mixture applied at the rate of 250 ml/m^2. What area will the contents of the bottle treat ?

MIXED EXERCISES

EXERCISE 2n

1. Ice cubes are made by freezing water in cuboid containers so that the frozen ice cube measures 2 cm by 3 cm by 2.5 cm. The water increases in volume by 5% when frozen.

a) What volume of water is needed to make one ice cube ?

b) How many ice cubes can be made from 1 litre of water ?

2. Three people stake £10 on a lottery and win £850. Peter paid £2, John paid £4.50 and Clare paid the rest towards the stake. The winnings are shared in the ratio of the contributions. How much does Clare get ?

3. What is the largest odd number that is a factor of 860 ?

4. Find the exact value of $\dfrac{15.2 \times 8.6}{0.05}$

5. From the set of numbers $\{1, 4, 5, 7, 9, 12, 15\}$ write down
   a) the prime numbers   c) factors of 60
   b) multiples of 3   d) perfect squares (square numbers).

6. A school fête raised £4800 and one quarter of this sum was paid out for expenses. Three-quarters of the remainder was given to the school fund and the rest was donated to a local charity. How much did the charity receive ?

7. Two planets A and B are respectively 1.8×10^{11} km and 8.9×10^{10} km from the Sun.
   a) How much further is one planet from the Sun than the other ?
   b) Find the ratio of the distances of A and B from the Sun in the form $1 : n$.
   c) If light travels at 3.00×10^5 km/s, find how long it takes to travel from the Sun to the more distant planet.

EXERCISE 2p

1. Express 441 as a product of its prime factors and hence find $\sqrt{441}$ without using a calculator.

2. A motorist is asked to pay a net premium of £280.50 for car insurance. This is after a discount of 45% on the gross premium. Find the gross premium.

3. A bottle of concentrated orange drink holds $32\frac{1}{2}$ fluid ounces. The recommended dilution is one capful to a glass of water. The cap holds $\frac{1}{3}$ gill and a gill is taken as 5 fluid ounces. How many glasses of orange drink can be obtained from one bottle ?

4. Find the exact value of $\dfrac{2\frac{1}{5} - 1\frac{3}{4}}{1\frac{1}{2} \times 2\frac{8}{11}}$

5. When Lord Worth died his estate was valued at £150 000. His will stated that 20% of his estate was to be given to charity and 5% of what was left was to be given to his housekeeper. The remainder was to be given to his only son. How much did his son receive ?

6. A road on a map is 2.5 cm long while the actual road is 4.8 km long. Find the map ratio in the form $1 : n$.

7. If 1 foot $= 0.31$ m and 1 fluid ounce $= 28.4$ ml, convert 240 ml per m^2 to fluid ounces per square foot.

EXERCISE 2q

1. Find
   a) the lowest number that is a common multiple of 9 and 12
   b) the highest number that is a common factor of 72 and 48
   c) the lowest number which when multiplied by 12 makes it into a perfect square.

2. The Red Brick Building Society states that it will give individuals a maximum mortgage of $2\frac{1}{2}$ times gross income. In certain circumstances it will increase the amount by up to $1\frac{1}{4}$ times the partner's income. The maximum mortgage the society will give on any property is 85% of its own valuation.

   Mr and Mrs Hope see a house which the society values at £68 000. Mr Hope has a gross income of £15 000 and his wife has an income of £4500.

   Find the difference between the maximum mortgage available on the house and the maximum mortgage the society will give Mr and Mrs Hope.

3. Don Lucky won £50 at bingo and decided to give it to his three children, in amounts that are in the same ratio as their ages. The children were 10, 12 and 18 years old respectively. How much did they each get?

4. Tom Peterson invested £500 in a deposit account which paid interest at 7.25% p.a. He left the interest in the account. How much was in the account at the end of two years?

5. Find the exact value of $2\frac{5}{11} \times 1\frac{2}{9} + \frac{5}{6}$

6. Mr Ford's gross motor insurance premium this year is £280. This represents an increase of 5% on last year's gross premium. In calculating the net premium that Mr Ford had to pay last year, a 30% no claims bonus was given. Find the net premium paid last year.

7. Use your calculator to find $\dfrac{6.3 + 7.92}{8.5 - 4.3}$ without using
   a) memory   b) brackets.

EXERCISE 2r

Do not use a calculator.

Each question is followed by several possible answers. Write down the letter that corresponds to the correct answer.

1. Correct to 3 s.f., the value of $\dfrac{1.87 \times 0.0073}{0.019}$ is

   A 7.18   **B** 0.0718   **C** 0.718   **D** 71.8

2. The third significant figure in 0.001 020 5 is

   A 0   **B** 2   **C** 5   **D** 1

3. The highest factor of 60 apart from itself is

A 2   **B** 5   **C** 10   **D** 30

4. In a sale, a store offers 15% off marked prices. When the marked price is £25, the sale price is

A £3.75   **B** £21.25   **C** £25   **D** £28.75

5. A common multiple of 6 and 9 is

A 18   **B** 3   **C** 15   **D** 12

6. The exact value of $(0.105)^2$ is

A 0.11025   **B** 0.011025   **C** 11025   **D** 0.011

7. Two-thirds of a class of children had school dinners. The remaining 8 children went home for lunch. The number who stayed for school dinner was

A 16   **B** 12   **C** 24   **D** 4

8. Correct to three significant figures, 87059.3479 is

A 87059.348   **B** 87100   **C** 87060   **D** 871

9. A good approximation for $\dfrac{89.37 \times 3.05}{0.92}$ is

A 300   **B** 30   **C** 0.3   **D** 3000

10. The value of 199×53 is

A 5353   **B** 10653   **C** 10547   **D** 5247

11. $a = 8 \times 10^6$, $b = 3 \times 10^3$ and $c = 2 \times 10^{-2}$
The value of $b + ac$ is

A 1.9×10^8 **B** 1.6×10^5 **C** 1.63×10^5 **D** 4.8×10^8

12. $x = 7.2 \times 10^{-4}$, $y = 2.8 \times 10^{-2}$ and $z = 8.4 \times 10^{-3}$. When placed in ascending order of size, the order is

A x, y, z **B** x, z, y **C** y, z, x **D** y, x, z

3 THE STANDARD ALGEBRAIC PROCESSES

In this chapter we revise the standard processes and methods of solving equations.

SIMPLIFYING EXPRESSIONS

Reminder x^2, $2x$ and 6 are *unlike* terms, so $x^2 + 2x + 6$ cannot be written more simply. $3x^2$ and $4x^2$ are *like* terms, so $3x^2 + 4x^2$ can be written as $7x^2$.

EXERCISE 3a

Simplify the following expressions.

1. $7x + 2 - 9x - 5 + 5x^2$ **6.** $3a - 7b - 4a - 5c + 10b + 6c$

2. $2x \times 3x$ **7.** $6x \times 7y$

3. $x \times x \times x$ **8.** $x \times x - x$

4. $x + x + x$ **9.** $x^2 \times x$

5. $2x^2 - 3x - x^2$ **10.** $x^2 \div x$

Expand and simplify, where possible, the following expressions.

11. $6(x - 2) + 4$ **14.** $x(x - 2) - 2(x + 4)$

12. $3(2a + 2b) - 2(b - 4)$ **15.** $c(a - b) + b(c - a)$

13. $4(3x - 1) - (2x - 3)$ **16.** $3(2x + 4) + x(3 - 4x)$

Expand the following expressions.

17. $(x + 3)(x + 4)$ **22.** $(a - b)(c - d)$

18. $(x - 3)(x + 4)$ **23.** $(2x + 5)^2$

19. $(x - 5)(x + 5)$ **24.** $(1 - 2x)(1 + 3x)$

20. $(x - 5)^2$ **25.** $(x + y)(x - 2y)$

21. $(2x + 3)(x - 4)$ **26.** $(2 - x)(3 + x)$

Simplify:

27. $(2x-3)^2-4x(x-4)$ **30.** $(x+3)^2+(x-1)^2$

28. $(a+b)^2-2ab$ **31.** $4-(x-2)^2$

29. $4(x-2)(x+1)$ **32.** $6(2x-1)(3-x)$

FACTORS

The factors of 10 are 2 and 5, i.e. $2 \times 5 = 10$. We need to be aware of this when we are, say, simplifying fractions.

In the same way we often need to know the factors of algebraic expressions in order to simplify the expressions and solve problems.

$3x^2-6x$ is made up of the factors $3, x$ and $(x-2)$ i.e. $3x^2-6x = 3x(x-2)$.

When you have decided on the factors, you should check, by multiplying out, that you have the correct ones.

Always start by looking for any common factors.

EXERCISE 3b

> Factorise $6x^2-15x$.
>
> $$6x^2-15x = 3x(2x-5)$$

Factorise the following expressions.

1. $2x-4$ **5.** x^2y+xy^2

2. $6a-9c$ **6.** x^2-x

3. $2x^2-6x$ **7.** $4x+20y$

4. $12a+18b-24c$ **8.** $9x^2y+18xy^2$

> Factorise $3ax-6ay-4bx+8by$.
>
> $$3ax-6ay-4bx+8by = 3a(x-2y)-4b(x-2y)$$
> $$= (x-2y)(3a-4b)$$

Factorise the following four-term expressions.

9. $ax + bx + ay + by$

13. $4uv + 3v - 12u - 9$

10. $pq - qr + ps - rs$

14. $ab + 4xy - 2bx - 2ay$

11. $2mn + pq - pn - 2mq$

15. $ax^2 + a^2x - ay - xy$

12. $x^3 + x^2 + x + 1$

16. $ab + 6cd - 2bc - 3ad$

FACTORS OF QUADRATIC EXPRESSIONS

Quadratic expressions will sometimes factorise into two brackets. Remember that the x term in each bracket must multiply to give the x^2 term and the product of the number terms (including their signs) from the brackets gives the number term in the quadratic expression.

Always check your factors by multiplying out.

EXERCISE 3c

Factorise   a) $x^2 - 10x + 16$ b) $x^2 - 16$

a) $x^2 - 10x + 16 = (x - 2)(x - 8)$ $-2x - 8x = -10x$

b) ($x^2 - 16$ is the difference of two squares)

$x^2 - 16 = (x - 4)(x + 4)$

Factorise the following expressions.

1. $x^2 + 12x + 32$

6. $y^2 - 18 + 7y$

2. $x^2 - 7x + 12$

7. $x^2 + 2x - 15$

3. $x^2 - 9$

8. $x^2 - 4x - 77$

4. $x^2 - 6x + 9$

9. $30 + 11x + x^2$

5. $49 + a^2 - 14a$

10. $x^2 - 9x$

Factorise $5x^2 - 15x - 20$.

(Look for the common factor first.)
$$5x^2 - 15x - 20 = 5(x^2 - 3x - 4)$$
$$= 5(x - 4)(x + 1) \qquad -4x + 1x = -3x$$

Factorise the following expressions by taking out the common factor first, then factorising the remaining expression if possible.

11. $3x^2 + 6x + 3$

12. $4x^2 + 8x - 12$

13. $9y^2 - 36$

14. $5y^2 - 40y + 35$

15. $12x^2 - 18x$

16. $2b^2 - 14b + 20$

17. $8x^2 + 8x - 48$

18. $3x^2 - 48$

Factorise $2x^2 - x - 1$.

(There is no common factor.)
$$2x^2 - x - 1 = (2x + 1)(x - 1) \qquad +x - 2x = -x$$

Factorise the following expressions.

19. $2x^2 + 7x + 3$

20. $3x^2 + 11x - 4$

21. $9x^2 - 4$

22. $6x^2 + 11x + 3$

23. $12x^2 - 29x + 15$

24. $5x^2 + 3x - 2$

25. $4x^2 + 4x - 3$

26. $12x^2 - 28x + 15$

27. $12x^2 - 41x + 15$

28. $25x^2 - 9$

29. $x^2 - 25x$

30. $25 - x^2$

31. $x^2 - 10x + 25$

32. $x^2 - 26x + 25$

33. $x^2 + 5ax + 5x + 25a$

34. $1 - x - 12x^2$

35. $10x^2 - 25x + 15$

36. $5x^2 + 50x + 125$

Factorise $2x^2 - 18$ and hence find the prime factors of 182.

$$2x^2 - 18 = 2(x^2 - 9)$$
$$= 2(x - 3)(x + 3)$$
$$182 = 2(91)$$
$$= 2(100 - 9)$$
$$= 2(10^2 - 3^2)$$
$$= 2(10 - 3)(10 + 3)$$
$$= 2 \times 7 \times 13$$

37. Factorise $101^2 - 99^2$ and hence work out its value.

38. Factorise $4x^2 - 9$ and hence find the prime factors of 391.

39. Factorise $3x^2 - 48$ and hence find the prime factors of 252.

40. Given that $8.12^2 - 1.88^2 = 10k$, find k.

41. Find the value of $7.86^2 - 2.14^2$

42. By expressing 899 as the difference between two perfect squares, find the prime factors of 899.

FINDING THE VALUE OF AN EXPRESSION

Remember that if $y^2 = 9$ then y can have two possible values i.e. 3 or -3.
We write $y = \pm 3$.
On the other hand, $y = \sqrt{9}$ means the *positive* square root of 9 i.e. $+3$.

EXERCISE 3d

Find, where possible, the value of each of the following expressions, given that $a = 6$, $b = -3$ and $c = 2$.

1. $2a + 3b + 4c$

2. $a^2 + b^2$

3. $2a^2$

4. $\sqrt{a + b + 3c}$

5. $\dfrac{a}{b + c}$

6. $(a + 3c)(b + 2c)$

7. $\dfrac{c}{a} + \dfrac{a}{c}$ **9.** $\dfrac{1}{a} + \dfrac{1}{b}$ **11.** $\sqrt{a^2 + b^2 + c^2}$

8. $\dfrac{1}{a + bc}$ **10.** $\sqrt{a - c}$ **12.** $\sqrt{c - a}$

13. Given that $z^2 = x^2 + y^2$, find the two possible values of z if
   a) $x = 5$ and $y = 12$
   b) $x = \sqrt{2}$ and $y = \sqrt{7}$

14. Given that $a = 3$, $b = -4$ and $c = -1$, evaluate
   a) $2a^2$ b) $a - c^2$ c) $a(b - c)$

15. If $y^2 = 4a(x + 5)$ find the two possible values of y when $a = \frac{1}{25}$ and $x = 4$.

INDICES

x^4 means $x \times x \times x \times x$

x^{-4} means the reciprocal of x^4, i.e. $\dfrac{1}{x^4}$

x^0 has the value 1

$x^{1/4}$ means the fourth root of x

MULTIPLICATION AND DIVISION

To *multiply* numbers in the same base we *add* the indices.

For example, $x^4 \times x^3 = x^7$

To *divide* numbers in the same base we *subtract* the indices.

For example, $x^6 \div x^4 = x^2$

EXERCISE 3e

If $x = 2$, $y = 3$ and $z = 5$, find the value of each of the following expressions.

1. x^5 **3.** $5x$ **5.** $\dfrac{1}{z^2}$ **7.** xy^2

2. z^0 **4.** y^3 **6.** y^{-2} **8.** $\left(\dfrac{y}{z}\right)^{-1}$

Complete the following statements.

9. $64 = 2^{\square}$ **10.** $125 = \square^3$ **11.** $4^{\square} = 1$ **12.** $\frac{1}{4} = 2^{\square}$

Simplify the following expressions where possible.

13. $a^5 \times a^2$ **16.** $a^5 \times a^{-2}$ **19.** $a^5 \div a^{-2}$

14. $a^5 \div a^2$ **17.** $a^5 + a^2$ **20.** $a^5 \div a^5$

15. $(a^5)^2$ **18.** $5a + 2a$ **21.** $(a^2)^{-5}$

Find the value of each of the following expressions.

22. $36^{1/2}$ **24.** $125^{1/3}$ **26.** $\left(\dfrac{9}{4}\right)^{1/2}$

23. $16^{1/4}$ **25.** $\left(\dfrac{27}{8}\right)^{1/3}$ **27.** $27^{1/3}$

Simplify the following expressions where possible.

28. $x^{1/2} \times x^{1/2}$ **32.** $6x^2 \times 3x^4$ **36.** $(x^3)^{1/3}$

29. $x^{1/3} \div x^{1/3}$ **33.** $\dfrac{x^2 \times x^4}{x^3 \times x}$ **37.** $a^{1/2} \times b^{1/3}$

30. $x^0 \times x^{1/4}$ **34.** $\dfrac{x^3 \times x^{-2}}{x^{1/2}}$ **38.** $x^{1/2} \div x^{1/4}$

31. $x^{1/2} + x^{1/3}$ **35.** $(x^{1/2})^4$ **39.** $x^{1/2} \times x^{1/2} \times x^{1/2} \times x^{1/2}$

Solve the equation $3^x = 9^3$.

(Before we can compare indices, the base must be the same on both sides.)

$$3^x = 9^3$$
$$3^x = (3^2)^3$$
$$3^x = 3^6$$
$$\therefore \quad x = 6$$

Find the value of x in each of the following equations.

40. $3^x = 81$ **42.** $5^x = 25^3$ **44.** $4^x = 2^6$

41. $2^x = 4^2$ **43.** $(2^x)^2 = 16$ **45.** $2^x \times 3^x = 6^3$

EXERCISE 3f

Evaluate   a) $27^{2/3}$ b) $4^{-1/2}$ c) $\left(\dfrac{81}{16}\right)^{-1/4}$

a) $(27^{2/3}) = (27^{1/3})^2$ b) $4^{-1/2} = \dfrac{1}{4^{1/2}}$

        $= 3^2$ $= \dfrac{1}{2}$

        $= 9$

c) $\left(\dfrac{81}{16}\right)^{-1/4} = \left(\dfrac{16}{81}\right)^{1/4} = \dfrac{2}{3}$

Find the value of each of the following expressions.

1. $4^{3/2}$ **4.** $8^{-1/3}$ **7.** $\left(\dfrac{4}{9}\right)^{-1/2}$

2. $81^{3/4}$ **5.** $125^{2/3}$ **8.** $1000^{2/3}$

3. $1^{1/3}$ **6.** $27^{4/3}$ **9.** $1000^{-4/3}$

Simplify the following expressions where possible.

10. $x^{3/2} \times x^{1/2}$ **13.** $x^{3/2} \times x^{-1/2}$ **16.** $\dfrac{1}{x^{-1/2}}$

11. $x^{3/2} + x^{1/2}$ **14.** $x^{3/2} \div x^{-1/2}$ **17.** $x \div x^{1/2}$

12. $x^{3/2} \div x^{1/2}$ **15.** $x^{-1/2} \div x^{3/2}$ **18.** $x \times x^{1/2}$

19. If $a = 2 \times 10^4$ and $b = 3 \times 10^6$, find the value of each of the following expressions, giving your answers in standard form.

   a) ab b) $\dfrac{b}{a}$ c) $a+b$ d) $b-a$

20. Given that $x = 2.4 \times 10^{-3}$ and $y = 1.6 \times 10^{-4}$, find in standard form, the value of

   a) xy b) $\dfrac{x}{y}$ c) $x+y$ d) $x-y$

EQUATIONS

When dealing with the simpler equations remember to tidy them first; then decide which side has the most xs.

EXERCISE 3g

Solve the following equations.

1. $2x + 4 = 8$ **4.** $7 - 2x = 5$

2. $6x - 3 = 7$ **5.** $5 - 6x = 2 - 2x$

3. $3x - 4 = 6 + x$ **6.** $4x - 8 = 2 - 6x$

7. $5x - 2 + 6x + 7 = 38$ **10.** $3(x-1) + 5(x-2) = x+1$

8. $3(2+y) = -18$ **11.** $x - 3 - 6(x-1) = 2(6-x)$

9. $5(2x-1) = 4(4-x)$ **12.** $7 = x - (4-x)$

13. I think of a number, double it and add 7. I take the same number and subtract it from 19. The two answers are the same. What is the number?

14. John is x years old now and his father is three times as old. In 12 years time, his father will be twice as old as John will be. Find x.

15. Two angles of a triangle are $x°$ and $2x°$ and the third angle is $42°$ more than the first angle. Find the sizes of the three angles.

SIMULTANEOUS EQUATIONS

Elimination method   Remember that if the signs are different we add the equations, and if the signs are the same we subtract.

EXERCISE 3h

Solve the equations $x + y = 10$
$$x - y = 6$$

$$x + y = 10 \qquad [1]$$
$$x - y = 6 \qquad [2]$$

[1] + [2] gives $\qquad 2x = 16$

$$x = 8$$

In [1] $\qquad\qquad 8 + y = 10$

$$y = 2$$

Check in [2] $x - y = 8 - 2 = 6$

The solution is $x = 8$, $y = 2$.

Solve the following pairs of equations.

1. $2x + y = 5$
$3x - y = 5$

4. $3x - 2y = 2$
$5x + 2y = -2$

2. $4x + y = 0$
$2x + y = 2$

5. $x - y = 7$
$3x - y = 31$

3. $x + 3y = -7$
$x + y = -1$

6. $4x - y = 8$
$6x - y = 0$

Sometimes one, or both, of the equations must be changed before adding or subtracting.

Solve the equations $6x - 5y = 8$

$4x - 3y = 6$

$$6x - 5y = 8 \qquad [1]$$

$$4x - 3y = 6 \qquad [2]$$

$[1] \times 3$ gives $18x - 15y = 24 \qquad [3]$

$[2] \times 5$ gives $20x - 15y = 30 \qquad [4]$

$18x - 15y = 24 \qquad [3]$

$[4] - [3]$ gives $2x = 6$

$x = 3$

In $[1]$ $18 - 5y = 8$

$18 = 8 + 5y$

$10 = 5y$

$y = 2$

Check in $[2]$ $4x - 3y = 12 - 6 = 6$

The solution is $x = 3, y = 2$.

Solve the following pairs of equations.

7. $4x + 6y = 50$
$3x + 2y = 30$

10. $3x - 5y = 13$
$2x - 3y = 8$

8. $2x + y = 7$
$5x - 3y = 12$

11. $x + 5y = 9$
$2x + 3y = 11$

9. $6x + 7y = 12$
$4x + 3y = 18$

12. $5x + 11y = -2$
$2x + 9y = 13$

In questions 13 to 18, some of the equations need rearranging first.

13. $x = 3 + y$
$x + y = 6$

16. $x + 3 = 2x + y$
$4x - y = 7$

14. $2y + x = 1$
$2x + y = -1$

17. $2x - y = -8$
$2y - x = 10$

15. $9 = 2x - 3y$
$3y + x = 9$

18. $4 + x = 9 + y$
$4 - x = 3 + y$

In each of the following questions form two equations. Remember to state first the meaning of the two letters that you use.

19. The sum of two numbers is 25 and the difference between them is 13. What are the numbers?

20. In a two-digit number the sum of the digits is 9 and the units digit is 5 more than the tens digit. What is the number?

21. The perimeter of a rectangle is 52 cm. The difference between the length and the width is 8 cm. Find the length and the width.

22. Three apples and five oranges cost 85 p; five apples and three oranges cost 83 p. How much does one apple cost?

QUADRATIC EQUATIONS

Some quadratic equations can be solved by factorising. If this is not possible then we can use the method of completing the square or we can use the formula.

For the equation $ax^2 + bx + c = 0$

$$x = \frac{-b \pm \sqrt{b^2 - 4ac}}{2a}$$

Whether factorisation or the formula is used it is necessary to arrange the equation with the terms in the correct order on one side and 0 on the other.

For example, $2x - 3 = 4 - x^2$ is rearranged as $x^2 + 2x - 7 = 0$.

Remember that the sum of the roots is $\dfrac{-b}{a}$

the product of the roots is $\dfrac{c}{a}$

EXERCISE 3i

Solve the equation $(x+4)(x-1) = 0$.

$$(x+4)(x-1) = 0$$

Either $x + 4 = 0$ or $x - 1 = 0$

$\qquad\qquad\qquad x = -4 \qquad\qquad\qquad x = 1$

Solve the following equations.

1. $(x-2)(x+3) = 0$

3. $2(x-1)(x-5) = 0$

2. $x(x-4) = 0$

4. $(1+4x)(7x-6) = 0$

Solve the equation $x^2 - 6x - 7 = 0$.

$$x^2 - 6x - 7 = 0$$

$$(x-7)(x+1) = 0$$

Either $x - 7 = 0$ or $x + 1 = 0$

$\qquad\qquad\qquad x = 7 \qquad\qquad\qquad x = -1$

Check   Sum of the roots $= 7 + (-1) = 6$, $\dfrac{-b}{a} = \dfrac{6}{1} = 6$

Product of the roots $= 7 \times (-1) = -7$, $\dfrac{c}{a} = \dfrac{-7}{1} = -7$

$\therefore$ the solution is $x = 7$ or $x = -1$.

Solve the following equations by factorising.

5. $x^2 - 7x + 12 = 0$

8. $2x^2 + 2x - 12 = 0$

6. $x^2 - 25 = 0$

9. $x^2 - 14x + 49 = 0$

7. $x^2 - 6x = 0$

10. $3x^2 + 9x = 0$

11. $x^2 - 2x = 8$ **14.** $4x^2 + 4x - 15 = 0$

12. $7x - x^2 = 10$ **15.** $5x^2 - 15x + 10 = 0$

13. $9x^2 = 9$ **16.** $2 - 4x^2 = 2x$

Solve the equation $2x^2 - 3x - 3 = 0$ by completing the square.

$$2x^2 - 3x - 3 = 0$$

$$x^2 - \tfrac{3}{2}x = \tfrac{3}{2}$$

$$x^2 - \tfrac{3}{2}x + \tfrac{3}{4} \times \tfrac{3}{4} = \tfrac{3}{2} + \tfrac{3}{4} \times \tfrac{3}{4}$$

$$\left(x - \tfrac{3}{4}\right)^2 = \tfrac{33}{16}$$

$$x - \tfrac{3}{4} = \pm\sqrt{\tfrac{33}{16}}$$

Either $x = \tfrac{3}{4} + \tfrac{\sqrt{33}}{4}$ or $x = \tfrac{3}{4} - \tfrac{\sqrt{33}}{4}$

$$= \tfrac{3}{4} + \tfrac{5.744}{4} \qquad\qquad = \tfrac{3}{4} - \tfrac{5.744}{4}$$

$$= 2.186 \qquad\qquad\qquad = -0.686$$

Check $2.186 + (-0.686) = 1.50$

$$-\frac{b}{a} = 1.5$$

The solution is $x = 2.19$ or $x = -0.69$ correct to 2 d.p.

Solve the following equations by completing the square.

Check your solution by comparing the sum of the roots with the value of $-\dfrac{b}{a}$

17. $x^2 - 2x - 7 = 0$ **20.** $3x^2 - x = 3$

18. $2x^2 + x = 1$ **21.** $x^2 = x + 4$

19. $x^2 + 3x + 1 = 0$ **22.** $7x = 2x^2 - 1$

Solve the equation $2x^2 - 3x - 3 = 0$ by using the formula.

$$2x^2 - 3x - 3 = 0$$

$$a = 2, \quad b = -3, \quad c = -3$$

$$x = \frac{-b \pm \sqrt{b^2 - 4ac}}{2a}$$

$$= \frac{3 \pm \sqrt{9 - (-24)}}{4}$$

$$= \frac{3 \pm \sqrt{33}}{4}$$

$$= \frac{3 \pm 5.744}{4}$$

Either $\quad x = \dfrac{8.744}{4} \qquad$ or $\quad x = \dfrac{-2.744}{4}$

$$= 2.186 \qquad\qquad = -0.686$$

Check Sum of roots $= 2.186 - 0.686 = 1.5$

$$\frac{-b}{a} = \frac{-(-3)}{2} = 1.5$$

Product of roots $= 2.186 \times (-0.686) = -1.499$

$$\frac{c}{a} = \frac{-3}{2} = -1.5$$

The solution is $x = 2.19$ or $x = -0.69$ correct to 2 d.p.

Solve the equations in questions 23 to 32 by completing the square or by using the formula. Give your answers correct to 2 decimal places.

23. $x^2 + 2x - 5 = 0$

24. $2x^2 + 4x + 1 = 0$

25. $x^2 - 3x - 1 = 0$

26. $3x^2 - 5x + 1 = 0$

27. $x^2 + 4x = 6$

28. $x^2 = x + 1$

29. $x^2 - 20 = 0$

30. $2x^2 - 7x + 2 = 0$

31. $6 - 4x - x^2 = 0$

32. $3x^2 = x + 6$

33. What happens when you try to solve the equation $x^2 - 2x + 5 = 0$ by

a) completing the square

b) using the formula ?

34. a) Repeat question 33 for the equations

  i) $x^2 - 3x + 3 = 0$ ii) $2x^2 + 5x + 4 = 0$.

b) Without attempting to find the solution, state whether the equation $x^2 + 7x + 15 = 0$ can be solved.

c) What is the condition for $ax^2 + bx + c = 0$ to have a solution ?

What is the condition for $2x^2 - px + q = 0$ to have a solution ?

$$2x^2 - px + q = 0$$

Using the formula with $a = 2$, $b = -p$ and $c = q$ gives

$$x = \frac{-(-p) \pm \sqrt{(-p)^2 - 4(2)(q)}}{4}$$

$$= \frac{p \pm \sqrt{p^2 - 8q}}{4}$$

To be able to find the square root, $p^2 - 8q$ must not be negative, i.e. values of x can be found if $p^2 - 8q \geqslant 0$

---

35. Give a condition for each equation to have a solution.

a) $x^2 + px + 3 = 0$

b) $x^2 + 5x + c = 0$

c) $px^2 + qx + r = 0$

d) $cx^2 + bx + a = 0$.

OTHER EQUATIONS AND PROBLEMS

We can solve the equation $x^4 = 5$ by finding $\sqrt[4]{5}$, but $x = 1.495\ldots$ is not the only solution; the other possible real solution is $-1.495\ldots$ because $(-1.495\ldots)^4 = 5$. Care must be taken to make sure that the correct solutions have been selected.

EXERCISE 3j

1. Solve the following equations if it is possible.

   a) $x^6 = 7$ b) $x^5 = -10$ c) $x^2 = 4.56$
   d) $x^2 - 7 = 0$ e) $x^4 - 8 = 0$ f) $x^5 - 6.87 = 0$
   g) $x^3 + 9 = 0$ h) $x^4 + 6 = 0$ i) $x^4 = 0.006\,78$.

2. Find x when $x^2 - 7 = 1 - x^2$.

3. The roots of the equation $x^2 + px + q = 0$ are both 5. Find the values of p and q.

4. Form the equation whose roots are 3 and 2.

5. The length of a rectangular carpet is 1 m more than the width, and its area is $10\,\text{m}^2$. Find its width correct to 3 significant figures.

6.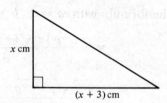

   x cm

   $(x + 3)$ cm

   The area of the triangle is $14\,\text{cm}^2$. Find x.

7. The product of two consecutive numbers is eleven more than the sum of the two numbers. Find the two numbers.

8. When a number is subtracted from its square, the remainder is 72. Find the two possible values of the number.

9. I travel 90 km at an average speed of x km/h.
   a) In terms of x how long does the journey take ?
   b) If the speed were 5 km/h greater, how long would the journey take ?
   c) By travelling at the faster speed I would take a quarter of an hour less than at the slower speed. Form an equation and find x.

10. I could save half an hour on a 45 mile journey if I travelled, on average, 15 m.p.h. faster than I had planned to do. Find the speed at which I had planned to travel.

11. Mary intends to spend £3.20 on balloons for a party, the balloons costing x pence each. However, she finds that the balloons each cost 2p more than she expected, so she will have to buy 8 fewer for her £3.20. Find x.

ALGEBRAIC FRACTIONS

Algebraic fractions are simplified by following the same rules as for arithmetic fractions: if we wish to add or subtract we look for a common denominator; if we wish to multiply or divide we look for factors to cancel.

In every case we first find the factors, if any.

MULTIPLICATION AND DIVISION

EXERCISE 3k

Simplify the following expressions.

1. $\dfrac{x}{2} \times \dfrac{y}{5}$

4. $1 \div \dfrac{a}{b}$

2. $\dfrac{5a}{c} \times \dfrac{c}{3a}$

5. $\dfrac{8pq}{r^2} \times \dfrac{r}{q^2}$

3. $\dfrac{1}{a} \times \dfrac{1}{b}$

6. $\dfrac{4a}{bc} \times \dfrac{3b}{a}$

7. $\dfrac{(x-1)}{4} \times \dfrac{3}{(x-1)}$

9. $\dfrac{x(x-1)}{x+2} \times \dfrac{3(x+2)}{x}$

8. $\dfrac{3(x+1)}{5} \div \dfrac{2(x+1)}{3}$

10. $\dfrac{x^2}{x-5} \div \dfrac{2x}{x-5}$

In the following questions factorise first, then cancel if possible. Remember that $(x-a) = -1(a-x)$.

11. $\dfrac{2x+4}{x^2+2x}$

16. $\dfrac{x^2-9}{3x-9}$

12. $\dfrac{x-2}{2-x}$

17. $\dfrac{ax+bx+ay+by}{ax-bx+ay-by}$

13. $\dfrac{x^2-4}{x^2+4x+4}$

18. $\dfrac{x^2-16}{x^2-x-20}$

14. $\dfrac{x^2-5x+6}{x^2-4x+3}$

19. $\dfrac{x^2-1}{2-2x}$

15. $\dfrac{x^2-x-12}{x^2-6x+8}$

20. $\dfrac{2x+4}{3x-9} \times \dfrac{2x-6}{3x+6}$

21. $\dfrac{x^2-16}{x+4} \div \dfrac{x-4}{2}$

23. $\dfrac{x^2+5x+6}{x^2-5x+6} \div \dfrac{x^2+6x+8}{x^2-6x+8}$

22. $\dfrac{x-a}{x+a} \times \dfrac{1}{x^2-a^2}$

24. $\dfrac{a^2-b^2}{a^2+b^2} \times \dfrac{a+b}{a-b}$

FRACTIONAL EXPRESSIONS AND EQUATIONS

$\dfrac{x+1}{6} - \dfrac{2x+1}{3} = 1$ is an *equation*. If we multiply every term by 6, the balance is not upset and the equation is still valid.

On the other hand, $\dfrac{x+1}{6} - \dfrac{2x+1}{3}$ is an *expression* and if we are simplifying it we must retain the common denominator, 6. We do *not* multiply it by 6 as this would make it six times as large, i.e. it would be changed.

EXERCISE 31

Simplify the expression $\dfrac{4x+1}{2} - \dfrac{2(x-2)}{3}$

$$\dfrac{(4x+1)}{2} - \dfrac{2(x-2)}{3} = \dfrac{3(4x+1)-4(x-2)}{6}$$

$$= \dfrac{12x+3-4x+8}{6}$$

$$= \dfrac{8x+11}{6}$$

Simplify the following expressions.

1. $\dfrac{x}{3} + \dfrac{2x}{5}$

4. $\dfrac{2(x-1)}{5} - \dfrac{3(1-x)}{2}$

7. $\dfrac{4}{x} + \dfrac{3}{2x}$

2. $\dfrac{x}{7} + \dfrac{1}{3} - \dfrac{2}{7}$

5. $\dfrac{x}{3} - \dfrac{x-1}{4}$

8. $\dfrac{1}{x+2} - \dfrac{1}{x-3}$

3. $\dfrac{x+1}{4} + \dfrac{x-1}{3}$

6. $\dfrac{1}{x} + \dfrac{x}{2}$

9. $\dfrac{x+2}{4} - \dfrac{2x-4}{5}$

Solve the equation $\dfrac{4x+1}{2} - \dfrac{2(x-2)}{3} = \dfrac{9}{2}$

$$\frac{4x+1}{2} - \frac{2(x-2)}{3} = \frac{9}{2}$$

$$\overset{3}{\cancel{6}} \times \frac{(4x+1)}{\cancel{2}_1} - \overset{2}{\cancel{6}} \times \frac{2(x-2)}{\cancel{3}_1} = \overset{3}{\cancel{6}} \times \frac{9}{\cancel{2}_1}$$

$$3(4x+1) - 4(x-2) = 27$$

$$12x + 3 - 4x + 8 = 27$$

$$8x + 11 = 27$$

$$8x = 16$$

$$x = 2$$

The solution is $x = 2$.

Solve the following equations.

10. $\dfrac{x}{3} + \dfrac{2x}{5} = 1$

11. $\dfrac{x}{7} + \dfrac{1}{3} - \dfrac{2}{7} = -\dfrac{2}{3}$

12. $\dfrac{x+1}{4} + \dfrac{x-1}{3} = \dfrac{17}{12}$

13. $\dfrac{2(x-1)}{5} - \dfrac{3(1-x)}{2} = \dfrac{19}{10}$

14. $\dfrac{x}{3} - \dfrac{x-1}{4} = 7$

15. $\dfrac{1}{x} + \dfrac{x}{6} = \dfrac{7}{6}$

16. $\dfrac{4}{x} + \dfrac{3}{2x} = \dfrac{11}{4}$

17. $(x+2) = \dfrac{(x+2)}{(x-3)}$

18. Express as a single fraction a) $\dfrac{3}{x-y} + \dfrac{2}{x+y}$ b) $\dfrac{a+b}{2} + \dfrac{2}{a-b}$

19. Solve the equation a) $\dfrac{x+1}{4} - \dfrac{x-1}{5} = 1$ b) $\dfrac{2}{3x} - \dfrac{6}{5x} = -8$

20. Find x if a) $\dfrac{1}{x} + \dfrac{x+1}{9} = \dfrac{11}{9}$ b) $\dfrac{3}{x-1} + \dfrac{4}{1-x} = 2$

21. Simplify a) $\dfrac{3}{x-1} + \dfrac{4}{1-x}$ b) $\dfrac{2}{x-y} + \dfrac{3}{y-x}$

SIMULTANEOUS EQUATIONS, ONE LINEAR, ONE QUADRATIC

To solve a pair of equations one of which contains terms in, say, x^2 or y^2 or xy, we need to use the method of *substitution* rather than elimination.

From the simpler equation (i.e. the linear equation), we find one letter in terms of the other and make a substitution in the more complicated equation.

EXERCISE 3m

Solve the pair of equations $x^2 + y^2 = 17$, $x + y = 3$.

$$x^2 + y^2 = 17 \qquad [1]$$
$$x + y = 3 \qquad [2]$$

(x and y are equally convenient to use.)

From [2] $\qquad\qquad x = 3 - y \qquad\qquad [3]$

$$x^2 = (3 - y)(3 - y)$$
$$= 9 - 6y + y^2$$

Substitute for x^2 in [1]

$$9 - 6y + y^2 + y^2 = 17$$
$$2y^2 - 6y + 9 = 17$$
$$2y^2 - 6y - 8 = 0$$
$$y^2 - 3y - 4 = 0$$
$$(y - 4)(y + 1) = 0$$

Either $y = 4$ or $y = -1$.

From [3], when $y = 4$, $x = -1$

when $y = -1$, $x = 4$

Check in [1]: when $x = 4$ and $y = -1$, $x^2 + y^2 = 16 + 1 = 17$

when $x = -1$ and $y = 4$, $x^2 + y^2 = 1 + 16 = 17$

The solution is $x = 4$, $y = -1$ or $x = -1$, $y = 4$.

Solve the following equations.

1. $x^2 + y^2 = 5$

    $x + y = 3$

2. $x^2 + y^2 = 10$

    $x - y = 4$

3. $2xy + y = 10$

    $x + y = 4$

4. $x^2 - 2xy = 32$

    $y = 2 - x$

5. $9 - x^2 = y^2$

    $x + y = 3$

6. $xy = 12$

    $x + y = 7$

In the previous equations either the choice of letter was obvious or it did not matter which was chosen. In the following equations, one letter is easier to use than the other, but it may not be obvious.

Solve the pair of equations $3xy + y^2 = 13$, $y = x - 3$.

$$3xy + y^2 = 13 \qquad\qquad [1]$$

$$y = x - 3 \qquad\qquad [2]$$

(It is simpler to substitute for x in [1], to avoid squaring.)

From [2] $x = y + 3$ [3]

In [1] $3y(y + 3) + y^2 = 13$

$$3y^2 + 9y + y^2 = 13$$

$$4y^2 + 9y - 13 = 0$$

$$(4y + 13)(y - 1) = 0$$

$\therefore$ either $4y + 13 = 0$ or $y = 1$.

$$4y = -13$$

$$y = -\tfrac{13}{4}$$

From [3], when $y = -3\tfrac{1}{4}$, $x = -3\tfrac{1}{4} + 3 = -\tfrac{1}{4}$

         when $y = 1$, $x = 4$.

Check   when $x = 4$ and $y = 1$, $3xy + y^2 = 12 + 1 = 13$

         when $x = -\tfrac{1}{4}$ and $y = -3\tfrac{1}{4}$, $3xy + y^2 = \tfrac{39}{16} + \tfrac{169}{16} = 13$

The solution is $x = 4$, $y = 1$ or $x = -\tfrac{1}{4}$, $y = -3\tfrac{1}{4}$.

Solve the following pairs of equations.

7. $xy - x = -10$

$2x + y = 2$

8. $xy = x$

$2x - y = 3$

9. $y^2 = 4x$

$x - y = 0$

10. $x + 3y = 14$

$xy = 8$

11. $13 - x^2 = y^2$

$x + y = 5$

12. $x^2 - y^2 = 24$

$x - 2y = 3$

Solve the equations $x^2 + y^2 = 13$, $2x + 3y = 13$.

$$x^2 + y^2 = 13 \qquad\qquad [1]$$

$$2x + 3y = 13 \qquad\qquad [2]$$

From [2] $\qquad\qquad 2x = 13 - 3y$

$$x = \frac{13 - 3y}{2} \qquad\qquad [3]$$

$$x^2 = \frac{(13 - 3y)(13 - 3y)}{4}$$

$$= \frac{169 - 78y + 9y^2}{4}$$

In [1] $\qquad\qquad \dfrac{169 - 78y + 9y^2}{4} + y^2 = 13$

Multiply both sides by 4 $\quad 169 - 78y + 9y^2 + 4y^2 = 52$

$$13y^2 - 78y + 117 = 0$$

Divide both sides by 13 $\qquad\qquad y^2 - 6y + 9 = 0$

$$(y - 3)(y - 3) = 0$$

$$\therefore \quad y = 3$$

From [3], when $y = 3$, $x = 2$.

Solve the following pairs of equations.

13. $x^2 + y^2 = 2$

$3x - 2y = 5$

14. $x^2 - y^2 = 0$

$3x + 2y = 5$

15. $xy = 6$

$4x - 3y = 6$

16. $xy + x = -3$

$2x + 5y = 8$

17. $x^2 = y + 3$

$2x - 3y = 8$

18. $\dfrac{3}{x} + \dfrac{6}{y} = 4$

$x + y = 5$

19. $x(x - y) = 6$

$x + y = 4$

20. $x^2 + xy + y^2 = 7$

$2x + y = 4$

MIXED EXERCISES

EXERCISE 3n

1. Simplify   a) $\dfrac{6a}{b} \times \dfrac{3a}{c}$ b) $\dfrac{6a}{b} \div \dfrac{3a}{c}$ c) $\dfrac{b}{6a} + \dfrac{c}{3a}$

2. Simplify $\dfrac{6x - 3x^2}{x}$

3. Solve the equations   a) $x^2 = 5x$ b) $\dfrac{3}{x} = 12$

4. Express $\dfrac{1}{x-2} - \dfrac{1}{x+3}$ as a single fraction.

5. Find the value of   a) 4^0 b) $4^{1/2}$ c) 4^{-3}

6. Solve the equation $2x^2 + 3x - 12 = 0$ giving your answers correct to 2 d.p.

7. Simplify the expression $\dfrac{x^2 + 2x - 8}{x^2 - 4}$

EXERCISE 3p

1. Find a value of x such that $\dfrac{3}{x} = \dfrac{x}{27}$

2. Simplify   a) $x^2 \times x^3$ b) $x^2 \div x^3$ c) $(x^2)^3$

3. Solve the equations $x + 2y = 12$, $3x - 4y = 1$

4. Factorise   a) $x^2 - x - 6$ b) $x^3 - x^2 + x - 1$

5. Express $\dfrac{4(x-1)}{3} - \dfrac{2(x+1)}{5}$ as a single fraction.

6. Solve the equation $x^2 - x - 42 = 0$

7. Give the condition for the equation $2x^2 + 5x + a = 0$ to have a solution.

EXERCISE 3q

1. Solve the equation $\dfrac{1}{2x} + \dfrac{x+1}{2} = 2\frac{1}{6}$

2. Factorise   a) $4x^2 - 16$ b) $4x^2 - 16x$ c) $4x^2 - 5x + 1$

3. Solve the equation $4(x-1) - 3(2x+1) = 3(x+4)$

4. Simplify   a) $2^4 \div 2^2$ b) $2^0 \div 2^3$ c) $(2^3)^2$

5. Solve the equations $2x - 3y = 2$, $3x - 2y = -7$

6. Solve the equation $x^2 - 6x + 1 = 0$, giving your solutions correct to 2 d.p.

7. The hypotenuse of a right-angled triangle is of length $3x + 4\,\text{cm}$ and the lengths of the other two sides are $x + 2\,\text{cm}$ and $4x\,\text{cm}$. Find x.

4 AREAS AND VOLUMES

Apart from revising previous work on areas and volumes this chapter considers the problems of errors and estimating.

We begin by summarising the most important results. Some of you may prefer to remember certain of these results in words rather than as formulae.

AREAS

Rectangle: Area = length × breadth

i.e. $A = lb$

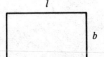

Triangle: Area = half base × perpendicular height

i.e. $A = \frac{1}{2}bh$

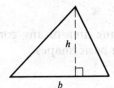

Parallelogram: Area = base × perpendicular height

i.e. $A = bh$

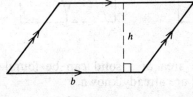

Trapezium: Area = half sum of parallel sides × distance between them

i.e. $A = \frac{1}{2}(a+b)h$

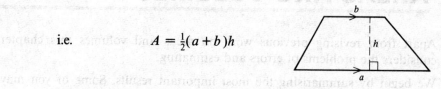

Circle: Area $= \pi r^2$

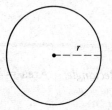

Sector of circle: Area $= \pi r^2 \times \dfrac{x}{360}$

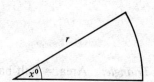

We can also find the area of any compound shape that is made up of a combination of the basic shapes

e.g.

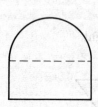  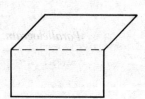

The surface area of a solid can be found if its plane faces are shapes whose areas are already known.

We can also find the surface area of a few curved surfaces.

Cylinder: Curved surface area $= 2\pi rh$

Therefore   total surface area $= 2\pi r^2 + 2\pi rh$

$$= 2\pi r(r + h)$$

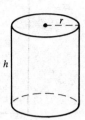

Sphere: Total surface area $= 4\pi r^2$

Cone: Curved surface area $= \pi rl$ where l is the slant height

Therefore   total surface area $= \pi r^2 + \pi rl$

$$= \pi r(r + l)$$

In the exercises that follow, if any answers are not exact, give them correct to three significant figures. Use the value of π on your calculator unless told otherwise.

EXERCISE 4a

Find the areas of the shapes given in questions 1 to 12. All measurements are given in centimetres.

1.

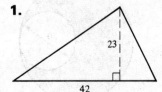

2.

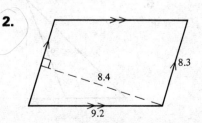

3.
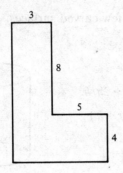

7.
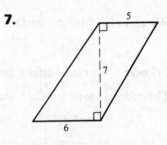

4.
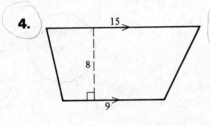

8.
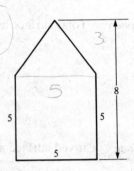

5.
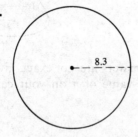

9.
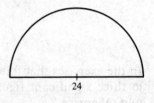

6.
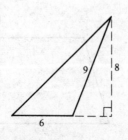

10.
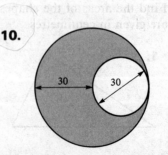

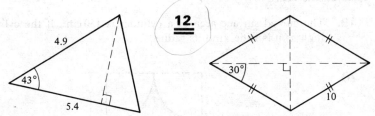

11. **12.**

13. a) Use $\pi = 3$ to give an approximate area for each of the shapes in questions 5, 9 and 10.

b) Find, in terms of π, the areas of the shapes in questions 5, 9 and 10.

14. The hands of a clock are 8 cm and 5 cm long.

a) What area does the minute hand pass over in half an hour?

b) What area does the hour hand pass over in half an hour?

15. Find the curved surface area of a solid cylinder of base radius 8 cm and height 12 cm. What is the total surface area of this cylinder?

16. Leanda uses her ruler to measure the sides of a page of a book and finds them to be 294 mm by 216 mm.

a) Express these measurements   i) in centimetres   ii) in metres.

b) Find the area of the page in square centimetres
   i) correct to one decimal place
   ii) correct to three significant figures.

The total surface area of a closed cylindrical metal can is 200 cm². If the diameter of the base of the can is 5 cm find its height.

$$A = 200 \qquad r = 2.5$$

$$A = 2\pi r(r + h)$$

$$200 = 2\pi \times 2.5(2.5 + h)$$

where h is the height in centimetres

$$2.5 + h = \frac{200}{2\pi \times 2.5}$$

$$2.5 + h = 12.73$$

$$h = 10.23$$

∴   the height of the can is 10.2 cm correct to 3 s.f.

---

17. Find the curved surface area of a right circular cone that has a base radius of 6 cm and a slant height of 10 cm. How high is the cone?

18. The total surface area of a sphere is 100 cm². Find its radius.

19. The curved surface area of a cylinder is 150 cm². If the cylinder is twice as high as it is wide, find its radius.

 20.

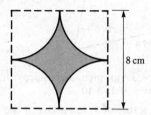

8 cm

The sketch shows the pressing, from a square sheet of metal of side 8 cm, required in the manufacture of a piece of machinery. The perimeter is formed from four quarter circles with equal radii.

a) Calculate   i) the perimeter of the pressing
                        ii) its area
                        iii) the percentage of the metal sheet wasted.

b) Several of these pressings have to be made. Can you suggest arrangements, using large sheets of metal, so that less metal is wasted ?

21. The scale of a map is 1 : 50 000. Find the actual area   a) in hectares,
b) in square kilometres, of a lake represented by an area of 3.8 square centimetres on the map.
(1 hectare = 10 000 m².)

22.

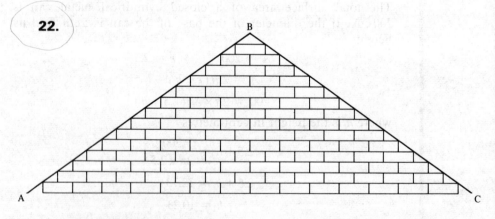

The sketch shows the gable end of a garage where bricks are used to fill the gable. Each brick measures 210 mm by 70 mm. If there are fourteen bricks in the first row and there are fourteen rows of bricks, find

a) the inclination of AB and BC to the horizontal

b) the distance AC, in metres

c) the height of B above the level of AC

d) the area of triangle ABC.

23.

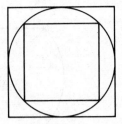

A square is inscribed in a circle of radius 10 cm and a second square is circumscribed to the circle. Find

a) the area inside the larger square but outside the circle

b) the area outside the smaller square but inside the circle.

Express your answer to (a) as a percentage of your answer to (b).

24.

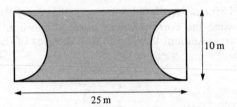

10 m

25 m

The diagram shows a rectangular garden, 25 m by 10 m. A semicircular flowerbed has been prepared at each end, and the remainder (the shaded area) put down to lawn. Using $\pi \approx 3$, calculate

a) the combined area of the two flowerbeds

b) the area of the lawn

c) the perimeter of the lawn.

25. Two teapot stands have exactly the same area. If the square stand has a side of 120 mm, what is the radius of the circular stand ?

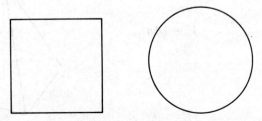

26.

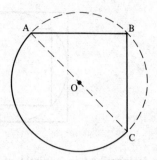

The shape of the top of a kitchen unit is part of a circle, centre O.
Angle ABC = 90° and AB = BC = 60 cm. Find

a) the area of the top in cm²

b) the perimeter of the top in centimetres

c) the cost of covering the top with a laminate costing £8 per square metre

d) the cost of plastic strip for the curved edge of the top at 24 p per metre.

27. Two similar triangles are such that every linear dimension in one triangle is twice the corresponding linear dimension in the other. If their combined areas amount to 500 cm², find the area of the larger triangle.

VOLUMES

1 litre = 1000 cubic centimetres.

Cuboid: Volume = length × breadth × height

i.e. $V = lbh$

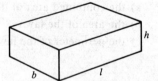

Pyramid: Volume = $\frac{1}{3}$ area of base × perpendicular height

i.e. $V = \frac{1}{3}Ah$

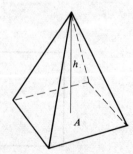

Cylinder: Volume = area of base × height

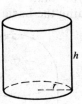

i.e. $V = \pi r^2 h$

Cone: Volume = $\frac{1}{3}$ area of base × perpendicular height

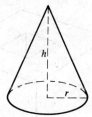

i.e. $V = \frac{1}{3}\pi r^2 h$

Sphere: $V = \frac{4}{3}\pi r^3$

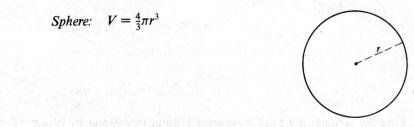

Prism: (solid with constant cross-section):

Volume = area of cross-section × length

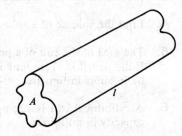

i.e. $V = Al$

It follows that we can find the volume of any solid that is made by combining the basic solids

e.g.

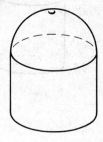

this salt cellar combines a cylinder with half a sphere (i.e. a hemisphere),

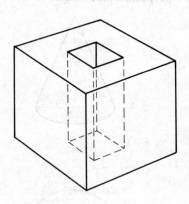

this solid wooden cube has had a cuboid removed from it.

EXERCISE 4b

1. Find the volume of a brick measuring 210 mm by 100 mm by 70 mm. Give your answer in cubic centimetres. How many such bricks are required to give a total volume that exceeds one cubic metre ?

2. A pyramid has a square base of side 12 cm and is 15 cm high. Find its volume.

3. A cone has a base radius of 3.8 cm and is 8 cm high. Find its volume.

4. Find the volume of a sphere of radius 15 cm.

5. The area of the end of a pencil with uniform cross section is $\frac{1}{5}$ cm^2. If the pencil is 17 cm long find its volume   a) in cubic centimetres b) in cubic millimetres.

6. A cylindrical can is 12 cm high and has a base radius of 25.8 mm. Find its capacity in millilitres.

7. The radius of a sphere and the radius of the circular base of a cylinder are each 5 cm. If both solids have the same volume, how high is the cylinder?

8. The volume of a circular cylinder is 500 ml. If its height is equal to twice its radius, find its radius.

9.

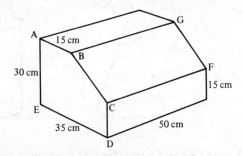

The sketch shows a closed wooden box of uniform cross-section, with a sloping front. The dimensions of the box are given on the sketch. Calculate
a) the length of BC
b) the area of the sloping front BCFG
c) the area of the end ABCDE
d) the total surface area of the box
e) the volume of the box.

10. The volume of a right circular cone is 1000 cm³. If its height is three times its radius, find its height.

11. The volume of a pyramid with a square base is 2187 cm³. If its height is 9 cm, find the length of a side of the base.

12. A cylindrical jam jar has a diameter of 70 mm, is 120 mm high, and is filled with water to a depth of 80 mm. 1200 identical spherical ball-bearings of radius 2.5 mm are placed in the jar and are completely immersed. By how much does the surface of the water rise?

13.

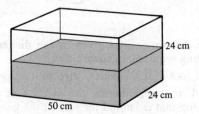

Water stands to a depth of 12 cm in a rectangular tank, measuring 50 cm × 24 cm × 24 cm. Five cubical heavy metal blocks, each of side 9 cm, are placed on the bottom of the tank. By how much does the water level rise?

14. A hemispherical cut-glass bowl has an internal diameter of 22 cm and is 7.5 mm thick throughout. If 5% of the original glass has been removed by the cutting of the design, calculate the volume of glass in the resulting bowl, giving your answer in cubic centimetres.

15.

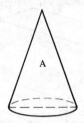 

A cone (A) and a cylinder (B) have equal bases and equal heights.

a) If the volume of the cylinder is 36 cm³, find the volume of the cone.

b) If the volume of the cone is 18.6 cm³, find the volume of the cylinder.

c) If the combined volume of the two solids is 64 cm³ find the volume of the cylinder.

16. The diagram shows the goalmouth and netting prepared for a football match. The netting is attached to the goal posts and crossbar, and also to two metal tubes, each in the form of a quarter of a circle.

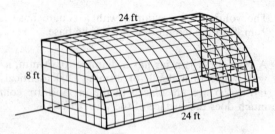

a) Use the dimensions given in the diagram to calculate the total area of netting required, in square feet.

b) If 1 foot = 0.305 metres, give your answer to (a) in square metres.

c) Find, in cubic metres, the volume of the space contained within the netting that is behind the face of the goal.

17. A solid metal cone of height 20 cm and radius 12 cm is melted down to form a cylinder of the same height. What is the radius of the cylinder?

18. A solid metal cylinder with diameter 2 cm and height 4 cm stands inside an empty cylindrical measuring jar with a diameter of 4 cm. Water is poured into the jar to a depth of 3 cm.

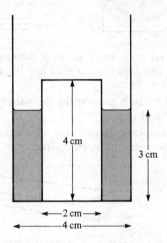

Find

a) the volume of water poured into the cylinder

b) the additional volume of water required just to cover the metal cylinder

c) the total volume of water required if the depth of water in the cylinder at its deepest point is 6 cm.

(Give all your answers as multiples of π.)

19. A salt cellar is in the form of a cylinder, of diameter 3 cm and height 3 cm, topped by a hemisphere. It contains salt to a depth of 2.5 cm. It is inverted with its outlet covered. Find the distance from the new level of the salt (assumed horizontal) to the flat base of the salt cellar.

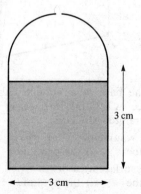

20.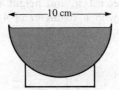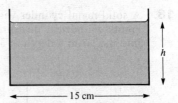

Soup placed in a bowl forms a hemisphere of diameter 10 cm. Six such bowls are filled with soup that has been warmed in a cylindrical saucepan with diameter 15 cm.

a) Find the depth of soup in the saucepan if there is just sufficient to fill all six bowls.

b) By what factor is the area of soup open to the atmosphere increased when the soup has been poured from the saucepan into the bowls ?

21.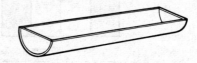

The diagram shows a 2 metre length of plastic gutter with semicircular end-stops of diameter 7 cm. The gutter is made by bending sheet plastic. Find

a) the maximum amount of water the gutter will hold
   i) in cubic centimetres   ii) in litres

b) the area, in square metres, of sheet plastic required to make the gutter, including the endstops. Assume that there is no overlap.

22.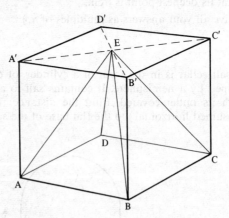

ABCD is the base of a wooden cube of side 6 cm. The diagonals of the opposite face A'B'C'D' intersect at E. Wood is removed from the cube to form the pyramid ABCDE.

a) Find the volume of
   i) the cube   ii) the pyramid   iii) the wood wasted.

b) Find the surface area of
   i) the cube   ii) the pyramid.

23.

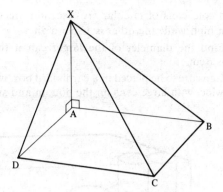

The diagram shows a pyramid which has a rectangular base ABCD, and a vertex X which is vertically above A. If AB = 40 cm, BC = 30 cm and $\widehat{ABX} = 32°$, find

a) the height of X above A

b) the length of AC

o) the angle $A\widehat{C}X$

d) the combined area of the *sloping* faces of the pyramid.

24.

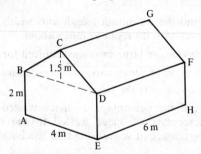

The diagram shows a workshop which stands on a rectangular base, and has a ridged roof. Its dimensions in metres are given on the diagram. Find

a) the area of the end ABCDE

b) the length CD, one of the sloping edges of the roof

c) the area of CDFG, one of the sloping faces of the roof

d) the capacity of the shed

e) the ground area on which the workshop stands

f) the volume of rain falling vertically on the roof of the shed during a storm of rainfall 2 cm.

25. Liquid is discharged from a pipe at a rate of 44.4 kilograms per minute. Express this rate in grams per second.

If the density of the liquid is 0.925 grams per cubic centimetre, calculate the volume of liquid discharged per second.

The liquid is discharged into cylindrical containers of height 72 cm and base radius 20 cm. Find the time taken, in seconds, to fill each container. (Give your answer as a multiple of π.)

26. Two cola cans of circular cross-section are similar in every respect. One is 8 cm high while the other is 12 cm high.

   a) Find the diameter of the larger can if the diameter of the smaller can is 6 cm.

   b) Cans are to be placed in a cardboard box, which is to be twice as long as it is wide, with large cans on the bottom and small cans on the top.

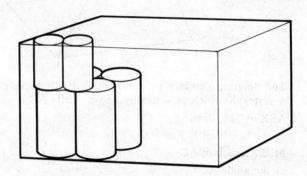

   i) Find the minimum length and width of the box if the cans at each level have no room to move about.

   ii) How many large cans are required for the bottom layer in the box ?

   iii) How many small cans are required for the top layer in the box ?

   iv) How deep is the box ?

   v) Find the percentage of space wasted in each layer. How does the percentage of space wasted in the upper layer compare with the percentage of space wasted in the bottom layer ?

27.

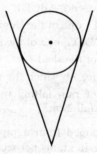

The sketch shows a cone of radius 4 cm and depth 12 cm on which rests a sphere of ice-cream of radius 2.5 cm. The ice-cream melts, and, without any loss or change in volume, runs into the cone. Find the depth of liquid in the cone when the ice-cream has melted completely.

DIMENSIONS OF LENGTH, AREA AND VOLUME

We can check formulae concerned with length, area and volume by checking the dimensions. Suppose that a formula for the area, A, of a shape is given as $A = \dfrac{V}{2a^2}$ where V is a number of volume units and a is a number of length units. We can see that $\dfrac{V}{2a^2}$ is only one dimensional, so the formula cannot be correct.

ROUGH ESTIMATES

There are many everyday situations in which we need to estimate. How long will it take to drive to London? How many tiles will we need to cover the bathroom walls? How many litres of paint will we require to paint the lounge? For most estimates of this kind we use our inbuilt knowledge of shape, size and units, or take advantage of the experience of other people. We also need to develop a feel for the size of an answer to a calculation, e.g. what, roughly, is $8.926 \times 0.042\,34$?

EXERCISE 4c

1. State whether each of the following quantities is a length, an area or a volume.

a) $9\,\text{cm}$ b) $11\,\text{m}^2$ c) $7\,\text{mm}^3$

d) $8\,\text{m}$ e) $5\,\text{in}^3$ f) $16\,\text{in}^2$

2. State whether each of the following quantities should be measured in length, area or volume units.

a) The circumference of a circle.

b) The space inside a cube.

c) The surface of a sphere.

3. The letters p, q and r each represent a number of centimetres. Write down a suitable unit (e.g. cm^2) for the subject of each of the following formulae.

a) $P = q + r$ b) $Q = 3\pi pq$ c) $R = \pi q^3$

d) $S = pqr$ e) $T = 4\pi r$ f) $U = rq + \pi pq$

In questions 4 and 5, a and b represent numbers of length units, A and B represent numbers of area units and V represents a number of volume units.

4. State whether Z represents a number of length, area or volume units.

a) $Z = \pi ac$ c) $Z = b^2 + c^2$ e) $Z = \pi bc^2$

b) $Z = \pi Ba$ d) $Z = \dfrac{V}{2ab}$ f) $Z = \dfrac{4V}{3c}$

5. Some of the following formulae are wrongly constructed. State, with a reason, which are incorrect.

a) $A = bc$ c) $B = \pi c$ e) $V = b + B$

b) $B = c(a + b)$ d) $V = 2a^2 + b^3$ f) $c = \dfrac{5V}{2b}$

6.

Which of these formulae could give the capacity of the vase in the diagram ?

A $2\pi rh$ **B** $\pi(r^2 + h)$ **C** $\dfrac{1}{2}\pi r^2 h$ **D** $\dfrac{\pi r^2}{h}$ **E** πrh

Write down an estimate for each of the following quantities. Where possible check your estimates by measuring or weighing or working them out.

7. How high is the door you used to come into the room ?

8. How wide is the blackboard ?

9. What are the dimensions of the room ?

10. What are the dimensions of this page ?

11. How high is the desk ?

12. How long is a new stick of chalk ?

13. How long is the school hall ?

14. Two hundred 1 kg bags of sugar are laid end to end on their sides. How far will they stretch ?

15. How heavy is   a) a pencil,   b) a shoe,   c) a 50 p coin,   d) an elephant, e) a coach,   f) a large ship ?

16. How high is a telegraph pole ? How could you calculate its height without climbing to the top ?

EVERYDAY ESTIMATES

We are used to numbers bombarding us from all sides:

80 000 at Wembley Stadium Last Night

Ruritania to spend £3.46m on defence next year

Population of China reaches 2000m

300 feared lost in air disaster.

These are typical headlines from our daily newspapers, but they do not mean exactly what they say! They are approximations or 'guesstimates'. Perhaps they are correct to the first figure. For example, '3000 feared dead in an earthquake' could mean anything between 2500 and 3499 if the figure is correct to the nearest thousand. If the number had been thought to be a few less than 2500 the estimate would have been 2000, whereas if the number had been thought to be 3500, or a few more, the estimate would have been 4000.

When we quantify something our value is often approximate. The length of our lounge is, perhaps, 4 m correct to the nearest metre, but 426 cm correct to the nearest centimetre. We estimate we spend £30 each week at the supermarket. Perhaps this means £27.40 one week but £34.72 the following week.

The next exercise considers the range within which given numbers lie.

EXERCISE 4d

> The attendance at a pop concert is given as 65 000, correct to the nearest thousand. Find
> a) the maximum number that could have been present
> b) the minimum number that could have been present.
>
> a) The largest number that could have been present is 65 499.
>   (This number correct to the nearest thousand is 65 000, whereas 65 500 correct to the nearest thousand would be 66 000.)
>
> b) The smallest number that could have been present is 64 500.

1. The attendance at a football match is given as 46 000 correct to the nearest thousand. Find

a) the greatest number of spectators that could have been present

b) the smallest number of spectators that could have been present.

2. It is reported that 1500 people have lost their lives in an earthquake. If this is correct to the nearest 100 what is the smallest possible number of deaths ?

3. A sports' club has 600 members, correct to the nearest 100. Between what numbers must the membership lie ?

4. The population of China is 2000 million, correct to the nearest 100 million.

a) What is the largest possible population ?

b) What is the smallest possible population ?

Give each answer correct to the nearest million.

5. Jenny spends £45 each week at the supermarket. If this is correct to the nearest £5, find

a) the largest amount she could spend

b) the smallest amount she could spend.

6. A local authority is to spend £750 000, correct to the nearest £10 000, on a new road project. What are the upper and lower limits within which they expect the expenditure to be ?

7. A motor manufacturer aims to produce 2000 cars a week, correct to the nearest 100. What are the upper and lower limits that satisfy this target ?

8. The Australian government decides that the number of immigrants next year, to the nearest thousand, is to be restricted to 35 000. What is the difference between the largest number that will be allowed and the smallest number that will be allowed ?

9. Copy and complete the following table, which shows corrected numbers and the smallest and largest values from which they can arise.

Number	Correct to nearest	Smallest possible value	Largest possible
4 560	10	4555	4564
1 800	100	1750	1849
5 000	1000		
80 000	10 000		
30 000	1000		
66 700	100		
	100		4549
	1000	3500	

FIRST ORDER APPROXIMATIONS

The approximations and estimates we have considered in the previous exercise have all concerned whole numbers. However, many of the measurements we make can involve decimal or fractional numbers. For example, the length of a room may be 3 m, correct to the nearest metre, but its length could be 3.24 m or 3.243 m, depending on the degree of accuracy possible in measuring.

If a length is given as 3 m, correct to the nearest whole number, then it is possible that the length could really be as low as 2.5 m or nearly as high as 3.5 m. So if the length is l cm

$$2.5 \leqslant l < 3.5$$

Similarly if the mass, m kg, of a bag of potatoes is 5.5 kg, correct to two significant figures, then

$$5.45 \leqslant m < 5.55$$

5.45 is called the lower bound of m and 5.55 is called the upper bound of m.

EXERCISE 4e

In questions 1 to 8 write down the values between which each of the given quantities lies.

1. The width of my protractor is 9.6 cm, correct to 2 s.f.

2. The height of my protractor is 5.6 cm, correct to 2 s.f.

3. The length of my ruler is 31 cm, correct to the nearest cm.

4. The length of my lounge is 8200 mm, correct to the nearest 100 mm.

5. The length of a rectangular field is 126 m, correct to the nearest metre.

6. The weight of a bag of cement is 50 kg, correct to the nearest kg.

7. The distance between Blackborough and Woodside is 300 miles, correct to the nearest 100 miles.

8. John's speed, correct to 3 s.f., was 8.35 m/s.

9. The length of my lounge is 4 m, correct to the nearest metre. If l metres is the actual length between what values must l lie ?

10. Ravi estimates that it is 3 miles from his home to school, correct to the nearest mile. If the actual distance is D miles, between what values must D lie ?

11. Shan is 166 cm tall, correct to the nearest cm. If Shan's actual height is h cm, between what values must h lie ?

12. The diameter of a spindle is given as within twelve thousandths of 0.5 cm. If the actual value is D cm use inequalities to show the range of possible diameters.

COMPOUND APPROXIMATIONS

If the side of a square field is given as 90 m, correct to the nearest 10 m, the area of the field could be anything within a fairly wide range of values.

The smallest value for the length of the side of the field is 85 m, which gives an area of 7225 m² for the field.

The largest value is the value just below 95 m, which gives an area just less than 9025 m². Thus if A m² is the area of the field

$$7225 \leqslant A < 9025$$

The upper bound is 25 % more than the lower bound, and clearly indicates why surveyors calculate their figures with great accuracy.

Similarly, if r is the radius of a sphere, and $r = 3$ cm correct to the nearest cm, then

$$2.5 \leqslant r < 3.5$$

and the volume of the sphere, V cm³ $(V = \frac{4}{3}\pi r^3)$, is such that

$$65 \leqslant V < 180$$

correct to the nearest cubic centimetre.

EXERCISE 4f

The sides of a rectangle are given as 5.2 cm and 3.8 cm, each correct to one decimal place.
Find   a) the upper bound of the possible area
        b) the minimum area
of the rectangle with these dimensions.

By what percentage does the upper limit of the area exceed the minimum area ?

The maximum length that gives a length of 5.2 cm, correct to the nearest tenth of a centimetre, is the length just less than 5.25 cm. Similarly the maximum width is just less than 3.85 cm.

Therefore the upper bound of the area is

$$5.25 \times 3.85 \, \text{cm}^2 = 20.21 \, \text{cm}^2$$

The minimum length that gives a length of 5.2 cm correct to the nearest tenth of a centimetre is exactly 5.15 cm. Similarly the minimum width is exactly 3.75 cm.

The minimum area is therefore $5.15 \times 3.75 \, \text{cm}^2$

$$= 19.31 \, \text{cm}^2$$

$$\text{Difference in areas} = (20.21 - 19.31) \, \text{cm}^2$$

$$= 0.90 \, \text{cm}^2$$

$$\text{Percentage difference} = \frac{0.90}{19.31} \times 100\%$$

$$= 4.7\% \quad (\text{correct to 1 d.p.})$$

---

1. The side of a square, correct to the nearest whole number, is 10 cm. For this square write down
   a) the upper limit for the length of a side of this square
   b) the smallest possible value for the length of a side
   c) the upper limit for the area of this square
   d) the smallest possible area.

2. A rectangle measures 20 cm by 15 cm, each measurement being given correct to the nearest whole number. Find
   a) the upper and lower bounds for its dimensions
   b) the upper and lower bounds for its area.

3. The side of a solid metal cube is 20 cm, correct to the nearest whole number. Find the upper and lower limits of the volume of metal used to make this cube.

4. A cuboid of platinum measures 3.2 cm by 1.3 cm by 2.2 cm. The density of platinum is 21.5 g/cm³. All these measurements including the density of the platinum are correct to 1 decimal place. A jewellery designer wishes to purchase this cuboid at a time when platinum costs £7 per gram.
   a) How much will he have to pay if he assumes that the measurements given are exact ?
   b) How much too much might he be paying for the platinum ?

In questions 5 to 13 all values are given correct to the nearest whole number. Use the given formula to find the upper and lower bounds for the values for the letter given on the left-hand side.

5. $A = l \times b$ if $l = 10$ and $b = 6$.

6. $A = 2(a+b)h$ if $a = 5$, $b = 7$ and $h = 6$.

7. $V = \frac{4}{3}\pi r^3$ if $r = 12$.

8. $s = \frac{1}{2}(a+b+c)$ if $a = 12$, $b = 15$ and $c = 17$.

9. $V = lbh$ if $l = 3$, $b = 4$ and $h = 5$.

10. $f = \frac{u+v}{2}$ if $u = 12$ and $v = 15$.

11. $C = 2\pi r$ if $r = 22$.

12. $A = \pi r^2$ if $r = 17$.

13. $z = \frac{y^2}{x}$ if $x = 10$ and $y = 12$.

14. Given $V = \frac{1}{3}\pi r^2 h$, $r = 1.25$ and $h = 4.93$, each correct to 2 d.p., find the maximum and minimum values for V. Give these values correct to 2 d.p.

15. If $x = 9$ and $y = 6$ correct to the nearest whole number, find the upper and lower bounds for the value of z given that $z = (x-y)^2$.
(Hint: z is largest when x is biggest and y is smallest.)

16. If $x = 1.4$ and $y = 2.8$, correct to one decimal place, find the largest and smallest values of   i) $2x+3y$ ii) $3y-x$ iii) $2xy$.

17. Two variables x and y are such that $7.5 \leqslant x \leqslant 10.5$ and $4 \leqslant y \leqslant 6$. Calculate the smallest and largest values of

a) $x+y$ b) $x-y$ c) xy d) $\dfrac{x}{y}$

18. Two variables y and z are such that $1.2 \leqslant y \leqslant 3.4$ and $4.3 \leqslant z \leqslant 6.8$.

Calculate the smallest and largest values of

a) $y+z$ b) yz c) $\dfrac{z}{y}$ d) y^2+z^2

19. The length of an edge of a cube is 5 cm, correct to the nearest whole number. Calculate the smallest and largest values of
a) an edge of the cube
b) the surface area of the cube
c) the volume of the cube.

A weights and measures inspector finds that the petrol pumps at a particular garage give 5% less petrol than is indicated on the meter.

a) How much petrol goes into the tank when a motorist thinks she has bought 5 gallons ?

b) If the marked price of the petrol is £2.20 per gallon, how much does the motorist actually pay per gallon ?

c) By how much was the motorist overcharged for the petrol she bought ?

a) For each gallon paid for, the motorist receives $(100-5)\%$ of a gallon.

$$1 \text{ gallon registered} \equiv 95\% \text{ of 1 gallon received}$$

$$5 \text{ gallons registered} \equiv 5 \times \frac{95}{100} \text{ gallons received}$$

$\therefore$ the motorist receives 4.75 gallons.

b) Price paid for 4.75 gallons is £5 × 2.20.

Therefore the price per gallon is

$$£\frac{5 \times 2.20}{4.75} = £2.32$$

c) The motorist should have paid

$$4.75 \times £2.20 = £10.45$$

Payment actually made $= 5 \times £2.20$

$$= £11$$

She was therefore overcharged by £11 − £10.45, i.e. by 55 p.

20. A right-angled triangle has sides of length 5 cm, 12 cm and 13 cm. In measuring these lengths Joan makes them too big by 2%, 5% and 4% respectively.

a) Find Joan's measurements and use them to find
   i) the perimeter   ii) the area.

b) Find the percentage error in Joan's calculation of
   i) the perimeter   ii) the area.

21.   A 30 cm wooden ruler is checked and found to be inaccurate. A line which is known to be exactly 10 cm long measures 10.1 cm according to this ruler.

a) What percentage error will result from measuring distances with this ruler ?

b) What measurement will this ruler give for the length of a box known to be 4 metres long ?

c) What is the true length of a distance measured as 3700 cm with this ruler ?

d) A rectangle is known to measure 72 cm by 84 cm. If its measurements are obtained using the ruler what percentage error will result in calculating
   i) the perimeter   ii) the area ?

22.   John was told that the width of a rectangle was 42 cm and the length was 85 cm and calculated the perimeter to be 254 cm. Unfortunately, it turned out that there was a possible error of 3 % either way in measuring the width and 2 % either way in measuring the length.

Find the maximum percentage error in giving the perimeter as 254 cm.

23.   Tim measures the space to replace a broken window using his mother's tape measure. He thinks that the piece of glass he requires measures 900 mm by 500 mm, but when he brings his glass home finds that it is too large. On checking the tape against a metal tape he finds that every 10 cm on the tape measure is actually 9.7 cm.

What measurements should he have given for the sheet of glass ?

24.   Three liquids *A, B* and *C* are mixed together to make an elixir. They are mixed in the proportions 1:2:3 using a ladle that holds 4% less liquid than its stated capacity. The most important ingredient is liquid *A*. If Zoe must take one teaspoonful of the elixir will she be taking

a) the exact amount of liquid *A*

b) too much of liquid *A*

c) too little of liquid *A* ?

Give a reason for your answer.

25.   a) A faulty electricity meter results in every 100 units of electricity I actually use being recorded as 106.

My bill for the units I used in a quarter, excluding the standing charge, was £90.10. By how much did I overpay ?

b) My neighbour also has a faulty meter. She paid £82.46 for the units when her bill should have been £86.80.

How many units does her meter record for each 100 units used ?

The radius of a circle is given as 4% greater than it really is. Find by what percentage the calculated area is greater than it should be.

Let the radius be r cm.

Then the given radius is 104% of r cm, i.e. $1.04r$ cm

$$\text{The calculated area} = \pi(1.04r)^2 \, \text{cm}^2$$

$$\text{Error} = (1.0816\,\pi r^2 - \pi r^2)\,\text{cm}^2$$

$$= (1.0816 - 1)\,\pi r^2 \,\text{cm}^2$$

$$= 0.0816\,\pi r^2 \,\text{cm}^2$$

$$\text{Percentage error} = \frac{0.0816\,\pi r^2}{\pi r^2} \times 100\%$$

$$= 8.16\%$$

Therefore the calculated area is 8.16% greater than it should be.

26. The length of a rectangle is 6% too long and the width is 5% too short.

a) By what percentage does the area differ from what it ought to be ?

b) Show that with this information it is not possible to find by what percentage the perimeter differs from what it ought to be.

27. The reading on a kitchen weighing machine is 20% more than the actual weight placed on it. For a particular recipe the requirements are

125 g butter
50 g sugar
175 g flour

How much of each ingredient should be indicated on these scales to give the correct amounts for the recipe ?

28. The sides of a rectangular piece of cardboard are each 10% too long. By what percentage is the area of the sheet too large ?

29. Use this temperature conversion table to complete the statements that follow.

°C	0	10	20	30	40	50	60	70	80	90	100
°F	32	50	68	86	104	122	140	158	176	194	212

a) 56 °C is approximately   °F.

b) 100 °F is approximately   °C.

c) A rise in temperature of 143 °F is approximately a rise of   °C.

d) A fall in temperature of 53 °C is approximately a fall of   °F.

30.

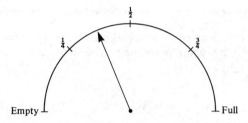

Empty — Full

The petrol tank on my car holds 16 gallons when full. The needle is in the position shown in the sketch. Approximately how far can I go if my car does, on average, 36 miles to the gallon ?

31. The table shows the area of a circle, A cm², for particular values of its radius, r cm.

r	3	5	10	15	20	25	30
A	28	79	310	710	1260	1960	2830

a) What is the approximate area of a circle with radius   i) 7 cm   ii) 23 cm ?

b) What is the approximate radius of a circle whose area is   i) 50 cm²   ii) 2500 cm² ?

32. On the continent petrol consumption is quoted in litres/100 km. In the United Kingdom it is given as miles per gallon. The table shows the connection between the two methods.

Petrol	in m.p.g.	26.4	32.8	39.2	45.5	52.3
consumption	in litres/100 km	10.7	8.6	7.2	6.2	5.4

a) Approximately what is the consumption in m.p.g. if the consumption in litres/100 km is
i) 9.5   ii) 7.9   iii) 5 ?

b) Approximately what is the consumption in litres/100 km if the consumption in m.p.g. is
i) 30   ii) 40   iii) 50 ?

EXERCISE 4g

In this exercise several alternative answers are given. Write down the letter that corresponds to the correct answer.

1. A circular garden pond has a perimeter of 12 metres. An approximate value for the area of its surface is

A   45 m²   **B**   12 m²   **C**   100 m²   **D**   75 m²

2. The area of a trapezium is 32 cm². If the parallel sides are of length 5.90 cm and 9.89 cm, the approximate distance between them is

A   4 cm   **B**   6 cm   **C**   8 cm   **D**   2 cm

3. The perimeter of the sector of a circle of radius 7.8 cm is 23.4 cm. The angle that the arc subtends at the centre is

   A about 60 °   **B** less than 45 °

   C between 90 ° and 180 °   **D** more than 180 °

4.

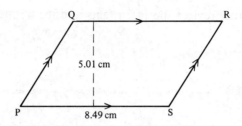

The area of parallelogram PQRS is approximately

   A 21 cm²   **B** 52 cm²   **C** 30 cm²   **D** 43 cm²

Questions 5 to 8 refer to the following diagram.

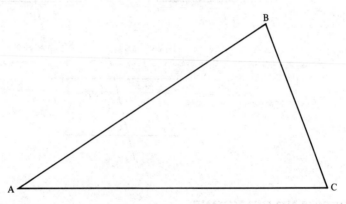

5. The length of AB is about

   A 5 cm   **B** 8 cm   **C** 12 cm   **D** 4 cm

6. The perimeter of the triangle ABC is about

   A 12 cm   **B** 32 cm   **C** 21 cm   **D** 40 cm

7. The value of $A\widehat{C}B$ is about

   A 70 °   **B** 45 °   **C** 60 °   **D** 50 °

8. The area of △ABC is about

   A 37 cm²   **B** 9 cm²   **C** 18 cm²   **D** 27 cm²

5 GEOMETRY AND DRAWING

This chapter revises the main facts and techniques.

PARALLEL LINES

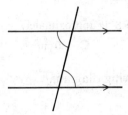 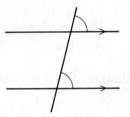

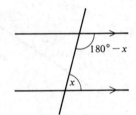

TRIANGLES AND POLYGONS

In any triangle,

the sum of the interior angles is $180°$
an exterior angle is equal to the
sum of the interior opposite angles.

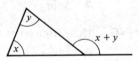

In a right-angled triangle,

the square on the hypotenuse is
equal to the sum of the squares
on the other two sides.

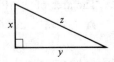

$z^2 = x^2 + y^2$

For any polygon,

the sum of the exterior angles is 360°.

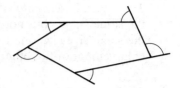

For a polygon with n sides,
the sum of the interior angles is $(180n - 360)° = (n - 2)180°$

A regular polygon has all its sides equal
and all its angles equal.

Two figures are *congruent* if they are
exactly the same shape and size.

To prove that two triangles are congruent, show that

either   the three sides of one triangle are equal to the three sides of the
other triangle.

or   two angles and one side of one triangle are equal to two angles
and the *corresponding* side of the other triangle.

or   two sides and the included angle of one triangle are equal to two
sides and the included angle of the other triangle.

or   both triangles have a right angle and two sides of one triangle are
equal to the two corresponding sides of the other triangle.

i.e.

Two figures are *similar* if they are
the same shape, but not necessarily
the same size (i.e. one figure is an
enlargement of the other).

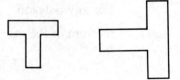

To prove that two triangles are similar, show that

either   the three angles of one triangle are equal to the three angles of
the other triangle.

or   the corresponding sides of each triangle are in the same ratio.

or   there is one pair of equal angles and the sides containing these
angles are in the same ratio.

i.e.

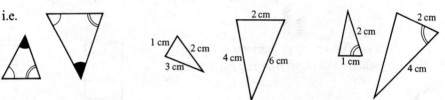

The ratio of the *areas* of similar figures is equal to the ratio of the *squares*
of corresponding lengths.

The ratio of the *volumes* of similar objects is equal to the ratio of the *cubes*
of corresponding lengths.

EXERCISE 5a

1. a)

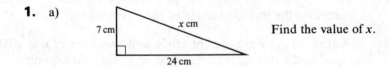

7 cm   *x* cm   Find the value of *x*.

24 cm

b) *x* cm is the length of the hypotenuse and *p* cm and *q* cm are the lengths
of the other two sides of a right-angled triangle. Copy and complete the
table.

p	*q*	*x*
3	4	
5		13
7	24	

c) The two shorter sides of a right-angled triangle are 70 mm and 240 mm.
Find the length of the other side.

2. Find the sizes of the angles marked *p, q* and *r*.

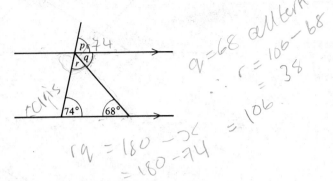

q = 68 alternative

r = 106 − 68
= 38

∴ *q* = 106

p = 180 − 74
= 106

[handwritten] *rq* = 180 − ?
= 180 − 74

3. These polygons are regular. Find the sizes of the marked angles.

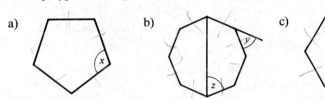

a)   b)   c)

4. Each of the following diagrams contains at least two triangles which are similar and/or congruent. Name these triangles and state, with reasons, which type they are.

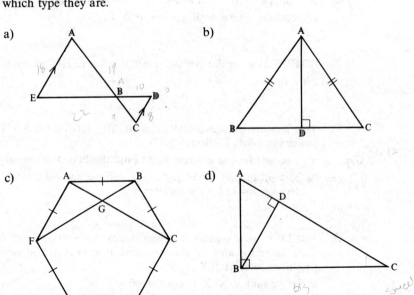

a)   b)

c)   d)

e)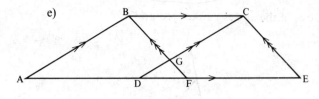

f)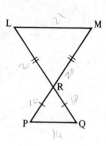

5.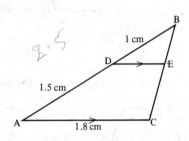

AD = 1.5 cm, DB = 1 cm and AC = 1.8 cm.

Find
a) BE : BC
b) the length of DE
c) the ratio of area △ABC to area △DBE.

6. In triangle ABC, AB = AC. L and M are the midpoints of AB and AC respectively. Show, with reasons, that $\widehat{BLC} = \widehat{CMB}$.

7. ABCDE is a regular pentagon. Sides AB and DC are extended to meet at F. Find the size of $\widehat{BFC}$.

8. Two jugs are mathematically similar. The smaller jug holds 0.8 litres and the larger jug holds 2.7 litres.
a) The smaller jug is 10 cm high. Find the height of the larger jug.
b) The lid on the larger jug has a surface area of 36 cm². Find the surface area of the lid for the smaller jug.

9. ABCDEF is a regular hexagon. Sides AB and DC are produced to meet at X. Sides BA and EF are produced to meet at Y and sides FE and CD are produced to meet at Z.
a) Prove that △XYZ is equilateral.
b) If AB is 8 cm long, find the length of XY.

10.

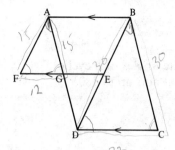

AB, EF and CD are parallel and equal. G is the midpoint of AD.

a) Show that △AFG is similar to △BDC.

b) Show that △AFG is congruent with △DEG.

c) Find the ratio of the area of △AFG to the area of △BDC.

d) Find the ratio of the area of △AFG to the area of ABCD.

CIRCLES

This section revises the angle and tangent properties of a circle.

The angle at the centre of a circle is equal to twice the angle subtended at the circumference by the same arc.

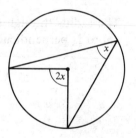

All the angles subtended at the circumference by an arc of a circle are equal.

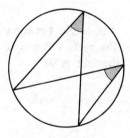

The angle in a semicircle is 90°.

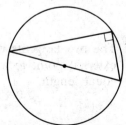

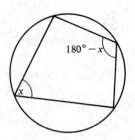

The opposite angles of a cyclic quadrilateral add up to 180°.

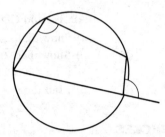

The exterior angle of a cyclic quadrilateral is equal to the interior opposite angle.

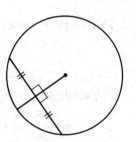

The radius through the midpoint of a chord is perpendicular to the chord.

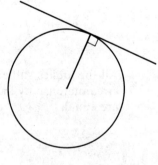

The angle between a tangent and the radius through the point of contact is 90°.

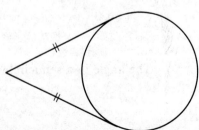

The two tangents drawn from an external point to a circle are of equal length.

The angle between a tangent and a chord drawn from the point of contact is equal to any angle in the alternate segment. (This is the alternate segment theorem.)

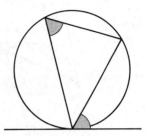

EXERCISE 5b

In questions 1 to 10 find the sizes of the marked angles. O is the centre of the circle in each case and AB is a tangent.

1.

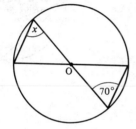

4.

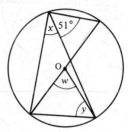

2.

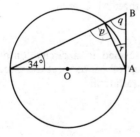

5.

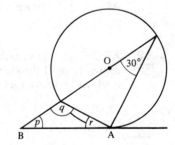

3.

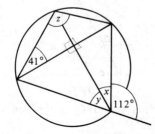

6.

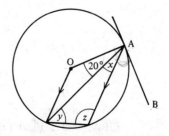

7.

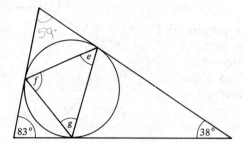

9.

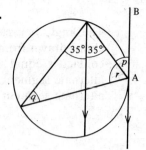

8.

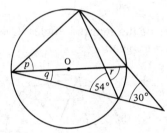

10.

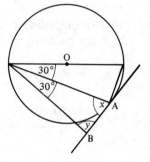

11. A, B, C and D are four points on the circumference of a circle, and $\widehat{ABC} = 90°$. Prove, with reasons, that $\widehat{ADC} = 90°$.

12. ABC is an equilateral triangle inscribed in a circle, centre O. A radius is drawn from O through the midpoint of AB to meet the circumference of the circle at D. Prove that $\triangle ODA$ is equilateral.

13.

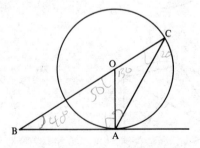

BA is a tangent to the circle at A and O is the centre of the circle. $\widehat{OBA} = 40°$. Find $\widehat{OAC}$.

14.

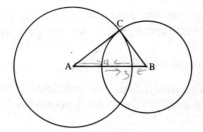

A is the centre of the larger circle whose radius is 4 cm and B is the centre of the smaller circle whose radius is 3 cm. AC is a tangent to the circle with centre B. Find the length of AB.

15.

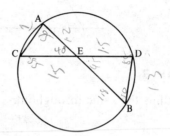

AB and CD are two chords of a circle that cut at E.

a) Prove that △AEC is similar to △DBE.

b) Hence show that AE × EB = CE × ED.

c) Use the result in (b) to find EB when AE = 6 cm, CE = 8 cm and ED = 9 cm.

16. ABC is an isosceles triangle inscribed in a circle. AB = AC. Prove that the tangent to the circle at A is parallel to BC.

17. Two chords of a circle, PQ and RS, when produced, meet outside the circle at M. Use a method similar to that in question 15 to prove that PM × MQ = RM × MS. (Hint: draw PR and QS.)

CONSTRUCTIONS USING RULER AND COMPASSES

Sometimes a construction has to be done without the aid of a protractor or a set square. Here is a reminder of the most useful 'ruler and compasses only' constructions.

In these diagrams, the positions where the point of the compasses have to be placed are marked P_1, P_2 ... for the first, second, ... positions.

To construct an angle of 60° at P_1

This involves constructing an equilateral triangle but drawing only two sides. Keep the radius the same throughout.

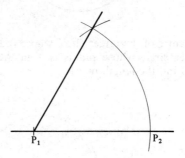

To bisect angle AP_1B

Keep the radius the same throughout.

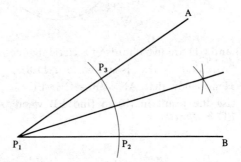

To construct an angle of 30° at P_1

Construct an angle of 60° at P_1 and then bisect it. Keep the radius the same throughout.

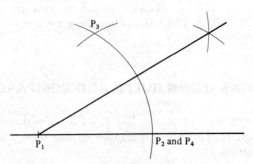

To construct an angle of 90° at P₁

Bisect an angle of 180° at P_1. Enlarge the radius for the arcs drawn from P_2 and P_3.

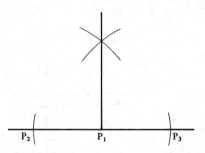

To construct an angle of 45° at P₁

Construct an angle of 90° at P_1 and then bisect it.

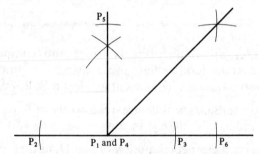

To draw a perpendicular from P₁ to the line AB

Keep the radius the same thoughout.

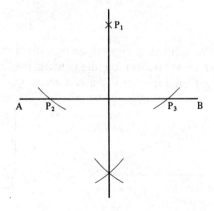

To bisect a line AB

Keep the radius the same throughout.

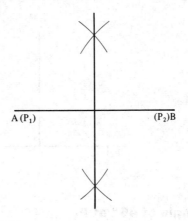

ACCURACY

When they are done properly, ruler and compasses constructions give more accurate results than those using the protractors and set squares commonly available. That accuracy depends, however, on

1. using compasses that are reasonably stiff (a loose joint means that the radius will change in use)

2. using a *sharp* pencil, preferably an H, and keeping it sharp

3. making the construction as large as is practical, in particular *not* using too small a radius on the compasses. (Aim for a minimum radius of about 5 cm, and do not rub out any arcs.)

EXERCISE 5c

Construct the following figures using only a ruler and a pair of compasses. Check your construction by measuring the length marked x. Your result should be within 1 mm of the given answer.

1.

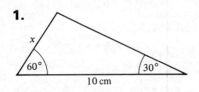

2.

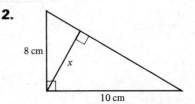

3.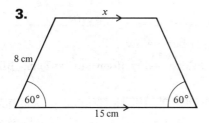

5.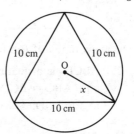

4.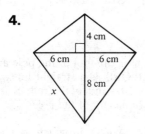

6.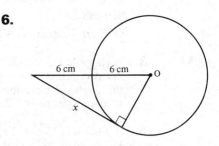

7. a) Construct △ABC with $\widehat{A}$ = 90°, AB = 24 cm, and AC = 10 cm.

b) Find by construction the centre of the circle which touches all three sides of △ABC.

c) Find by construction the radius of this circle and hence draw the circle. (This circle is the inscribed circle of △ABC.)

SKETCHES

In the last exercise, a sketch was given of the shape to be drawn accurately. Sometimes, however, only a description of the figure is given. In this case a sketch is essential because it gives some understanding of the shape and properties of the accurate drawing that has to be produced.

A sketch should be drawn freehand, but neatly. It should be big enough for essential information to be marked. Sometimes a first attempt at a sketch does not fit the given information. When this happens make another sketch.

The next exercise gives practice in producing useful sketches and getting information from them. Questions on loci are included.

EXERCISE 5d

Draw sketches of the figures described below.

1. ABCD is a quadrilateral in which AB = 10 cm, BC = 8 cm, BD = 10 cm and $\widehat{ABC} = \widehat{BCD} = 90°$.

a) Find CD.   b) Find the area of ABCD.

2. ABC is an equilateral triangle of side 6 cm. The line which bisects $\widehat{B}$ cuts AC at D and BD is produced to E so that DE = BD.

a) What type of quadrilateral is ABCE ? Give reasons.

b) Find BE.

c) Find the area of ABCE.

3. A flagpole PQ stands on level ground. Q is the foot of the pole and R and S are two points on the ground such that QRS is a straight line. RS = 12 m, the angle of elevation of P from R is 60° and of P from S is 30°. Find

a) the angles of △PRS   b) PR   c) the height of the pole.

4. A garden is in the shape of a trapezium ABCD in which AB = 50 m and DC = 40 m. AD is the back of the house; it is perpendicular to both AB and DC and is of length 20 m. The owner wants to plant a tree that is at least 40 m from the house and at least 5 m from any fence. Describe the shape of the region in which the tree can be planted.

5. A first-floor window A is 4 m above ground level, and overlooks a level garden with a tree PQ standing in it. From A, the angle of depression of Q, the foot of the tree, is 30° and the angle of elevation of P, the top of the tree, is 60°.

Find   a) the angles in △APQ

b) the length AQ

c) the height of the tree.

6. P is a point on a sheet of paper. The sum of the distances of P from the left hand edge of the paper and the bottom edge of the sheet is 10 cm. Sketch the locus of P and describe it.

7. Two lookout points A and B lie one on each side of a sea-channel of width 30 km. The sea-channel runs east to west and B is due north of A.

A light-buoy is to be placed so that it is equidistant from A and B but not more than 20 km from either.

Show on a sketch the possible positions of the light-buoy.

8. A circle is rolled along a straight line.

a) What is the locus of the centre C of the circle ?

b) Sketch the locus of P, a point on the edge of the circle.

c) Repeat with a square in place of the circle and with the point P
   i) at a vertex   ii) at a midpoint of a side.

9.

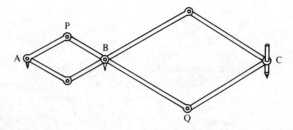

The drawing shows a pantograph, which is a linkage that can be used for enlarging drawings. The point A is fixed while point B traces out the drawing to be copied. The pencil at C will then draw an enlarged version. AP = PB = 8 cm, PQ = 24 cm and QC = 16 cm.

If B traces out a square of side 4 cm, sketch the square and the drawing produced by C. What are the measurements of this drawing ?

SCALES

The construction of a scale drawing usually requires the choice of a scale and the calculation of lengths to be used. The following exercise gives practice in these techniques, and in interpreting information from scale drawings. Remember to draw a sketch first.

EXERCISE 5e

1. A quadrilateral PQRS is to be drawn to scale. PQ = 92 m and QR = 76 m.

a) Find what the lengths of PQ and QR should be if the scale is
   i) 1 cm to 10 m   ii) 1 cm to 8 m.

b) On a drawing using a scale of 1 cm to 10 m, the measured length of PR is 6.8 cm. What is the real length of PR ?

c) On a drawing using a scale of 1 cm to 8 m, the measured length of QS is 7.2 cm. What is the real length of QS ?

d) Which scale was easier to use ? Would a scale of 1 cm to 5 m be easier to use than 1 cm to 8 m ? Give your reasons.

2. A map is drawn to a scale of 1 : 50 000. Two towns A and B are 36 km apart.

a) What real length does 1 cm on the map represent ?

b) How far apart are the points on the map representing A and B ?

c) On the map, town C is 42 cm from A. How far apart are the towns C and A ?

3.

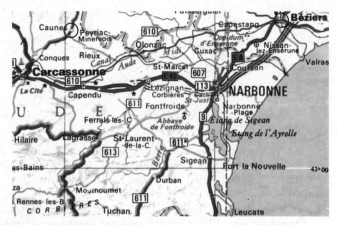

This is an extract from an Esso road map of France. The scale is 1 : 1 000 000.
Find, in kilometres, the straight line distance between

a) Beziers and Narbonne

b) Carcassonne and Narbonne

c) Caunes and Sigean.

4.

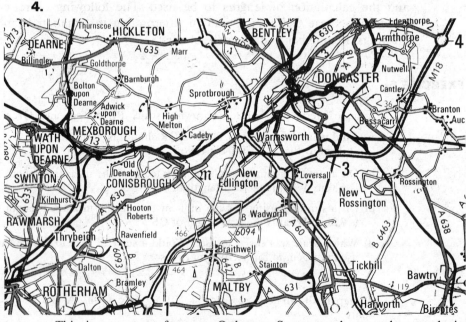

This is an extract from an Ordnance Survey road map whose scale is
1 inch : 3 miles. Find, in miles, the straight line distance between

a) junctions 3 and 4 on the M18

b) junctions 1 and 4 on the M18

c) junction 1 on the M18 and Hickleton.

5. A length which represents 800 km is drawn to a scale of 1 cm to 100 km but an error of 1 mm is made.

a) What error, in kilometres, does the error represent ?

b) What is the percentage error ?

The length is redrawn to a different scale but an error of 1 mm is again made. What length, in kilometres, does the error represent if the scale is

c) 1 cm to 200 km

d) 1 cm to 50 km ?

What advice would you give to someone who has to choose the scale for a drawing ?

6. A triangle PQR is to be constructed using a scale of 1 cm to 5 m. PR = 48 m and $\widehat{Q} = 90°$.

a) If $\widehat{R} = 25°$, calculate the length of PQ on the drawing.

b) When drawing the triangle to scale, an error is made in drawing $\widehat{R}$ as 26° instead of 25°. The other measurements are correct. Calculate the drawn length of PQ in this case and hence find the percentage error in PQ.

c) Construct $\triangle PQR$ accurately when $\widehat{R} = 25°$. Comment on any difference between your measured length of PQ and the calculated answer in (a).

BEARINGS

Bearings are measured from a north-pointing line in a clockwise direction.

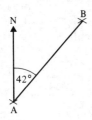

The bearing of B from A is 042°.

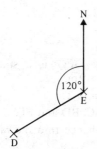

The bearing of D from E is $(360 - 120)°$, i.e. 240°.

SCALE DRAWING

Remember never to draw right angles or parallel lines by eye. Use a protractor, a pair of compasses or a ruler and set square after you have studied the rough sketch and decided on a method.

LINKAGES

A linkage is a mechanism for producing a locus. An example is the wheel and rod below, where the circular motion of point Q about O gives the linear motion of P along the rod. The reverse of this linkage is used in a steam engine where the linear motion of the piston produces the circular motion of the wheels.

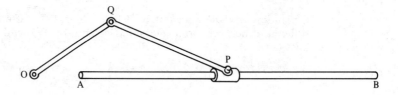

EXERCISE 5f

The illustrations in this exercise are not drawn to scale.

1.

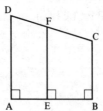

The diagram shows the plan of two gardens. DFC is a straight line. AD = 15 m, AB = 20 m, BC = 11 m and AE = 9 m.

a) Draw the plan accurately, using a scale of 1 cm to 2 m.

b) Use your drawing to find the real lengths of AC, BD and EF.

c) Calculate the areas of the two gardens, and hence find the ratio of the area of ADFE to that of EFCB.

2.

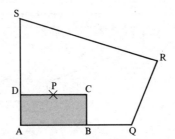

The diagram shows the grounds of a school, with the school building in one corner. There is a door at P, the midpoint of CD, and there are gates at Q, R and S. AS = 83 m, AQ = 80 m, QR = 41 m, $\hat{Q}$ = 95°, AB = 42 m and AD = 20 m.

a) Draw the plan accurately, using a scale of 1 cm to 10 m.

b) Andrew comes out of the door at P. If he can cross the grounds as he pleases, which of the three gates is nearest to P? (Give reasons for your answer.)

c) Draw a perpendicular from R to ABQ produced. Calculate the true area of AQRS, measuring from the drawing any lengths that you need.

3.

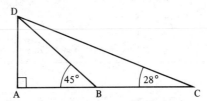

AD is a pole standing on level ground. The angle of elevation of D from B is 45° and of D from C is 28°. BC is 8.4 m.

a) Choose your own scale and draw an accurate diagram (start by drawing △BCD).

b) How high is the flagpole?

4.

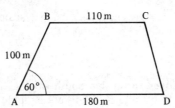

ABCD represents a paddock, which is in the shape of a trapezium with BC parallel to AD. Using a scale of 1 cm for 10 m, make a scale drawing of the paddock.

a) Find the perimeter and area of the paddock.

b) The owner wants to plant some trees in the paddock. They must be at least 70 m from D, and not more than 40 m from BC. Shade the area in which the trees can be planted.

5.

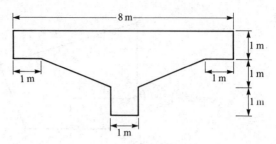

The diagram shows the cross-section of a girder for a motorway bridge.

The girder has one line of symmetry.

Use a scale of 1 cm to 0.5 m to make a scale drawing of the cross-section.

a) Take measurements from your drawing to find the perimeter of this cross-section.

b) Find the volume of concrete needed to make a girder 40 m long.

6.

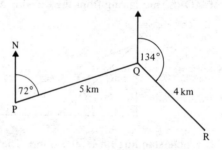

Abel walks 5 km on a bearing of 072° from a point P to point Q and then for 4 km on a bearing of 134° to point R.

a) Find $P\widehat{Q}R$.

b) Draw △PQR accurately using a scale of 2 cm to 1 km, and find how far R is from P.

7. Baxter drives 36 km due South from L to M and then he drives 28 km on a bearing of 292° to K. Choose a suitable scale and use an accurate drawing to find the direct distance from K to L.

8. Carlos sails from port A for 20 nautical miles on a bearing of 040° to a port B. He then sails for 40 nautical miles on a bearing of 290° to a port C. Choose a suitable scale and use an accurate drawing to find the distance and bearing of C from A.

9.

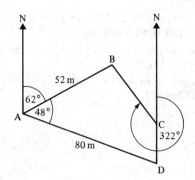

The diagram shows part of a park with two large trees A and B and the positions C and D where new trees are to be planted.

a) Sketch the diagram and calculate the remaining angles of the quadrilateral.

b) What is the bearing of A from D ?

c) Draw the quadrilateral accurately using a scale of 1 cm to 10 m. (Notice that there is no need to draw the north-pointing lines; start with AD.)

d) Use your drawing to find the distance between the trees at A and C.

e) Use your drawing to find the bearings of C from A and of B from D.

10. Two people set out from a point P at the same time. The first person, A, walks at 3.5 km/h on a bearing of 025° and the second person, B, walks at 4.5 km/h on a bearing of 065°.

a) Draw a sketch showing the positions of A and B twenty minutes after leaving P.

b) Make an accurate drawing of your sketch, using a scale of 10 cm to 1 km.

c) Use your drawing to find the distance and bearing of A from B twenty minutes after leaving P.

11. A and B are two points on a coast, 12 km apart. B is due east of A. The bearing of a ship C from A is 042° and from B is 330°. Draw a sketch to show the position of C.

It turns out that the possible error in each instrument gives bearings such that the angles may be as much as 10° out, either bigger or smaller. On your sketch show the region in which the ship must lie.

Use an accurate scale drawing to find the range of possible distances of the ship from the shore.

12. ABC is a field in the shape of an equilateral triangle of side 80 m. The position of P is such that it is less than 60 m from A and nearer to B than to C.

a) Show on an accurate drawing the locus of P.

b) How near can P be to C ?

c) How far can P be from C ?

13. Three towns A, B and C are such that A is 50 km due north of B, and C is 45 km from B on a bearing of 060°.

a) Use an accurate drawing to find the locus of P, where P is equidistant from A and B.

b) A radio transmitter is equidistant from A, B and C. How far is it from each town ?

14.

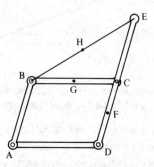

ABCDE is a freely jointed linkage; A and D are fixed points; DCE is rigid and BE is an elastic string. F, G and H are the midpoints of DC, BC and BE respectively.

AB = DC = CE = 6 cm and AD = BC = 8 cm.

a) Sketch and describe the locus of
  i) B   ii) E   iii) F, as AB rotates about A.

b) Make an accurate drawing of these loci and draw the locus of
  i) G   ii) H.

c) Describe the loci of G and H.

15.

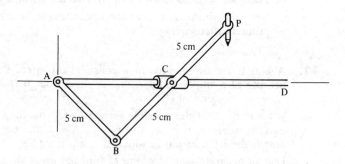

A linkage is formed of three rods AB, AD and BP, freely jointed at A and B. AD is fixed but C is free to slide along AD. A pencil P traces out a curve as C moves along AD.

Draw AD about 20 cm long. Choose a position for C, say C_1, and find the corresponding position, B_1, of B. Now mark the position of P.

By plotting about ten more points find the locus of P. Make sure that you have found the extreme positions. Assume that C can actually reach a position at A.

16.

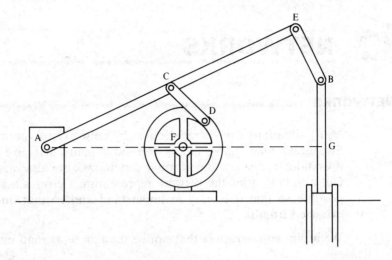

The diagram shows a 'nodding donkey', which can be used to pump oil from the ground. An engine causes the wheel, centre F, to rotate and this constrains the beam AE to move so that point E moves through an arc of a circle; this in turn makes the piston move up and down in a vertical shaft.

The linkage is freely jointed at points A, B, C, D and E.   AC = CE = 3 m, CD = 1 m, EB = 1.25 m   and the radius of the wheel is 0.75 m. AFG is horizontal and AF = FG = 3 m.

a) Draw on a sketch the line AFG, the locus of D, the arcs of the circles on which the loci of C and E lie, and the vertical line on which the locus of B lies.

b) By reference to the sketch drawn for part (a), make an accurate scale drawing. Use 2 cm to represent 1 m. Mark a position for D at the lowest point of the wheel and construct the corresponding position of B.

c) Now mark D at the highest point on the wheel and find the corresponding position of B. What is the distance between the two positions of B ?

d) Are these the extreme positions of B ?

6 NETWORKS

NETWORKS

Many situations can be represented by networks, i.e. points joined by arcs. Simplified road maps, family trees and plans that give the order of the operations necessary to perform a certain task are all examples of networks. Our aim is to draw the network representing a given situation as simply as possible so that it is easy to understand and so that information can be extracted from it.

We begin with networks that can be thought of as road maps.

EXERCISE 6a

1. a)

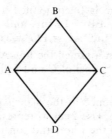

Copy this network, starting at A. Do not lift your pen from the paper and do not go over any line more than once. (If a network can be drawn in this way it is said to be traversable or unicursal.)

b) Try to copy, in this way, the network in (a) starting at B. Can it be done?

c) Are the following networks traversable? In (i) start at A. For the rest, choose your own starting point.

i)

ii)

iii)
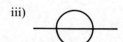

iv)

v)

vi)
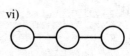

120

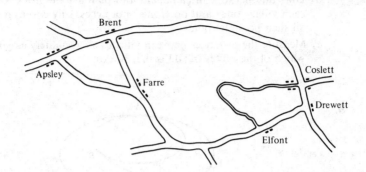

Represent the road system in this section of a road atlas by a simple network. Ignoring the incoming roads, is the network traversable ?

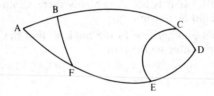

The network is not traversable.

 2.

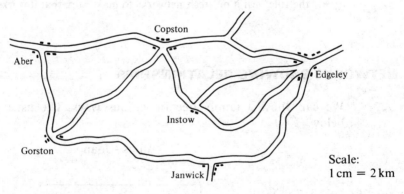

Scale:
1 cm = 2 km

a) Represent the road system given above by a simple network showing only whether or not there are roads between points. No directions or distances need be preserved.

b) Ignoring the incoming roads, is the network traversable ? Who might be interested in the answer to this ?

c) If it is not traversable, add a road to make it so.
If it *is* traversable, add a road to make it non-traversable.

d) Draw the network in (a) again and plan a route from A which will visit each village once and only once, not necessarily covering every road. List all such possible routes.

e) Measure the distances between villages as accurately as you can and find which of the routes in (d) is the shortest.

3.

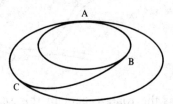

The diagram shows the layout of a model railway track.

a) Is it possible to run an engine from A over every part of the track once only ? If it is not possible, is there another starting point from which it would be possible ?

b) Add another line to the track so that the resulting complete track is not traversable by the train.

*4. It is possible to decide whether a network is traversable without actually drawing it.

Use the networks already drawn and consider the number of points (sometimes called nodes, or vertices), the number of arcs and the number of arcs meeting at each point. Some of this information will help you to find the rule; test it on fresh networks to make sure that it works.

NETWORKS SHOWING RELATIONSHIPS

We can show a family tree in various ways. The usual form is shown below.

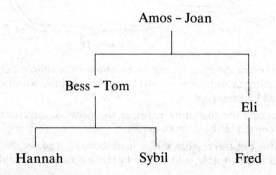

A selection from this information could be represented in a different way as shown below (A is for Amos etc.)

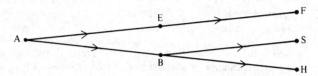

Here a line with an arrow means 'is a parent of' so we can see that B is a parent of H.

EXERCISE 6b

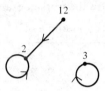

A line with an arrow means 'is a multiple of'. The network is not complete.

Add a point to represent 4 and complete the network.

(Notice 2 is a multiple of 2; a loop is needed to represent this.)

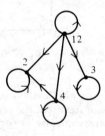

1. a) Draw a network for points representing the people Abel, Bart, Carol, Danielle and Englebert. A line with an arrow means 'is taller than'. Show the following information.
Danielle is taller than Carol.
Englebert is the tallest.
Bart is the shortest.
Abel is shorter than Danielle.
b) How does Abel compare in height with Carol?

2.

Andrew   Barbara

Joan   Colin   Ruth – Len   David

Gilly   Sue   Nick   Trish   Max

Select information from this family tree to draw a network where a line with an arrow means 'is a cousin of'. (Note that each line will have to be marked with two arrowheads.)

3. Draw a network with points representing the numbers 2, 3, 6, 8, 9 and 12. A line with an arrow means 'is a factor of'. If the network becomes impossible to draw without lines crossing, use a bridge: ⟶⟩⟵ .

4. The information in the worked example could be shown in a table

'Is a multiple of'	2	3	4	12
2	1	0	0	0
3	0	1	...	...

1 means 'true', 0 means 'false'.

Complete the table and form similar tables for the relationships in questions 2 and 3.

5.

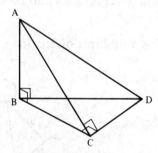

Name three lines to which AB is perpendicular.
Draw a network to represent the relationship of lines in the given tetrahedron. A line with an arrow means 'is perpendicular to'.

6.

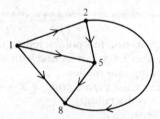

What relationship could be represented by a line with an arrow in this network?

PLANNING NETWORKS

Networks can be used to represent the order in which activities are to be carried out.

Consider the preparation of a meal involving the following activities. The time needed for each activity is given in brackets in minutes.
Cook meat   (35)
Cook potatoes   (25)
Prepare and cook peas   (20)
Make the gravy after cooking meat and peas   (4)
Lay the table   (10)
Bring food to table   (4)

We could represent this by the following diagram.

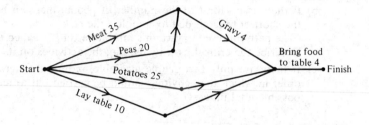

We can now see that the total time taken will be at least 43 minutes.

The unlabelled lines represent dummy activities. They are used to make it easier to show on the diagram that one activity needs to be finished before another starts.

The activities involved do not need continuous attention so one person might manage the whole task. If however each activity needed individual supervision and we had three people available, we could go on to redraw the planning network to allow for this, e.g.

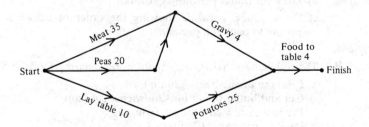

The use of networks for planning, in particular for minimising the time taken, is called *critical path analysis*.

EXERCISE 6c

1.

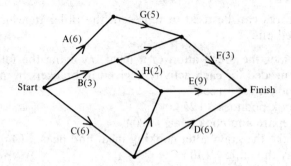

This network shows eight activities, lettered A to H, involved in completing a task, and the time in minutes needed for each activity.

a) Are there any dummy activities represented in the diagram?

b) If there is no limit to the number of people that can be called on, find the shortest time needed to complete the task.
(The path followed to give this minimum time is called the *critical path*.)
Describe the critical path by naming the activities on it.

c) If there are only two people available, redraw the network showing the order in which the activities should be carried out to require the shortest possible total time.

2. Given below is a list of activities involved in wrapping a present. They are in no particular order.
A Wrap the present in paper.
B Tie wrapped present with ribbon and cut the ribbon.
C Write the label before tying it on.
D Tie label on.
E Find wrapping paper and ribbon.
F Find label.
G Find pen and scissors.

a) Make a list of the activities and beside each of them write the reference letters of the activities that must take place before that activity can be carried out. (G must be completed before C for example.)

b) Draw an initial planning network.

c) Draw a new network showing the order of activities if there are two people to pack the present.

3. The following activities are involved in preparing food for a picnic.
Find the picnic bag   (1 min)
Cut and butter bread for sandwiches   (8 min)
Prepare sandwich filling   (6 min)
Pack picnic bag   (2 min)
Complete the sandwiches   (6 min)
Select drinks   (2 min)
Select cups and cutlery   (3 min)

a) Draw an initial planning network to show the preparation for the picnic.
b) Draw a new planning network to show the order of activities if there are three people to carry them out.
   What is the minimum time required ?
c) Repeat (b) for two people.
d) Is there any great advantage in having three people rather than two people ? How much time will the participants spend standing around waiting in each of the two cases ?

4. In Pamplonia, red tape is rife. A company who wished to make gidgets wrote to the Ministry of Gidget Making for advice and received the following helpful information.

To apply for a licence to make gidgets, you need to send Forms A, B and C to this Ministry.

To get Form A, apply to Office X. Time to receive Form A from Office X: 2 weeks.

To get Form B, apply to Office Y, enclosing Form D. Time: 4 weeks.

To get Form C, apply to Office Z with Forms D and E. Time: 2 weeks.

To get Form D, apply to Office T with Form A. Time: 4 weeks.

To get Form E, apply to Office U. Time: 7 weeks.

When the Ministry receives your application, it will take 5 weeks to deal with it. Photocopies of forms D and E may be used instead of the originals.

a) Construct a planning network; assume that when the forms are received by the would-be gidget makers they are dealt with immediately.
b) What is the minimum number of weeks, if there are no hold-ups, before the company can expect to receive its licence ? Describe the critical path by listing the activities on it in order.

7 TRIGONOMETRY

THE TRIGONOMETRIC RATIOS

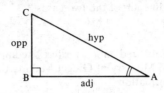

In a right-angled triangle ABC in which $\widehat{B} = 90°$,

$$\sin A = \frac{\text{opp}}{\text{hyp}} = \frac{BC}{AC} \qquad \cos A = \frac{\text{adj}}{\text{hyp}} = \frac{AB}{AC} \qquad \tan A = \frac{\text{opp}}{\text{adj}} = \frac{BC}{AB}$$

To help decide which ratio to use, mark the sides of the triangle as opp, adj, hyp, with respect to the angle to be found or used.

Remember that, if two angles in a triangle are known, the third angle can be found from the angle sum of a triangle.

Remember also that, in a right-angled triangle, if two sides are known, the third side can be calculated using Pythagoras' Theorem.

PROBLEMS IN TWO DIMENSIONS

To calculate angles or lengths, first identify a right-angled triangle containing the unknown quantity. This often involves adding lines to a diagram.

For example, if we are asked to find the radius of the smallest circle within which a regular octagon of side 4 cm will fit, we start with the octagon and the circle and add two radii.

We can then see that we need to add a line to divide the resulting isosceles triangle into two right-angled triangles.

128

EXERCISE 7a

In $\triangle ABC$, $\widehat{B} = 90°$, $AB = 7.2\,cm$ and $AC = 9.3\,cm$.
Find a) BC   b) $\widehat{C}$

a) $AC^2 = BC^2 + AB^2$ (Pythag. th.)

$9.3^2 = BC^2 + 7.2^2$

$86.49 = BC^2 + 51.84$

$BC^2 = 86.49 - 51.84$

$= 34.65$

$BC = 5.886$

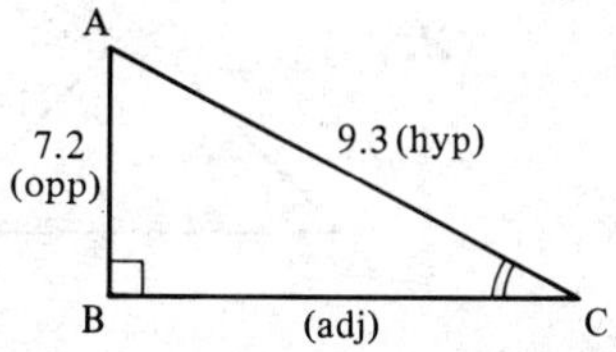

$\therefore$ $BC = 5.89\,cm$ correct to 3 s.f.

b) $\sin C = \dfrac{opp}{hyp} = \dfrac{7.2}{9.3}$

$= 0.7742$

$\therefore$ $\widehat{C} = 50.7°$

In $\triangle PQR$, $\widehat{P} = 90°$, $\widehat{R} = 38°$, $RP = 4.3\,cm$. Find RQ.

$\cos 38° = \dfrac{adj}{hyp} = \dfrac{4.3}{x}$

$0.7880 = \dfrac{4.3}{x}$

$x \times 0.7880 = 4.3$

$x = \dfrac{4.3}{0.7880}$

$= 5.456$

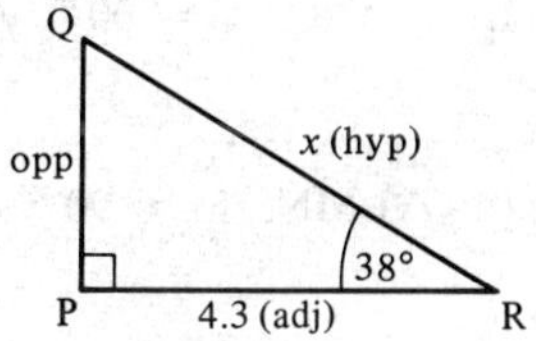

$RQ = 5.46\,cm$ correct to 3 s.f.

In questions 1 to 6, all lengths are in centimetres. Calculate x, giving angles correct to 1 d.p. and lengths correct to 3 s.f.

1.

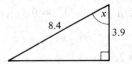

4.

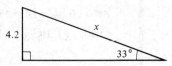

2.

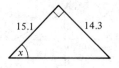

5.

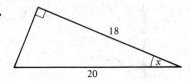

3.

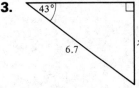

6.

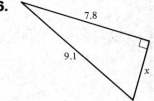

7. In $\triangle PQR$, $\widehat{P} = 90°$, $PQ = 3.2$ cm and $QR = 5.7$ cm. Find $\widehat{Q}$ and $\widehat{R}$.

8. In $\triangle XYZ$, $\widehat{X} = 90°$, $XY = 2.5$ cm, $XZ = 3.2$ cm. Find YZ and $\widehat{Y}$.

9. In $\triangle ABC$, $\widehat{C} = 90°$, $AB = 4.3$ cm and $\widehat{A} = 54°$. Find $\widehat{B}$ and AC.

10. In $\triangle LMN$, $\widehat{M} = 90°$, $LM = 48$ cm, $LN = 64$ cm. Find $\widehat{L}$ and $\widehat{N}$.

11. A is the point $(4, -3)$, B is the point $(4, 3)$ and C is the point $(-2, -3)$. Find AC and $A\widehat{C}B$.

12. From the top of a cliff, the angle of depression of a boat at sea is $23°$. The cliff is 40 m high. Calculate the distance of the boat from the foot of the cliff.

13.

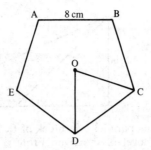

ABCDE is a regular pentagon. The point O is equidistant from all five vertices. Find

a) $O\hat{C}D$ b) the distance of O from DC   c) the area of the pentagon.

14. In a circle, centre O, radius 9 cm, a chord AB of length 12 cm is drawn. Find the distance of the chord from O.

15. Two tangents are drawn from a point P to a circle centre O. The radius of the circle is 8.2 cm and P is 12.4 cm from O. Find the angle between the tangents.

16. A rectangular frame measures 6 m by 2.5 m. The frame is kept in shape by two diagonal struts. Find

a) the length of a strut   b) the angle between the struts.

17.

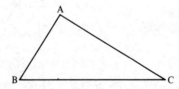

The diagram shows a vertical section through an asymmetrical roof.

The ridge A is 2.5 m above the base BC. AC is inclined at 30° to BC and AB is inclined at 60° to BC. Find the width (BC) of the base of the roof.

18. The road from village A runs due west for 5 miles to a fort B. A television mast is due south of B and 4 miles from B. Find the distance and bearing of the mast from A.

19. A is the point (1,1), B is the point (4,5) and C is the point (5,3). Find

a) the angle between AB and a line parallel to the *y*-axis

b) the angle between BC and a line parallel to the *y*-axis.

c) Hence find $A\hat{B}C$.

20.

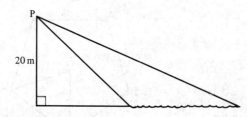

A river runs parallel to a block of flats. The roof of this block is 20 m above the water level of the river. From a point P on the roof, looking directly across the river, the angle of depression of the nearer bank is 43° and the angle of depression of the farther bank is 23°. Find the width of the river.

PROBLEMS IN THREE DIMENSIONS

To find angles or lengths in solid figures, a right-angled triangle containing the unknown quantity has to be identified. This triangle should then be drawn separately from the solid figure.

EXERCISE 7b

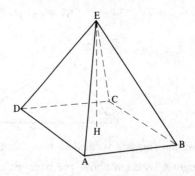

The figure is a pyramid on a square base ABCD. The edges of the base are 30 cm long and the height EH of the pyramid is 42 cm. Find   a) the length of AC   b) the angle EÂH.

a)

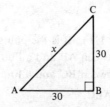

AC is a diagonal of the square base ABCD.

Using $\triangle ABC$, $\widehat{B} = 90°$, $AB = BC = 30\,cm$

$$AC^2 = AB^2 + BC^2 \quad (\text{Pythag. th.})$$

$$\therefore \qquad x^2 = 900 + 900$$

$$= 1800$$

$$x = 42.42$$

$$\therefore \qquad AC = 42.4\,cm \text{ correct to 3 s.f.}$$

b)

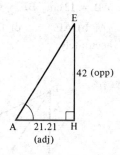

$E\widehat{A}H$ is in $\triangle AHE$, in which $\widehat{H} = 90°$ and
$AH = \frac{1}{2}AC = 21.21\,cm$

$$\tan \widehat{A} = \frac{opp}{adj} = \frac{42}{21.21}$$

$$= 1.9802$$

$$\therefore \qquad \widehat{A} = 63.2°$$

$$\text{i.e.} \quad E\widehat{A}H = 63.2°$$

1.

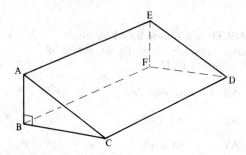

ABCDEF is a prism with a triangular cross-section. $A\widehat{B}C = 90°$, $BC = 8\,m$, $AB = 6\,m$ and $CD = 20\,m$.

Find a) AC   b) BD   c) $A\widehat{C}B$ d) $A\widehat{D}B$
      e) the surface area of the prism.

2.

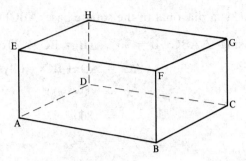

In the cuboid, $AB = 12\,cm$, $BF = 6\,cm$ and $BC = 8\,cm$.

Find   a) FC   b) AF   c) DB   d) $\widehat{HBD}$.

Draw $\triangle AFC$ accurately.

3.

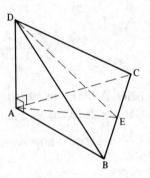

ABCD is a pyramid on an equilateral triangular base ABC of side 15 cm. AD is perpendicular to AC and AB, and is also 15 cm long. E is the midpoint of BC.

Find   a) AE   b) $\widehat{ABD}$ c) $\widehat{AED}$.

4.   VABCD is a square-based pyramid with V vertically above O, the centre of the square ABCD.

If $AB = 15\,cm$ and $VO = 20\,cm$ find

a) AC   b) $\widehat{VAO}$

c) AV   d) $\widehat{VAB}$.

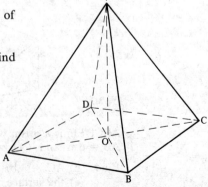

5.

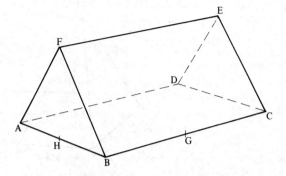

ABCDEF is a prism with cross-section an equilateral triangle of side 2 cm. BC = 5 cm, G is the midpoint of BC and H is the midpoint of AB.

Find   a) FG   b) $B\widehat{F}G$ c) $A\widehat{G}B$ d) $F\widehat{G}H$.

Sketch the solid whose vertices are F, H, G and B.

6.

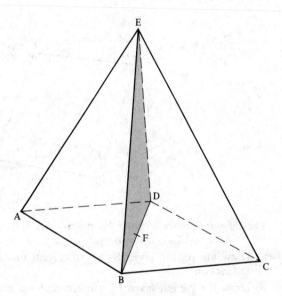

The diagram shows a square pyramid. Its base is horizontal and E is vertically above F, the centre of the base. AB = 8 cm and EF = 10 cm.

a) Sketch section EBD. What type of triangle is it ? Find BD and the area of the section.

b) Sketch the vertical section through EF, parallel to BC. Find its area.

7.

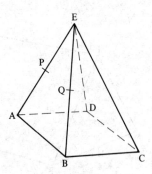

The diagram shows a square pyramid. Its base is horizontal and E is vertically above the centre of the base. AB = 6 cm and AE = 10 cm. P and Q are midpoints of EA and EB.

a) Find the length of PQ.

b) Sketch the horizontal section through PQ. What shape is it? Find its area.

c) Sketch the vertical section through PQ. What shape is it?

d) Give the ratio of the volumes of the two solids into which section (b) cuts the pyramid.

8.

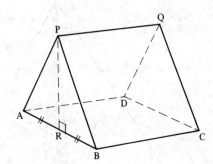

The diagram shows a triangular prism. AB = 6 cm, AP = PB = 5 cm and PQ = 8 cm. ABCD is horizontal.

a) Draw the section given by a vertical cut through PQ. Find the area of the section.

b) Draw the section given by a horizontal cut through the midpoint of AP and find its area.

c) Find the surface area of the prism.

d) Find the volume of the prism.

e) Find the volume of the smaller of the two solids into which the cut in (b) divides the prism.

f) Which of the cuts described in (a) and (b) is in a plane of symmetry?

9.

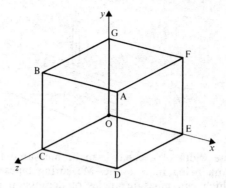

ABCDEFGO is a cube. A is the point $(4,4,4)$

Find   a) $B\hat{D}C$ b) $B\hat{O}C$ c) AG   d) $O\hat{A}G$

10.

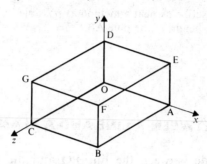

The diagram shows a cuboid. F is the point $(5,3,6)$

Find   a) $E\hat{B}A$ b) $G\hat{O}C$ c) OB   d) $F\hat{O}B$

11.

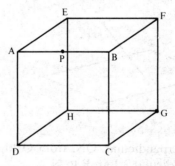

The diagram shows a cube of edge 6 inches. P is the midpoint of AB. An insect starts from P and crawls to G over the surface of the cube and crossing the edge BF.

a) Find the length of the shortest route it can take and the angle with the horizontal at which the insect is crawling when it is on the vertical face BCGF.

b) Show that there is an alternative shortest route from P to G. What angle does this route make with the horizontal when the insect is on the vertical face BCGF ?

*12.

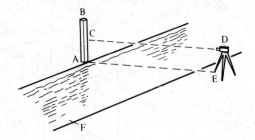

The width of a canal is to be measured from the near side, the opposite bank being inaccessible. Measuring tapes are available; also a theodolite which can measure angles of depression and elevation, and the angle of rotation in a horizontal plane (so that, for example, $B\widehat{D}C$ and $A\widehat{E}F$ can be measured).

Describe as neat a method as possible for finding the width of the canal and the height of the pole AB.

THE ANGLE BETWEEN A LINE AND A PLANE

The angle between the line PQ and the plane ABCD is defined as the angle between PQ and its projection on the plane ABCD.

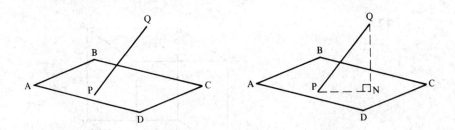

Draw a perpendicular, QN, from Q to the plane. (N is called the foot of the perpendicular.) Join P to N

The required angle is $Q\widehat{P}N$. (This angle is tucked under the line.)

The line PN is called the *projection* of the line PQ on the plane.

(Note: if the plane does not look horizontal, it may help you to see which line is the perpendicular if you turn the page and look at the diagram from a different angle.)

THE ANGLE BETWEEN TWO PLANES

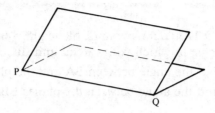

To find the angle between two planes we need to find two lines to act as the arms of the angle.

The two lines, one in each plane, must meet on the joining line, PQ, of the two planes and each must be at right angles to the joining line.

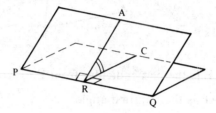

One possible angle is $A\widehat{R}C$.

Notice that there are any number of pairs of lines that meet at a given point on the joining line but only a pair at right angles to PQ gives the required angle. $D\widehat{E}F$ is *not* a possible angle but $D\widehat{Q}F$ is possible.

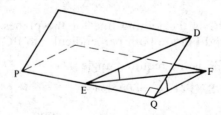

It can be helpful to use a section through a solid when trying to identify the angle between two of its faces. The section, or cut, must be made at right angles to the edge where the two faces meet, cutting this edge at P, say. Then the angle between the faces is the angle at Q in the section. For example, in a right pyramid, the angle between the base and a sloping face can be found from a section formed by a cut through the vertex perpendicular to the base.

EXERCISE 7c

ABCD is a right pyramid of height 5 cm. Its base ABCD is a rectangle in which AB = 6 cm and BC = 8 cm.

a) Find the angle between EA and the plane ABCD.

b) Find the angle between the planes EBC and ABCD.

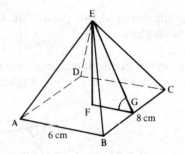

a) (EF is the perpendicular from E to ABCD)

EÂF is the required angle.

$AF = \frac{1}{2}AC$

In △ABC, AC = 10 cm (3, 4, 5 △)

∴ AF = 5 cm

∴ EÂF = 45° (rt-angled isos. △)

The angle between EA and ABCD is 45°.

b) (BC is the joining line for the planes. From symmetry, EG and FG are both perpendicular to BC at G.)

EĜF is the required angle.

In △EFG, F̂ = 90°

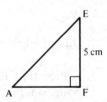

$$\tan G = \frac{opp}{adj} = \frac{5}{3}$$

$$= 1.666\,66\ldots$$

$$E\widehat{G}F = 59.0°$$

The angle between the planes is 59.0°.

Questions 1 to 3 are concerned with identifying angles, question 4 onwards require the sizes of the angles to be calculated.

1.

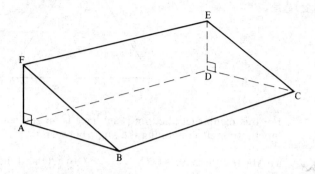

For this wedge, sketch and label a triangle containing the angle between

a) FB and the base ABCD

b) FC and the base ABCD

c) FC and the face ADEF

d) BE and the base ABCD

e) the planes BCEF and ABCD

f) the planes FAC and FAB.

2.

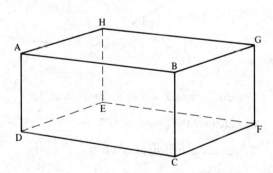

For this cuboid, sketch and label a triangle containing the angle between

a) AC and the base CDEF

b) AC and the face ADEH

c) HC and the face EFGH

d) the planes CDHG and CDEF

e) the planes ACFH and CDEF

f) the planes ABFE and EFGH.

3.

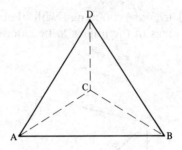

For this regular tetrahedron (each face is an equilateral triangle), sketch and label a triangle containing the angle between

a) AD and the base ABC

b) CD and the base ABC

c) AB and the face ACD

d) the planes ABC and DBC.

4.

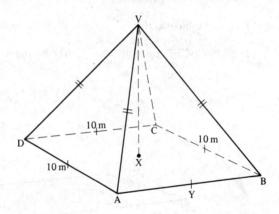

For this pyramid, whose height is 10 m,

a) calculate the length of DB

b) calculate the length of VB

c) find the angle that VB makes with the base ABCD

d) calculate the length of VY, where Y is the midpoint of AB

e) draw the section containing the angle between VY and the face ABCD

f) calculate the angle described in (e)

g) find the angle between the planes VAB and ABCD.

5.

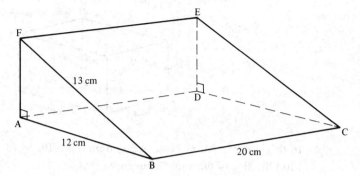

For this wedge,

a) calculate the lengths of AF and FC

b) draw the section containing the angle between the diagonal FC and the base ABCD

c) find the size of the angle that FC makes with the base ABCD

d) find the size of the angle between the planes FBCE and ABCD.

6.

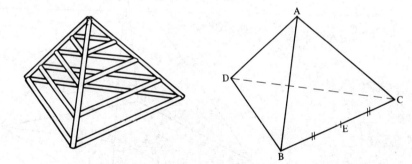

This is a sketch of a playground climbing structure. The basic shape is a pyramid with each face an equilateral triangle of side 3 m. It is possible to climb to the top in various ways.

a) Find the distance from the bottom to the top, starting at
   i) a corner   ii) the midpoint of a side.

b) Find and sketch a section that contains both the angle that AD makes with the base and the angle that AE makes with the base.

c) Using a scale of 4 cm to 1 m, draw this section accurately.

d) By taking measurements from your drawing find the angles described in (b) and the height of the structure.

7.

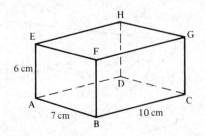

In this cuboid, AB = 7 cm, AE = 6 cm and BC = 10 cm.

Find the size of the angle between

a) EC and the plane ABCD

b) FD and the plane ABFE

c) the planes EBCH and AEHD

d) the planes EFCD and CDHG.

8. A is the point $(6, 4, 2)$.

Find   a) OA   b) the angle between OA and the *xy* plane.

9.

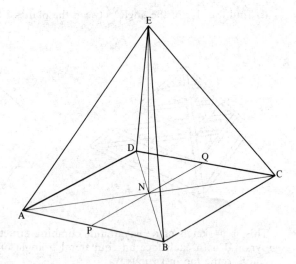

The great pyramid of Cephren at Gizeh in Egypt has a square base of side 215 m and is 225 m high. In the diagram E is the vertex of the right pyramid and ABCD is its base. The diagonals of the base intersect at N; P and Q are the midpoints of AB and DC respectively.

a) A tunnel runs from the entrance P to the burial chamber at N. Find PN. How far is N from A ?

b) How far is it   i) from P to the top   ii) from A to the top ?

c) A climber wishes to climb from the base of the pyramid to the top. Where should he start   i) to make the shortest climb
ii) to climb in one straight line at the smallest angle to the horizontal ?

10.

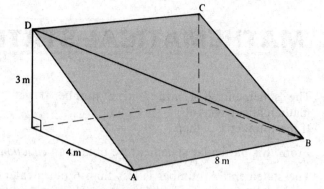

The diagram shows a part of a sea wall whose constant cross-section is a right-angled triangle.

The road is at the level of the top, DC, and the beach starts at AB.

Jim clambers from the road to the beach straight down the path DA whereas Pete goes along the path DB. Find

a) the length of each path

b) the inclination to the horizontal of each path.

11.

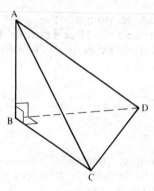

The diagram shows a corner block of a concrete edging system.

AB = BC = BD = 6 cm.

Find the angle that the sloping face, ACD, makes with the horizontal base, BCD.

8 MATHEMATICAL STATEMENTS

The statement 'if I add 7 to a number I get 11' can be written in mathematical symbols.
If the number is x then $x + 7 = 11$.

From this particular statement we obtain an *equation* in x.

The statement 'A number is less than 6 but greater than 3' can be written as $3 < x < 6$ where x is the number. This time we have an *inequality*.

The statement 'the expenses for my car journey are made up of the number of miles I have travelled multiplied by 30 p, added to a fixed sum' can be simplified to $E = 30a + S$ provided we make it clear what each letter represents. We can call this a *formula* for E.

FORMULAE

A formula can be thought of as a set of instructions for finding the value of a particular quantity. For example, the formula $A = \pi r^2$ tells us to find the area of a circle by multiplying π by the square of the radius.

USING FORMULAE

EXERCISE 8a

1. The perimeter, P metres, of a rectangle of length l metres and width w metres is given by the formula $P = 2(l + w)$.
   a) Find P if $l = 2.4$ and $w = 1.7$
   b) Find l if $P = 23.4$ and $w = 4.2$
   c) Find w if $P = 0.06$ and $l = 0.024$

2. The formula for the volume, V, of a cone of radius r and height h is $V = \frac{1}{3}\pi r^2 h$.
   a) Calculate the value of V if $r = 7$, $h = 9$ and $\pi = \frac{22}{7}$
   b) Calculate h if $V = 14\frac{2}{3}$, $r = 2$ and $\pi = \frac{22}{7}$

3. The equation of a straight line is $y = mx + c$ where m is the gradient and c the intercept on the y-axis.
   a) Find y if $m = 1\frac{1}{2}$, $x = 7$ and $c = -3$
   b) Find x if $y = 9$, $m = -\frac{1}{2}$ and $c = 4$

4. The formula for converting F degrees Fahrenheit to C degrees Celsius is $C = \frac{5}{9}(F-32)$.

a) Convert 77 °F to degrees Celsius.

b) Convert 15 °C to degrees Fahrenheit.

5. The number, N, of diagonals of a polygon is given by the formula $N = \frac{1}{2}n(n-3)$ where n is the number of sides of the polygon.

a) How many diagonals are there in a seven-sided polygon ?

b) How many diagonals are there in an octagon ?

c) If a polygon has 54 diagonals, how many sides has it ?

6. The equation of a curve is $y = 2x^3 - \dfrac{3}{x}$. Copy and complete the following table.

x	-3	-2	-1.5	-1	-0.25
y					

7. The formula for the time, T seconds, taken by a pendulum bob to swing from one end of its path to the opposite end is given by

$$T = \pi \sqrt{\frac{l}{g}}$$

where l metres is the length of the pendulum and $g\,\text{m/s}^2$ is the acceleration due to gravity.

a) Find the value of T when $l = 0.56$ and $g = 9.81$

b) Find the value of l when $T = 2$ and $g = 9.8$

c) If l is measured incorrectly as $l+r$, find an expression for the error in the calculated value of T.

d) Find the percentage error in the value of T if $g = 9.81$ and if l is measured as 0.72 instead of the correct value of 0.78

8. Given that $p \circ q$ means $p - 2(p^2 - q)$, find

a) $2 \circ 3$ b) $3 \circ -1$ c) $(2 \circ 2) \circ (-1 \circ -2)$

9. If $a \square b$ means $\dfrac{(a^2 - b^2)}{a}$ find

a) $5 \square 2$ b) $-3 \square 4$ c) $(2 \square 1) \square (-1 \square -2)$

LITERAL EQUATIONS AND FORMULAE

When we solve an equation like $5x + 2 = 3x - 1$, we find x in terms of numbers.

For a literal equation such as $ax = bx + c$ we can find x in terms of a, b and c by the same method:

1.   Get rid of fractions and brackets.

2.   Collect the x terms on one side.

3.   Collect the non-x terms on the other side.

4.   Divide both sides by the number of x s.

EXERCISE 8b

Solve $ax + b = bx + c$ for x.

$$ax + b = bx + c$$

Subtract bx from each side $\qquad ax - bx + b = c$

Take b from each side $\qquad\qquad ax - bx = c - b$

(Decide how many x s there are) $\qquad x(a - b) = c - b$

Divide both sides by $(a - b)$ $\qquad\qquad x = \dfrac{c - b}{a - b}$

Solve the following equations for x.

1. $ax + bx = c$ **4.** $ax + x = c$

2. $ax + b = c$ **5.** $x = bx - c$

3. $ax = c - bx$ **6.** $a = b - cx$

Solve the following equations for x. Get rid of fractions first, then brackets.

7. $a(x + 2) = c$ **11.** $a(x - b) + b(x + a) = c$

8. $\dfrac{x}{a} + \dfrac{x}{b} = 1$ **12.** $\dfrac{x + 1}{a} + \dfrac{x - 1}{b} = 1$

9. $\dfrac{x + a}{b} + \dfrac{x}{b} = c$ **13.** $\dfrac{x - b}{b} = \dfrac{x - a}{a}$

10. $a(x + 1) = b(x - 1)$ **14.** $a(x - 1) = b(x - 1)$

In questions 15 to 36, make the letter in the brackets the subject of the formula, i.e. solve the literal equations for the letter in the brackets.

15. $v = u + at$ $[u]$ **20.** $S = 4a^2 + 4al$ $[l]$

16. $A = 2\pi r(r + h)$ $[h]$ **21.** $l = a + (n - 1)d$ $[d]$

17. $y - k = m(x - h)$ $[m]$ **22.** $l = a + (n - 1)d$ $[n]$

18. $v = u + at$ $[a]$ **23.** $S = \dfrac{(u + v)}{2}t$ $[t]$

19. $A = \frac{1}{2}h(a + b)$ $[a]$ **24.** $\dfrac{1}{u} + \dfrac{1}{v} = \dfrac{1}{f}$ $[f]$

25. $v^2 = u^2 - 2as$ $[u]$ **29.** $a = \frac{1}{2}\sqrt{t}$ $[t]$

26. $T = \pi\sqrt{\dfrac{l}{g}}$ $[g]$ **30.** $p^2 = q^2 - r^2$ $[r]$

27. $V = \pi r^2 h$ $[r]$ **31.** $h = a - \sqrt{t}$ $[t]$

28. $b = \sqrt{a^2 - c^2}$ $[c]$ **32.** $p^2 = 3 - \dfrac{r}{a^2}$ $[a]$

33. $A = bc + bd$ $[b]$ **35.** $s = \dfrac{t}{3}(2 - v)$ $[v]$

34. $A = \pi r(r - h)$ $[h]$ **36.** $x(y - z) = z(x - y)$ $[x]$

37. $F + V = E + 2$, $E = \frac{1}{2}nF$ and $V = \frac{1}{3}nF$. Find F in terms of n.

38. If $A = \pi r^2$ and $C = 2\pi r$ express A in terms of C.

39. Given that $V = \pi r^2 h$ and $A = 2\pi r^2 + 2\pi rh$, express V in terms of A and r.

40. $v = u + at$ and $s = ut + \frac{1}{2}at^2$. Find s in terms of v, u and a.

MAKING FORMULAE

If you cannot see how to make a formula, first think what you would do if you had numbers in place of the letters.

EXERCISE 8c

1. The sum of three numbers, a, b and c, is T. Give a formula for
   a) T in terms of a, b and c
   b) a in terms of T, b and c.

2. Six exercise books cost p pence each and 8 pencils cost q pence each. Give a formula for C if C pence is the total cost of books and pencils.

3. A ladder has N rungs. The rungs are 20 cm apart and the top and bottom rungs are 20 cm from the ends of the ladder. If the length of the ladder is y cm, give a formula for y in terms of N. (Draw a diagram to help.)

4. The sum of two numbers is x. One of the numbers is 6.
   a) What is the second number in terms of x?
   b) The product of the two numbers is P. Give a formula for P in terms of x.

5. A furniture shop buys chairs at £C each and sells them for £S each. N chairs are sold for a total profit of £T. Give a formula for T in terms of C, S and N.

6. A room measures x cm by y cm. The area of the floor is A m². Give a formula for A in terms of x and y.

7. A sequence of numbers begins $4, 7, 10, 13, \ldots$
   a) Find the eighth number in the sequence.
   b) The nth term is x. Find a formula for x in terms of n. (Check your formula by using $n = 8$ and comparing the result with your answer to (a).)

8.

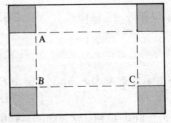

The diagram shows a rectangular piece of card measuring 40 cm by 30 cm, from which the four shaded squares each of side x cm have been cut.

The remaining piece is folded up to form an open box.
a) Give the lengths of AB and BC in terms of x.
b) If the volume of the box is V cm³, give a formula for V in terms of x.

9. Two opposite sides of a rectangular field are each of length x metres. The perimeter of the field is 600 m.

a) Find the area of the field in terms of x.

b) If the area is 21 600 m², find the dimensions of the field.

10.

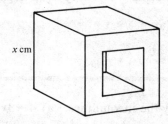

x cm

A cube of edge x cm has a hole of cross-sectional area 5 cm² cut through it in a direction perpendicular to one pair of faces.

a) Find in terms of x the remaining area of each of these faces.

b) Find in terms of x the volume of the remaining solid.

c) If the volume is also equal to $\frac{4}{5}x^3$, find the value of x.

11. The volume of a rectangular box is 288 cm³. The base of the box measures x cm by $2x$ cm.

a) Find the height of the box in terms of x.

b) If the height is $4\frac{1}{2}$ cm, find the other dimensions of the box.

12. The number of diagonals of an n-sided polygon is $\frac{1}{2}n(n-3)$. If the number of diagonals is 35, find the number of sides of the polygon.

13. The sides of a right-angled triangle are x cm, $(x+1)$ cm and $(x+2)$ cm. Find the value of x.

14. A clock shows the time to be exactly 2 o'clock. A few minutes later the hour hand has moved through x degrees.

a) Through what angle, in terms of x, has the minute hand moved ?

b) What angle does each hand make with the vertical line from the centre through 12 ?

c) If the minute hand is exactly over the hour hand, what is the value of x ?

15. If x and y are positive integers such that $(x+y)$ is divisible by 4, show why $(5x+y)$ is also divisible by 4.

INEQUALITIES

Not all mathematical statements are as restricting as

$$x+2 = 6$$

We must also be able to put into symbols a statement such as 'A number is less than 10' and be able to handle it algebraically.

The following exercise reminds you of the meaning of inequalities and the methods for simplifying them.

Remember to use the rules for solving equations to simplify inequalities. You cannot multiply or divide by a negative number without upsetting the inequality.

EXERCISE 8d

Simplify the inequalities   a) $4 - 3x \leqslant 3$ b) $3 + x < 5 < 4 + 3x$.
In each case represent x on a number line.

a) $4 - 3x \leqslant 3$

Add $3x$ to each side $4 \leqslant 3 + 3x$

$$1 \leqslant 3x$$

$$x \geqslant \tfrac{1}{3}$$

(The solid circle ● shows that $x = \tfrac{1}{3}$ is included.)

b) $3 + x < 5 < 4 + 3x$

(We have two inequalities, which must be dealt with separately.)

$3 + x < 5$ and $5 < 4 + 3x$

$x < 2$ $1 < 3x$

$\tfrac{1}{3} < x$

so $\tfrac{1}{3} < x < 2$

(The hollow circles ○ show that $x = \tfrac{1}{3}$ and $x = 2$ are not included.)

Simplify the following inequalities and in each case represent the result on a number line.

1. $2x + 7 \geqslant 11$ **4.** $9 - 4x < 4 - x$ **7.** $18 < 2x + 1 < 24$

2. $3 - 5x > -7$ **5.** $3 < x + 2 < 7$ **8.** $2 + 3x < 8 < 15 + x$

3. $6 - 4x \leqslant 5 + x$ **6.** $-4x > 9$ **9.** $2 - x \leqslant 7 \leqslant 9 - 2x$

10. Simplify the inequality $3 + 2x < 10$ and give the largest integer which satisfies it.

11. Simplify $4 - x < 6 < 7 - 2x$ and list the integers which satisfy the inequalities.

12. Find the smallest integer which satisfies the inequality $5x - 7 > 3x + 11$.

13. Simplify the inequality $20x + 10y \geqslant 50$. If x and y are both positive, give two more inequalities concerning x and y.

14. If $x + y < 6.5$ give three pairs of integers x and y which satisfy the inequality.

15. x and y are positive integers and $2x - y > 7$. Give pairs of values of x and y which satisfy this inequality.

16. Simplify the inequalities   a) $6 - x \leqslant 4 \leqslant 8 - 2x$ b) $6 - x < 4 < 8 - 2x$. Comment on the results.

17. a) On the same diagram sketch the graphs of $y = x^2$ and $y = 16$.
b) Give the values of x for which $x^2 = 16$.
c) Give the range of values of x for which $x^2 < 16$.

18. Use sketch graphs to give the range(s) of values of x for which
a) $x^2 \geqslant 49$ b) $x^2 - 1 < 0$ c) $x^2 > 3x$.

19. a) Factorise $x^2 - 5x + 6$.
b) Sketch the graph of $y = x^2 - 5x + 6$.
c) Find the range of values of x for which $x^2 - 5x + 6 \leqslant 0$.

20. Find the range of values of x for which
a) $x^2 - 3x - 10 \geqslant 0$ b) $x^2 < 5x + 6$.

MATHEMATICAL STATEMENTS

EXERCISE 8e

Susan wishes to buy x red pens at 26 p each and y green pens at 18 p each. She cannot spend more than £1.40. Give three inequalities concerning x and/or y.

The cost of the pens is $(26x + 18y)$ p

$\therefore$ one inequality is $26x + 18y \leqslant 140$

i.e. $13x + 9y \leqslant 70$

She cannot buy a negative number of pens

$\therefore$ $x \geqslant 0$ and $y \geqslant 0$

(Since you cannot buy part of a pen, x and y are integers, so further possible inequalities are $x \leqslant 5$ and $y \leqslant 7$)

1. I think of a number and add 3. I take the first number and double it. The first result is greater than the second.

   a) Write an inequality to represent this statement and simplify it.

   b) Give a positive integer which satisfies the conditions.

2. Anne is more than twice as old as Mary and Mary is more than 4 years older than Sally.

   a) If Anne, Mary and Sally are a, m and s years old respectively, give inequalities to represent the given conditions.

   b) Suggest possible ages for the three girls if Anne is less than 16 years old.

3. A man buys x stamps at 15 p each and y stamps at 20 p each.

   a) Give the total cost in pence.

   b) He cannot spend more than £2. Give as many inequalities as you can think of, concerning x and/or y.

   c) If the man buys seven 15 p stamps, how many 20 p stamps could he buy ?

   d) If the man spends £1.15, what numbers of stamps might he be buying ?

4. The mathematics teacher wishes to order books for the school library. Each book is published in hardback and in paperback, the hardbacks costing £6 each and the paperbacks £2.50 each.

He decides to buy x books in hardback and y books in paperback.

   a) Make a formula for the total cost $£C$ of the books.

   b) If he cannot spend more than £100 on the books, give as many inequalities as you can concerning x and/or y.

   c) If he spends £89 and buys 23 books altogether, give two equations in x and y, and find how many books of each sort he buys.

5. For a party, the Browns buy x cans of cola and y bottles of orange squash. Each child drinks one can of cola or two glasses of orange squash. One bottle of squash gives 12 drinks.

   a) If there are 36 children of whom 9 drink cola, how many bottles of squash must the Browns buy ?

   b) If there are C children and all the drink is consumed, give a formula for C in terms of x and y.

   c) If there are 30 children and they don't mind which drink they have, give as many relationships as you can concerning x and/or y.

   d) If there are 30 children and they have a free choice of drink, give a new set of relationships concerning x and/or y.

6. A classroom is equipped with x desks and y tables. Two people can sit at a table but only one at a desk.

   a) Give a formula for the number of pupils, P, that can be accommodated in this classroom.

   b) If there are more than three times as many desks as there are tables give an inequality to represent this statement.

   c) If a class of 22 can use the room, give an inequality concerning x and y.

   d) If the room will take at the most 27 pupils and there are 16 of these pieces of furniture, find how many desks and how many tables there are.

MIXED EXERCISES

EXERCISE 8f

1. x grams of flour are mixed with y grams of lard. Find the total mass in kilograms.

2. $a = -2$, $b = 3$, $c = 4$. Find the value of

   a) $a + 2b$ b) $b^2 + c^2$ c) $3bc^2$ d) a^2.

3. Simplify the inequality $7 - 2x < 9 + x$.

4. Make p the subject of the formula $A = \pi(p^2 + 3q^2)$.

5. If $\dfrac{a+2b}{a} = \dfrac{7}{3}$,

a) find b in terms of a

b) find the value of $\dfrac{b}{a}$.

6. Give the range of values of x for which $4x^2 - 9 < 0$.

EXERCISE 8g

1. Find the largest integer which satisfies the inequality $14 < 7 - 2x$.

2. Find a when $b = 3.6$ and $c = -2.2$, if $b^2 = c^2 + a^2$.

3. Given that $a * b$ denotes $\dfrac{a+b}{a}$, evaluate

a) $3 * 1$ b) $1 * 3$ c) $(3 * 1) * (1 * 3)$.

4. Make h the subject of the formula $A = 2\pi rh + ah$.

5. A canteen has x chairs and y tables. A chair is allowed $\frac{1}{2}\,\text{m}^2$ of floor space and a table $2\,\text{m}^2$. If there is $70\,\text{m}^2$ of floor space available, give an inequality concerning x and y.

6. For what values of x is $x^2 - 2x \leqslant 15$?

EXERCISE 8h

1. Solve for x the equation $p(x-4) + q(x-2) = p + q$.

2. In a two-digit number, the first digit is x and the units digit is y. What is the value of the number in terms of x and y ?

3. Find the smallest even number which satisfies the inequality $5x + 9 > -11$.

4. a) Find the values of $x^2 - x - \dfrac{1}{x}$ when $x = 1$ and when $x = 2$.

b) Give a value of x for which the value of $x^2 - x - \dfrac{1}{x}$ is roughly zero.

5. If $y = ax^2$ and $x = \dfrac{b}{z}$, express y in terms of a, b and z.

6. Make h the subject of the formula $A = \pi r \sqrt{r^2 + h^2}$

STRAIGHT LINE GRAPHS AND INEQUALITIES

9

The gradient, or slope, of the straight line joining the points A and B is

$$\frac{\text{increase in } y \text{ value from A to B}}{\text{increase in } x \text{ value from A to B}}$$

The equation $y = mx + c$ represents a straight line, where m is the gradient and c is the y intercept.

The larger the value of m, the steeper is the slope.

If m is positive, the line slopes *up* from left to right and makes an acute angle with the positive x-axis.

If m is negative, the line slopes *down* from left to right and makes an obtuse angle with the positive x-axis.

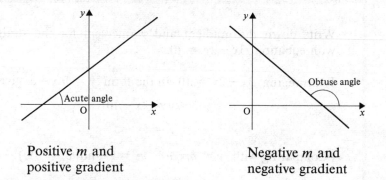

Positive m and positive gradient

Negative m and negative gradient

If the y intercept, c, is *positive*, the line crosses the y-axis c units *above* the origin.

If c is *negative*, the line crosses the y-axis c units *below* the origin.

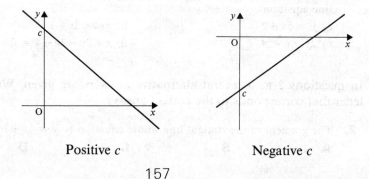

Positive c

Negative c

157

The equation $x = a$ represents a straight line parallel to the y-axis, passing through the point $(a, 0)$.

The equation $y = b$ represents a straight line parallel to the x-axis, passing through the point $(0, b)$.

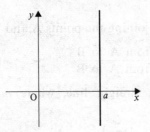

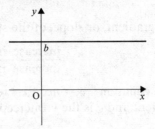

a may be positive or negative.

b may be positive or negative.

EXERCISE 9a

> Write down the gradient and y intercept for the straight line with equation $3x - 2y = 10$.
>
> Rearranging $3x - 2y = 10$ in the form $y = mx + c$ gives
>
> $$2y = 3x - 10$$
>
> $$y = \tfrac{3}{2}x - 5$$
>
> (Comparing with $y = mx + c$, $m = \tfrac{3}{2}$ and $c = -5$.)
>
> $\therefore$ gradient is $\tfrac{3}{2}$ and y intercept is -5.

1. Write down the gradient and y intercept for each of the following straight line equations.

a) $y = 5x + 2$

b) $5y = 2x + 1$

c) $2y - x = 4$

d) $x + 2y - 2y - 4 = 0$

In questions 2 to 6 several alternative answers are given. Write down the letter that corresponds to the correct answer.

2. The gradient of the straight line whose equation is $y = \tfrac{1}{2}x + 7$ is

A 2   **B** $\tfrac{1}{2}$ **C** 7   **D** $-\tfrac{1}{2}$

3. The gradient of the straight line whose equation is $x + 3y - 6 = 0$ is

    A $\frac{1}{3}$ **B** -3 **C** $-\frac{1}{3}$ **D** -2

4. The y intercept for the straight line whose equation is $3y = 5x - 9$ is

    A 3 **B** -3 **C** -9 **D** $\frac{5}{3}$

5. The sketch of the straight line with equation $y = 2x - 4$ is

    A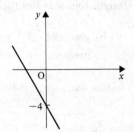   **C**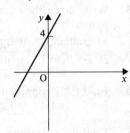

    B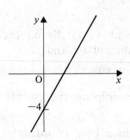   **D**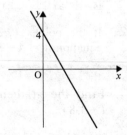

6. The sketch of the straight line whose equation is $3x + y = 4$ is

    A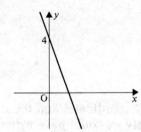   **C**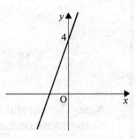

    B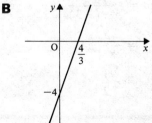   **D**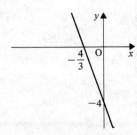

7. Sketch the straight line with the given equation.

a) $y = 4x + 2$

b) $y = -2x - 5$

c) $y = 8 + \frac{1}{2}x$

d) $2y = 2x + 5$

e) $2x + y = 4$

f) $x - 4y + 7 = 0$

8. Determine whether or not the following pairs of equations represent parallel lines.

a) $y = 3x - 7$, $y = 3x + 2$

b) $2x + 3y = 4$, $6y = 3 + 4x$

9. Write down the equation of the straight line that has the given gradient and y intercept.

a) gradient 2, y intercept 3

b) gradient -3, y intercept 4

c) gradient $\frac{1}{2}$, y intercept -2

d) gradient $-\frac{2}{3}$, y intercept $\frac{1}{3}$

10. Find the y coordinate of the point on the line $y = 6 - 3x$ whose x coordinate is   a) 1   b) 3   c) -4.

11. Find the x coordinate of the point on the line $y = 5x + 2$ whose y coordinate is   a) 2   b) 7   c) -8.

12. If the points $(2, a)$, $(-2, b)$ and $(c, 4)$ lie on the straight line with equation $y = 4 - 2x$, find the values of a, b and c.

Find the gradient of the line joining the points $(5, 4)$ and $(-3, 8)$.

$$\text{Gradient} = \frac{\text{difference in } y \text{ coordinates}}{\text{difference in } x \text{ coordinates}}$$

$$= \frac{8 - 4}{-3 - 5}$$

$$= \frac{4}{-8}$$

$$= -\frac{1}{2}$$

Note Be careful to take the y coordinates and the x coordinates in the same order. Alternatively we could have written

$$\text{Gradient} = \frac{4 - 8}{5 - (-3)}$$

$$= \frac{-4}{8}$$

$$= -\frac{1}{2}$$

13. Find the gradient of the straight line passing through the points

    a) $(2,4)$ and $(6,6)$ b) $(3,2)$ and $(2,-5)$

    c) $(8,2)$ and $(2,4)$ d) $(-1,-2)$ and $(-5,-5)$

In questions 14 and 15, write down

a) the coordinates of A and B

b) the gradient of the straight line shown

c) the y intercept

d) the equation of the line AB in the form $y = mx + c$.

14.

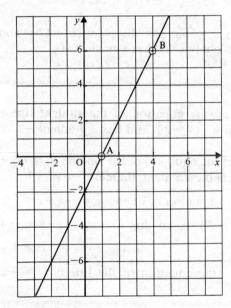

15.

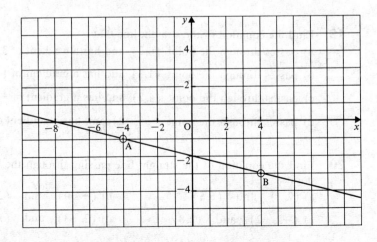

16. Plot on a graph the points A(6,2), B(8,4) and C(−2,−6), and draw the straight line that passes through them.

Use your graph to find the gradient of this line and its y intercept. Hence write down the equation of the line in the form $y = mx + c$.

For questions 17 and 18 draw x and y axes scaled from −6 to 6 using 1 cm for 1 unit on both axes.

17. On a graph, plot the point A(2,1) and through this point draw the straight line that has a gradient of 2.

18. On a graph, plot the point P(−4,2) and through this point draw the straight line that has a gradient of $\frac{1}{2}$.

Find the equation of the straight line that passes through the point $(4,-3)$ and has a gradient -1.

Let the equation of the line be $y = mx + c$
m is the gradient, therefore $m = -1$.

$\therefore$ equation of line is $y = -x + c$

$(4,-3)$ is on this line so $-3 = -4 + c$

$\therefore$ $c = 1$

$\therefore$ the equation of the line is $y = -x + 1$

---

19. Find the equation of the straight line that
a) passes through the point $(0,2)$ and has a gradient of 3

b) passes through the point $(1,3)$ and has a gradient of $\frac{1}{2}$

c) passes through the point $(4,2)$ and has a gradient of -2

d) passes through the point $(-5,-2)$ and has a gradient of $-\frac{3}{4}$.

20. Find the equation of the straight line passing through the following pairs of points.

a) $(2,3)$ and $(6,5)$ b) $(-4,0)$ and $(2,-2)$

c) $(-2,-2)$ and $(2,8)$ d) $(2,-3)$ and $(7,-1)$.

Does the point $(5, -2)$ lie on the line whose equation is $y = -2x + 7$?

On the given line,

when $x = 5$, $y = -2 \times 5 + 7$

$\qquad\qquad = -3$

For the given point,

when $x = 5$, $y = -2$

So the point $(5, -2)$ is not on the given line.

21. In each of the following questions determine whether or not the given point lies on the given straight line.

a) $(3, 8)$, $\quad y = 3x - 1$ b) $(-2, 3)$, $\quad y = 2x + 7$

c) $(3, 0)$, $\quad y = 2x - 5$ d) $(-4, -3)$, $\quad x + y + 1 = 0$.

22. The graph of the line with equation $4x + 3y = 12$ cuts the x-axis at A and the y-axis at B.

a) Find the coordinates of   i) A,   ii) B.

b) Find the gradient of AB.

c) Use Pythagoras' theorem to find the length of AB.

d) Find the area of triangle OAB where O is the origin.

23. The diagram shows a line p which meets the x-axis at the point $(-1, 0)$ and the y-axis at $(0, 3)$. When p is reflected in the line $x = 1$, its image is the line q.

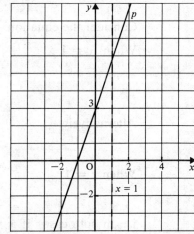

a) What is the gradient of p?

b) Copy the diagram and draw the line q on your diagram.

c) Write down the equation of the line q.

24.

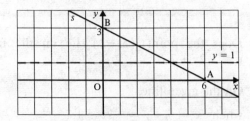

The diagram shows a line s which meets the x-axis at the point $A(6,0)$ and the y-axis at the point $B(0,3)$. When s is reflected in the line $y = 1$ its image is the line s'.

a) What is the gradient of s ?

b) Copy the diagram and draw the line s' on it.

c) Write down the gradient of s' and the coordinates of C, the point where s' crosses the y-axis.

d) What is the equation of s' ?

e) Find the area of triangle ABC.

GRAPHICAL SOLUTION OF SIMULTANEOUS LINEAR EQUATIONS

If we draw two straight lines on a graph the values of x and y at the point of intersection of the two lines satisfy both the given equations, that is they are the solutions of the two simultaneous equations which are represented by the straight line graphs.

To plot a point that lies on a straight line with a given equation we can *either* substitute our chosen value of x in the given equation to find the corresponding value of y, *or* we can rearrange the equation before we make the substitution.

Consider the equation $3x + 4y = 13$

When $x = 1$
$$3 + 4y = 13$$
$$4y = 10$$
$$y = 2.5$$

Alternatively
$$4y = 13 - 3x$$
$$y = \tfrac{1}{4}(13 - 3x)$$

When $x = 1$
$$y = \tfrac{1}{4}(13 - 3)$$
$$y = 2.5$$

i.e. in both cases, if $x = 1, y = 2.5$

EXERCISE 9b

Using graph paper, draw axes for $-4 \leqslant x \leqslant 8$ and $-3 \leqslant y \leqslant 10$.
Take 1 cm for 1 unit on both axes.

Solve graphically the simultaneous equations

$$2x + y = 4$$
$$5x - 8y = -8$$

	$2x + y = 4$		$5x - 8y = -8$
i.e.	$y = -2x + 4$		$5x + 8 = 8y$
			$8y = 5x + 8$
		i.e.	$y = \frac{5}{8}x + 1$

x	-2	0	2
y	8	4	0

x	-4	0	8
y	-1.5	1	6

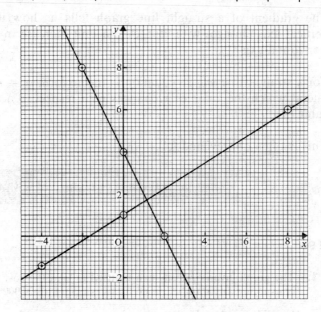

The straight lines intersect at the point $(1.1, 1.7)$.

The solutions of the given equations are $x = 1.1$ and $y = 1.7$.

Solve the following equations graphically. In each case draw axes for x and y, and use values in the ranges indicated, taking 1 cm for 1 unit.

1. $2x + 3y = 12$ $-4 \leqslant x \leqslant 6, \quad -2 \leqslant y \leqslant 8$
        $x - 2y = -2$

2. $8x + 5y = 40$ $-4 \leqslant x \leqslant 6, \quad -2 \leqslant y \leqslant 12$
        $5x - 2y = 2$

3. $6x - 5y = 30$ $-4 \leqslant x \leqslant 8, \quad -10 \leqslant y \leqslant 4$
        $2x + y = 4$

4. $3y - 8x + 24 = 0$ $-6 \leqslant x \leqslant 6, \quad -10 \leqslant y \leqslant 4$
        $5y + 2x + 10 = 0$

INTERPRETING GRADIENTS

The gradient of a straight line graph tells us how the quantity on the vertical axis changes with respect to a unit increase in the quantity on the horizontal axis.

For a straight line whose equation is in the form $y = mx + c$, m gives the rate at which the value of y changes with respect to a unit increase in the value of x.

This is often abbreviated to:

> Gradient is the rate of change of y w.r.t. x.

EXERCISE 9c

1. The graph given opposite can be used to find the cost to the householder of consuming any number of kWh of gas from 0 to 24 000.

Use this graph to find
a) the cost of using 17 600 kWh
b) the number of kWh a householder could buy for £36
c) the payment due before any gas is paid for
d) the gradient of the line. Can you attach a meaning to this value ?

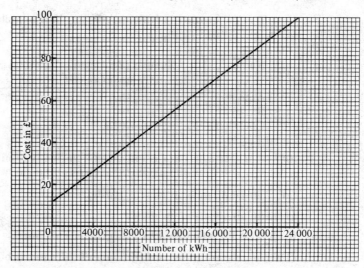

2. The graph shows the cost of electricity to the domestic user for two different tariffs, Tariff A and Tariff B. Use it to answer the questions below.

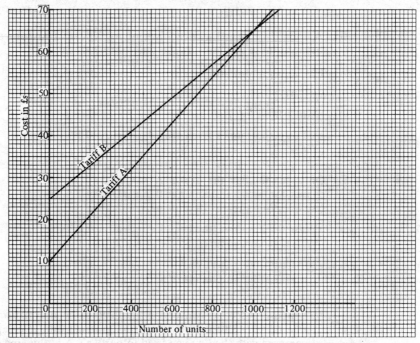

a) What is the cost of 500 units using tariff A ?

b) How many units can I buy for £ 55 using tariff B ?

c) For how many units is the cost the same, whichever tariff is used ?

d) Find the gradient and vertical intercept for the straight line representing each tariff. Attach a meaning to each of these values.

3. Details of the quarterly telephone bills for three households are given in the table.

Name	Number of metered units used (x)	Total cost in £s (y)
Arnott	500	55
Burley	800	76
Compton	1200	104

Represent this data on a graph using 1 cm for 100 units for x and 1 cm for £10 for y. Draw the straight line that passes through these points.

Use your graph to find

a) the quarterly standing charge

b) the cost for a householder using 640 metered units

c) the number of units used by a householder whose bill is £100

d) the slope of the straight line. How can you use this to find the cost of one metered unit ?

4. A tonne, i.e. 1000 kg, is equivalent to 2200 lb. Draw a conversion graph between these two units, in the range 0 to 2000 kg.

Use your graph to find

a) 1700 kg in lb

b) 1950 lb in kg

c) 1.5 tons in tonnes given that 1 ton = 2240 lb.

5. On a certain day the exchange value of £1 in dollars was $1.40. Draw a conversion graph in the range 0 to £20.
Use 8 cm to represent 10 units on both axes.

a) Use the graph to find
  i) how many dollars could be bought for £8.50
  ii) how many pounds it cost to buy 24 dollars
  iii) the value in pounds of $15
  iv) the value in dollars of £16.25

b) Suppose a second conversion graph is to be drawn using an exchange rate of £1 ≡ $1.55. How would the gradient and intercepts for this line compare with the line you used in part (a). Add this line to your graph.

c) Julie returned from holiday and wanted to change $25 into pounds. She could have exchanged her dollars when the rate was £1 ≡ $1.40 but decided not to and eventually exchanged them when the rate was £1 ≡ $1.55. Use your graph to find how much more (or less) she received by waiting.

INEQUALITIES AND REGIONS

These topics were dealt with thoroughly in Chapter 21 of Book 3A. The most important points to remember are:

a continuous line is used for a boundary which is included but a broken line is used for a boundary which is not included. When we have the choice we will shade the region that we do *not* want.

e.g. we represent $x \geqslant 3$ by the following diagram.

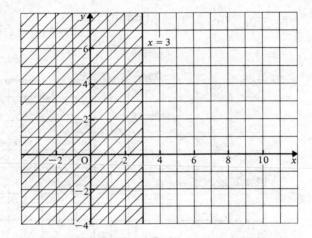

The inequality $x > -1$ tells us that x may not take the value -1. In this case we use a broken line for the boundary, e.g.

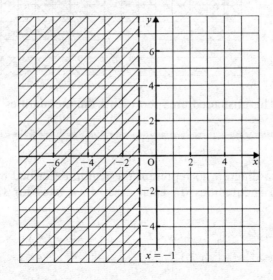

EXERCISE 9d

Draw a diagram to represent the region defined by the set of inequalities $-4 \leqslant x \leqslant 2$, $-3 \leqslant y < \frac{3}{2}$.

The boundary lines are

$x = -4$ and $x = 2$

$y = -3$ and $y = \frac{3}{2}$ (not included)

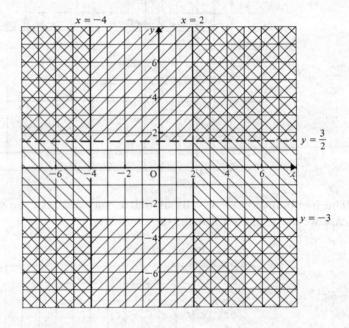

The unshaded area represents the inequalities.

Draw a diagram to represent the region described by each of the following sets of inequalities. In each case, draw axes for values of x and y from -5 to 5.

1. $-3 < x < 0$, $-4 < y < 2$

2. $x \geqslant 2$, $-1 \leqslant y \leqslant 3$

3. $1 < x \leqslant 5$, $-5 \leqslant y < -2$

4. $-4 \leqslant x < 3$, $y < 3$

Give the set of inequalities that describes each of the following unshaded regions.

5.
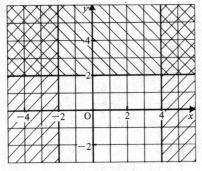

6.
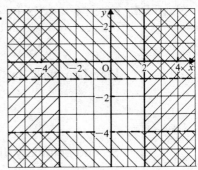

Leave unshaded the region defined by the inequality $x + y > 5$.

The boundary line (not included) is $x + y = 5$

x	0	3	5
y	5	2	0

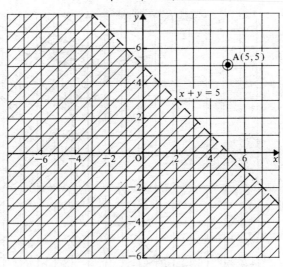

(Test the point A$(5,5)$: when $x = 5$ and $y = 5$, $x + y > 5$ so the required region is above the line.)

In questions 7 and 8 leave unshaded the region defined by the inequality.

7. $x + y < 3$

8. $2x - 3y \leqslant 6$

Leave unshaded the regions defined by the set of inequalities $y > x$, $y < 4x$, $x + y \leqslant 5$. Give the points whose coordinates are integers and which lie in the region.

First boundary line (not included) $y = x$

x	-3	0	3
y	-3	0	3

Second boundary line (not included) $y = 4x$

x	-2	0	2
y	-8	0	8

Third boundary line (included) $x + y = 5$

x	-2	0	5
y	7	5	0

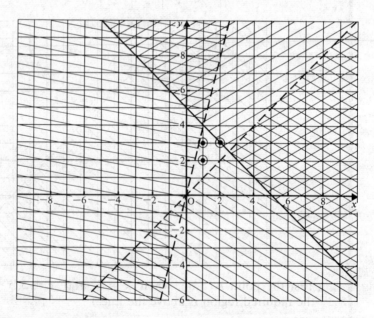

Points on the broken lines do not lie in the region; there are only three points in the region whose coordinates are integers: $(1, 2)$, $(1, 3)$, $(2, 3)$.

In questions 9 to 11 leave unshaded the region defined by the given set of inequalities and find the coordinates of the vertices of the region.

9. $y \geqslant 0$, $x \geqslant 0$, $x + y \leqslant 2$

10. $x > -1$, $-1 < y < 4$, $x + y < 6$

11. $x + y \leqslant 4$, $3x + y \geqslant 3$, $y \geqslant 0$, $x \leqslant 3$

In questions 12 to 14 shade the region defined by the set of inequalities and give the points whose coordinates are integers and that lie in the region.

12. $x < 4$, $y \leqslant 3$, $x + y > 1$

13. $y > \frac{1}{2}x$, $0 < x < 3$, $x + y < 5$, $y < 3$

14. $5x + 2y \leqslant -10$, $y \geqslant -2$, $x \geqslant -5$

In questions 15 and 16 give the inequalities that define the unshaded region.

15.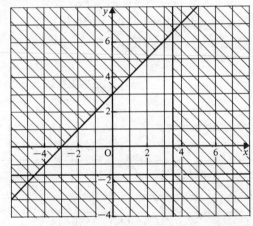

16.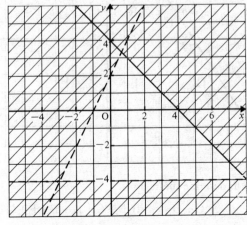

17.

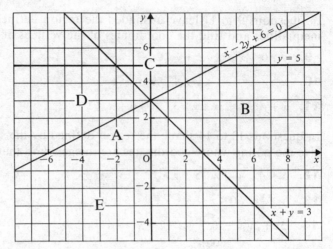

Use inequalities to describe the regions.

a) A   b) B   c) C   d) A + B

(The *y*-axis is not a boundary line but the *x*-axis is.)

18.

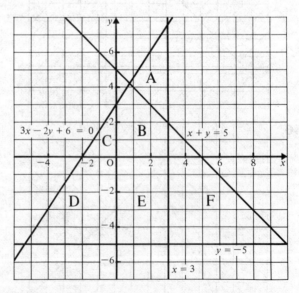

Use inequalities to describe the regions.

a) A   b) B   c) C + D   d) B + C + D + E + F + G

In the unshaded region defined in the diagram find the greatest value of $2x - 3y$ for integer values of x and y.

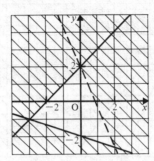

(In Book 3A we found that, for integer values of x and y, the greatest or least value of an expression occurred at or near one of the vertices of a region. So the only points that we need to check are $(-3, -1)$, $(1, -2)$, and $(0, 1)$. Remember that points on the broken line are *not* included in the region.)

At $(-3, -1)$, $2x - 3y = 7$

At $(1, -2)$ $2x - 3y = 8$

At $(0, 1)$ $2x - 3y = -3$

Therefore, for integer values of x and y, the greatest value of $2x - 3y$ is 8 which occurs when $x = 1$ and $y = -2$.

For each region R, find, for integer values of x and y, the greatest and least values of (a) $x + y$ (b) $2x + y$ giving the values of x and y at which these occur. If there is more than one set of values for x and y, give all of them.

19.

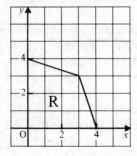

20.

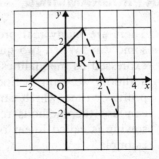

21.

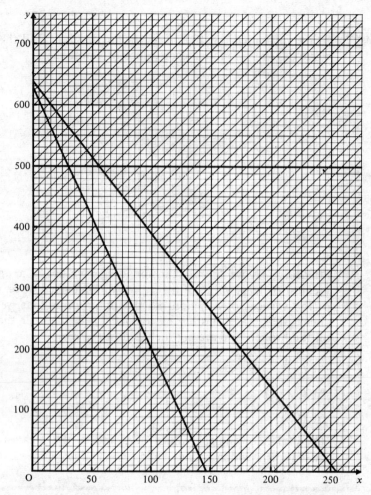

a) From the diagram find the coordinates of the vertices of the unshaded region.

b) Find the vertex at which the value of $3x + y$ is i) greatest   ii) least.

LINEAR PROGRAMMING

There are many real problems in which quantities have to be limited in some way. When two quantities are involved the restrictions can often be expressed as inequalities and illustrated as a region in the xy-plane. If, in addition, we want to find the greatest or least value of a quantity such as profit, or time, which can be expressed in terms of the other quantities, we can use the methods revised in this chapter. This method for problem solving is called linear programming and is illustrated in the next worked example.

EXERCISE 9e

A caterer wants to buy at least 100 chocolate cakes and at least 200 apple pies. A chocolate cake costs £1.50 and an apple pie costs £1. If the caterer does not want to spend more than £500, find the largest total number of cakes and pies that can be bought.

If x chocolate cakes are bought, then $x \geqslant 100$

If y apple pies are bought, then $y \geqslant 200$

The total cost is £$(1.5x + y)$, so $1.5x + y \leqslant 500$.

Illustrating these graphically gives this diagram.

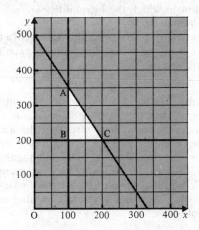

The values of x and y that satisfy these inequalities lie in the unshaded region or on its boundary.

The total number of cakes and pies that can be bought is $x + y$

The greatest value of $x + y$ occurs at one of the vertices.

At A, $x = 100$ and $y = 350$,   so $x + y = 450$

At B, $x = 100$ and $y = 200$,   so $x + y = 300$

At C, $x = 200$ and $y = 200$,   so $x + y = 400$

Therefore the largest total number of cakes and pies that can be bought is 450.

1. A factory produces x plain pencils and y fancy pencils each day.

a) At least 100 plain pencils but no more than 500 fancy pencils are made each day. Draw axes for x and y values from 0 to 1000, using 1 cm for 100 on each axis, and illustrate the inequalities.

b) No more than twice as many plain pencils as fancy pencils are made. Express this as an inequality and illustrate it on your graph. Hence show the region in which the possible numbers of plain and fancy pencils made each day are shown.

c) The profit on one plain pencil is 2 p and the profit on the fancy pencil is 3 p. Express the daily profit, £P, in terms of x and y.

d) Use your graph to find the number of each type of pencil that should be made to give the most profit. What is this profit ?

2. A canteen needs stocks of x canned fizzy drinks and y tetra-paks of fruit juices. There is room for a total of 200 drinks. The minimum order is for 100 drinks. At least twice as many cans as tetra-paks have to be ordered.

a) Express these statements as inequalities and use a graph to show the region in which the inequalities are satisfied. On each axis use a scale of 1 cm to 20 drinks .

b) If the cost of a can is 40 p and the cost of a tetra-pak is 25 p, find an expression for cost of the order. How many of each type of drink should be ordered to minimise the cost ?

3. A builder has a 5000 m^2 plot of land and outline planning permission to build a mixture of two-bedroomed houses and two-bedroomed bungalows. The planning regulations state that the area of a plot for a bungalow must be at least 300 m^2 and the area of a plot for a house must be at least 250 m^2. It takes 260 man-days to build a bungalow and 180 man-days to build a house. The builder wants to keep as many of his work force employed as possible so plans to use at least 2000 man-days. He plans to build at least 6 bungalows. What is the greatest number of dwellings that he can build on this plot ?

4. A haulage contractor has 10 lorries and 20 vans. On a particular day, when only 15 drivers turn up for work, some crates have to be moved from a factory to a rail depot. The distance is such that each driver can make one journey only in the day.

a) If x lorries and y vans are used, express these statements as inequalities and illustrate them on a graph, using a scale of 5 cm to 5 vehicles on each axis.

b) A lorry can carry 100 crates, a van can carry 50 crates and at least 1050 crates have to be moved that day. Express this condition as an inequality and add it to your graph. Hence show the region in which all the conditions are satisfied.

c) What is the minimum number of drivers required ?

d) If it costs £300 for a lorry to make the journey and £120 for a van to make the trip, how many of each vehicle should be used to minimise costs ?

5. A school wants to upgrade its computer storage capacity. It can buy either Brand A or Brand B hard disc and drive combinations, provided at least half of the drives are Brand A. The A drive has a hard disc capacity of 40 megabytes and costs £250 while the B drive has a capacity of 60 megabytes and costs £340. The school requires a total capacity of at least 1200 megabytes. How many of each brand should be bought to give the cheapest solution for the school's requirements ?

6. A biscuit manufacturer is planning a presentation box containing plain and chocolate biscuits. There must be at least 10 chocolate biscuits, the total weight of biscuits must be at least 500 grams and the cost must be less than £1. Other factors to consider are given in the table.

	No. in pack	Weight (g)	Cost (p)	Profit (p)
Chocolate	n	15	3	1
Plain	m	10	1	1

a) Show that $3n + 2m \geqslant 100$ and that $3n + m < 100$.

b) Illustrate all the inequalities as a region in a plane.

c) Find the numbers of each type of biscuit to maximise profit.

7. Greenfly on cabbage plants can be controlled using a spray. It is found that a solution containing x grams of chemical will kill y greenfly where y is up to $50x - x^2$.

a) Plot the graph of $y = 50x - x^2$ for values of x from 0 to 50 using a scale of 1 cm for 10 units on the x-axis and 1 cm for 50 units on the y-axis.

b) Express the statement given at the beginning of the question as an inequality. Show the region of your graph which satisfies this inequality.

c) What dose should give the maximum kill ? Why do you think the effectiveness falls off after this dose ?

d) The benefit, B, to the grower is a relationship based on the number of greenfly killed set against the cost of the spraying and is given by

$$B = y - 20x$$

How many grams of chemical give the maximum benefit ?

e) What is the range of values of x for which there is positive benefit ?

10 CURVES AND EQUATIONS

CURVE SKETCHING

Curved graphs were considered in detail in Book 4A, where it is shown that the general shape of a curve can often be deduced from its equation.

QUADRATIC GRAPHS

All the graphs that have equations of the type $y = ax^2 + bx + c$ $(a \neq 0)$ are curves of the same basic shape. They are called parabolas.

If a is positive the vertex is at the bottom and there is no highest value of y.

On the other hand when a is negative the vertex is at the top and there is no lowest point.

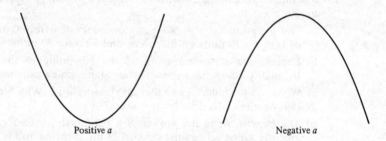

Positive a Negative a

CUBIC GRAPHS

All the graphs that have equations of the type $y = ax^3 + bx^2 + cx + d$ $(a \neq 0)$ are curves of the same general shape. They are called cubic curves.

If a is a positive they look like

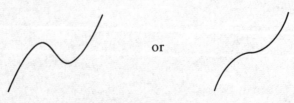

or

180

while if *a* is negative they look like

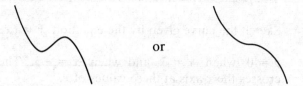

or

EQUATIONS OF THE FORM $y = \dfrac{a}{x}$

Equations of the form $y = \dfrac{a}{x}$ give distinctive 'two part' curves. There is no value for y when $x = 0$.

If *a* is positive it looks like this

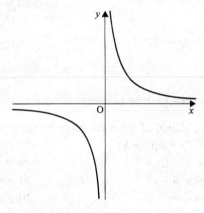

while if *a* is negative it looks like this

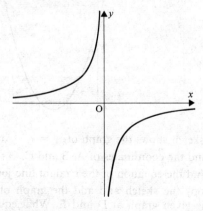

(These curves are called hyperbolas.)

EXERCISE 10a

Sketch the curve given by the equation $y = (x - 3)(x + 5)$.

$y = 0$ when $x = 3$ and when $x = -5$. The graph therefore crosses the x-axis at these values of x.

$y = x^2 + 2x - 15$.

The x^2 term is positive, so the vertex is at the bottom and there is no highest value of y.

When $x = 0$, $y = -15$.

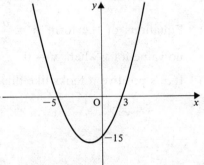

1. Draw a sketch of the curve given by the equation

a) $y = (x - 1)(x - 6)$

b) $y = (x + 4)(x + 7)$

c) $y = x^2 - 2x - 3$

d) $y = x^2 + 8x + 12$

e) $y = x(4 - x)$

f) $y = x^2 + 5$

g) $y = 4 - x^2$

h) $y = (4 - x)(5 + x)$.

2.

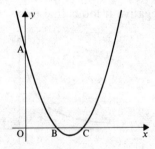

The sketch shows the graph of $y = x^2 - 5x + 6$.

a) Find the coordinates of A, B and C.

b) Find the equation of the straight line joining A and C.

c) Copy the sketch and add the graph of $y = x$. Let this graph intersect the given graph at D and E. What equation will have the x-coordinates of D and E as roots ?

3.

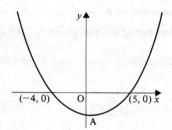

The equation of the curve shown in the sketch is $y = x^2 + px + q$.
Find   a) p and q b) the coordinates of A.

4.

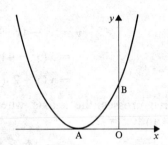

The sketch shows the graph of $y = x^2 + 6x + 9$.
a) Find the coordinates of A and B.
b) Without plotting points sketch, on the same axes, the graph of $y = x^2 - 6x + 9$.

5. Sketch, on the same axes, the graphs of $y = x^2 - 1$, $y = x^2$ and $y = x^2 + 2$, clearly distinguishing between them.

6. On the same axes sketch the graphs of $y = x^2$ and $y = -x^2$. Describe a transformation that maps the first curve to the second.

7. Sketch, on the same axes, the graphs of $y = x^2 - 4$ and $y = -x^2 + 4$. Describe a transformation that maps the first curve to the second.

8.

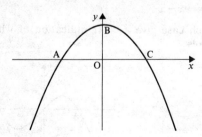

The sketch shows the graph of $y = 9 - x^2$.
a) Find the coordinates of A, B and C.
b) Without plotting points, sketch on the same axes the graph of $y = x^2 - 9$.

Sketch the cubic graph given by the equation $y = x^3 - 4x$.

The x^3 term is positive and therefore the shape of the curve is either

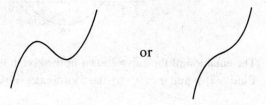

or

$$y = x^3 - 4x$$
$$= x(x^2 - 4)$$
$$= x(x+2)(x-2)$$

The curve crosses the x-axis when $y = 0$, i.e. when $x = 0$, $x = -2$ and $x = 2$.

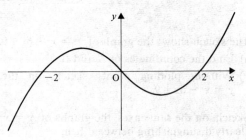

9. Draw a sketch of the curve given by the equation
a) $y = (x-1)(x-3)(x-5)$
b) $y = (x+1)(x-2)(x+7)$
c) $y = 9x - x^3$
d) $y = 3x(4-x^2)$
e) $y = x^3 - 2x^2 + x$.

In each case give a clear indication of where the graph crosses or touches the axes.

10.

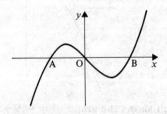

The sketch shows the graph of $y = x^3 - x^2 - 12x$. Find the coordinates of A and B.

11.

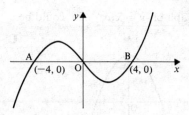

The equation of the cubic curve shown in the sketch is $y = x^3 + ax^2 + bx$. If the curve passes through the points $A(-4,0)$ and $B(4,0)$ find the values a and b.

12. Sketch the graph of $y = \dfrac{10}{x}$ for values of x between 1 and 10.

13. Sketch the graph of $y = -\dfrac{12}{x}$ showing clearly the two parts of the curve.

In questions 14 to 17 several possible answers are given. Write down the letter that corresponds to the correct answer.

14. The graph of $y = x^2 + 6x + 8$ could be

A

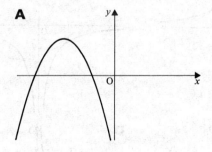

C

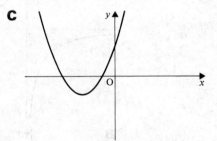

B

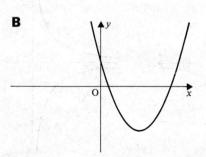

D

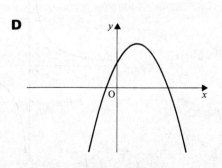

15. The graph of $y = x(x^2 - 9)$ could be

A

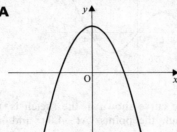

C

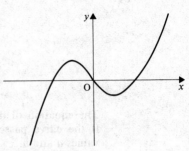

B

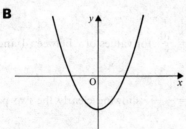

D

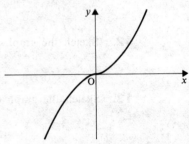

16. The graph of $y = -\dfrac{15}{x}$ could be

A

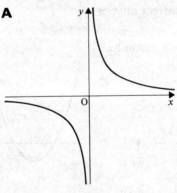

C

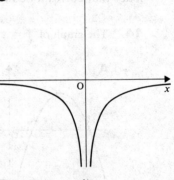

B

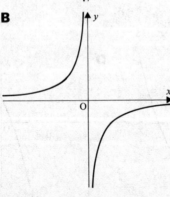

D

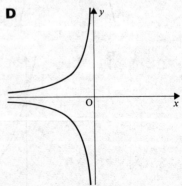

17.

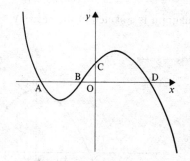

The sketch shows the graph of $y = (x+5)(x+1)(4-x)$.

The coordinates of C are

A $(0,5)$ **B** $(0,1)$ **C** $(0,4)$ **D** $(0,20)$

*18. This diagram is a sketch of the curve $y = x^3 + 2$.

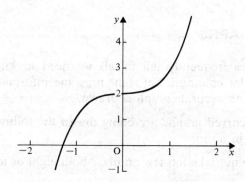

a) Copy the sketch and, on the same diagram, sketch the graph of $y = x^2$.

b) Estimate the value of x where the curves intersect.

c) Write down the equation for which this value of x is a root.

d) Test your estimate in the equation and draw conclusions about the accuracy of your estimate.

e) Can you deduce any information about other possible roots of the equation ?

19. This diagram is a sketch of the curve $y = 3 - x^2$.

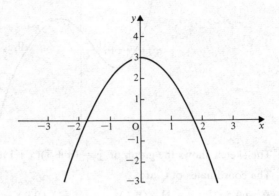

a) Copy the diagram and superimpose a sketch of the curve $y = \dfrac{1}{x}$.

b) Show that the values of x at the points of intersection of the two graphs are the roots of the equation $x^3 - 3x + 1 = 0$.

c) How many roots does the equation have ? Estimate their values.

* **20.** Investigate the roots of the equation $x^3 = 1 - x^2$.

DRAWING GRAPHS

Sketches frequently tell us all we need to know about the curve for a particular equation, but sometimes the information we seek can be found only if an accurate graph is drawn.

When curved graphs are being drawn the following advice should be kept clearly in mind.

1. Do not take too few points. About eight or ten are usually required.

2. To decide where to draw the y-axis look at the range of x-values, and vice versa.

3. In some questions you will be given most of the y-values but you may have to calculate a few more for yourself. If so, always plot first those points that you were given and, from these, get an idea of the shape of the curve. Then you can plot the points you calculated and see if they fit on to the curve you have in mind. If they do not, go back and check your calculations. Always have a clear idea of the shape of the resulting curve before you begin to draw it.

4. When you draw a smooth curve to pass through the points, always turn the page into a position where your wrist is on the inside of the curve.

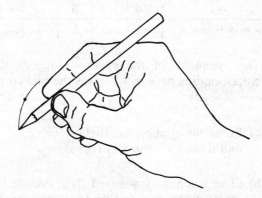

There are graphics programs available for computers that will plot curves and give the coordinates of points of intersection as accurately as anyone could want. There is also a pocket calculator on the market which has this facility. If you have access to either of these, you may like to use them to answer some of the following questions. If you explore these graphics capabilities further, you will find that you can do many of the remaining questions in this chapter far more accurately than it is possible to do by drawing.

EXERCISE 10b

Draw the graph of $y = 5 + 3x - x^2$ for whole number values of x from -2 to 5.

Use your graph to find the highest value of $5 + 3x - x^2$, and the corresponding value of x.

Draw, on the same axes, the graph of $y = \frac{1}{3}x - 1$.

a) Write down the values of x at the points of intersection of the two graphs.

b) Use your graph to find the range of values of x for which $5 + 3x - x^2$ is greater than $\frac{1}{3}x - 1$.

c) Find, in its simplest form, the equation whose roots are the values of x at the points of intersection.

d) What other straight line graph should be drawn to solve the equation $x^2 - 2x - 4 = 0$?

x	-2	-1	0	1	2	3	4	5
5	5	5	5	5	5	5	5	5
$3x$	-6	-3	0	3	6	9	12	15
$-x^2$	-4	-1	0	-1	-4	-9	-16	-25
$y = 5 + 3x - x^2$	-5	1	5	7	7	5	1	-5

The symmetry of the y-values suggests that the value of y corresponding to $x = 1.5$ gives the highest point of the graph.

a) From the graph, the highest value of $5 + 3x - x^2$ is 7.25 and it occurs when x is 1.5.

b) (The graph of $y = \frac{1}{3}x - 1$ is a straight line, so we take only three values of x and find the corresponding values of y.)

x	-2	0	3
$y = \frac{1}{3}x - 1$	$-1\frac{2}{3}$	-1	0

The graphs intersect when $x = -1.46$ and 4.12.
From $x = -1.46$ to $x = 4.12$ the curve $y = 5 + 3x - x^2$ is above the straight line $y = \frac{1}{3}x - 1$.

Therefore $5 + 3x - x^2 > \frac{1}{3}x - 1$ for $-1.46 < x < 4.12$.

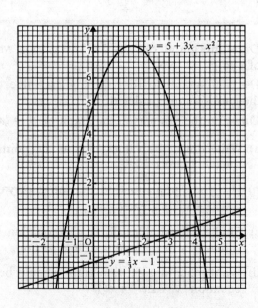

c) At $x = -1.46$ and $x = 4.12$, the values of y for the curve and for the straight line are equal,

i.e.
$$5 + 3x - x^2 = \tfrac{1}{3}x - 1$$
$$15 + 9x - 3x^2 = x - 3$$
$$3x^2 - 8x - 18 = 0$$

Therefore $3x^2 - 8x - 18 = 0$ is the equation whose roots are the values of x at the points of intersection of the two graphs.

d) (To solve the equation $x^2 - 2x - 4 = 0$ we convert it so that one side becomes $5 + 3x - x^2$.)

$$x^2 - 2x - 4 = 0$$
$$0 = 4 + 2x - x^2$$
$$1 + x = 5 + 3x - x^2$$

(Therefore we draw the line with equation $y = x + 1$ on the same axes as the curve $y = 5 + 3x - x^2$.)

The points of intersection of the curve whose equation is $y = 5 + 3x - x^2$ and the straight line that has equation $y = x + 1$ will give the roots of the equation $x^2 - 2x - 4 = 0$.

1. Draw the graph of $y = x^2 - 5x + 3$ for values of x from 0 to 5 at half-unit intervals. Take 4 cm as 1 unit on the x-axis and 2 cm as 1 unit on the y-axis. Use your graph to find

   a) the value of y when x is 3.2

   b) the values of x when the value of $x^2 - 5x + 3$ is -2

   c) the lowest value of $x^2 - 5x + 3$ and the value of x for which it occurs

   d) the values of x when $x^2 - 5x + 3 = 0$.

2. Draw the graph of $y = 5 - 2x - x^2$ for values of x from -4 to 3 at unit intervals, but adding other values if you think that they are needed. Take 2 cm as 1 unit on the x-axis and 1 cm as 1 unit on the y-axis. Use your graph to find

   a) the value of y when x is -2.4

   b) the highest value of $5 - 2x - x^2$ and the value of x for which it occurs

   c) the values of x when $5 - 2x - x^2 = 0$.

3. Use the graph of $y = 4 - 2x - x^2$, which is given below, to solve the equations

a) $4 - 2x - x^2 = 0$ b) $x^2 + 2x - 4 = 0$

c) $2 - 2x - x^2 = 0$ d) $13 - 2x - x^2 = 0$

e) $x^2 + 2x - 10 = 0$.

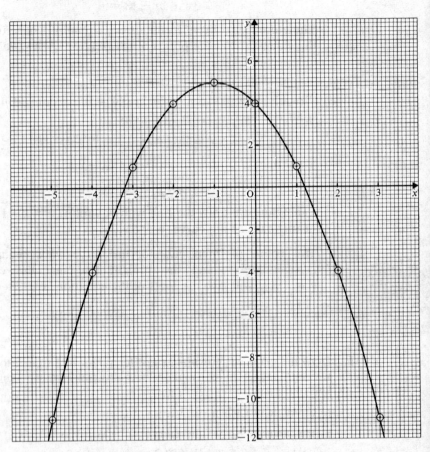

4. Complete the following table which gives values of $3x^2 - 3x - 2$ for values of x from -2 to 3.

x	-2	$-1\frac{1}{2}$	-1	$-\frac{1}{2}$	0	$\frac{1}{2}$	1	$1\frac{1}{2}$	2	$2\frac{1}{2}$	3
$3x^2$	12	$6\frac{3}{4}$		$\frac{3}{4}$		$\frac{3}{4}$	3	$6\frac{3}{4}$		$18\frac{3}{4}$	27
$-3x$	6	$4\frac{1}{2}$		$\frac{3}{2}$		$-\frac{3}{2}$	-3	$-4\frac{1}{2}$		$-7\frac{1}{2}$	-9
-2	-2	-2		-2		-2	-2	-2		-2	-2
$3x^2 - 3x - 2$	16	$9\frac{1}{4}$		$\frac{1}{4}$			-2	$\frac{1}{4}$		$9\frac{1}{4}$	16

Hence draw the graph of $y = 3x^2 - 3x - 2$ for values of x from -2 to 3. Take 3 cm as 1 unit for x and 1 cm as 1 unit for y.

Use your graph to solve the equations

a) $3x^2 - 3x - 2 = 0$

b) $3x^2 - 3x - 5 = 0$

c) $x^2 - x - 3 = 0$.

5. Draw the graph of $y = x^2 - 4x - 4$ for whole number values of x from -1 to 5. Take 2 cm as 1 unit on both axes.

Use your graph to find

a) the value of y when $x = 3.3$

b) the values of x when $y = -2.4$

c) the values of x when the graph crosses the x-axis, and the equation that has these x values as roots.

Draw, on the same axes, the graph of $y = x - 6$.

d) Write down the values of x at the points of intersection of the two graphs, and find, in its simplest form, the equation whose roots are these x values.

e) Use your graph to find the range of values of x for which $x^2 - 4x - 4$ is less than $x - 6$.

Copy and complete the following table, which gives values of $x(x + 2)(x - 4)$ for values of x from -3 to 4.

x	-3	-2	-1	0	1	2	3	4
$x(x+2)(x-4)$	-21	0		0	-9	-16		

Hence draw the graph of $y = x(x + 2)(x - 4)$ for values of x from -3 to 4. Take 2 cm as 1 unit for x and 2 cm as 5 units for y.

Draw, on the same axes, the graph of $y = 2x - 10$.

Write down the values of x at the points of intersection of the two graphs and find, in its simplest form the equation for which these values are the roots.

x	-1	3	4
x	-1	3	4
$x+2$	1	5	6
$x-4$	-5	-1	0
$x(x+2)(x-4)$	5	-15	0

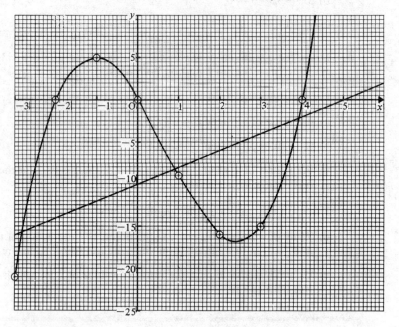

(The graph of $y = 2x - 10$ is a straight line, so we take only three values of x and the corresponding values of y.)

x	-2	0	3
$y = 2x - 10$	-14	-10	-4

The graphs intersect when x is -2.8, -0.9 and 3.9.

When x has these values, the values of y for the curve and for the straight line are equal.

i.e. $$x(x+2)(x-4) = 2x - 10$$

i.e. $$x^3 - 2x^2 - 8x = 2x - 10$$

i.e. $$x^3 - 2x^2 - 10x + 10 = 0$$

Therefore the roots of the equation $x^3 - 2x^2 - 10x + 10 = 0$ are the values of x at the points of intersection of the two graphs.

6. The following table gives values of $4(x^3-x^2-6x)$ for values of x from -3 to 4.

x	-3	$-2\frac{1}{2}$	-2	$-1\frac{1}{2}$	-1	$-\frac{1}{2}$	0	$\frac{1}{2}$
$4(x^3-x^2-6x)$	-72	$-27\frac{1}{2}$	0	$13\frac{1}{2}$		$10\frac{1}{2}$		$-12\frac{1}{2}$

x	1	$1\frac{1}{2}$	2	$2\frac{1}{2}$	3	$3\frac{1}{2}$	4
$4(x^3-x^2-6x)$	-24	$-31\frac{1}{2}$	-32	$-22\frac{1}{2}$	0	$38\frac{1}{2}$	

a) Write down the three missing values.

b) Draw the graph of $y = 4(x^3-x^2-6x)$ for values of x from -3 to 4. Take $2\,\text{cm}$ as 1 unit on the x-axis and $1\,\text{cm}$ as 10 units on the y-axis. Draw on the same axes the graph of $y = 5(4-x)$.

c) Write down the value(s) of x at the point(s) of intersection of the two graphs.

d) Use your graph to find the range of values of x for which $4(x^3-x^2-6x)$ is greater than $5(4-x)$.

e) Find, in its simplest form, the equation whose roots are the values of x at the points of intersection of the two graphs.

7. Copy and complete the following table, which gives values of $\frac{1}{5}x^3$ for values of x from -4 to 4.

x	-4	-3.5	-3	-2.5	-2	-1.5	-1	0
$\frac{1}{5}x^3$	-12.8	-8.6	-5.4	-3.2	-1.6	-0.68	-0.2	0

x	1	1.5	2	2.5	3	3.5	4
$\frac{1}{5}x^3$		0.68		3.2		8.6	12.8

Hence draw the graph of $y = \frac{1}{5}x^3$ for values of x from -4 to 4. Take $2\,\text{cm}$ as 1 unit on the x-axis and $1\,\text{cm}$ as 1 unit on the y-axis.

Use your graph to solve the equations

a) $\frac{1}{5}x^3 = -8$ b) $x^3 = 35$ c) $x^3 + 20 = 0$.

8. Draw, on the same axes, the graphs of $y = x^3$ and $y = 9x-4$ for values of x from -4 to 4. Take $2\,\text{cm}$ as 1 unit on the x-axis and $2\,\text{cm}$ as 10 units on the y-axis.

a) Write down the values of x at the points where the two graphs intersect.

b) Write down and simplify the equation whose roots are these x values.

c) Without drawing any more graphs determine the number of roots of the equation $x^3 + 3x - 2 = 0$.

9. Draw the graph of $y = \dfrac{24}{x}$ for values of x from 1 to 12. Take 1 cm as 1 unit on both axes. Draw on the same axes the graph of $x + y = 13$.

a) Write down the values of x at the points where the graphs intersect.

b) What equation has these x values as its roots ?

c) Write down the range of values of x for which $13 - x \geqslant \dfrac{24}{x}$.

d) Why do we not continue the graph of $y = \dfrac{24}{x}$ towards the y-axis ?

10. Draw the graph of $y = \dfrac{12}{x+1}$ taking 0, 1, 2, 3, 5, 7, 9, 11 and 13 as the values for x in the table. Take 1 cm as 1 unit on the x-axis and 2 cm as 1 unit on the y-axis.

a) Use your graph to solve the equation $\dfrac{12}{x+1} = 5.2$.

On the same axes draw the graph of $x + y = 10$.

b) Write down the values of x at the points where these graphs intersect.

c) What equation has these values as its roots ?

11. Copy and complete the table which gives values of $\dfrac{1}{x^2}$ for values of x from 0.5 to 4.

x	0.5	0.6	0.75	1	1.5	2	2.5	3	3.5	4
$\dfrac{1}{x^2}$		2.78	1.78		0.44	0.25	0.16	0.11	0.08	0.06

a) Draw the graph of $y = \dfrac{1}{x^2}$ for values of x from 0.5 to 4, taking 4 cm as 1 unit on both axes.

12. Sketch the graph of $y = 1 + \dfrac{1}{x^2}$ for values of x from 0.5 to 4.

13. Sketch the graph of $y = 1 - \dfrac{1}{x^2}$ for values of x from 0.5 to 4.

14. Sketch the graph of $y = \dfrac{1}{x^2} - 1$ for values of x from 0.5 to 4.

15. a) Draw the graph of $y = x + \dfrac{1}{x}$ for values of x from $\frac{1}{2}$ to 4, taking the x values at half-unit intervals. Take 4 cm as 1 unit on both axes.

b) Draw, on the same axes, the graph of $x + y = 4$.

c) Write down the value of x at the point where the graphs intersect.

d) Write down, and simplify, the equation which is satisfied by this value of x.

PROBLEM SOLVING USING GRAPHS

The types of graph studied in the two previous exercises can help us to solve certain real life problems. The next exercise considers some typical problems.

EXERCISE 10c

1. A subsidiary of a large company produces electric switchboards. When it produces x thousand switchboards it makes a profit of y thousand pounds, where $y = 7x - (x^2 + 2)$.

Corresponding values of x and y are given in the following table.

x	0	1	2	3	4	5	6
y	-2	4	8	10	10	8	4

Draw a graph to represent this data using 4 cm as the unit for x and 1 cm as the unit for y. You may find it an advantage to plot additional points.

Use your graph to find

a) the maximum profit the company can make and the number of switchboards it must produce to give this profit

b) the minimum number of switchboards the company must produce in order at least to break even.

c) The parent company decides that the subsidiary must make a minimum profit of £6000 to remain in production. Within what range must the number of switchboards lie in order to achieve this?

2. After t seconds, the height of a stone above its point of projection is s metres, where $s = 35t - 5t^2$. Draw a graph to represent this data for values of t from 0 to 7. Take 2 cm as 1 unit for t and 2 cm as 5 units for s.

Use your graph to find

a) the height of the stone after 2.6 s

b) at what times the stone is 40 m above the ground

c) the maximum height the stone reaches and the time it takes to reach this height.

d) the height of the stone after 7 s ?

3. A farmer has a roll of wire 140 metres long, and wishes to make a rectangular enclosure using a straight wall as one side.

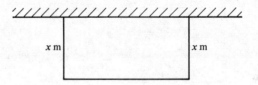

If the rectangle is x metres wide, find its length in terms of x, and hence show that the area of the enclosure, A m², is given by $A = 2x(70-x)$.

Complete the following table to find the values for A corresponding to the given values for x.

x	0	10	20	30	40	50	60	70
$A = 2x(70-x)$	0	1200		2400		2000	1200	

Draw the graph of $A = 2x(70-x)$ for values of x from 0 to 70. Take 1 cm to represent 5 units for x and 1 cm to represent 100 units for A.

Use your graph to find

a) the width of the enclosure when its area is 1500 m²

b) the maximum area that the farmer can enclose and the corresponding value of x

c) the area enclosed when the width of the enclosure is 56 m

d) the area enclosed when the length of the enclosure is 56 m.

4.

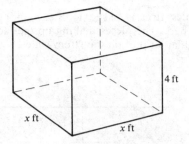

4 ft

x ft

x ft

The diagram shows a four-foot-deep water tank with a square base of side x feet.

a) Show that the capacity of the tank, C cubic feet, is given by the formula $C = 4x^2$.

b) Complete the table below which shows the value of C for various values of x.

x	0.5	1	1.3	1.7	2	2.3	2.7	3	3.3	3.6	4
C	1	4	6.76	11.56			29.2	36	43.6	51.8	64

c) Draw the graph of $C = 4x^2$ for values of x from 0 to 4. Take 4 cm as 1 unit on the x-axis and choose your own scale for the C-axis.

d) What value for x will give a capacity of 40 ft³.

e) A householder needs a new tank with a capacity between 30 ft³ and 40 ft³. To fit the tank into the available space the side of the base must be less than 3 feet. What range of values for x will satisfy these conditions?

5. A piece of wire, 16 cm long, is cut into two pieces. One piece is $8x$ cm long and is bent to form a rectangle measuring $3x$ cm by x cm. The other piece is bent to form a square.

a) Find, in terms of x,
    i) the length of wire used to make the square
    ii) the length of a side of this square
    iii) the area of the rectangle
    iv) the area of the square.

b) Show that the combined area of the rectangle and the square is A cm² where $A = 7x^2 - 16x + 16$.

Corresponding values for x and A are given below.

x	0	0.5	1	1.5	2	2.5	3	3.5
A	16	9.75	7	7.75	12	19.75	31	45.75

c) Draw the graph of $A = 7x^2 - 16x + 16$ for values of x in the range 0 to 3.5. Take 4 cm as the unit on the x-axis and 4 cm as 10 units on the A-axis.

d) Use your graph to find the value of x for which the combined area of the rectangle and the square is smallest.

6. A plastics firm is asked to make an open rectangular container with a square base. The pieces making up the faces of the container are cut from a rectangular strip of plastic 20 cm wide.

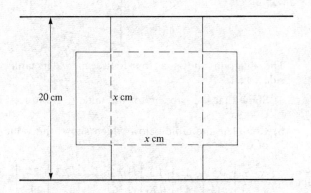

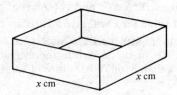

a) If the side of the base is x cm write down, in terms of x, an expression for the depth of the container.

b) Show that the capacity of the container, C cm^3, is given by the formula
$$C = x^2\left(10 - \frac{x}{2}\right).$$

c) Construct a table which shows the value of C for various values of x from 0 to 20.

d) Draw the graph of $C = x^2\left(10 - \frac{x}{2}\right)$ for values of x from 0 to 20. Take 1 cm as 1 unit on the x-axis and choose your own scale for the C-axis.

e) What is the capacity when x is 3.75 ?

f) What values of x will give a capacity of 400 cm^3 ?

g) What is the largest capacity possible for this container ? For what value of x does this occur ?

7. The graph below shows the price of Brited plc shares at the close of business each week day over a twelve week period.

a) During which periods is the price of the share rising ?

b) During which periods is the price of the share falling ?

c) After week 3 when would the best time have been   i) to buy   ii) to sell ?

d) What do you think is likely to happen to the price of the share during week 13 ?

e) "The price of the share doubled in the first six weeks." Is this statement true or false ?

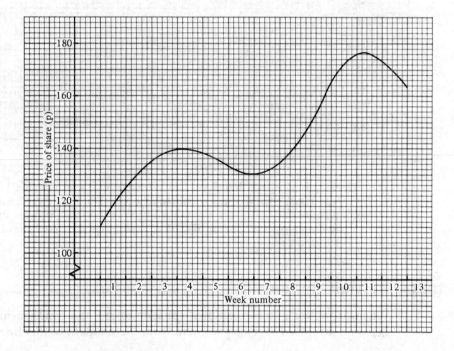

8. As soon as Peter was admitted to hospital he was linked up to a machine that recorded his temperature every five minutes. The graph overleaf shows his temperature for the first ten hours after being admitted.

a) At what time was Peter admitted.

b) For how long did his temperature continue to rise ?

c) What was the highest temperature recorded ?

d) How much did it fall before it began to rise again ?

e) Peter's normal temperature is 37 °C. At what time should his temperature become normal if it continues to fall at the same rate ?

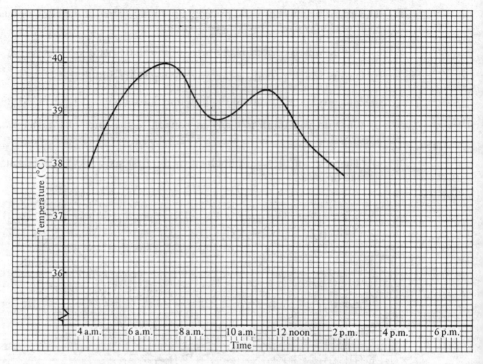

f) Suppose instead that Peter was admitted at 5 a.m. and his temperature was taken then and every subsequent four hours. If these readings were recorded as points on a graph and joined by straight lines, explain the different type of picture that this would give for the behaviour of his temperature.

DISTANCE-TIME GRAPHS

When an object is travelling at a constant speed, the distance–time graph is a straight line. The speed is found from the gradient of this line.

i.e.
$$\text{Speed} = \frac{\text{distance travelled}}{\text{time taken}}$$

When the velocity of an object is constantly changing, the distance–time graph is a curved line.

The *average velocity* from time t_1 to time t_2 may be found from this graph by finding the gradient of the chord joining the points on the curve that correspond to times t_1 and t_2.

The *velocity* at the instant when the time is t is given by the gradient of the tangent to the distance–time curve at the point where the time is t. To find the velocity from a graph, the tangent has to be drawn by eye. The gradient can then be found from the graph.

VELOCITY-TIME GRAPHS

The acceleration at time t is represented by the gradient of the tangent to the velocity–time graph at the point where the time is t.

The *distance travelled* in an interval of time is represented by the area under the velocity–time graph for that interval.

To find the area under the curve, the area is divided into a number of vertical strips. A chord is drawn across the top of each strip to give a set of trapeziums. The sum of the areas of these trapeziums is approximately equal to the required area.

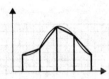

EXERCISE 10d

1. The table shows the distance, d metres, of a ball from its starting point, t seconds after being thrown into the air.

t	0	0.5	1	1.5	2	2.5	3	3.5	4
d	0	8.75	15	18.75	20	18.75	15	8.75	0

Draw the graph of d against t using 4 cm as 1 unit on the t-axis and 1 cm as 1 unit on the d-axis.

From your graph find
a) when the ball returns to the starting point
b) the average velocity of the ball from $t = 1$ to $t = 2$
c) the average velocity of the ball from $t = 1.5$ to $t = 2$
d) the velocity of the ball when $t = 1$
e) the velocity of the ball when $t = 3$
f) the velocity of the ball when $t = 2.5$
g) what kind of relationship there is between d and t.

2. A ball was thrown vertically upwards and, after t seconds, its height, h metres, above the ground was given by $h = 10(2-t)(1+t)$
a) Sketch the distance–time graph for values of t from 0 to 4.
b) From your graph estimate the velocity of the ball
   i) at the start   ii) when $t = 2.5$
c) What is the greatest distance of the ball from the ground ?
d) How long does the ball take before it hits the ground ?

3. A particle travels in a straight line and its speed, v metres per second, after t seconds, is given by $v = t(1-t)$. Sketch the graph of $v = t(1-t)$ for values of t from 0 to 1.

Use your graph to estimate

a) the maximum value of v

b) the acceleration of the particle, in metres per second per second, when $t = 0.2$

c) the time at which the acceleration is zero

d) the total distance covered by the particle in the first second.

4.

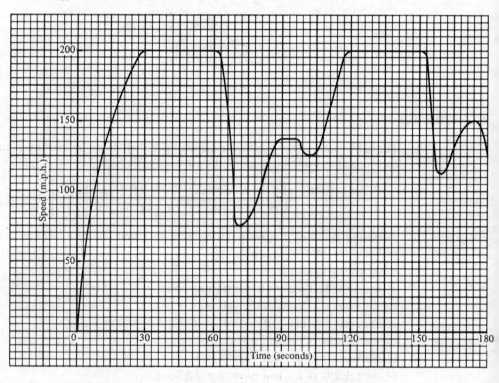

The sketch shows the velocity-time graph for a racing car during the first three minutes of a race.

a) During which period does the acceleration have its greatest positive value ?

b) What is the maximum speed of the car ?

c) For how long is the car driven at this maximum speed ?

d) What is the lowest speed to which the car slows ?

e) How far does the car travel in the first minute ?

5. A rocket is fired and its velocity, v km/minute, t minutes after firing is given by

$$v = t^3 - \tfrac{1}{2}t^2$$

Copy and complete the following table.

t	0	1	1.5	2	2.5	3	3.5	4
v	0	0.5	2.25		12.5		36.75	56

Use scales of $4\,\text{cm} \equiv 1\,\text{minute}$ and $4\,\text{cm} \equiv 10\,\text{km/min}$ to draw the velocity–time graph. From your graph find

a) the acceleration 3 minutes after firing

b) the velocity after $2\frac{3}{4}$ minutes

c) the time when the velocity is 30 km/min

d) the distance covered in the first 3 minutes

e) the distance covered in the third minute.

INTERPRETATION OF RATES OF CHANGE

The graph shows the distance travelled by a hill-climb cyclist from the time he leaves the bottom of a hill until he reaches the top.

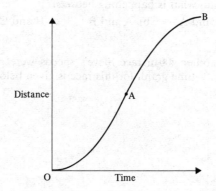

The gradient of any tangent to this curve gives the rate of change of distance with respect to time, i.e. it gives the speed of the cyclist at that instant.

From O to A the gradient of the tangent is increasing, i.e. the speed is increasing. From A to B the gradient of the tangent is decreasing, until at B it has become very small. This indicates that the speed is gradually decreasing as the cyclist travels towards the top of the hill. By the time he reaches the top his speed is quite slow.

In general terms, if we draw the graph of a variable y plotted against a variable x, and the graph is a smooth curve, the gradient of the tangent at any point on the curve gives the rate of change of y with respect to x.

EXERCISE 10e

1. Steve is a 400 metre runner. The distance–time graph for one of his races is given below.

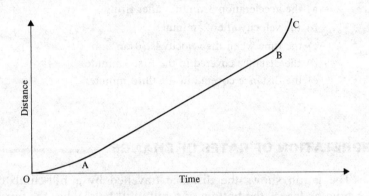

Explain what is happening between

a) O and A   b) A and B   c) B and C.

2. In another 400 m race Steve's speeds were recorded at different times. The velocity–time graph for this race is given below.

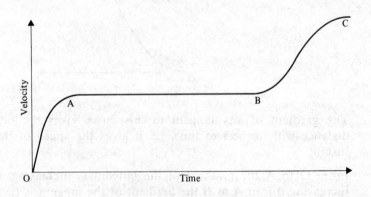

Explain what is happening between

a) O and A   b) A and B   c) B and C.

3. 'The rate of inflation is slowing down'. Which ONE of these graphs best represents this statement ?

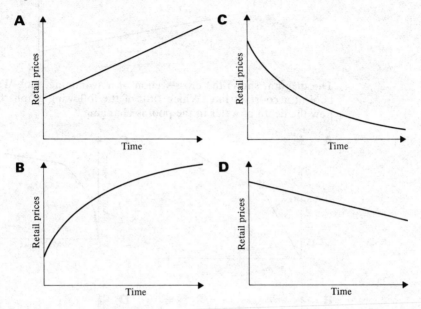

4. 'Building Society interest rates rose several times during the year'. Which ONE of the following graphs best represents this statement ?

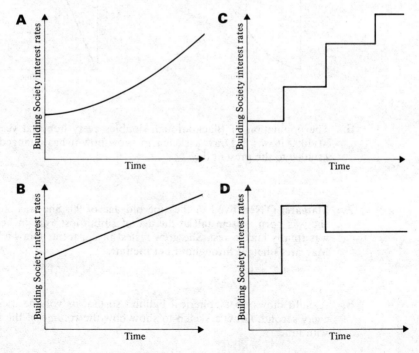

5.

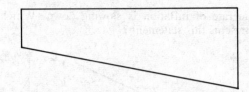

The diagram shows the cross-section of a swimming pool. Water enters the pool at a constant rate. Which ONE of the following graphs best represents how the depth of water in the pool is changing ?

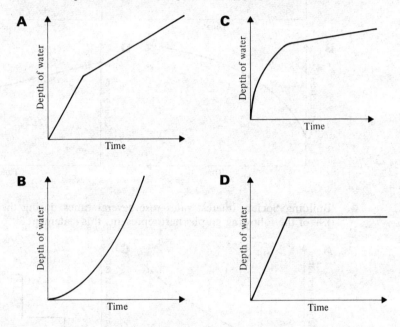

6. The population of Blackborough doubles every hundred years. In the year AD 1000 it was 8. Draw a sketch to show how it has changed from the year AD 1000 to the present day.

7. Margaret O'Neil lived to the ripe old age of 90. She was 50 cm long when she was born, 150 cm tall at the age of 30 but lost 5 cm in height before she was finally laid to rest. She grew fastest in her teens. Draw a sketch to show Margaret's height throughout her lifetime.

8. A child blows up a spherical balloon so that its volume increases by 5 cm³ every second. Draw a sketch to show how the volume of the sphere changes with time.

9. The radius of a circle is increasing at a constant rate of 2 centimetres each second. The graph shows how the area of the circle A, changes with time (t).

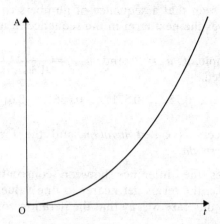

State whether each of the following statements is true or false.

a) The area increases with time.

b) The area increases at constant rate.

c) The area increases at an ever increasing rate.

10. A car accelerates from rest to a maximum speed of 100 m.p.h. in 32 seconds. What would you expect the velocity–time graph to look like. (Any suitable sketch will do.)

11. A sprinter covers 100 metres at a constant speed.
Sketch   a) the distance–time graph,   b) the velocity–time graph.

12. Rabbits colonise a hitherto rabbit-free common. To begin with, the numbers are small, but soon they treble in number every year until a population of approximately two thousand is reached after five years. This number remains stable for three years when, unfortunately, the viral disease of myxomatosis is introduced into the colony. The size of the colony falls, slowly at first, but then with increasing rapidity, until the common is once again rabbit-free after ten years.

Draw a sketch graph to show how the rabbit population on the common changes with time.

13. Water is poured at a constant rate into a variety of containers. For each of the containers shown below, sketch a graph showing how the depth of water in the container varies with time.

a)   b)   c)   d)

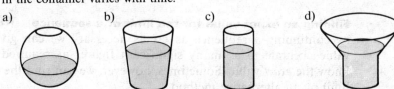

ITERATION

We have seen that a sequence of numbers can be produced by a formula which gives the next term in the sequence in terms of the one before it.

For example, if $u_1 = 2$ and $u_{n+1} = \dfrac{1}{1+u_n}$, then the following sequence is generated.

$$2,\ 0.333\ldots,\ 0.75\ldots,\ 0.571\ldots,\ 0.636\ldots,\ 0.611\ldots,\ 0.620\ldots,\ 0.617\ldots,\ \ldots$$

This process is called *iteration* and the formula $u_{n+1} = \dfrac{1}{1+u_n}$ is an *iteration formula*.

Sometimes the difference between consecutive terms gets smaller and smaller, i.e. the terms get nearer to one value, as happens in the example above. In this case we say that the iteration converges.

This does not always happen as we can see from the sequence generated by

$$u_{n+1} = \frac{u_n^2 + 1}{u_n} \quad \text{when} \quad u_1 = 3$$

i.e. $3,\ 9.33\ldots,\ 87.21\ldots,\ 7607.0\ldots,\ \ldots$

The limit of a sequence   When the terms of a sequence converge to one value, this value is called the *limit* of the sequence.

For example, $u_{n+1} = \dfrac{4}{5 - u_n}$ with $u_1 = 2$ generates the sequence

$$2,\ \frac{4}{3},\ \frac{12}{11},\ \frac{44}{43},\ \frac{172}{171},\ \frac{688}{687}\cdots$$

i.e.,

$$2,\ 1.333\ldots,\ 1.0909\ldots,\ 1.0232\ldots,\ 1.0058\ldots,\ 1.0014\ldots$$

The terms are getting closer in value to 1 so the limit of this sequence is 1.

The first sequence discussed clearly has a limit, but its exact value is not obvious. However we can say that the limit is 0.6 correct to 1 s.f. To give the limit more accurately than this, say to three significant figures, we need to continue the sequence until the value of the fourth significant figure is clear.

Finding an exact value for the limit of a sequence   We have seen that by continuing a sequence as far as necessary we can give its limit as a value accurate to as many significant figures as required but we cannot know the *exact* value. Sometimes, however, we can find the exact value of a limit by an alternative method.

Consider again the sequence given by $u_{n+1} = \dfrac{1}{1+u_n}$ when $u_1 = 2$, i.e.

2, $0.333\ldots$, $0.75\ldots$, $0.571\ldots$, $0.636\ldots$, $0.611\ldots$, $0.620\ldots$, $0.617\ldots$, $\ldots$

Suppose that the exact limit is x.

If we continue the sequence far enough, we will get to the point where u_{n+1} and u_n are so close to x that the difference between them is negligible, i.e. we get to the point where we can replace both u_{n+1} and u_n by x in the iteration formula.

This gives $x = \dfrac{1}{1+x}$.

Hence the value of x is a solution of the equation $x = \dfrac{1}{1+x}$.

Multiplying both sides by $(1+x)$ gives

$$x(1+x) = 1$$

and rearranging gives

$$x^2 + x - 1 = 0$$

This is a quadratic equation, and using the formula gives $x = \dfrac{-1 \pm \sqrt{1+4}}{2}$

i.e.

$$x = \frac{-1+\sqrt{5}}{2} \quad \text{or} \quad x = \frac{-1-\sqrt{5}}{2}$$

We know that the limit of the sequence is positive (it is $0.6\ldots$) so the positive value of x, i.e. $\dfrac{-1+\sqrt{5}}{2}$, is the exact value of the limit.

Notice that the limit is an irrational number, which is why it is not obvious from the sequence.

Notice also that we can check our working by finding $\dfrac{-1+\sqrt{5}}{2}$ as a decimal and comparing it with the observed value of the limit from the first few terms of the sequence.

To summarise:

> *if* an iteration converges, the limit of the sequence generated is a solution of the equation formed by replacing u_{n+1} and u_n by x in the iteration formula.

EXERCISE 10f

1. Write down the first five terms generated by each iteration formula. If the iteration converges, give the limit of the sequence.

    a) $u_1 = 1$ and $u_{n+1} = \dfrac{6}{5 - u_n}$ b) $u_1 = 2$ and $u_{n+1} = 2 - 3u_n^2$

2. Determine whether the sequence has a limit and, if it has, find it correct to two significant figures.

    a) $u_1 = 0.5$ and $u_{n+1} = \dfrac{1}{1 + 3u_n}$ b) $u_1 = 1.5$ and $u_{n+1} = \dfrac{u_n^2}{1 - u_n}$

3. For each of the sequences defined in questions 1 and 2, write down the equation for which the limit, if it exists, is a solution.

4. Find the limit, if it exists, of the sequence given by $u_{n+1} = (u_n)^2 - \frac{1}{2}$
    when   a) $u_1 = 0.5$ b) $u_1 = 2$ c) $u_1 = 1$.

    Give your answers as irrational numbers if necessary.

Using iteration to solve equations   In the last section we saw that if an iteration converges, the limit of the sequence is a solution to the equation given by replacing u_{n+1} and u_n by x in the iteration formula. There are many equations that cannot be solved exactly, but if we can change the equation into an iteration formula that converges, we can use the sequence generated to find an approximation for a solution to the equation and this approximation can be correct to as many significant figures as we wish.

Consider the equation $x^3 + 2x - 1 = 0$.

The first step is to rearrange the equation in the form

$$x = (\text{everything else})$$

This can be done in several ways, but we will choose $x = \dfrac{1 - x^3}{2}$.

We now change this into the iteration formula $u_{n+1} = \dfrac{1 - u_n^3}{2}$

Now we need a value for u_1. It is sensible to choose a value fairly close to the solution we want, so we need a rough value of the solution; we can find this by using sketch graphs.

Rearranging the equation as $x^3 = 1 - 2x$ gives straightforward sketches.

From the sketch we see that there is only one root and it is roughly 0.5, so will take this as our first approximation, i.e. $u_1 = 0.5$

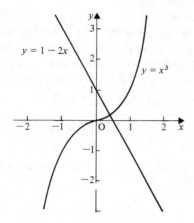

The iteration formula then gives

$$u_2 = \frac{1-(0.5)^3}{2} = 0.4375$$

$$u_3 = \frac{1-(0.4375)^3}{2} = 0.4581\dots$$

$$u_4 = \frac{1-(0.4581)^3}{2} = 0.4519\dots$$

$$u_5 = \frac{1-(0.4519)^3}{2} = 0.4538\dots$$

$$u_6 = \frac{1-(0.4538)^3}{2} = 0.4532\dots$$

This sequence clearly has a limit and, if this limit is x, then x is the solution of the equation.

The pattern so far justifies saying that $x = 0.45$ correct to 2 s.f.

The iteration can be continued to give $u_7 = 0.4534\dots$

Comparing u_6 with u_7 we see that $0.4534 < x < 0.4532$, i.e. $x = 0.453$ correct to three significant figures.

Notice that four significant figures only are used in each iteration. This is enough to give a result correct to three significant figures. If greater accuracy is required more significant figures need to be used.

The advantage of the method is that, once the iteration has started, no judgements or decisions have to be made. This makes it ideal for computer programming. Another advantage is that even a fairly wild first approximation may lead to a result.

The disadvantage of the method is that the iteration may not converge. This could be because the first value chosen is too wild an approximation or the iteration formula chosen may not give a sequence which converges, however close the approximation. For any given equation there are several arrangements which will give it in the form $x = $ (everything else),
e.g. $x^3 + 2x - 1 = 0$ can be written as

$$x = \sqrt[3]{1 - 2x}, \quad x = \frac{1}{x^2 + 2} \quad \text{or} \quad x = \frac{1 - x^3}{2}$$

Each of these gives a different iteration formulae so if the first choice does not work, try another.

EXERCISE 10g

1. Use each of the three arrangements given above of the equation
$$x^3 + 2x - 1 = 0$$
to derive an iteration formula. Test these to find which of them gives the solution to the equation when
   a) $u_1 = 0.5$ b) $u_1 = 2$.

2. a) Show that $x = 0.5$ is an approximate solution of the equation
$$x^2 + 7x - 5 = 0$$

   b) By rearranging the equation as $x = \dfrac{5 - x^2}{7}$, find an iteration formula.

   c) Use the formula with 0.5 as the start value to give the first five terms of a sequence. Comment on your result.

3. a) An iteration formula is $u_{n+1} = 2 + \dfrac{3}{u_n}$. Starting with $u_1 = 2$, find the first ten numbers generated by the sequence. What is the limit of the sequence?

   b) Starting with $u_1 = 0$, use the iteration formula $u_{n+1} = \dfrac{3}{u_n - 2}$ to write down the first ten numbers of a sequence. What is the limit of this sequence?

   c) Show that both iterations give solutions to the same equation. Explain why there are two solutions.

4. You are given the equation $x^2 - 2x - 9 = 0$
   a) Write down as many arrangements as you can in the form
$x = $ (everything else).

   b) Given that 4 is an approximate value of a root of the equation, find which of the arrangements give iteration formulae that converge. Hence find the value of this root correct to 2 decimal places.

   c) Is the root found in (b) the larger or smaller root?

5. For the equation $x^3 - x^2 - 3 = 0$

    a) use sketch graphs to find the number of roots and their rough values

    b) use iteration to find the value(s) of the root(s) correct to 3 significant figures.

* 6. You will need access to a computer with BASIC for this question.

This computer program, which is written in BASIC, solves the equation $x^2 - 5x + 2 = 0$ using iteration.

```
10 INPUT A
20 PRINT A
30 LET B = 5 - 2/A
40 PRINT B
50 IF ABS(A - B) < 0.000001 THEN GOTO 80
60 LET A = B
70 GOTO 30
80 STOP
```

    a) What is the iteration formula that the program uses ?

    b) Find an approximate value for the larger root of the equation. This is the value of A. What is the second number that appears on the screen ?

    c) Type in the program and run it, entering the value of A found in (b).

    d) How accurate is the root given by the program ? How could you change the program to alter this accuracy ?

    e) Alter line 30 to `LET B = A * A - 1` Which equation is this intended to solve ?

    f) Try running the program with the new line 30 and with $A = 5$. Describe what happens. Can you find a way of altering the program to stop this ?

11 VECTORS

DEFINITION OF A VECTOR

A vector quantity has magnitude (i.e. size) and direction and can be represented by a directed line segment.

Velocity is a vector (e.g. 16 m.p.h. west) but mass (e.g. 4 kg) is not. We can represent 16 m.p.h. west by a line.

The length of the line represents the magnitude, and the direction of the line represents the direction, of the vector.

EXERCISE 11a

1. Which of the following quantities are vectors?

a) The length of a piece of string.

b) The force needed to move a lift up its shaft.

c) A move from the door to your chair.

d) The speed of a galloping horse.

e) The distance between Bristol and Edinburgh.

2. Represent each of the following vector quantities by a suitable directed line.

a) A force of 6 newtons acting vertically downwards.

b) A velocity of 3 m/s on a bearing of 035°.

c) An acceleration of 2 m/s^2 northwest.

d) A displacement of 7 km due south.

216

REPRESENTATION OF A VECTOR

If we use squared paper then the line representing the vector can be described by the displacements parallel to the x and y axes.

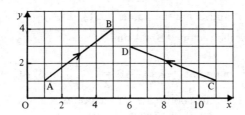

The vector can be named either by using the end letters or by using a small letter in heavy type. In writing we cannot use heavy type so the letter is underlined, e.g. $\underline{a}$.

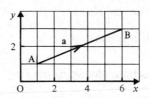

$$\overrightarrow{AB} = \mathbf{a} = \underline{a} = \begin{pmatrix} 5 \\ 2 \end{pmatrix}$$

DISPLACEMENT

We have already used vectors to describe translations. A translation is a *displacement,* or shift of position from one point to another.

EXERCISE 11b

1.

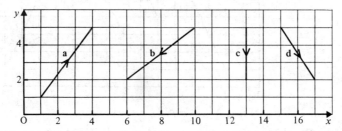

Give the vectors **a**, **b**, **c** and **d** in the form $\begin{pmatrix} x \\ y \end{pmatrix}$.

2. Draw lines to represent the following vectors. Remember to include the arrow.

a) $\begin{pmatrix} 1 \\ 4 \end{pmatrix}$ b) $\begin{pmatrix} -6 \\ -4 \end{pmatrix}$ c) $\begin{pmatrix} -1 \\ 5 \end{pmatrix}$ d) $\begin{pmatrix} 3 \\ -4 \end{pmatrix}$ e) $\begin{pmatrix} 4 \\ 0 \end{pmatrix}$

3. A, B and C are the points $(2,1)$, $(5,7)$ and $(3,-2)$. Draw a diagram and give the vectors $\overrightarrow{AB}$, $\overrightarrow{BA}$ and $\overrightarrow{AC}$.

4. A is the point $(-2,1)$. $\overrightarrow{AB} = \begin{pmatrix} 4 \\ -3 \end{pmatrix}$ and $\overrightarrow{AC} = \begin{pmatrix} 5 \\ 2 \end{pmatrix}$.

   a) Find the coordinates of the points B and C.

   b) Give the vector $\overrightarrow{BC}$.

5. B is the point $(2,1)$, $\overrightarrow{AB} = \begin{pmatrix} 6 \\ -4 \end{pmatrix}$. Give the coordinates of A.

6. A, B and C are the points $(-2,1)$, $(2,0)$ and $(1,3)$.

   a) $\triangle ABC$ is translated using the vector $\begin{pmatrix} 4 \\ 1 \end{pmatrix}$. Label the image $A_1B_1C_1$.

   b) $\triangle ABC$ is translated using the vector $\begin{pmatrix} -3 \\ 2 \end{pmatrix}$. Label the image $A_2B_2C_2$.

   c) Give the vector defining the translation which maps
      i) $\triangle A_1B_1C_1$ to $\triangle A_2B_2C_2$ ii) $\triangle A_2B_2C_2$ to $\triangle A_1B_1C_1$

EQUAL AND PARALLEL VECTORS

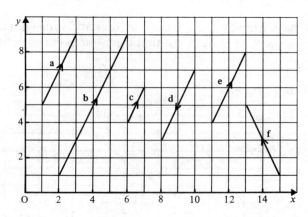

From the diagram, $\mathbf{a} = \begin{pmatrix} 2 \\ 4 \end{pmatrix}$ and $\mathbf{e} = \begin{pmatrix} 2 \\ 4 \end{pmatrix}$ so we can say that $\mathbf{a} = \mathbf{e}$.

The lines representing $\mathbf{a}$ and $\mathbf{e}$ are parallel and equal in length.

Now $\mathbf{b} = \begin{pmatrix} 4 \\ 8 \end{pmatrix}$ and $\mathbf{c} = \begin{pmatrix} 1 \\ 2 \end{pmatrix}$ so $\mathbf{b} = 2\mathbf{a}$ and $\mathbf{c} = \frac{1}{2}\mathbf{a}$.

$\mathbf{a}$, $\mathbf{b}$ and $\mathbf{c}$ are parallel but $\mathbf{b}$ is twice the size of $\mathbf{a}$ and $\mathbf{c}$ is half the size of $\mathbf{a}$.

$\mathbf{d} = \begin{pmatrix} -2 \\ -4 \end{pmatrix}$ so $\mathbf{d} = -\mathbf{a}$.

$\mathbf{d}$ and $\mathbf{a}$ are parallel and the same size but they are in opposite directions.

$\mathbf{f} = \begin{pmatrix} -2 \\ 4 \end{pmatrix}$.

$\mathbf{f}$ is the same size as $\mathbf{a}$ but is not parallel to $\mathbf{a}$ so $\mathbf{a} \neq \mathbf{f}$.

EXERCISE 11c

1.

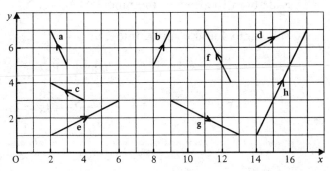

a) Give the vectors in the diagram above in the form $\begin{pmatrix} x \\ y \end{pmatrix}$.

b) Find the relationships between as many pairs of vectors as possible, giving them in the form $\mathbf{p} = k\mathbf{q}$.

2.

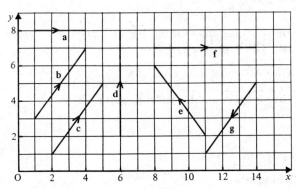

Repeat question 1 for the vectors in the diagram above.

$\overrightarrow{PQ} = p = \begin{pmatrix} 10 \\ 5 \end{pmatrix}$ and R is a point on PQ such that PR : RQ = 2 : 3. Give $\overrightarrow{PR}$ and $\overrightarrow{RQ}$ in terms of **p**.

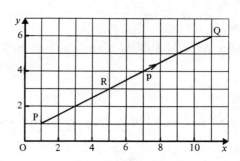

(Divide both 10 and 5 in the ratio 2 : 3.)

10 splits into 4 and 6, and 5 into 2 and 3

so $\overrightarrow{PR} = \begin{pmatrix} 4 \\ 2 \end{pmatrix}$ and $\overrightarrow{RQ} = \begin{pmatrix} 6 \\ 3 \end{pmatrix}$

$\overrightarrow{PR} = \frac{2}{5}p$ and $\overrightarrow{RQ} = \frac{3}{5}p$

3. $\overrightarrow{AB} = a = \begin{pmatrix} 12 \\ 9 \end{pmatrix}$.

a) Draw a diagram showing $\overrightarrow{AB}$ and mark the point C on AB such that AC : CB = 1 : 2.

b) Give $\overrightarrow{AC}$ and $\overrightarrow{CB}$ in terms of **a**.

c) Give $\overrightarrow{BA}$, $\overrightarrow{CA}$ and $\overrightarrow{BC}$ in terms of **a**.

4. $\overrightarrow{PQ} = p = \begin{pmatrix} 8 \\ 12 \end{pmatrix}$ and R is a point on PQ such that $\overrightarrow{PR} = \frac{3}{4}p$. Give the following ratios.

a) PR : RQ   b) PR : PQ   c) RQ : PQ

5. $\vec{AB} = \mathbf{a} = \begin{pmatrix} -4 \\ 6 \end{pmatrix}$ and C is a point on AB produced such that $\vec{AC} = \frac{3}{2}\vec{AB}$. Give the following ratios.

a) AB : BC   b) AC : AB   c) AC : BC

6. In a quadrilateral ABCD, A and B are the points $(-1,0)$ and $(3,1)$, $\vec{BC} = \begin{pmatrix} -3 \\ 3 \end{pmatrix}$, BC is parallel to AD and $AD = \frac{4}{3}BC$. Find $\vec{AD}$ and give the coordinates of D.

7. $\vec{AB} = \mathbf{a}$. C is on AB produced such that $\frac{AB}{AC} = \frac{3}{5}$. Give $\vec{AC}$ in terms of **a**.

THE MAGNITUDE OF A VECTOR

When a vector is represented by a line segment, the *magnitude* of the vector is the *length* of the line, e.g. if $\mathbf{a} = \begin{pmatrix} 4 \\ 2 \end{pmatrix}$ then the magnitude of **a**, which is written as $|\mathbf{a}|$, is equal to the length of the line representing **a**.

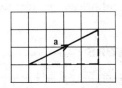

$$|\mathbf{a}| = \sqrt{4^2 + 2^2} \quad (\text{Pythag. th.})$$
$$= \sqrt{20}$$
$$= 4.47 \quad \text{correct to 3 s.f.}$$

EXERCISE 11d

1. Find the magnitude of each of the vectors in Exercise 11c, question 1.

2. Find the magnitude of each of the vectors in Exercise 11c, question 2.

ADDITION OF VECTORS

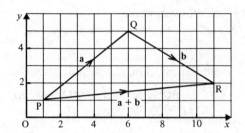

The displacement from P to Q followed by the displacement from Q to R is equivalent to the displacement from P to R, so we write

$$\overrightarrow{PQ} + \overrightarrow{QR} = \overrightarrow{PR}$$

or

$$\begin{pmatrix} 5 \\ 4 \end{pmatrix} + \begin{pmatrix} 5 \\ -3 \end{pmatrix} = \begin{pmatrix} 10 \\ 1 \end{pmatrix}$$

The vector $\overrightarrow{PR}$ is equivalent to $\overrightarrow{PQ}$ together with $\overrightarrow{QR}$ and is called the *resultant* of $\overrightarrow{PQ}$ and $\overrightarrow{QR}$.

To add two vectors we add the corresponding numbers. Notice that a vector in the form $\begin{pmatrix} x \\ y \end{pmatrix}$ is a 2×1 matrix. Vector addition is similar to matrix addition.

Note that in vector addition, $+$ means 'together with'.

SUBTRACTION OF VECTORS

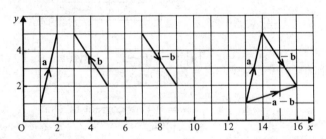

We may think of $\mathbf{a} - \mathbf{b}$ as $\mathbf{a} + (-\mathbf{b})$.

$$\mathbf{a} + (-\mathbf{b}) = \begin{pmatrix} 1 \\ 4 \end{pmatrix} + \begin{pmatrix} 2 \\ -3 \end{pmatrix} = \begin{pmatrix} 3 \\ 1 \end{pmatrix}$$

or

$$\mathbf{a} - \mathbf{b} = \begin{pmatrix} 1 \\ 4 \end{pmatrix} - \begin{pmatrix} -2 \\ 3 \end{pmatrix} = \begin{pmatrix} 3 \\ 1 \end{pmatrix}$$

EXERCISE 11e

In this exercise $a = \begin{pmatrix} 6 \\ 2 \end{pmatrix}$, $b = \begin{pmatrix} -3 \\ 4 \end{pmatrix}$ and $c = \begin{pmatrix} 4 \\ -5 \end{pmatrix}$.

Draw diagrams to represent the following vectors and calculate the resultant vectors. Check that your calculations agree with your diagrams.

1. a	**4.** a + b	**7.** b + c	**10.** c − a
2. b	**5.** b + a	**8.** c + a	**11.** c + b
3. c	**6.** a − b	**9.** a − c	**12.** b − a

13. Is vector addition *commutative,* i.e. does the order of adding a and b make no difference ?

14. Is vector subtraction commutative ?

15. Draw diagrams to represent

a) a + b + c   b) b + a + c

c) Are the two resultant vectors the same ?

d) In how many different orders could you add a, b and c ? Would the resultant vectors be different from those in (a) and (b) ?

16. Draw diagrams to represent

a) 2a   b) 2b   c) 2a + 2b   d) a + b

e) What can you say about the lines representing a + b and 2a + 2b ?

VECTORS AND GEOMETRY

Because a vector can be represented by a line segment, we can use the sides of triangles and polygons to represent vectors, and other lines in the figure can represent combinations of these vectors.

Consider, for example, a triangle XYZ.

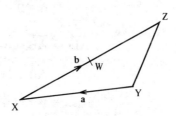

By comparing this with previous diagrams, we can see that the displacement from Y to Z, i.e. $\overrightarrow{YZ}$, is equivalent to a together with b.

i.e. $\overrightarrow{YZ} = a + b$

If **W** is the midpoint of XZ, then $XW = \frac{1}{2}XZ$

so $$\overrightarrow{XW} = \tfrac{1}{2}\mathbf{b}$$

Remember also that if one line represents the vector **c**, say, and another line represents 2**c** then the lines are parallel and the second line is twice the length of the first.

EXERCISE 11f

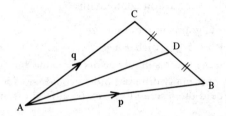

$\overrightarrow{AB} = \mathbf{p}$, $\overrightarrow{AC} = \mathbf{q}$ and D is the midpoint of BC.

Give $\overrightarrow{BC}$ and $\overrightarrow{AD}$ in terms of **p** and **q**.

(Give an alternative route from B to C first.)

$$\overrightarrow{BC} = \overrightarrow{BA} + \overrightarrow{AC}$$
$$= -\mathbf{p} + \mathbf{q}$$
$$= \mathbf{q} - \mathbf{p}$$

$$\overrightarrow{AD} = \overrightarrow{AB} + \overrightarrow{BD}$$
$$= \overrightarrow{AB} + \tfrac{1}{2}\overrightarrow{BC}$$
$$= \mathbf{p} + \tfrac{1}{2}(\mathbf{q} - \mathbf{p})$$
$$= \tfrac{1}{2}\mathbf{p} + \tfrac{1}{2}\mathbf{q}$$
$$= \tfrac{1}{2}(\mathbf{p} + \mathbf{q})$$

1.

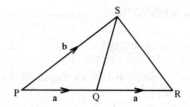

a) Is PQR a straight line ?

b) Give in terms of **a** and **b**

    i) $\overrightarrow{QS}$ ii) $\overrightarrow{SR}$ iii) $\overrightarrow{RS}$

2.

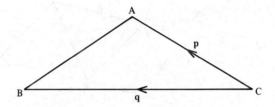

If D is the midpoint of BC, give in terms of **p** and **q**

  a) $\overrightarrow{AB}$ b) $\overrightarrow{CD}$ c) $\overrightarrow{DB}$ d) $\overrightarrow{AD}$

3.

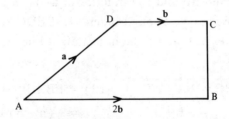

a) What type of quadrilateral is ABCD ?

b) Give in terms of **a** and **b**

    i) $\overrightarrow{BC}$ ii) $\overrightarrow{BD}$ iii) $\overrightarrow{AC}$

4. $\overrightarrow{AB} = \begin{pmatrix} 5 \\ 3 \end{pmatrix}$ and $\overrightarrow{AC} = \begin{pmatrix} -2 \\ 5 \end{pmatrix}$.

Draw a diagram and find $\overrightarrow{BC}$ and $\overrightarrow{CB}$.

5. $\mathbf{p} = \begin{pmatrix} 3 \\ 1 \end{pmatrix}$, $\mathbf{q} = \begin{pmatrix} -2 \\ 3 \end{pmatrix}$ and $\mathbf{r} = \begin{pmatrix} 0 \\ 11 \end{pmatrix}$.

If $\mathbf{r} = h\mathbf{p} + k\mathbf{q}$, find h and k.

GEOMETRY USING VECTORS ——————————————

The following fact is useful.

If $a = kb$ (i.e. if a is a multiple of b) then a and b are parallel and $|a| = k|b|$.

EXERCISE 11g

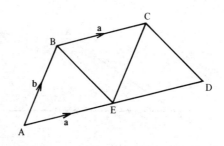

$\overrightarrow{AB} = b$, $\overrightarrow{AE} = a$, $\overrightarrow{BC} = a$ and $\overrightarrow{CD} = a - b$.

a) Find $\overrightarrow{BE}$ and $\overrightarrow{ED}$ in terms of a and b.

b) What type of quadrilateral is BEDC ?

c) Do A, E and D lie in a straight line ?

a) $\overrightarrow{BE} = \overrightarrow{BA} + \overrightarrow{AE}$ $\overrightarrow{ED} = \overrightarrow{EB} + \overrightarrow{BC} + \overrightarrow{CD}$

$\quad = -b + a$ $\quad = -(a - b) + a + (a - b)$

$\quad = a - b$ $\quad = a$

b) $\overrightarrow{BE} = \overrightarrow{CD}$

$\quad \therefore$ CD is parallel to BE and CD = BE.

$\quad \therefore$ BEDC is a parallelogram.

c) Both $\overrightarrow{AE}$ and $\overrightarrow{ED}$ represent a.

$\quad \therefore$ ED is parallel to AE.

Also the point E is on both lines.

$\quad \therefore$ A, E and D lie in a straight line.

1.

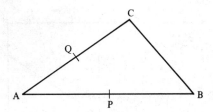

$\overrightarrow{AB} = \mathbf{b}$ and $\overrightarrow{AC} = \mathbf{c}$. P and Q are the midpoints of AB and AC respectively. Give in terms of **b** and **c**

a) $\overrightarrow{AP}$ b) $\overrightarrow{AQ}$ c) $\overrightarrow{BC}$ d) $\overrightarrow{PQ}$

e) Show that PQ is parallel to BC.

f) What can you say about the lengths of PQ and BC ?

2.

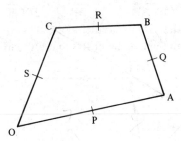

$\overrightarrow{OA} = \mathbf{a}$, $\overrightarrow{OB} = \mathbf{b}$ and $\overrightarrow{OC} = \mathbf{c}$. P, Q, R and S are the midpoints of OA, AB, BC and OC respectively.

Give in terms of **a**, **b** and **c**

a) $\overrightarrow{OP}$ b) $\overrightarrow{AB}$ c) $\overrightarrow{AQ}$ d) $\overrightarrow{PQ}$ e) $\overrightarrow{SR}$

f) Show that PQ is parallel to SR.

g) What type of quadrilateral is PQRS ?

3.

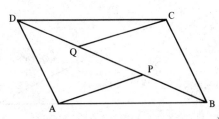

ABCD is a parallelogram. $\overrightarrow{AB} = \mathbf{a}$ and $\overrightarrow{AD} = \mathbf{b}$. P and Q are points on BD such that BP = PQ = QD.

Give in terms of **a** and **b**

a) $\overrightarrow{BD}$ b) $\overrightarrow{BP}$ c) $\overrightarrow{BQ}$ d) $\overrightarrow{AP}$ e) $\overrightarrow{QC}$

f) Show that APCQ is a parallelogram.

4.

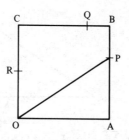

OABC is a square. $\overrightarrow{OA} = \mathbf{a}$ and $\overrightarrow{OC} = \mathbf{b}$.

P is the point on AB such that AP : PB = 2 : 1.

Q is the point on BC such that BQ : QC = 1 : 3.

R is the midpoint of OC.

Find in terms of **a** and **b**

a) $\overrightarrow{AB}$ b) $\overrightarrow{AP}$ c) $\overrightarrow{OP}$ d) $\overrightarrow{OR}$ e) $\overrightarrow{CQ}$ f) $\overrightarrow{RQ}$

g) Show that RQ is parallel to OP.

h) How do the lengths of RQ and OP compare ?

5.

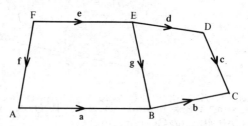

The diagram shows a rough sketch of two quadrilaterals.

a) If $\mathbf{a} = 2\mathbf{b}$ what can you say about A, B and C ?

b) If $\mathbf{a} = \mathbf{b} = \mathbf{e} = \mathbf{d}$ what type of figure is ABCDEF ?

c) If $\mathbf{g} = 2\mathbf{c}$ what type of figure is BCDE ?

d) If $\mathbf{d} + \mathbf{c} = \mathbf{e} + \mathbf{g}$ name four points that are vertices of a parallelogram.

6.

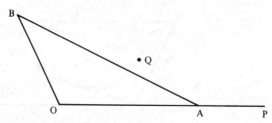

$\overrightarrow{OA} = 4\mathbf{a}$, $\overrightarrow{OB} = 2\mathbf{b}$, $AP = \frac{1}{2}OA$ and $\overrightarrow{OQ} = 3\mathbf{a} + \mathbf{b}$.

Give in terms of **a** and **b**

a) $\overrightarrow{BP}$ b) $\overrightarrow{BQ}$

c) Show that B, Q and P lie in a straight line.

d) Find BQ : BP.

7. In $\triangle PQR$, $\overrightarrow{PQ} = \mathbf{q}$ and $\overrightarrow{PR} = \mathbf{r}$. S is the point such that $\overrightarrow{PS} = 3\mathbf{r}$ and T is the mid-point of QS.

a) Find, in terms of $\mathbf{q}$ and $\mathbf{r}$, the vectors

(i) $\overrightarrow{QS}$ (ii) $\overrightarrow{QT}$ (iii) $\overrightarrow{PT}$.

b) U is the point such that $\overrightarrow{PU} = 2\overrightarrow{PT}$. Find $\overrightarrow{QU}$.

c) What type of quadrilateral is
(i) QUSP   (ii) QURP ?

POSITION VECTORS

In general, vectors are not fixed in position. They are *free* vectors.

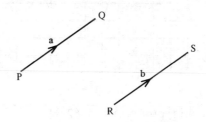

If PQ is parallel to RS and PQ = RS then we say

$$\overrightarrow{PQ} = \overrightarrow{RS} \quad \text{and} \quad \mathbf{a} = \mathbf{b}$$

If, however, we wish to fix the position of one point relative to another, we can use a *position vector*.

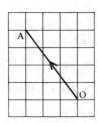

Relative to O the position vector of A is $\begin{pmatrix} -3 \\ 4 \end{pmatrix}$.

Position vectors have already been used to describe the positions of points. We used them when matrix transformations were discussed in Book 4A.

EXERCISE 11h

The position vectors, relative to O, of A, B and C are

$\begin{pmatrix} 7 \\ 1 \end{pmatrix}$, $\begin{pmatrix} -3 \\ 5 \end{pmatrix}$ and $\begin{pmatrix} -1 \\ -1 \end{pmatrix}$ respectively. Mark points A, B and C

on a diagram and find   a) the position vectors of the midpoints of AB and BC   b) the area of △ABC.

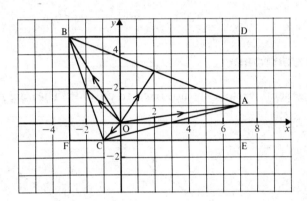

a) The midpoint of AB is (2,3).

Its position vector is $\begin{pmatrix} 2 \\ 3 \end{pmatrix}$.

The midpoint of BC is (−2,2).

Its position vector is $\begin{pmatrix} -2 \\ 2 \end{pmatrix}$.

b) (The area of △ABC can be found by enclosing it in a rectangle BDEF)

Area △ABC = area BDEF − area (△BDA + △AEF + △CFB)

= 60 − (20 + 8 + 6) sq units

= 26 sq units

1. The position vectors of P and Q relative to O are $\begin{pmatrix} 6 \\ 2 \end{pmatrix}$ and $\begin{pmatrix} 1 \\ 8 \end{pmatrix}$.

Find the midpoint of PQ and the area of △POQ.

2. Relative to O the position vectors of A and B are $\begin{pmatrix} 3 \\ 5 \end{pmatrix}$ and $\begin{pmatrix} -6 \\ 8 \end{pmatrix}$.

Find the position vector of the midpoint of
a) AB   b) OA   c) OB.

3. Relative to O the position vectors of L and M are $\begin{pmatrix} 4 \\ 3 \end{pmatrix}$ and $\begin{pmatrix} 6 \\ 9 \end{pmatrix}$.

Find the position vector of
a) the midpoint of LM
b) the midpoint of OL
c) the point N on OM such that ON : NM = 1 : 2.

The position vectors, relative to O, of A and B are $\begin{pmatrix} 5 \\ 1 \end{pmatrix}$ and $\begin{pmatrix} -3 \\ 3 \end{pmatrix}$. If $\overrightarrow{OA}$ = **a**, find the point D such that $\overrightarrow{BD}$ = 2**a**.

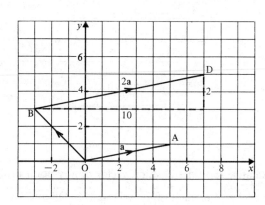

$$2\mathbf{a} = \begin{pmatrix} 10 \\ 2 \end{pmatrix}$$

Therefore, from the diagram, D is the point (7,5).

---

4. The position vectors relative to O of A and B are **a** and **b**.
$\mathbf{a} = \begin{pmatrix} 2 \\ 4 \end{pmatrix}$ and $\mathbf{b} = \begin{pmatrix} -3 \\ 1 \end{pmatrix}$.

a) Find the point C such that $\overrightarrow{AC}$ = 3**b**.

b) Find the point D such that $\overrightarrow{BD} = \frac{1}{2}\mathbf{a}$.

c) Find the point E such that $\overrightarrow{AE}$ = **b** − **a**.

d) Find the area of △BCD.

5.

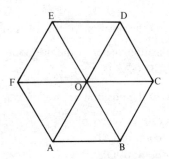

ABCDEF is a regular hexagon. Relative to O the position vectors of A and B are **a** and **b**.

a) Give the position vectors of C, D, E and F in terms of **a** and **b**.

b) Give in terms of **a** and **b** the vectors

i) $\overrightarrow{AB}$ ii) $\overrightarrow{BC}$ iii) $\overrightarrow{CD}$ iv) $\overrightarrow{DE}$ v) $\overrightarrow{EF}$ vi) $\overrightarrow{FA}$

6.

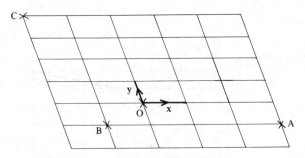

Relative to O the position vector of any point in this diagram is of the form $h\mathbf{x} + k\mathbf{y}$. For each of the vectors $\overrightarrow{OA}$, $\overrightarrow{OB}$ and $\overrightarrow{OC}$ give the values of h and k.

7.

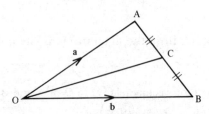

a and **b** are the position vectors of A and B relative to O.
C is the midpoint of AB. Give in terms of **a** and **b**

a) $\overrightarrow{BA}$ b) $\overrightarrow{AB}$ c) $\overrightarrow{BC}$ d) $\overrightarrow{AC}$

e) $\overrightarrow{OC}$ can be given as $\overrightarrow{OB} + \overrightarrow{BC}$ or $\overrightarrow{OA} + \overrightarrow{AC}$. Use each of these two versions to find $\overrightarrow{OC}$ in terms of **a** and **b**. Are your two answers the same ?

8.

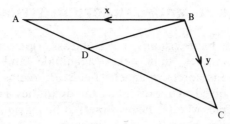

$\overrightarrow{BA} = \mathbf{x}$ and $\overrightarrow{BC} = \mathbf{y}$. D is the point on AC such that AD : DC = 1 : 2.

Give in terms of **x** and **y**

a) $\overrightarrow{AC}$ b) $\overrightarrow{AD}$ c) $\overrightarrow{CA}$ d) $\overrightarrow{CD}$

e) $\overrightarrow{BD}$ can be given as $\overrightarrow{BA} + \overrightarrow{AD}$ or $\overrightarrow{BC} + \overrightarrow{CD}$.

   Find $\overrightarrow{BD}$ in terms of **x** and **y** by the two different ways.

9.

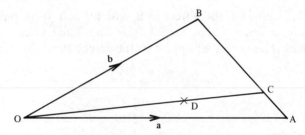

Relative to O the position vectors of A and B are **a** and **b**. C is on AB such that AC : CB = 1 : 3. D is on OC such that OD : DC = 2 : 1.

Give the following vectors in terms of **a** and **b**.

a) $\overrightarrow{AB}$ b) $\overrightarrow{BA}$ c) $\overrightarrow{AC}$ d) $\overrightarrow{BC}$ e) $\overrightarrow{OC}$ f) $\overrightarrow{OD}$ g) $\overrightarrow{DC}$

10.

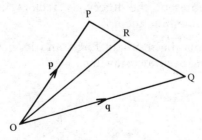

Relative to O the position vectors of P and Q are **p** and **q**. R is the point on PQ such that $\overrightarrow{PR} = k\overrightarrow{PQ}$.

Give in terms of **p** and **q**

a) $\overrightarrow{PQ}$ b) $\overrightarrow{PR}$ c) $\overrightarrow{RQ}$ d) $\overrightarrow{OR}$

USING VECTORS TO MODEL PRACTICAL SITUATIONS

So far we have visualised vectors as displacements but there are many other quantities that have magnitude and direction, e.g. velocities, accelerations, forces, magnetic fields. Problems involving any of these can often be solved by representing the quantities as vectors.

For example, when a heavy object is being pulled by two ropes, the object is only going to move in one direction.

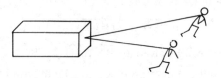

If we consider the force with which each rope pulls, we can find one *resultant* force which would have the same effect as the two combined forces. The object will move in the direction of this resultant force.

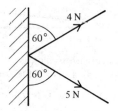

We can represent the forces as vectors in a diagram and use vector addition to combine them.

$\overrightarrow{AC}$ represents the resultant force, and its magnitude and direction can be found (using accurate drawing).

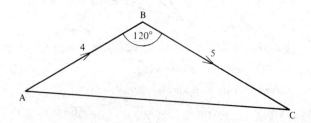

EXERCISE 11i

1. Use the information given on page 234 to make an accurate drawing of △ABC. Hence find the direction in which the block moves. Give your answer as an angle made with the face to which the ropes are attached.

2. p and q are two forces acting on a body.

Draw a diagram to show the resultant force, **p** + **q**.

3.

a) Sketch a vector diagram to show the two forces and their resultant.

b) Calculate the magnitude of the resultant force.

4. The diagram shows a boat crossing a river. Its motion is made up of two velocities. One is the current in the river. The other is the speed and direction set by the boatman.

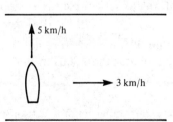

a) Draw an accurate vector diagram to show the resultant velocity.

b) Find the angle between the resultant velocity and the direction of the current.

A plane needs to travel due north at 300 km/h. There is a cross wind of 90 km/h blowing from the east. Find the direction which the pilot should set.

(We know the resultant velocity (300 km/h due north) of the plane and one of the two velocities that contribute to the resultant. First sketch the two known velocities separately.)

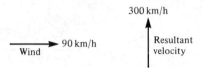

(Now we can draw a second combined diagram.)

$\overrightarrow{CB}$ is the resultant and $\overrightarrow{CA}$ is the second contributing velocity. To find the direction of $\overrightarrow{CA}$ we need to calculate $A\widehat{C}B$.

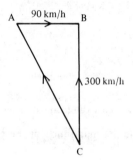

In $\triangle ABC$, $\tan C = \dfrac{90}{300} = 0.3$

∴ $\widehat{C} = 16.7°$ correct to 1 d.p.

The pilot has to set course on a bearing
$$(360° - 16.7°) = 343.3°$$

(Notice that, if the wind were not blowing, the speed of the plane would be greater than 300 km/h.)

---

5. A pilot sets course due south at 120 km/h but, because of the wind, the plane actually flies at 130 km/h on a bearing of 150°. Find the speed and direction of the wind.

6. A pallet with bricks loaded on it is pulled by two ropes, each inclined at 30° to the direction in which the pallet moves. The force in one rope is 10 Newtons. Find the force in the other rope.

7. A boat, whose speed is set to 3 m/s (this is the speed it would have in still water) is driven across a river which is flowing at 1.5 m/s. Use scale drawings to answer the following questions.

a) If the boat is pointed straight across the river, in what direction does it actually move ?

b) The boat actually needs to go across the river at right angles to the bank. In which direction should it be pointed ?

c) The speed of the current changes so that when the boat is pointed upstream at 70° to the bank, it actually moves downstream at 80° to the bank. What is the speed of the current ?

HARDER PROBLEMS

Given two non-parallel vectors **a** and **b** there is only one way to express a third vector in terms of **a** and **b**,

i.e.   if $3\mathbf{a} + 2\mathbf{b} = h\mathbf{a} + k\mathbf{b}$

then $h = 3$ and $k = 2$

Sometimes the expressions need rearranging first but all the questions in the next exercise use this idea.

EXERCISE 11j

a and b are non-parallel vectors

a) If $3\mathbf{a} - \mathbf{b} = h\mathbf{a} + k\mathbf{b}$ find h and k.

b) If $p\mathbf{a} + \mathbf{b} = 2\mathbf{a} + q(\mathbf{a} + \mathbf{b})$ find p and q.

(There is only one way to express a given vector in terms of **a** and **b**. Therefore the coefficients of **a** are equal and the coefficients of **b** are equal.)

a) $3\mathbf{a} - \mathbf{b} = h\mathbf{a} + k\mathbf{b}$

∴ $h = 3$ and $k = -1$

b) $p\mathbf{a} + \mathbf{b} = 2\mathbf{a} + q(\mathbf{a} + \mathbf{b})$

i.e. $p\mathbf{a} + \mathbf{b} = (2 + q)\mathbf{a} + q\mathbf{b}$

∴ $p = 2 + q$ and $1 = q$

So $p = 3$ and $q = 1$.

In each question from 1 to 9, **x** and **y** are non-parallel vectors.
Find h and k.

1. $5\mathbf{x} + h\mathbf{y} = k\mathbf{x} - 4\mathbf{y}$

2. $h\mathbf{x} - 6\mathbf{y} = 7\mathbf{x} + k\mathbf{y}$

3. $h\mathbf{x} + k\mathbf{y} = 6\mathbf{x} + 2h\mathbf{y}$

4. $2\mathbf{x} + h(\mathbf{x} + \mathbf{y}) = k\mathbf{x} + 5\mathbf{y}$

5. $h\mathbf{x} + \mathbf{x} + k\mathbf{y} = k\mathbf{x} + 6\mathbf{y}$

6. $\frac{1}{3}\mathbf{x} + h(\frac{2}{3}\mathbf{x} + \frac{1}{3}\mathbf{y}) = \frac{2}{3}\mathbf{x} + (k + 1)\mathbf{y}$

7. $h(\frac{1}{4}\mathbf{x} + \frac{3}{4}\mathbf{y}) = (k + \frac{1}{2})\mathbf{y} + \frac{1}{2}\mathbf{x}$

8. $(h - \frac{2}{5})\mathbf{x} + \mathbf{y} = k(\mathbf{x} + \mathbf{y})$

9. $(h + 4k)\mathbf{x} + 2k\mathbf{y} = 2h\mathbf{x} + \mathbf{y}$

Given that $\mathbf{p} = 4\mathbf{a} + k\mathbf{b}$ and $\mathbf{q} = 6\mathbf{a} + 9\mathbf{b}$ and that $\mathbf{p}$ and $\mathbf{q}$ are parallel, find the value of k.

(As $\mathbf{p}$ and $\mathbf{q}$ are parallel, $\mathbf{q}$ is a multiple of $\mathbf{p}$, so the coefficients of $\mathbf{a}$ and $\mathbf{b}$ are in the same ratio.)

$$\frac{4}{6} = \frac{k}{9}$$

$$\frac{9 \times 4}{6} = k$$

i.e. $k = 6$.

In each question from 10 to 16, given that $\mathbf{p}$ and $\mathbf{q}$ are parallel vectors, find k.

10. $\mathbf{p} = 6\mathbf{a} + 18\mathbf{b}, \quad \mathbf{q} = k\mathbf{a} + 6\mathbf{b}$

11. $\mathbf{p} = 12\mathbf{a} + k\mathbf{b}, \quad \mathbf{q} = 9\mathbf{a} - 21\mathbf{b}$

12. $\mathbf{p} = (k + 1)\mathbf{a} + (k - 1)\mathbf{b}, \quad \mathbf{q} = 10\mathbf{a} + 6\mathbf{b}$

13. $\mathbf{p} = k\mathbf{a} + 12\mathbf{b}, \quad \mathbf{q} = 3\mathbf{a} + k\mathbf{b}$.

14. $\mathbf{p} = (k - 2)\mathbf{a} + 4\mathbf{b}; \quad \mathbf{q} = 6\mathbf{a} + k\mathbf{b}$

15. $\mathbf{p} = \mathbf{a} + k\mathbf{b}; \quad \mathbf{q} = (k - 3)\mathbf{a} + (k + 5)\mathbf{b}$

16. $\mathbf{p} = k\mathbf{a} + (1 - 2k)\mathbf{b}; \quad \mathbf{q} = (2 - 3k)\mathbf{a} + (k + 4)\mathbf{b}$

$\overrightarrow{OQ} = q$, $\overrightarrow{OP} = p$, $\overrightarrow{OR} = \frac{1}{3}p + kq$, $\overrightarrow{OS} = hp + \frac{1}{2}q$ and R is the midpoint of QS. Find h and k.

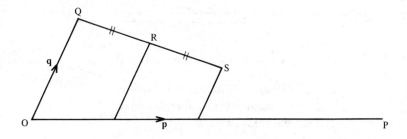

(We need to find $\overrightarrow{QR}$ and $\overrightarrow{RS}$.)

$$\overrightarrow{QR} = \overrightarrow{QO} + \overrightarrow{OR}$$

$$= -q + \frac{1}{3}p + kq$$

$$= \frac{1}{3}p + (k-1)q$$

$$\overrightarrow{RS} = \overrightarrow{RO} + \overrightarrow{OS}$$

$$= -(\frac{1}{3}p + kq) + hp + \frac{1}{2}q$$

$$= (h - \frac{1}{3})p + (\frac{1}{2} - k)q$$

But $\overrightarrow{QR} = \overrightarrow{RS}$ (R is the midpoint of QS.)

$\therefore$ $\qquad \frac{1}{3}p + (k-1)q = (h - \frac{1}{3})p + (\frac{1}{2} - k)q$

Comparing coefficients of p, $\frac{1}{3} = h - \frac{1}{3}$

$\therefore$ $\qquad\qquad\qquad\qquad h = \frac{2}{3}$

Comparing coefficients of q, $k - 1 = \frac{1}{2} - k$

$$2k = 1\frac{1}{2}$$

$\therefore$ $\qquad\qquad\qquad\qquad k = \frac{3}{4}$

So $h = \frac{2}{3}$ and $k = \frac{3}{4}$.

17.

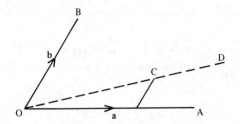

$\overrightarrow{OA} = \mathbf{a}$, $\overrightarrow{OB} = \mathbf{b}$, $\overrightarrow{OC} = \frac{2}{3}\mathbf{a} + \frac{1}{3}\mathbf{b}$. D is the point such that $\overrightarrow{OD} = k\overrightarrow{OC}$.

a) Find $\overrightarrow{OD}$ and $\overrightarrow{BD}$ in terms of **a** and **b**.

b) If BD is parallel to OA, find the value of k.

c) Find the ratio OC : CD.

18.

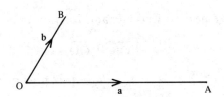

$\overrightarrow{OA} = \mathbf{a}$, $\overrightarrow{OB} = \mathbf{b}$, C and D are the points such that $\overrightarrow{OC} = \mathbf{a} - \frac{1}{2}\mathbf{b}$ and $\overrightarrow{OD} = k\mathbf{a} + \frac{3}{4}\mathbf{b}$.

a) Find $\overrightarrow{BD}$ in terms of **a** and **b**.

b) If BD is parallel to OC find the value of k.

c) Find $\dfrac{BD}{OC}$.

19.

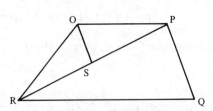

OPQR is a trapezium with OP parallel to RQ. $\overrightarrow{OP} = \mathbf{p}$, $\overrightarrow{OR} = \mathbf{r}$, RQ = hOP and PS = kPR. Express in terms of **p** and **r**

a) $\overrightarrow{RQ}$ b) $\overrightarrow{PR}$ c) $\overrightarrow{PQ}$ d) $\overrightarrow{PS}$ e) $\overrightarrow{OS}$

f) If OS is parallel to PQ, find h in terms of k.

g) If, in addition, $\dfrac{PS}{PR} = \dfrac{1}{2}$, find k and h.

20.

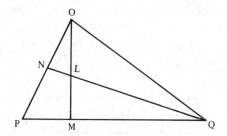

$\overrightarrow{OP} = \mathbf{p}$, $\overrightarrow{OQ} = \mathbf{q}$, M is a point on PQ such that PM : MQ = 1 : 2. N is the midpoint of OP. LQ = hQN.

Give in terms of **p, q** and h

a) $\overrightarrow{PQ}$ b) $\overrightarrow{PM}$ c) $\overrightarrow{OM}$ d) $\overrightarrow{ON}$ e) $\overrightarrow{QN}$ f) $\overrightarrow{QL}$ g) $\overrightarrow{OL}$

h) If OL = kOM, express $\overrightarrow{OL}$ in terms of **p, q** and k.

i) Using the two versions of $\overrightarrow{OL}$, find the values of h and k.

UNIT VECTORS

When using x and y coordinates, writing $\mathbf{a} = \begin{pmatrix} 6 \\ 4 \end{pmatrix}$ means that **a** is equivalent to a displacement of 6 units in the direction Ox (i.e. parallel to the x-axis) together with a displacement of 4 units in the direction Oy.

If we use **i** to represent a displacement of 1 unit in the direction Ox and **j** for a displacement of 1 unit in the direction Oy then we can express **a** in terms of **i** and **j**.

i.e. $\mathbf{a} = 6\mathbf{i} + 4\mathbf{j}$

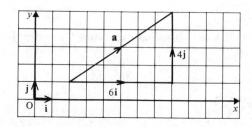

Similarly

$$a = \begin{pmatrix} 4 \\ 3 \end{pmatrix} = 4i + 3j, \quad b = \begin{pmatrix} 4 \\ -2 \end{pmatrix} = 4i - 2j$$

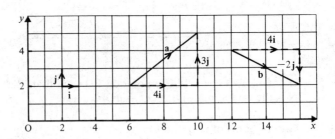

i and **j** are called *unit base vectors*.

EXERCISE 11k

$$p = i + 2j, \quad q = 3i - 5j, \quad r = -4i + 3j$$

Express $p + q$, $q - r$ and $3r$ in terms of **i** and **j**.

$$p + q = (i + 2j) + (3i - 5j)$$
$$= 4i - 3j$$
$$q - r = (3i - 5j) - (-4i + 3j)$$
$$= 3i - 5j + 4i - 3j$$
$$= 7i - 8j$$
$$3r = -12i + 9j$$

1. $a = 3i + 4j, \quad b = -2i - 5j \quad$ and $\quad c = 5i - j$

Express in terms of **i** and **j**

a) $2a$ b) $-b$ c) $a + b$

d) $c - b$ e) $b - c$ f) $a - b$

g) $a + b + c$ h) $2b + c$ i) $-3b$

2. a = 5i − 3j,   b = 4i + 3j,   c = 2i

Draw diagrams to represent the following vectors.

a) a   b) b   c) c
d) 2c   e) a + b   f) −b
g) a − c   h) b − 2c   i) a + b + c

j) Find the magnitudes of **a**, **b** and **c**.

3. Give, in terms of **i** and **j**, the position vectors relative to the origin of the points (2, 4), (−3, 9) and (−6, −4).

4.

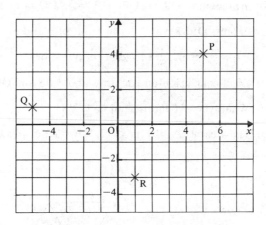

a) Give, in terms of **i** and **j**, the position vectors relative to O of the points P, Q and R.

b) Express, in terms of **i** and **j**, the vectors $\overrightarrow{PQ}$, $\overrightarrow{QR}$ and $\overrightarrow{RQ}$.

c) Find the position vectors of the midpoints of PQ and QR.

d) If $\overrightarrow{OS} = 8i + 2j$, find the vectors $\overrightarrow{PS}$ and $\overrightarrow{QS}$.

e) Show that PS is parallel to QR and find $\dfrac{PS}{QR}$.

5. The position vectors relative to O of A and B are 4i + 3j and 5j. C is the midpoint of AB and D is the midpoint of OC.

a) Find the position vector and the coordinates of C.

b) Find the position vector of D.

c) E is the midpoint of OB. Show that EC is parallel to OA.

FURTHER PROBLEMS

EXERCISE 11I

1.

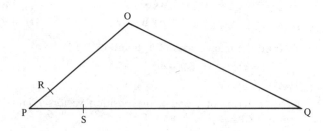

In the diagram $OR = \frac{4}{5}OP$, $\overrightarrow{OP} = p$, $\overrightarrow{OQ} = q$ and $PS : SQ = 1 : 4$.

a) Express $\overrightarrow{OR}$, $\overrightarrow{RP}$ and $\overrightarrow{PQ}$ in terms of p and q.

b) Express $\overrightarrow{PS}$ and $\overrightarrow{RS}$ in terms of p and q.

c) What conclusion do you draw about RS and OQ ?

d) What type of quadrilateral is ORSQ ?

e) The area of $\triangle PRS$ is $5\,cm^2$. What is the area of ORSQ ?

2.

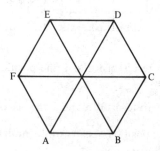

ABCDEF is a regular hexagon, $\overrightarrow{AB} = a$ and $\overrightarrow{AC} = b$.

G is the point such that $\overrightarrow{CG} = b$ and H is the point such that $\overrightarrow{CH} = 2a - b$.

Find, in terms of a and b,

a) $\overrightarrow{AD}$ b) $\overrightarrow{BE}$ c) $\overrightarrow{EG}$ d) $\overrightarrow{HG}$

e) Show that HG is parallel to EF.

f) What type of quadrilateral is ADGH ?

3.

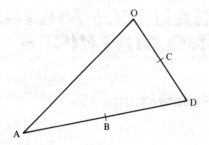

Relative to O the position vectors of A, B and C are **a**, **b** and **c**. B and C are the midpoints of AD and OD.

a) Give $\overrightarrow{OD}$ and $\overrightarrow{AD}$ in terms of **a** and **c**.

b) Find **b** in terms of **a** and **c**.

c) E is a point on OA produced such that $\overrightarrow{OE} = 4\overrightarrow{AE}$. If $\overrightarrow{CB} = k\overrightarrow{AE}$ find the value of k.

4. O, A and B are the points $(0,0)$, $(3,4)$ and $(4,-6)$ respectively.

a) C is the point such that $\overrightarrow{OA} = \overrightarrow{OC} + \overrightarrow{OB}$. Find the coordinates of C.

b) D is the point $(1,24)$ and $\overrightarrow{OD} = h\overrightarrow{OA} + k\overrightarrow{OB}$. Find the values of h and k.

5. ABCD is a parallelogram. Relative to O the position vector of A is $\begin{pmatrix} 2 \\ -1 \end{pmatrix}$, $\overrightarrow{AB} = \begin{pmatrix} 3 \\ 4 \end{pmatrix}$ and $\overrightarrow{AD} = \begin{pmatrix} -2 \\ 5 \end{pmatrix}$.

Find the coordinates of the four vertices of the parallelogram, and its area.

12 TRANSFORMATIONS AND MATRICES

COMMON TRANSFORMATIONS

REFLECTION

A reflection is defined by the mirror line.

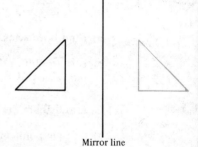

Mirror line

ROTATION

A rotation is defined by the centre and the angle of rotation.

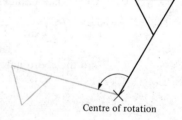

Centre of rotation

TRANSLATION

A translation is defined by a description of the displacement, usually in the form of a vector.

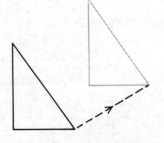

ENLARGEMENT

An enlargement is defined by the centre
of enlargement and the scale factor.

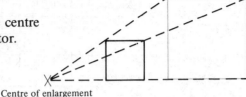

Centre of enlargement

EXERCISE 12a

For questions 1 to 4, draw x and y axes, each for values from -6 to 6.
Use 1 cm to 1 unit.

1. Draw $\triangle ABC$ with A(3, 2), B(5, 2) and C(5, 5). Draw the image of $\triangle ABC$
   a) under a reflection in the line $x = 1$. Label it $\triangle A_1B_1C_1$
   b) under a rotation of 90° clockwise about (0, 0). Label it $\triangle A_2B_2C_2$
   c) under an enlargement, centre (6, 6) and scale factor 3. Label it $\triangle A_3B_3C_3$.

2. Draw $\triangle PQR$ with P(-1, 2), Q(-1, 5) and R(-3, 2).
   Draw the image of $\triangle PQR$
   a) under a reflection in the line $y = x$. Label it $\triangle P_1Q_1R_1$
   b) under a reflection in the y-axis. Label it $\triangle P_2Q_2R_2$
   c) under a reflection in the x-axis. Label it $\triangle P_3Q_3R_3$.
   Describe the transformation
   d) that maps $\triangle P_2Q_2R_2$ to $\triangle P_3Q_3R_3$.
   e) that maps $\triangle P_3Q_3R_3$ to $\triangle P_1Q_1R_1$.

3. Draw rectangle ABCD with A(1, 1), B(4, 1), C(4, 3) and D(1, 3).
   Draw the four images of ABCD under the translations described by the
   vectors
   a) $\begin{pmatrix} -5 \\ 3 \end{pmatrix}$ b) $\begin{pmatrix} -7 \\ -1 \end{pmatrix}$ c) $\begin{pmatrix} -5 \\ -7 \end{pmatrix}$ d) $\begin{pmatrix} 2 \\ -5 \end{pmatrix}$
   Label the images $A_1B_1C_1D_1$, $A_2B_2C_2D_2$, $A_3B_3C_3D_3$ and $A_4B_4C_4D_4$
   respectively.
   e) Describe the transformation that maps $A_4B_4C_4D_4$ to $A_1B_1C_1D_1$.
   f) Describe the transformation that maps $A_2B_2C_2D_2$ to ABCD.

4. Draw $\triangle LMN$ with L(3, 2), M(5, 2) and N(5, 5).
   Draw the image of $\triangle LMN$
   a) under a reflection in the line $y = -x$. Label it $\triangle L_1M_1N_1$
   b) under a rotation of 180° about (0, 2). Label it $\triangle L_2M_2N_2$
   c) under a translation described by the vector $\begin{pmatrix} -4 \\ 1 \end{pmatrix}$. Label it $\triangle L_3M_3N_3$.
   What is the image of $\triangle LMN$ under a rotation of 360° about O ?

248   *ST(P) Mathematics 5A*

5.

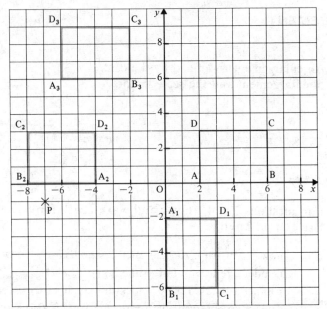

Give the transformation that maps rectangle ABCD to

a) $A_1B_1C_1D_1$ b) $A_2B_2C_2D_2$ c) $A_3B_3C_3D_3$

$A_1B_1C_1D_1$ is mapped to $A_3B_3C_3D_3$ by a rotation about $P(-7,-1)$.

d) What is the angle of rotation ?

6.

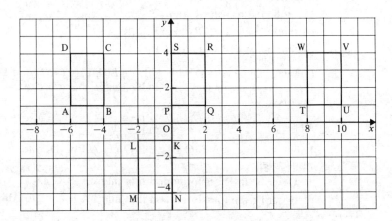

Give the transformation that maps PQRS to

a) ABCD   c) MNKL   e) TUVW

b) KLMN   d) BADC   f) UTWV

Give the transformation that maps ABCD to

g) PQRS   h) QPSR   i) KLMN

7. P is the point (3, 3) and Q is (1, 2). Find the coordinates of the point to which P is mapped under

a) an enlargement, centre Q, scale factor 2

b) an enlargement, centre Q, scale factor -1

c) a clockwise rotation of $90°$ about Q.

8. A translation maps the point (6, 2) to the point (7, 5) and the mirror line of a reflection is the line $x + y = 2$. Find the image of the point (1, 2) under

a) the translation   b) the reflection.

9.

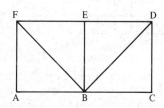

ABEF and BCDE are squares.

a) Under a rotation, $\triangle CDB$ is mapped to $\triangle ABF$. Give the centre of rotation and the angle of rotation.

b) Under a reflection, $\triangle CDB$ is mapped to $\triangle AFB$. Give the mirror line.

c) Under another rotation, square CDEB is mapped to FABE. Give the centre of rotation and the angle of rotation.

10.

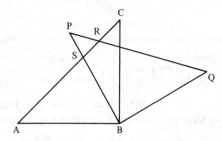

In $\triangle ABC$, $AB = BC$ and $A\widehat{B}C = 90°$. $\triangle ABC$ is mapped to $\triangle PBQ$ by a rotation of $60°$ clockwise about B.

a) Name all the lengths equal to AB and to AC.

b) Through what angle has BC rotated in this transformation? What is the size of $C\widehat{B}Q$?

c) Through what angle has AC rotated? What is the size of $A\widehat{R}P$?

d) Calculate $C\widehat{S}B$.

e) If $AB = 6\,cm$, give the length of CQ.

11.

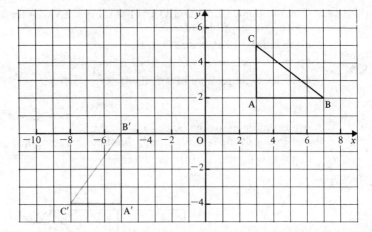

Copy the diagram, using 1 cm to 1 unit. △A'B'C' is the image of △ABC under a rotation, centre P, where P is the intersection of the perpendicular bisectors of AA', BB' and CC'. Use compasses to construct the perpendicular bisectors of CC' and BB'.

a) Give the coordinates of the centre of rotation and the angle of rotation of this transformation.

b) Explain why the centre of rotation lies on the perpendicular bisectors.

NOTATION

It is useful to have a symbol to describe a transformation.

For example we can use Y to denote a reflection in the y-axis. Then the image of a triangle (called P) under the reflection is named Y(P).

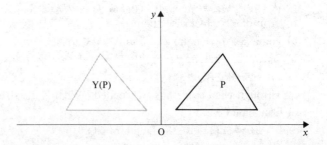

EXERCISE 12b

R₁ is a rotation of 90° anticlockwise about O. The object P is
△ABC with vertices A(1,1), B(4,1) and C(4,5).
Draw P and R₁(P)

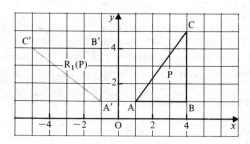

In this exercise,

R₁ is a rotation of 90° anticlockwise about O

R₂ is a rotation of 180° about O

R₃ is a rotation of 90° clockwise about O

X is a reflection in the *x*-axis

Y is a reflection in the *y*-axis

T is a translation defined by the vector $\begin{pmatrix} 1 \\ 3 \end{pmatrix}$

For each question, draw *x* and *y* axes, each for values from −6 to 6.

1. P, Q and R are the points (2, 1), (5, 1) and (5, 3).
Draw △PQR and label it A.
Draw and label the following images
a) R₁(A)   b) R₂(A)   c) R₃(A)

2. A, B and C are the points (−2, 1), (−4, 1) and (−2, 5).
Draw △ABC and label it Q.
Draw and label the following images
a) X(Q)   b) Y(Q)

3. P is the triangle with vertices $(-5, 0)$, $(-3, 0)$ and $(-3, 2)$.
Q is the triangle with vertices $(1, 0)$, $(3, 0)$ and $(1, 2)$.
R is the triangle with vertices $(-2, -6)$, $(0, -6)$ and $(0, -4)$.
Draw and label   a) T(P)   b) T(Q)   c) T(R)

4. L is a reflection in the line $x + y = 2$ and M is a reflection in the line $y = x + 2$. The object A is the triangle with vertices $(1, 2)$, $(4, 2)$ and $(4, 4)$.
Find   a) L(A)   b) M(A)

5. N is a rotation of $90°$ anticlockwise about $(1, 1)$.
R is a rotation of $90°$ clockwise about $(0, -1)$.
The object B is the triangle with vertices $(-2, 1)$, $(-5, 1)$ and $(-2, 2)$.
Find   a) N(B)   b) R(B)

COMPOUND TRANSFORMATIONS

If we reflect the object P in the x-axis and then reflect the resulting image in the y-axis, we are carrying out a compound transformation. The letters defined in exercise 12b can be used to describe the final image.

The first image is X(P). The second image is Y(X(P)) but the outer set of brackets is not usually used and it is written YX(P).

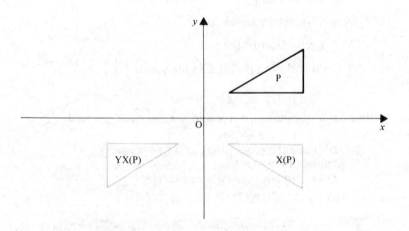

Notice that the letter X, denoting the transformation used first, is nearer to the object P. We work outwards from the bracket containing the object.

EXERCISE 12c

In this exercise,

R_1 is a rotation of $90°$ anticlockwise about O

R_2 is a rotation of $180°$ about O

R_3 is a rotation of $90°$ clockwise about O

X is a reflection in the x-axis

Y is a reflection in the y-axis

T is a translation defined by the vector $\begin{pmatrix} 4 \\ 3 \end{pmatrix}$

A, B and C are the points $(4, 1)$, $(6, 1)$ and $(6, 4)$.
Draw $\triangle ABC$ and label it P. Draw and label $R_1(P)$, $XR_1(P)$ and $YR_1(P)$.

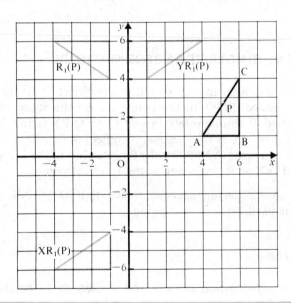

In each of the following questions draw x and y axes, each for values from -6 to 6.

1. P, Q and R are the points $(1, 3)$, $(3, 3)$ and $(1, 6)$. Draw $\triangle PQR$ and label it A. Draw and label

a) $R_3(A)$ b) $XR_3(A)$ c) $X(A)$ d) $R_3X(A)$

e) Describe the single transformation that will map A to $R_3X(A)$.

2. L, M and N are the points $(-2, 1)$, $(-4, 1)$ and $(-2, 5)$. Draw $\triangle LMN$ and label it P. Draw and label

a) $R_1(P)$ b) $R_2R_1(P)$ c) $R_3R_1(P)$

d) What is the single transformation that will map P to $R_2R_1(P)$?

e) What is the single transformation that will map $R_2R_1(P)$ to $R_1(P)$?

3. A, B and C are the points $(-5, 2)$, $(-2, 2)$ and $(-5, 4)$. Draw $\triangle ABC$ and label it P. Draw and label

a) $X(P)$ b) $YX(P)$ c) $R_2(P)$ d) $Y(P)$ e) $XY(P)$

f) Is $YX(P)$ the same triangle as $XY(P)$?

g) Is $R_2(P)$ the same triangle as $XY(P)$?

h) What single transformation is equivalent to a reflection in the x-axis followed by a reflection in the y-axis?

4. L, M and N are the points $(-3, 0)$, $(-1, 0)$ and $(-1, 3)$. Draw $\triangle LMN$ and label it Q. Find

a) $T(Q)$ b) $XT(Q)$ c) $X(Q)$ d) $TX(Q)$

e) Describe the single transformation that will map $X(Q)$ to $XT(Q)$.

f) Describe the single transformation that will map $XT(Q)$ to $TX(Q)$.

EQUIVALENT SINGLE TRANSFORMATIONS

We have seen that if we reflect an object P in the x-axis and then reflect the image $X(P)$ in the y-axis we get the same final image as if we had rotated P through $180°$ about O. $YX(P)$ is the same as $R_2(P)$ and the effect of YX is the same as the effect of R_2.

We can write $YX(P) = R_2(P)$ referring to the images
and $YX = R_2$ referring to the transformations.

In the following exercise notice that $X^2 = XX$, i.e. the transformation X is used twice in succession.

EXERCISE 12d

In each question draw x and y axes, each for values from -6 to 6. Use 1 cm for 1 unit.

1. A is a reflection in the line $x = -1$ and B a reflection in the line $y = 2$. Label as Z the triangle PQR where P is the point $(1, 4)$, $Q(4, 6)$ and $R(1, 6)$.

a) Find $A(Z)$, $B(Z)$, $AB(Z)$ and $BA(Z)$.

b) Describe the single transformations given by AB and BA. Is AB equal to BA?

c) Find $A^2(Z)$ and $B^2(Z)$.

2. T is a reflection in the line $x = 1$.
U is a reflection in the line $y = 2$.
V is a rotation of $180°$ about the point $(1, 2)$.
Label with A the triangle PQR where P is the point $(1, 1)$, Q is $(3, 1)$ and R is $(3, -2)$.

a) Draw T(A), U(A), TU(A) and UT(A).

b) Are TU and UT the same transformation?

c) Is it true that V = TU?

3. R_1 is a rotation of $90°$ anticlockwise about O.
R_2 is a rotation of $180°$ about O.
R_3 is a rotation of $90°$ clockwise about O.
Label with P the triangle ABC where A is the point $(1, 2)$, B is $(4, 2)$ and C is $(1, 4)$.

a) Draw $R_1(P)$, $R_1{}^2(P)$, $R_2(P)$, $R_2R_1(P)$ and $R_3(P)$.
Complete the following statements

$$R_1{}^2 = \qquad \text{and } R_2R_1 =$$

b) Draw whatever images are needed and complete the following statements

$$R_3{}^2 = \qquad R_2R_3 = \qquad \text{and } R_3R_2 =$$

THE IDENTITY TRANSFORMATION

If an object is rotated through $360°$ or translated using the vector $\begin{pmatrix} 0 \\ 0 \end{pmatrix}$, the final image turns out to be the same as the original object. We are back where we started and might as well not have performed a transformation at all. This operation is called the *identity transformation* and is usually denoted by I.

EXERCISE 12e

In this exercise

R_1 is a rotation of $90°$ anticlockwise about O

R_2 is a rotation of $180°$ about O

R_3 is a rotation of $90°$ clockwise about O

A is a reflection in the x-axis

B is a reflection in the y-axis

C is a reflection in the line $y = x$

D is a reflection in the line $y = -x$

I is the identity transformation.

P is the triangle with vertices $(2, 1)$, $(5, 1)$ and $(2, 3)$.
Find $B(P)$ and $B^2(P)$. Name the single transformation which is
equal to B^2.

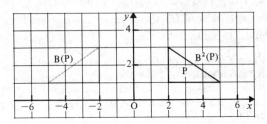

$$B^2(P) = P$$

$$\therefore \qquad B^2 = I$$

For each question draw x and y axes, each for values from -6 to 6.
Use $1\,\text{cm}$ to 1 unit.

1.   P is the triangle with vertices $(2, 1)$, $(5, 1)$ and $(5, 5)$.
   a) Find $R_1(P)$, $R_2(P)$, $R_3(P)$, $R_1R_3(P)$ and $R_3R_1(P)$.
   Name the single transformation which is equal to both R_1R_3 and R_3R_1.
   b) Complete the following statements with a single letter.
   i) $R_2{}^2 =$ ii) $R_2R_3 =$ iii) $R_1R_2 =$

2.   Q is the triangle with vertices $(-2, 1)$, $(-5, 1)$ and $(-4, 5)$.
   a) Find $A(Q)$, $B(Q)$, $AB(Q)$, $R_2(Q)$ and $B^2(Q)$.
   b) Complete the following statements with a single letter.
   i) $B^2 =$ ii) $AB =$

3.   N is the triangle with vertices $(1, 3)$, $(1, 6)$ and $(5, 6)$.
   a) Find $C(N)$, $DC(N)$, $C^2(N)$, $AC(N)$, $BC(N)$ and $IC(N)$.
   b) Complete the following statements with a single letter.
   i) $DC =$ ii) $C^2 =$ iii) $AC =$
   iv) $BC =$ v) $IC =$

4. M is the triangle with vertices $(3, 2)$, $(5, 2)$ and $(5, 6)$.
   a) Find $R_1(M)$, $A(M)$, $A^2(M)$, $AR_1(M)$ and $R_1A(M)$.
   b) Complete the following statements with a single letter.
      i) $A^2 =$ ii) $AR_1 =$ iii) $R_1A =$
   c) Is the statement $AR_1 = R_1A$ true or false?

5. L is the triangle with vertices $(3, 1)$, $(4, 4)$ and $(1, 4)$.
   a) Find $I(L)$, $AI(L)$, $BI(L)$, $IA(L)$ and $IB(L)$.
   b) Simplify AI, BI, IA and IB.

6. P is the rectangle with vertices $(-2, -2)$, $(-5, -2)$, $(-5, -4)$ and $(-2, -4)$.
   a) Find $I(P)$, $CI(P)$, $DI(P)$ and $D^2(P)$.
   b) Simplify CI, DI and D^2.

7. Q is the rhombus with vertices $(-3, -3)$, $(-4, -1)$, $(-3, -1)$ and $(-2, -1)$.
   a) Find $R_1(Q)$, $R_2R_1(Q)$ and $R_1R_2R_1(Q)$.
   b) Simplify R_2R_1 and $R_1R_2R_1$.
   c) Is it true that $R_1R_3 = R_3R_1 = R_2{}^2$?

MATRICES

A matrix is a rectangular array of numbers and can be used in many different ways.

The size of a matrix is given in terms of the number of rows and the number of columns, e.g. a 2×3 matrix has 2 rows and 3 columns. Matrices of the same size can be added or subtracted by adding, or subtracting, corresponding elements, e.g.

$$\begin{pmatrix} 1 & 4 \\ 2 & 3 \end{pmatrix} + \begin{pmatrix} 5 & -2 \\ 1 & 0 \end{pmatrix} = \begin{pmatrix} 6 & 2 \\ 3 & 3 \end{pmatrix} \quad \text{and} \quad 3\begin{pmatrix} 1 & 4 \\ 2 & 3 \end{pmatrix} = \begin{pmatrix} 3 & 12 \\ 6 & 9 \end{pmatrix}$$

Some matrices can be multiplied, but only when they are *compatible* for multiplication: the number of columns in the first matrix must be the same as the number of rows in the second matrix because each entry in a row of the first matrix is multiplied by the corresponding entry in a column of the second matrix.

e.g.
$$\begin{pmatrix} 4 & 2 \\ 1 & 6 \\ 3 & 4 \end{pmatrix} \times \begin{pmatrix} 4 \\ 1 \end{pmatrix} = \begin{pmatrix} 4 \times 4 + 2 \times 1 \\ 1 \times 4 + 6 \times 1 \\ 3 \times 4 + 4 \times 1 \end{pmatrix} = \begin{pmatrix} 18 \\ 10 \\ 16 \end{pmatrix}$$

3×2 2×1 3×1

When the sizes of the two matrices are written down, the two middle numbers must be the same. The outer two numbers give the size of the product matrix.

$$\begin{pmatrix} 3 & 1 \\ 4 & 5 \end{pmatrix} \times (1 \quad 4 \quad -1) \quad \text{cannot be found.}$$

$$\underset{2 \times 2}{} \qquad \qquad \underset{1 \times 3}{}$$

Except in a very few cases the order of multiplication does matter. In general, **AB ≠ BA**.

UNIT MATRIX

$\begin{pmatrix} 1 & 0 \\ 0 & 1 \end{pmatrix}$ is an example of a unit matrix.

Multiplying a matrix by $\begin{pmatrix} 1 & 0 \\ 0 & 1 \end{pmatrix}$ does not change the matrix.

e.g.
$$\begin{pmatrix} 1 & 0 \\ 0 & 1 \end{pmatrix} \times \begin{pmatrix} 6 & 2 & 1 \\ 4 & 3 & 2 \end{pmatrix} = \begin{pmatrix} 6 & 2 & 1 \\ 4 & 3 & 2 \end{pmatrix}$$

and
$$\begin{pmatrix} 2 & 4 \\ 6 & 8 \end{pmatrix} \times \begin{pmatrix} 1 & 0 \\ 0 & 1 \end{pmatrix} = \begin{pmatrix} 2 & 4 \\ 6 & 8 \end{pmatrix}$$

EXERCISE 12f

1. $A = \begin{pmatrix} 3 \\ 2 \end{pmatrix}$ $B = (4 \ 2)$ $C = \begin{pmatrix} 4 & -1 \\ 0 & 3 \end{pmatrix}$ $D = \begin{pmatrix} 1 & 2 & 1 \\ 4 & 3 & 2 \end{pmatrix}$

$I = \begin{pmatrix} 1 & 0 \\ 0 & 1 \end{pmatrix}$

Find, where possible,

a) **AB**   b) **BA**   c) **AC**

d) **CA**   e) **DA**   f) **AD**

g) A^2 h) C^2 i) **BD**

j) **IA**   k) **CI**   l) I^2

2. If $\begin{pmatrix} a & 1 \\ 2 & b \end{pmatrix}\begin{pmatrix} 2 & 1 \\ 3 & 1 \end{pmatrix} = \begin{pmatrix} 5 & 2 \\ 10 & 4 \end{pmatrix}$, find a and b.

3. If $\begin{pmatrix} x+1 & 2 \\ 3 & y \end{pmatrix}\begin{pmatrix} 1 \\ 4 \end{pmatrix} = \begin{pmatrix} 11 \\ 7 \end{pmatrix}$, find x and y.

4. If $\begin{pmatrix} p & 2 \\ 3 & -1 \end{pmatrix}\begin{pmatrix} p & -1 \\ p & r \end{pmatrix} = \begin{pmatrix} q & -2 \\ 4 & -3 \end{pmatrix}$, find p, q and r.

5. If $3A = \begin{pmatrix} 1 & 0 \\ 2 & 3 \end{pmatrix}\begin{pmatrix} 3 & 3 \\ -1 & 0 \end{pmatrix}$, find A.

MATRIX TRANSFORMATIONS

If we use a transformation matrix to find the image of point A(2,3) under a transformation then it is really the image of the position vector that we are finding.

If the transformation matrix is $\begin{pmatrix} 1 & 3 \\ 1 & 0 \end{pmatrix}$ then $\begin{pmatrix} 1 & 3 \\ 1 & 0 \end{pmatrix}\overset{A}{\begin{pmatrix} 2 \\ 3 \end{pmatrix}} = \overset{A'}{\begin{pmatrix} 11 \\ 2 \end{pmatrix}}$

The position vector of A' is $\begin{pmatrix} 11 \\ 2 \end{pmatrix}$ and A' is the point (11, 2)

We can save time when finding the images of several points, by lining up their position vectors side by side

$$\begin{pmatrix} 1 & 3 \\ 1 & 0 \end{pmatrix}\overset{A \quad B \quad C}{\begin{pmatrix} 2 & -3 & 1 \\ 3 & 1 & 4 \end{pmatrix}} = \overset{A' \quad B' \quad C'}{\begin{pmatrix} 11 & 0 & 13 \\ 2 & -3 & 1 \end{pmatrix}}$$

Then we can see that the position vectors of the images of B' and C' are $\begin{pmatrix} 0 \\ -3 \end{pmatrix}$ and $\begin{pmatrix} 13 \\ 1 \end{pmatrix}$ respectively, so B' is the point (0,−3) and C' is the point (13, 1).

EXERCISE 12g

Draw △ABC with A(2, 1), B(5, 1) and C(4, 4). Find the image of △ABC under the transformation defined by the matrix $\begin{pmatrix} -1 & 0 \\ 0 & 1 \end{pmatrix}$. Describe the transformation.

$$\begin{pmatrix} -1 & 0 \\ 0 & 1 \end{pmatrix} \overset{\text{A B C}}{\begin{pmatrix} 2 & 5 & 4 \\ 1 & 1 & 4 \end{pmatrix}} = \overset{\text{A}'\ \text{B}'\ \text{C}'}{\begin{pmatrix} -2 & -5 & -4 \\ 1 & 1 & 4 \end{pmatrix}}$$

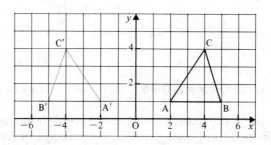

The transformation is a reflection in the y-axis.

For each question from 1 to 3 draw x and y axes for values in the given ranges and draw △ABC with A(1,0), B(4,0) and C(4,2).

1. Use $-4 \leqslant x \leqslant 4$ and $-4 \leqslant y \leqslant 4$.

Find the images of △ABC under the transformations defined by the matrices

a) $\begin{pmatrix} 0 & -1 \\ 1 & 0 \end{pmatrix}$ b) $\begin{pmatrix} -1 & 0 \\ 0 & -1 \end{pmatrix}$ c) $\begin{pmatrix} 0 & 1 \\ -1 & 0 \end{pmatrix}$ d) $\begin{pmatrix} 1 & 0 \\ 0 & -1 \end{pmatrix}$

Describe each of the four transformations.

2. Use $-4 \leqslant x \leqslant 4$ and $-4 \leqslant y \leqslant 4$.

Find the images of △ABC under the transformations defined by the matrices

a) $\begin{pmatrix} 0 & 1 \\ 1 & 0 \end{pmatrix}$ b) $\begin{pmatrix} -1 & 0 \\ 0 & 1 \end{pmatrix}$ c) $\begin{pmatrix} 0 & -1 \\ -1 & 0 \end{pmatrix}$

Describe each of the three transformations.

3. Use $-12 \leqslant x \leqslant 8$ and $-6 \leqslant y \leqslant 4$.

Find the images of $\triangle ABC$ under the transformations defined by the matrices

a) $\begin{pmatrix} 2 & 0 \\ 0 & 2 \end{pmatrix}$　　b) $\begin{pmatrix} -3 & 0 \\ 0 & -3 \end{pmatrix}$　　c) $\begin{pmatrix} -\frac{1}{2} & 0 \\ 0 & -\frac{1}{2} \end{pmatrix}$

Describe each transformation.

4. Draw x and y axes for $-6 \leqslant x \leqslant 6$ and $0 \leqslant y \leqslant 4$.

Draw rectangle PQRS with P(1, 0), Q(3, 0), R(3, 3) and S(1, 3).

Find the images of PQRS under the transformations defined by the matrices

a) $\begin{pmatrix} 1 & 1 \\ 0 & 1 \end{pmatrix}$　　b) $\begin{pmatrix} 1 & -2 \\ 0 & 1 \end{pmatrix}$

5. Draw x and y axes each for values from 0 to 6. Draw the rectangle ABCD where A is (0, 1), B is (3, 1), C is (3, 3) and D is (0, 3).

Find the images of ABCD under the transformations defined by the matrices

a) $\begin{pmatrix} 1 & 0 \\ 0 & 2 \end{pmatrix}$　　b) $\begin{pmatrix} 3 & 0 \\ 0 & 1 \end{pmatrix}$

6. Draw x and y axes each for values from -6 to 6. Use the square OABC as the object, where O is (0, 0), A is (1, 0), B is (1, 1) and C is (0, 1).

Make up two enlargement matrices and test them on the square OABC. Describe the enlargement in each case.

COMMON TRANSFORMATION MATRICES

It is useful to know the following facts.

a)　An enlargement matrix is of the form $\begin{pmatrix} k & 0 \\ 0 & k \end{pmatrix}$

b)　Reflection in the x or y-axis or lines $y = \pm x$ and rotations of multiples of $90°$ about the origin are produced by matrices with zeros in one diagonal and 1 or -1 elsewhere,

e.g. $\begin{pmatrix} -1 & 0 \\ 0 & -1 \end{pmatrix}$ gives a rotation of $180°$ about O.

c)　There are no matrices that produce reflections in lines other than lines through the origin. Nor are there any matrices that produce rotation or enlargement about points other than the origin.

d)　The unit matrix $\begin{pmatrix} 1 & 0 \\ 0 & 1 \end{pmatrix}$ maps an object to itself. This matrix gives the identity transformation (for instance, a rotation of $360°$ about O).

e)　A translation is *not* produced by a 2×2 matrix but is defined by a vector.

INVERSE MATRICES AND DETERMINANTS

When a matrix is multiplied by its inverse, the result is the *identity matrix*.

To find the inverse of **M**, where $\mathbf{M} = \begin{pmatrix} 2 & 1 \\ 4 & 3 \end{pmatrix}$, we first interchange the

entries in the leading diagonal, $\begin{pmatrix} 3 & \\ & 2 \end{pmatrix}$, and change the sign of the entries

in the other diagonal, $\begin{pmatrix} & -1 \\ -4 & \end{pmatrix}$.

Then we divide the resulting matrix, $\begin{pmatrix} 3 & -1 \\ -4 & 2 \end{pmatrix}$, by the *determinant* of **M**.

The determinant of a matrix can be found from a formula,

i.e. the determinant of $\begin{pmatrix} a & b \\ c & d \end{pmatrix}$ is $ad - bc$

In the example given in the previous section the determinant of **M** is

$$2 \times 3 - 1 \times 4 \qquad \text{i.e. } 2$$

Alternatively the determinant may be found by multiplying the original

matrix $\begin{pmatrix} 2 & 1 \\ 4 & 3 \end{pmatrix}$ by the first attempt at the inverse i.e. $\begin{pmatrix} 3 & -1 \\ -4 & 2 \end{pmatrix}$.

In this case, $\qquad \begin{pmatrix} 3 & -1 \\ -4 & 2 \end{pmatrix}\begin{pmatrix} 2 & 1 \\ 4 & 3 \end{pmatrix} = \begin{pmatrix} 2 & 0 \\ 0 & 2 \end{pmatrix}$

and we can see that the determinant is 2.

The inverse of $\begin{pmatrix} 2 & 1 \\ 4 & 3 \end{pmatrix}$ is $\frac{1}{2}\begin{pmatrix} 3 & -1 \\ -4 & 2 \end{pmatrix} = \begin{pmatrix} \frac{3}{2} & -\frac{1}{2} \\ -2 & 1 \end{pmatrix}$

Similarly, for $\begin{pmatrix} 5 & -6 \\ -4 & 4 \end{pmatrix}$, the determinant given by the formula is

$$5 \times 4 - (-6) \times (-4) = -4$$

Hence the inverse of $\begin{pmatrix} 5 & -6 \\ -4 & 4 \end{pmatrix}$ is $-\frac{1}{4}\begin{pmatrix} 4 & 6 \\ 4 & 5 \end{pmatrix} = \begin{pmatrix} -1 & -\frac{3}{2} \\ -1 & -\frac{5}{4} \end{pmatrix}$

EXERCISE 12h

Find the determinant of the matrix $\begin{pmatrix} 3 & 4 \\ 1 & 2 \end{pmatrix}$

First method   (Using the formula)

The determinant of $\begin{pmatrix} 3 & 4 \\ 1 & 2 \end{pmatrix}$ is $(3 \times 2) - (4 \times 1)$

$$= 6 - 4$$
$$= 2$$

Second method   (Start by trying to find the inverse)

Try $\begin{pmatrix} 2 & -4 \\ -1 & 3 \end{pmatrix}$ as the inverse

$$\begin{pmatrix} 3 & 4 \\ 1 & 2 \end{pmatrix}\begin{pmatrix} 2 & -4 \\ -1 & 3 \end{pmatrix} = \begin{pmatrix} 2 & 0 \\ 0 & 2 \end{pmatrix}$$

∴ the determinant is 2.

Find the determinants of the following matrices.

1. $\begin{pmatrix} 3 & 2 \\ 1 & 2 \end{pmatrix}$ **4.** $\begin{pmatrix} 4 & -2 \\ 1 & 1 \end{pmatrix}$ **7.** $\begin{pmatrix} 5 & -1 \\ -3 & 2 \end{pmatrix}$

2. $\begin{pmatrix} 9 & 2 \\ 4 & 1 \end{pmatrix}$ **5.** $\begin{pmatrix} 4 & -2 \\ 1 & -1 \end{pmatrix}$ **8.** $\begin{pmatrix} -1 & 0 \\ 0 & -1 \end{pmatrix}$

3. $\begin{pmatrix} 4 & 2 \\ 3 & 1 \end{pmatrix}$ **6.** $\begin{pmatrix} -2 & 4 \\ 1 & -3 \end{pmatrix}$ **9.** $\begin{pmatrix} 2 & 6 \\ 1 & 3 \end{pmatrix}$

In each question from 10 to 15, draw x and y axes each for values from −2 to 6. Draw the object OABC where A is $(2, 0)$, B is $(2, 1)$ and C is $(0, 1)$.

Find

a) the image of OABC under the transformation by the given matrix

b) the areas of OABC and the image OA′B′C′.

c) the value of $\dfrac{\text{area of OA′B′C′}}{\text{area of OABC}}$

d) the determinant of the transformation matrix. What do you notice?

10. $\begin{pmatrix} -1 & 0 \\ 0 & -1 \end{pmatrix}$ **12.** $\begin{pmatrix} 3 & 0 \\ 0 & 3 \end{pmatrix}$ **14.** $\begin{pmatrix} 0 & 0 \\ 0 & 0 \end{pmatrix}$

11. $\begin{pmatrix} 1 & 2 \\ 0 & 1 \end{pmatrix}$ **13.** $\begin{pmatrix} \frac{1}{2} & 0 \\ 0 & \frac{1}{2} \end{pmatrix}$ **15.** $\begin{pmatrix} 2 & 2 \\ 0 & 3 \end{pmatrix}$

AREA SCALE FACTOR

The fraction $\dfrac{\text{area of the image}}{\text{area of the object}}$ is the *area scale factor,* and we see from the results of the previous exercise that it is given by the determinant of the transformation matrix.

If we know the area of the object, the determinant can be used to calculate the area of the image.

UNIT VECTORS AND THE UNIT SQUARE

In question 6 of Exercise 12g the object was taken as the square OABC where A is the point (1, 0) and C is (0, 1).

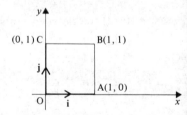

This is a particularly easy object to use, as the position vectors of A and C are $\begin{pmatrix} 1 \\ 0 \end{pmatrix}$ and $\begin{pmatrix} 0 \\ 1 \end{pmatrix}$ and, lined up together, they form the unit matrix $\begin{pmatrix} 1 & 0 \\ 0 & 1 \end{pmatrix}$.

The vectors $\begin{pmatrix} 1 \\ 0 \end{pmatrix}$ and $\begin{pmatrix} 0 \\ 1 \end{pmatrix}$ are called the *base vectors* for the coordinates.

Often O, A′ and C′ are enough to identify the image of the unit square but, if the shape of the image is still not clear, we can also find the image of B(1, 1).

EXERCISE 12i

Using the unit square as the object, in each question from 1 to 6 find the image under the transformation defined by the given matrix. If it is possible to do so, identify the transformation, describing it fully.

1. $\begin{pmatrix} 0 & -1 \\ 1 & 0 \end{pmatrix}$ **3.** $\begin{pmatrix} -1 & 0 \\ 0 & -1 \end{pmatrix}$ **5.** $\begin{pmatrix} 1 & 2 \\ 0 & 1 \end{pmatrix}$

2. $\begin{pmatrix} 1 & -2 \\ 0 & 1 \end{pmatrix}$ **4.** $\begin{pmatrix} 2\frac{1}{2} & 0 \\ 0 & 2\frac{1}{2} \end{pmatrix}$ **6.** $\begin{pmatrix} 3 & 12 \\ 1 & 4 \end{pmatrix}$

7. Find the area scale factor of each transformation in questions 1 to 6.

8. Given the matrix $\begin{pmatrix} 4 & -8 \\ -1 & 2 \end{pmatrix}$ find

    a) the image of the unit square under the transformation given by the matrix

    b) the determinant of the matrix and the area scale factor of the transformation

    c) the area of the image.

9. A rectangle ABCD has area 6 square units. It is transformed using the matrix $\begin{pmatrix} 3 & 1 \\ 1 & 2 \end{pmatrix}$.

    a) Find the determinant of the matrix and the area scale factor of the transformation.

    b) Find the area of the image of ABCD.

10. A, B, C and D are the points (0, 2), (0, 4), (3, 4) and (3, 2) respectively.

    a) Find the area of rectangle ABCD.

    b) ABCD is transformed using the matrix $\begin{pmatrix} 4 & 5 \\ 1 & 2 \end{pmatrix}$.

    Calculate the area of the image of ABCD (do *not* find and draw the image).

INVERSE TRANSFORMATIONS

A rotation of 90° anticlockwise about O maps △OAB to △OPQ. The *inverse* transformation is a rotation of 90° clockwise about O. It maps △OPQ back to △OAB.

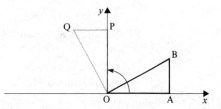

Some transformations, such as reflections, are their own inverses. Some transformations have no inverses as the next exercise will show.

EXERCISE 12j

Describe the inverses of the following transformations.

1. A rotation of 60° clockwise about the point (1, 1).

2. A reflection in the *x*-axis.

3. An enlargement, centre (0, 0) and scale factor 2.

4. A translation defined by the vector $\begin{pmatrix} 2 \\ 3 \end{pmatrix}$.

5. A rotation of 180° about O.

For each question from 6 to 9, draw *x* and *y* axes for values from −4 to 4. Use the unit square OABC as the object. A is the point (1, 0), B is (1, 1) and C is (0, 1).

6. You are given the matrix $\begin{pmatrix} 0 & 1 \\ -1 & 0 \end{pmatrix}$

    a) Find the image of the unit square under the transformation given by the matrix.

    b) Describe the transformation.

    c) Describe the inverse transformation.

    d) Find the inverse of the matrix $\begin{pmatrix} 0 & 1 \\ -1 & 0 \end{pmatrix}$

    e) Transform OA'B'C' using the inverse matrix. What happens?

    f) Describe the transformation given by the inverse matrix in part (e).

    g) Are the transformations described in parts (c) and (f) the same? What is the matrix of the inverse transformation?

7. Repeat question 6 with the matrix $\begin{pmatrix} 2 & 0 \\ 0 & 2 \end{pmatrix}$

8. Repeat question 6 with the matrix $\begin{pmatrix} 0 & -1 \\ 1 & 0 \end{pmatrix}$

9. Repeat question 6 parts (a) to (d) with the matrix $\begin{pmatrix} 0 & -1 \\ -1 & 0 \end{pmatrix}$

10. Repeat question 6 parts (a) to (d) with the matrix $\begin{pmatrix} -1 & 0 \\ 0 & 1 \end{pmatrix}$

11. Comment on the results obtained in questions 9 and 10.

12. Draw x and y axes, each for values from -6 to 6. The object is the unit square.
Repeat question 6 parts (a) and (b) with the matrices

i) $\begin{pmatrix} 3 & 6 \\ 1 & 2 \end{pmatrix}$ ii) $\begin{pmatrix} 3 & 2 \\ 6 & 4 \end{pmatrix}$

What goes wrong in each case when you try to describe the inverse transformation?

FINDING A TRANSFORMATION MATRIX

EXERCISE 12k

A is the point $(2, 1)$, B is $(3, 4)$, P is $(5, 3)$ and Q is $(10, 12)$.
Find the matrix of the transformation under which
AB is mapped to PQ.

Let the transformation matrix be $\begin{pmatrix} a & b \\ c & d \end{pmatrix}$

then

$$\begin{pmatrix} a & b \\ c & d \end{pmatrix}\begin{pmatrix} 2 & 3 \\ 1 & 4 \end{pmatrix} = \begin{pmatrix} 5 & 10 \\ 3 & 12 \end{pmatrix}$$

(columns labelled A B and P Q)

$$\begin{pmatrix} 2a+b & 3a+4b \\ 2c+d & 3c+4d \end{pmatrix} = \begin{pmatrix} 5 & 10 \\ 3 & 12 \end{pmatrix}$$

Comparing entries in the first row gives

$$2a + b = 5 \qquad (1)$$
$$3a + 4b = 10 \qquad (2)$$

$(1) \times 4$

$$8a + 4b = 20 \qquad (3)$$
$$3a + 4b = 10 \qquad (2)$$

$(3) - (2)$

$$5a = 10$$
$$a = 2$$

In (1)

$$b = 1$$

Comparing entries in the second row gives

$$2c + d = 3 \qquad (4)$$
$$3c + 4d = 12 \qquad (5)$$

(4) × 4

$$8c + 4d = 12 \qquad (6)$$
$$3c + 4d = 12 \qquad (5)$$

(6) − (5)

$$5c = 0$$
$$c = 0$$

In (5)

$$d = 3$$

∴ the matrix is $\begin{pmatrix} 2 & 1 \\ 0 & 3 \end{pmatrix}$

In each question from 1 to 6 find the matrix of the transformation which maps AB to PQ.

1. A is (1, 1), B is (2, 1), P is (1, 2) and Q is (2, 2)

2. A is (1, 1), B is (3, 1), P is (3, 2) and Q is (5, 6)

3. A is (4, 2), B is (1, 1), P is (12, 2) and Q is (3, 2)

4. A is (2, 1), B is (1, 1), P is (1, 5) and Q is (0, 5)

5. A is (2, 2), B is (1, 3), P is (−6, 6) and Q is (−11, 9)

6. A is (1, 2), B is (1, −2), P is (1, 0) and Q is (17, −4)

7.

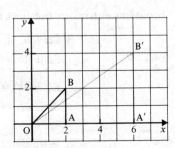

A transformation maps △OAB to △OA′B′. Find the matrix that defines this transformation. (Use AB and its image A′B′.)

8.

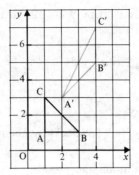

A transformation maps △ABC to △A'B'C'. Find the matrix that defines this transformation. (Use two points to find the matrix. The third point may be used for a check.)

Find the matrix that defines reflection in the *y*-axis.

(We may choose our own object so we use the unit square.)

Let the matrix be $\begin{pmatrix} a & b \\ c & d \end{pmatrix}$

$$\begin{matrix} & \mathbf{A} & \mathbf{B} & & \mathbf{A'} & \mathbf{B'} \end{matrix}$$
$$\begin{pmatrix} a & b \\ c & d \end{pmatrix}\begin{pmatrix} 1 & 0 \\ 0 & 1 \end{pmatrix} = \begin{pmatrix} -1 & 0 \\ 0 & 1 \end{pmatrix}$$

$\therefore \qquad \begin{pmatrix} a & b \\ c & d \end{pmatrix} = \begin{pmatrix} -1 & 0 \\ 0 & 1 \end{pmatrix}$

i.e. the transformation matrix is $\begin{pmatrix} -1 & 0 \\ 0 & 1 \end{pmatrix}$

In each question from 9 to 12, find the matrix that defines the transformation.

9. Reflection in the x-axis.

10. Rotation of $90°$ clockwise about O.

11. Rotation of $90°$ anticlockwise about O.

12. Reflection in the line $y = x$.

COMPOUND TRANSFORMATIONS

EXERCISE 12I

1. A square ABCD has vertices at A(2,0), B(4,0), C(4,2) and D(2,0).

$$P = \begin{pmatrix} 1 & 0 \\ 0 & -1 \end{pmatrix} \quad \text{and} \quad Q = \begin{pmatrix} 0 & 1 \\ -1 & 0 \end{pmatrix}.$$

a) Find the images of ABCD under the two transformations given by P and Q and identify the transformations. Label the two images $A_1B_1C_1D_1$ and $A_2B_2C_2D_2$.

b) Find the image of $A_1B_1C_1D_1$ under the transformation given by Q. Label the image $A_3B_3C_3D_3$.

c) Describe the transformation that maps ABCD to $A_3B_3C_3D_3$.

d) Find the matrices R and S where $R = QP$ and $S = PQ$.

e) Find the image of ABCD under the transformation given by R.

f) Find the image of ABCD under the transformation given by S.

g) Comment on the results of (b), (e) and (f). Explain the significance of the order in which P and Q occur.

2. The vertices of a triangle P are $(2,1), (4,1)$ and $(4,4)$.

$$M = \begin{pmatrix} -1 & 0 \\ 0 & -1 \end{pmatrix} \quad \text{and} \quad N = \begin{pmatrix} -1 & 0 \\ 0 & 1 \end{pmatrix} \quad \text{define transformations M and}$$
N respectively.

a) Find M(P) and NM(P).

b) Describe the transformations M and NM.

c) Find the matrix L, given that $L = NM$.

d) The matrix L defines a transformation L. Find L(P) and describe the transformation L.

e) Is L the same transformation as NM?

3.

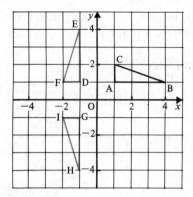

Find the matrices **P**, **Q** and **R** if

a) **P** is the matrix of the transformation which maps △ABC to △ADEF'

b) **Q** is the matrix of the transformation which maps △DEF to △GHI

c) **R** is the matrix of the transformation which maps △ABC to △GHI.

d) Give an equation linking **P**, **Q** and **R**.

4. If $Q = \begin{pmatrix} 0 & -1 \\ 1 & 0 \end{pmatrix}$ find $Q\begin{pmatrix} x \\ y \end{pmatrix}$

a) Draw a diagram and describe the transformation given by **Q**.

b) Hence, or otherwise, write Q^8 as a single matrix.

DEFINING TRANSFORMATIONS AS MATRIX EQUATIONS

The matrix $\begin{pmatrix} 2 & 3 \\ 0 & -1 \end{pmatrix}$ maps the point A whose position vector is $\begin{pmatrix} 2 \\ 4 \end{pmatrix}$ to

the point A′ whose position vector is given by the product $\begin{pmatrix} 2 & 3 \\ 0 & -1 \end{pmatrix}\begin{pmatrix} 2 \\ 4 \end{pmatrix}$,

i.e. $\begin{pmatrix} 16 \\ -4 \end{pmatrix}$

In general the matrix will map any point P whose position vector is $\begin{pmatrix} x \\ y \end{pmatrix}$

to the point P′ whose position vector is $\begin{pmatrix} x' \\ y' \end{pmatrix}$ where

$$\begin{pmatrix} 2 & 3 \\ 0 & -1 \end{pmatrix}\begin{pmatrix} x \\ y \end{pmatrix} = \begin{pmatrix} x' \\ y' \end{pmatrix}$$

We can use this matrix equation to define the transformation.

A translation cannot be defined in terms of a 2×2 matrix, but we can still use a matrix equation if we consider a position vector in the form $\begin{pmatrix} x \\ y \end{pmatrix}$ as a 2×1 matrix.

Consider a translation defined by the vector $\begin{pmatrix} 3 \\ -1 \end{pmatrix}$.

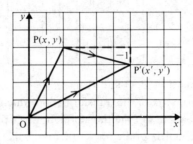

This vector will move any point 3 units to the right and 1 unit down, i.e. it will move P to P'.

Using vector addition, the relationship between OP and OP' is

$\overrightarrow{OP} + \begin{pmatrix} 3 \\ -1 \end{pmatrix} = \overrightarrow{OP'}$, i.e. the translation can be defined by the equation

$$\begin{pmatrix} x \\ y \end{pmatrix} + \begin{pmatrix} 3 \\ -1 \end{pmatrix} = \begin{pmatrix} x' \\ y' \end{pmatrix}$$

COMPOUND TRANSFORMATIONS AND MATRICES

From the last exercise we can see that the matrix for a compound transformation ST is given by the matrix product ST.

For example, if S is defined by the matrix $\begin{pmatrix} 2 & 3 \\ -1 & 0 \end{pmatrix}$ and T is defined by $\begin{pmatrix} 0 & 2 \\ -1 & 0 \end{pmatrix}$ then the matrix for the compound transformation ST is given by the product $\begin{pmatrix} 2 & 3 \\ -1 & 0 \end{pmatrix}\begin{pmatrix} 0 & 2 \\ -1 & 0 \end{pmatrix}$, which is equal to the matrix $\begin{pmatrix} -3 & 4 \\ 0 & -2 \end{pmatrix}$.

Hence the transformation ST is defined by $\begin{pmatrix} -3 & 4 \\ 0 & -2 \end{pmatrix}\begin{pmatrix} x \\ y \end{pmatrix} = \begin{pmatrix} x' \\ y' \end{pmatrix}$.

This is true *only* if S and T are both 2×2 matrices.

Now consider the compound transformation of a reflection in the x-axis followed by a translation given by the vector $\begin{pmatrix} 4 \\ 2 \end{pmatrix}$. The diagram shows the effect on a triangle A.

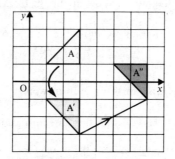

The matrix which maps A to A' is $\begin{pmatrix} 1 & 0 \\ 0 & -1 \end{pmatrix}$.

This matrix maps any point $\begin{pmatrix} x \\ y \end{pmatrix}$ to the point given by $\begin{pmatrix} 1 & 0 \\ 0 & -1 \end{pmatrix}\begin{pmatrix} x \\ y \end{pmatrix}$

which is then translated to the point given by $\begin{pmatrix} 1 & 0 \\ 0 & -1 \end{pmatrix}\begin{pmatrix} x \\ y \end{pmatrix} + \begin{pmatrix} 4 \\ 2 \end{pmatrix}$.

Hence if $\begin{pmatrix} x \\ y \end{pmatrix}$ is mapped to $\begin{pmatrix} x' \\ y' \end{pmatrix}$ then the combined transformation can be expressed as the matrix equation

$$\begin{pmatrix} 1 & 0 \\ 0 & -1 \end{pmatrix}\begin{pmatrix} x \\ y \end{pmatrix} + \begin{pmatrix} 4 \\ 2 \end{pmatrix} = \begin{pmatrix} x' \\ y' \end{pmatrix}$$

EXERCISE 12m

Questions 1 to 5 refer to $\triangle ABC$ with $A(1,1)$, $B(4,1)$ and $C(2,3)$.

1. Draw the image of $\triangle ABC$ under the transformation defined by

a) $\begin{pmatrix} -1 & 0 \\ 0 & -1 \end{pmatrix}\begin{pmatrix} x \\ y \end{pmatrix} = \begin{pmatrix} x' \\ y' \end{pmatrix}$

b) $\begin{pmatrix} 1 & 0 \\ 0 & 3 \end{pmatrix}\begin{pmatrix} x \\ y \end{pmatrix} = \begin{pmatrix} x' \\ y' \end{pmatrix}$.

c) $\begin{pmatrix} 3 & 0 \\ 0 & -3 \end{pmatrix}\begin{pmatrix} x \\ y \end{pmatrix} = \begin{pmatrix} x' \\ y' \end{pmatrix}$.

d) $\begin{pmatrix} -1 & 0 \\ 0 & 2 \end{pmatrix}\begin{pmatrix} x \\ y \end{pmatrix} = \begin{pmatrix} x' \\ y' \end{pmatrix}$

2. Describe in words each of the transformations defined in question 1.

3. A transformation is defined by the matrix equation $\begin{pmatrix} -1 & 4 \\ 1 & 2 \end{pmatrix}\begin{pmatrix} x \\ y \end{pmatrix} = \begin{pmatrix} x' \\ y' \end{pmatrix}$.

Draw a diagram to show the image of $\triangle ABC$ under this transformation.

4. Draw a diagram to show the image of $\triangle ABC$ under the transformation

defined by $\begin{pmatrix} 2 & 0 \\ 0 & 2 \end{pmatrix}\begin{pmatrix} x \\ y \end{pmatrix} + \begin{pmatrix} 3 \\ -1 \end{pmatrix} = \begin{pmatrix} x' \\ y' \end{pmatrix}$.

Describe this transformation in words.

5. Repeat question 4 with the transformation defined by

$$\begin{pmatrix} 0.5 & 0 \\ 0 & -0.5 \end{pmatrix}\begin{pmatrix} x \\ y \end{pmatrix} + \begin{pmatrix} -3 \\ 2 \end{pmatrix} = \begin{pmatrix} x' \\ y' \end{pmatrix}$$

For each of the following diagrams

a) describe the transformation that maps A to A'

b) give a matrix equation that defines the transformation.

The side of one square is one unit.

6.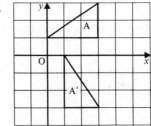

7.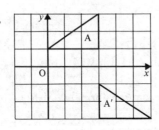

8.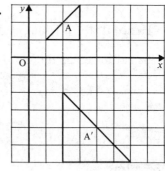

9.

10. A point whose coordinates are $(2,5)$ is translated by the vector $\begin{pmatrix} 2 \\ 4 \end{pmatrix}$ and then reflected in the y-axis. What is the image of the point? Express the transformation as a matrix equation.

ROUTE MATRICES

We saw in Book 4A that matrices can be used to store and process information.

We can also use matrices to represent information about routes between points.

Consider the following network showing roads that link A, B and C.

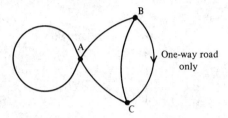

One-way road only

The matrix below shows the number of one-stage routes from one point to another, i.e. routes which do not go through any other point. There are two routes from A to A because the loop road can be travelled in either direction

$$\begin{array}{c} & & \text{To} \\ & & \text{A} \quad \text{B} \quad \text{C} \\ \text{From} & \begin{array}{c} \text{A} \\ \text{B} \\ \text{C} \end{array} & \begin{pmatrix} 2 & 1 & 1 \\ 1 & 0 & 2 \\ 1 & 1 & 0 \end{pmatrix} \end{array}$$

EXERCISE 12n

In each question from 1 to 4 give a matrix to show the number of one-stage routes from one point to another.

1.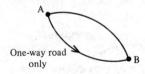

One-way road only

3.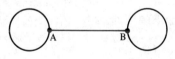

2.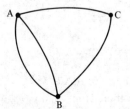

4.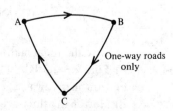

One-way roads only

In each question from 5 to 8 draw networks using the information given by the matrices. (There may be several possible networks in each case.)

5.

$$\text{From} \quad \begin{array}{c} \\ A \\ B \end{array} \begin{array}{cc} \text{To} \\ A & B \\ \begin{pmatrix} 0 & 1 \\ 2 & 0 \end{pmatrix} \end{array}$$

7.

$$\text{From} \quad \begin{array}{c} \\ A \\ B \\ C \end{array} \begin{array}{ccc} \text{To} \\ A & B & C \\ \begin{pmatrix} 0 & 1 & 1 \\ 1 & 0 & 1 \\ 1 & 1 & 0 \end{pmatrix} \end{array}$$

6.

$$\text{From} \quad \begin{array}{c} \\ A \\ B \\ C \end{array} \begin{array}{ccc} \text{To} \\ A & B & C \\ \begin{pmatrix} 1 & 1 & 1 \\ 1 & 1 & 1 \\ 1 & 1 & 1 \end{pmatrix} \end{array}$$

8.

$$\text{From} \quad \begin{array}{c} \\ A \\ B \\ C \\ D \end{array} \begin{array}{cccc} \text{To} \\ A & B & C & D \\ \begin{pmatrix} 0 & 1 & 2 & 1 \\ 1 & 0 & 1 & 0 \\ 2 & 1 & 0 & 1 \\ 1 & 0 & 1 & 0 \end{pmatrix} \end{array}$$

9.

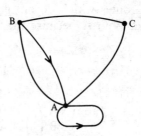

a) Give the route matrix **R** for this network.
b) Find R^2.
c) How many two-stage routes are there from A to C i.e. that involve passing through one other point on the way ? (AAC is one example.)
d) Give the two-stage routes from A to B, A to A, B to A, etc. Compare these with the matrix R^2. What information does R^2 contain ?
e) What information would R^3 give you ?

10.

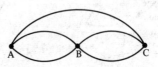

a) Give the route matrix R for this network.
b) Find R^2 and R^3.
c) How many two-stage routes are there from A to C ?
d) How many three-stage routes are there from A to C ?

MIXED EXERCISES

EXERCISE 12p

1. Find the value of a for which the matrix $\begin{pmatrix} a-2 & 0 \\ 0 & 3 \end{pmatrix}$

a) has no inverse

b) represents an enlargement. State the scale factor of this enlargement.

2. Under a certain transformation, (x', y') is the image of (x, y) and

$$\begin{pmatrix} x' \\ y' \end{pmatrix} = \begin{pmatrix} 3 & 1 \\ 1 & 1 \end{pmatrix}\begin{pmatrix} x \\ y \end{pmatrix}$$

a) Find the coordinates of the image of the point $(2, 3)$.

b) Find the coordinates of the image of the point $(-1, 2)$.

c) Find the coordinates of the point of which $(7, 3)$ is the image.

3. A transformation T is defined by the matrix $\begin{pmatrix} 4 & 2 \\ 7 & 4 \end{pmatrix}$

a) Find the inverse of the matrix.

b) Given that T maps the point A to the point $(8, 15)$, find the coordinates of A.

4. Find the matrix product $\begin{pmatrix} 0 & 1 \\ 1 & 0 \end{pmatrix}\begin{pmatrix} x \\ y \end{pmatrix}$ and describe the transformation

defined by $\begin{pmatrix} 0 & 1 \\ 1 & 0 \end{pmatrix}\begin{pmatrix} x \\ y \end{pmatrix} = \begin{pmatrix} x' \\ y' \end{pmatrix}$

5. A transformation is defined by the matrix $\begin{pmatrix} 1 & 0 \\ 3 & 1 \end{pmatrix}$.

a) Express as a single matrix $\begin{pmatrix} 1 & 0 \\ 3 & 1 \end{pmatrix}\begin{pmatrix} x \\ y \end{pmatrix}$.

b) Find the coordinates of the image of the point (p, p) under the transformation.

c) The transformation maps the line $y = x$ to the line $y = mx$. Find the value of m.

EXERCISE 12q

1. $A = \begin{pmatrix} 6 & 2 \\ 5 & 2 \end{pmatrix}$ and $B = \begin{pmatrix} 2 & -3 \\ -1 & 2 \end{pmatrix}$

Give as a single matrix

a) **AB**   b) **BA**   c) A^{-1} d) B^{-1}

e) A^2 f) B^3 g) **2A**   h) **3B**

2. $A = \begin{pmatrix} 0 & 1 \\ 1 & 0 \end{pmatrix}$. Find

   a) $2A$ b) A^{-1} c) A^2 d) A^3
   e) A^4 f) A^5 g) $|A|$ h) $|A^2|$
   i) A^n if n is even   j) A^n if n is odd

3.   If $4\begin{pmatrix} 6 & -3 \\ 1 & 0 \end{pmatrix} + \begin{pmatrix} 2 & -1 \\ 3 & 4 \end{pmatrix}\begin{pmatrix} 1 & -2 \\ 3 & 0 \end{pmatrix} = \begin{pmatrix} a & b \\ c & d \end{pmatrix}$ find a, b, c and d.

4. $A = \begin{pmatrix} 2 & 0 \\ 3 & 1 \end{pmatrix}$ and $B = \begin{pmatrix} 1 & 0 \\ 2 & k \end{pmatrix}$.

   a) Find AB and BA.
   b) If $AB = BA$ find k.
   c) If $k = 0$ why does B have no inverse ?

5.   If $\begin{pmatrix} 1 & 2 \\ 3 & 8 \end{pmatrix} P = \begin{pmatrix} 4 & 0 \\ 0 & 4 \end{pmatrix}$ find P.

EXERCISE 12r

In this exercise, several alternative answers are given. Write down the letter that corresponds to the correct answer.

1.   The determinant of the matrix $\begin{pmatrix} 4 & 6 \\ 2 & 4 \end{pmatrix}$ is

   A 16   **B** 4   **C** -16 **D** $\frac{1}{4}$

2.   The inverse of the matrix $\begin{pmatrix} 3 & 1 \\ 4 & 2 \end{pmatrix}$ is

   A $\begin{pmatrix} 1 & -\frac{1}{2} \\ -2 & 1\frac{1}{2} \end{pmatrix}$ **B** $\begin{pmatrix} 2 & -1 \\ -4 & 3 \end{pmatrix}$ **C** $\begin{pmatrix} 1\frac{1}{2} & \frac{1}{2} \\ 2 & 1 \end{pmatrix}$ **D** $\begin{pmatrix} \frac{1}{5} & \frac{1}{10} \\ -\frac{2}{5} & \frac{3}{10} \end{pmatrix}$

3.   The inverse of rotation of $270°$ clockwise about O is

   A rotation of $90°$ clockwise about O
   B rotation of $270°$ anticlockwise about $(1, 0)$
   C rotation of $90°$ anticlockwise about O
   D rotation of $270°$ clockwise about O

4.   The area scale factor of the transformation defined by

   $\begin{pmatrix} 3 & -1 \\ 2 & 1 \end{pmatrix}\begin{pmatrix} x \\ y \end{pmatrix} = \begin{pmatrix} x' \\ y' \end{pmatrix}$ is

   A 1   **B** $\frac{1}{5}$ **C** 2   **D** 5

5.

The matrix which maps OABC to OA′B′C′ is

A $\begin{pmatrix} 1 & 0 \\ 0 & 1 \end{pmatrix}$ **B** $\begin{pmatrix} 2 & 0 \\ 0 & 2 \end{pmatrix}$ **C** $\begin{pmatrix} 0 & 2 \\ 2 & 0 \end{pmatrix}$ **D** $\begin{pmatrix} \frac{1}{2} & 0 \\ 0 & \frac{1}{2} \end{pmatrix}$

6. $A = \begin{pmatrix} 2 & 0 \\ 0 & 2 \end{pmatrix}$, A^n is

A $\begin{pmatrix} 2n & 0 \\ 0 & 2n \end{pmatrix}$ **B** $\begin{pmatrix} n^2 & 0 \\ 0 & n^2 \end{pmatrix}$ **C** $\begin{pmatrix} 2^n & 0 \\ 0 & 2^n \end{pmatrix}$ **D** $\begin{pmatrix} 2 & 0 \\ 0 & 2 \end{pmatrix}$

13 NUMBERS

INTEGERS

The numbers we use for counting are called the *natural numbers*,

i.e. $1, 2, 3, 4, \ldots$

Whole numbers, both positive and negative, are called integers,

i.e. $\{\text{integers}\} = \{\ldots -3, -2, -1, 0, 1, 2, 3, \ldots\}$

SEQUENCES AND PATTERNS

The simplest sequence is the sequence of natural numbers,

i.e. $1, 2, 3, 4, 5, 6, \ldots$

Other simple sequences are

$1, 3, 5, 7, 9, \ldots$ (odd numbers)

$2, 4, 6, 8, 10, \ldots$ (even numbers)

$2, 3, 5, 7, 11, 13, \ldots$ (prime numbers)

To continue a sequence we need to recognise a pattern. Consider, for example,

$2, 5, 8, 11, \ldots$

Each number in this sequence is three units greater than the preceding number. Hence the sequence continues $14, 17, 20, \ldots$

The pattern is not always so obvious. If you cannot immediately see a pattern, try looking for sums, products, multiples, plus or minus a number, squares, etc.

THE *n*th TERM OF A SEQUENCE

In a sequence the terms occur in a *particular order,* i.e. there is a first term, a second term and so on. The value of each term depends upon its position in that order. (This is the difference between a sequence of numbers and a set of numbers in which the members can be in any order.)

We use the notation $u_1, u_1, u_3, \ldots$ for the first, second, third, ... term in a sequence.

Thus u_{10} means the 10th term

u_{100} means the 100th term

u_n means the nth term

If we are given a formula for u_n in terms of n, e.g. $u_n = n(n+1)$, then we can find any term of the sequence.

In this case, the first term, u_1, is found by substituting 1 for n in $n(n+1)$,

i.e. $$u_1 = 1(2) = 2$$

Similarly $$u_2 = 2(2+1) = 6, \qquad \text{(substituting 2 for } n\text{)}$$

$$u_3 = 3(3+1) = 12,$$

$$u_4 = 4(4+1) = 20$$

$$\ldots\ldots\ldots\ldots\ldots\ldots$$

$$u_{10} = 10(10+1) = 110,$$

and so on.

Therefore the sequence defined by $u_n = n(n+1)$ is

$$2, \ 6, \ 12, \ 20, \ \ldots$$

FINDING THE nth TERM

When the pattern in a sequence is known, a formula for u_n can often be found.

It is helpful to start by trying to recognise the connection between each term and the number of its position order (i.e. between u_1 and 1, u_2 and 2, etc.)

This can often be done by writing the sequence in the form shown in the following example which uses the sequence of natural numbers; 1, 2, 3, ...

$$u_1, \ u_2, \ u_3, \ u_4, \ \ldots, \ u_n, \ \ldots$$
$$\downarrow \quad \downarrow \quad \downarrow \quad \downarrow$$
$$1 \quad 2 \quad 3 \quad 4$$

In this case it is obvious that the value of a term is the same as its position number, e.g. $u_{20} = 20$ and $u_n = n$.

Now consider the sequence of even numbers:

$$u_1, \ u_2, \ u_3, \ u_4, \ \ldots$$
$$\downarrow \quad \downarrow \quad \downarrow \quad \downarrow$$
$$2 \quad 4 \quad 6 \quad 8$$

This time the value of a term is twice its position number, so the nth term is $2n$, i.e. $u_n = 2n$.

Finally look at the sequence of odd numbers:

$$u_1, \ u_2, \ u_3, \ u_4, \ \ldots \ u_n, \ \ldots$$
$$\downarrow \quad \downarrow \quad \downarrow \quad \downarrow$$
$$1 \quad 3 \quad 5 \quad 7$$

Comparing this sequence with the last one we see that each term here is 1 less than the corresponding term in the previous sequence.
Therefore the nth term of this sequence is $2n - 1$ i.e. $u_n = 2n - 1$.

Note that it is sensible to check that a formula obtained for u_n gives the correct values for $u_1, u_2, \ldots$

FLOW CHARTS

In Book 2A, Chapter 17 we used flow charts to generate sequences. An example of such a flow chart is given below.

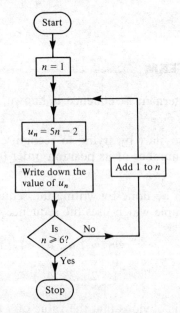

This flow chart gives the first six terms of the sequence $3, 8, 13, 18, 23, 28 \ldots$

Notice that a decision box, i.e. a question with a 'yes' or 'no' answer, is shown as a diamond shape, whereas statements and instructions are shown within rectangles. Each flow chart should begin with $\left(\text{Start} \right)$ and end with $\left(\text{Stop} \right)$.

EXERCISE 13a

Find the next two terms in the following sequences.

1. 3, 7, 11, 15,...

2. 3, −6, 12, −24,...

3. 4, 9, 16, 25,...

4. $1 + 3, 1 + 3 + 5, 1 + 3 + 5 + 7,...$

5. $1, -\frac{1}{3}, \frac{1}{9}, -\frac{1}{27},...$

6. 2, 4, 6, 10, 16, 26,...

7. Give the first four terms of the sequence for which
   a) $u_n = 2n + 1$
   b) $u_n = 2^n$
   c) $u_n = (n-1)(n+1)$.

Find a formula for the nth term of the sequence

a) $2 \times 3, 3 \times 4, 4 \times 5, \ldots$ b) 5, 8, 11, 14, ...

a) $u_1, \quad u_2, \quad u_3, \ldots$
                   $\downarrow \qquad \downarrow \qquad \downarrow$
                $2 \times 3 \quad 3 \times 4 \quad 4 \times 5$

(Each term is the product of the two integers that follow the position number.)

Hence $u_n = (n+1)(n+2)$

[Check: $u_1 = (1+1) \times (1+2) = 2 \times 3,$

                $u_2 = (2+1) \times (2+2) = 3 \times 4]$

b)
$$u_1, \ u_2, \ u_3, \ u_4, \ \ldots$$
$$\downarrow \quad \downarrow \quad \downarrow \quad \downarrow$$
$$5 \quad 8 \quad 11 \quad 14$$

(Each term is 3 greater than the term before, so these terms involve multiples of 3.)

Rearranging each term gives

$$u_1, \quad u_2, \quad u_3, \quad \quad u_4,$$
$$\downarrow \quad \downarrow \quad \downarrow \quad \quad \downarrow$$
$$5 \quad 5+3 \quad 5+2(3) \quad 5+3(3)$$

From the pattern above $\quad u_n = 5 + (n-1)3$
$$= 5 + 3n - 3$$
$$= 2 + 3n$$

[Check: $\quad u_1 = 2 + 3(1) = 5, \quad u_2 = 2 + 3(2) = 8$]

Find a formula for the nth term of each of the following sequences.

8. $5, 7, 9, 11, \ldots$

9. $0, 3, 6, 9, 12, \ldots$

10. $4, 8, 16, 32, 64, \ldots$

11. $1 \times 3, 2 \times 4, 3 \times 5, \ldots$

12. $1, 8, 27, 64, 125, \ldots$

13. $2, 5, 10, 17, 26, \ldots$

14. Draw a simple flow chart for working out the nth term of the sequence in question 7(c). Use this flow chart to find the tenth term.

15. Draw a simple flow chart for working out the nth term of each of the following sequences. Use your flow chart to find the tenth term.
a) $11, 15, 19, 23, \ldots$
b) $4, 7, 12, 19, \ldots$
c) $3, 8, 15, 24, \ldots$

16. This is a sequence of pairs of numbers: $(1, 2), (2, 5), (3, 10), (4, 17), \ldots$
Find
a) the next pair in the sequence
b) the 10th pair in the sequence
d) the nth pair in the sequence.

In questions 17 and 18 write down the terms given by the flow chart.

17.

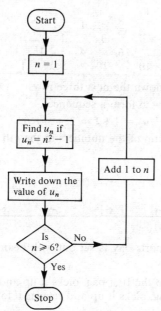

18.

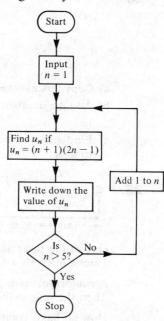

19. Draw a flow chart with a decision box and a loop for working out the first six terms of the sequence whose nth term is $(n+1)^2$.

20. Draw a flow chart to work out the first five terms of the sequence whose nth term is $\dfrac{n}{n+1}$.

21. Draw a flow chart to give the first five terms of the sequence 4, 9, 14, 19,...

22. Draw a flow chart to give the first six terms of the sequence 2, 6, 12, 20,...

23. John made these patterns with matchsticks

 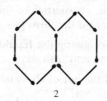 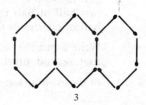

      1   2   3

a) Write down the number of matchsticks required for each of the first five patterns in the sequence.

b) How many matchsticks are needed for
   i) the nth term in the sequence
   ii) the 30th term in the sequence ?

c) John has a box of 200 matchsticks. How many patterns can he make in this sequence ? How many matchsticks are left over ?

*24.

```
              1
           1     1
        1     2     1
     1     3     3     1
   1     4     6     4     1
 1     5    10    10    5     1
```

a) Copy this pattern and write down the next three rows.

b) Add the numbers in each row to form a sequence,

i.e. $u_1 = 1$, $u_2 = 1 + 1 = 2$, ...

c) Find an expression for the sum of the numbers in the nth row of Pascal's triangle.

25.

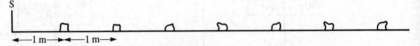

One of the races at a school sports day is set out with bean bags placed at 1 metre intervals along the track.

A competitor starts at S, runs to the first bag, picks it up and returns it to S. Then she runs to the second bag, picks it up and returns it to S, and so on.

How far has a competitor run when she has returned

a) 1 bean bag   b) 4 bean bags   c) n bean bags ?

26. These three triples are known as Pythagorean triples.

$$(3, 4, 5), \quad (5, 12, 13), \quad (7, 24, 25)$$

a) What is the relationship between the three numbers? (Their name should give you a clue!)

b) Find one more Pythagorean triple (not a multiple of those given above).

27. A boy is given a large bar of chocolate and decides to make it last by eating half of what is left each day. Thus he eats half the bar on the first day; he eats half of half the bar, i.e. quarter of the bar, on the second day; he eats half of quarter of the bar on the third day, and so on.

Write down the sequence giving the fraction of the bar left at the end of the first, second, third, fourth and fifth days.

In theory, how long will the bar of chocolate last?

*28. Start a sequence by choosing any two integers. Continue the sequence so that each subsequent term is the difference between the previous two terms. End the sequence when zero appears as a term. Repeat this with several different pairs of integers, sometimes starting with the smaller number and sometimes starting with the larger number.

Can you find a relationship between the way a sequence ends and the pair of integers it begins with?

29. A sequence is defined by $u_n = \frac{1}{2}n(n+1)$. Find
   a) the first five terms of the sequence
   b) the 20th term of the sequence
   c) an expression for the term before u_n (i.e. u_{n-1})
   d) an expression for $u_n - u_{n-1}$
   e) values of $u_2 - u_1$, $u_3 - u_2$, $u_4 - u_3$, $u_5 - u_4$
   f) the 20th term of the sequence in part (e).

30. Repeat question 29 when $u_u = \frac{1}{6}(n+1)(2n+1)$

DIFFERENCES

Sometimes the rule or formula to find the next few terms in a sequence is too difficult to spot. In this case a *difference table* may be helpful.

The first difference sequence is found by subtracting u_1 from u_2, u_2 from u_3, and so on.

As a simple example consider the sequence 5, 6, 9, 14, 21,...

| The terms are | 5 | 6 | 9 | 14 | 21 | 30 | 41 |

| 1st difference | | 1 | 3 | 5 | 7 | 9 | 11 |

We can see that the first difference row will continue with 9 and 11 and hence the sequence will continue 30 (i.e. $21+9$) and 41 (i.e. $30+11$). The sequence is now 5, 6, 9, 14, 21, 30, 41,...

A less obvious example is 2, 5, 13, 31, 64,... We find that we need a second difference row before the pattern becomes clear.

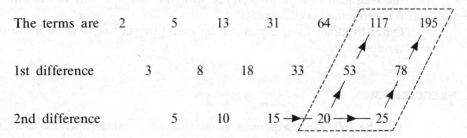

| The terms are | 2 | 5 | 13 | 31 | 64 | 117 | 195 |

| 1st difference | | 3 | 8 | 18 | 33 | 53 | 78 |

| 2nd difference | | | 5 | 10 | 15 | 20 | 25 |

In some cases it may be necessary to add a third difference line before being able to see the pattern.

Note that a difference table does not always help because there are some sequences whose first differences, second differences, etc., do not show an obvious pattern.

Sometimes too few terms in a sequence are given for us to be certain that the intended rule has been found.

For example, suppose that we have in mind to define a sequence in the following way: start with 1; multiply each term by 2 to give the next term. The first three terms in this sequence are 1, 2, 4 and the next three terms are 8, 16, 32. Someone else looking at the first three terms might think that the rule was: start with 1, add 1 to get the second term, then add 2 to get the third term, then add 3 to get the fourth term, and so on. The next three terms using this rule would be 7, 11, 16. To reduce the possibility of ambiguity we normally give at least four terms in a sequence.

CONVERGENT AND DIVERGENT SEQUENCES

Consider the sequence 1, 4, 7, 10,... where 3 is added each time. It is clear that the terms are getting larger and larger. We say that the sequence *diverges*. On the other hand if $u_{n+1} = \sqrt{1+u_n}$ and the first term is 3, then the sequence starts 3, 2, 1.732 05..., 1.652 89..., 1.628 76..., 1.621 34..., and we can see that the terms are getting closer together in value. We say that they are *converging*.

FIBONACCI SEQUENCES

In Exercise 13a, the terms in question 6 were generated by starting with 2 and 4, and obtaining the rest by adding the previous two terms. This is called a Fibonacci sequence.

The simplest Fibonacci sequence is 1, 1, 2, 3, 5, 8,... These numbers crop up frequently in nature. For example, if you count the number of spirals in the seedhead of a sunflower you will find that it is one of the numbers in this sequence, say 55 or 89.
Other Fibonacci sequences can be found by starting with different pairs of numbers.

EXERCISE 13b

For the following sequences make difference tables and use them to find the next two terms in each sequence.

1. 4, 5, 10, 19, 32,...

2. 1, 2, 5, 10, 17,...

3.   2, 3, 7, 15, 28,...   **5.**   1, 0, 5, 28, 81, 176,...

4.   11, 17, 33, 71, 143, 261,...   **6.**   1, 2, −1, −5, −7, −4,...

For each of the following sequences, there are at least two possible rules or formulae for generating it. Find two possibilities and in each case give three more terms.

    7.   3, 9, 27,...   **8.**   3, 6, 12,...   **9.**   1, 2, 5,...

Use any method to continue each of the following sequences for three more terms. Give a rule or formula if possible.

*10.   100, 99, 95, 79, 15,...   **12.**   2, 9, 28, 65,...   **14.**   1, −2, 4, −8,...

11. $\frac{1}{2}, \frac{2}{3}, \frac{3}{4}, \frac{4}{5},...$ **13.**   1.3, 2.4, 3.5, 4.6,...   **15.** $\frac{1}{2}, \frac{3}{5}, \frac{2}{3}, \frac{5}{7}, \frac{3}{4},...$

16.   The numbers 87, 7, 2, 18, 58, 121, 35, 210, 163 when written in order of size, smallest first, would form a sequence if the value of one of them was changed. Find which one should be changed and gives its correct value.

17.   Copy and complete the sequence and rows of differences. Start at the bottom line and work up.

Terms	8	10	?	20	?	58	?	148	220
1st differences		2	?	7	?	24	?	?	?
2nd differences			1	4	?	?	13	?	?
3rd differences				3	3	?	3	3	?

18.   The nth term of a sequence is given by $u_n = 3n - 4$.
    a) Find the 50th term.
    b) Find the value of n when $u_n = 293$.
    c) What is the smallest value of n such that $u_n > 1000$?

Questions 19 to 25 refer to the sequence 2, 7, 12, 17,...

19.   Write down the next two terms and give the rule used to obtain them.

20.   Give the formula for the nth term in terms of n.

21.   Give the first five terms of the sequence formed by multiplying each term of the given sequence by the term following it.
    (The first term is 2×7, i.e. 14.)

22. Use a difference table on the five terms of the new sequence formed in question 21, to find the sixth and seventh terms.

Check that you are correct by using the rule given in question 21.

23. Give the first five terms of the sequence formed by adding each term of the original sequence to the term following it.

24. Give the formula for the nth term of the sequence in question 23.

25. a) The nth term of a sequence is equal to the sum of the first n terms of the given sequence (e.g. the third term is $2+7+12$, i.e. 21). Write down the first five terms.

b) A new sequence is formed when the nth term of the sequence in (a) is divided by n. Write down the first five terms of this sequence using fractions where necessary.

c) Give a formula for the nth term of the sequence in (b).

d) Hence give a formula for the nth term of the sequence in (a).

Investigate whether the terms of each of the following sequences appear to be converging or not. If converging, state what value they appear to be approaching.

26. $u_1 = 4,\ u_{n+1} = \sqrt{u_n}$

27. $u_n = \dfrac{n}{n+1}$

28. $u_1 = 3,\ u_{n+1} = u_n^2 - 4$

29. $u_{n+1} = 4 + \dfrac{1}{u_n}$ where $u_1 = 4$

30. $u_{n+1} = 4 - u_n^2$ where $u_1 = -4$

31. $u_{n+1} = \dfrac{1}{2}\left(u_n + \dfrac{10}{u_n}\right)$ where $u_1 = 5$

32. Form a Fibonacci sequence from each of the following pairs of numbers. Give the first six terms.

a) 1,3   b) 2,3   c) 3,4

33. Form a difference table for the sequence you obtained in part (c) of question 32. What do you notice?

Does the same thing happen if you use the sequence obtained for part (b) of the same question?

34. a) Give the first eight terms of the Fibonacci sequence that begins 1, 1,...

    b) Form a sequence by expressing each term of the sequence in (a) as a fraction of its following term. Give the first ten terms.

    c) Give the fractions in (b) as decimals correct to 4 decimal places. What do you notice?

USING A COMPUTER

If we have a rule or a formula for generating a sequence, then it is possible to write a simple program for a computer.

The following programs are in BBC Basic and will run under most forms of BASIC. Both generate the same sequence.

```
10 PRINT "Rule: Start with 2 and add 5 to each term."
20 PRINT TAB(9); "N" TAB(15); "Nth TERM"
30 X = 2
40 N = 1
50 PRINT N, X
60 N = N1
70 X = X + 5
80 IF N < 11 THEN GOTO 50
```

```
10 PRINT "Nth TERM = 2 + 5(N−1)"
20 PRINT TAB(9); "N" TAB(15); "Nth TERM"
30 FOR N = 1 TO 10
40 X = 2 + 5*(N−1)     (or X = 5*N−3)
50 PRINT N, X
60 NEXT N
```

There may be more refined ways of writing programs, but these two are simple and self-explanatory. If you have not written a program before, you could use them as an introduction. Type RUN and press Return and you should see the first ten terms of the sequence appear on the screen. Either program can be adapted for other rules and formulae, and to give any number of terms. Try to write a program and use a computer to produce some of the sequences given in Exercise 13a.

Computer programs can also be used to test for convergence, as any number of terms can be calculated for inspection. It is also possible to incorporate a test for convergence into a program so that terms will continue to be produced until it is obvious whether or ot their values are converging.

A program is given below to test the convergence of the sequence for which

$$u_{n+1} = \frac{1}{2}\left(u_n + \frac{3}{u_n}\right).$$

```
10  B = 1
20  N = 1
30  A = B
40  PRINT N; TAB(12); A
50  B = 0.5*(A+3/A)
60  N = N+1
70  IF ABS (A − B) > 0.00000001 AND N < 20 GOTO 30
```

Try checking questions 26 to 31 in Exercise 13b.

RATIONAL NUMBERS

In the last section, the majority of the sequences involved integers only. When we include the positive and negative fractions with the integers, we have a much larger set of numbers called the *rational numbers*, i.e.

any rational number can be expressed as $\dfrac{p}{q}$ where p and q are integers.

Notice that this statement includes the integers, since, for example, 2 can be expressed as $\dfrac{2}{1}$. Examples of rational numbers are $\dfrac{3}{4}, \dfrac{5}{1}, \dfrac{12}{5}$.

RATIONAL NUMBERS AS DECIMALS

As a rational number is a fraction, it can be expressed as a decimal if we divide the numerator by the denominator.

Any fraction can be expressed either as an exact decimal or as a recurring decimal. This is because, on division, there will at some point either be zero remainder or the remainders will form a repeating sequence.

Conversely   any decimal which is either exact or recurring is a rational number.

For some fractions, the recurring decimal is quick to obtain by division. Some of the simpler ones should be recognised, e.g.

$$\frac{1}{3} = 0.\dot{3}, \quad \frac{2}{3} = 0.\dot{6}, \quad \frac{1}{6} = 0.1\dot{6}, \quad \frac{1}{9} = 0.\dot{1}$$

Note that for practical applications it is not necessary to find the repeating pattern in a recurring decimal. The decimal should be given correct to a number of significant figures.

EXERCISE 13c

> Express $\frac{1}{7}$ as a recurring decimal and hence write $\frac{1}{70}$ as a recurring decimal.
>
> Dividing 1 by 7 gives
> $$\frac{1}{7} = 0.\dot{1}4285\dot{7}$$
>
> $$\begin{array}{r} 0.142857\,14 \\ 7\overline{)1.0^30^20^60^40^50^10^30\ldots} \end{array}$$
>
> Now $\quad \frac{1}{70} = \frac{1}{7} \div 10$
>
> $$= 0.\dot{1}4285\dot{7} \div 10$$
>
> $$= 0.0\dot{1}4285\dot{7}$$

1. Express the following fractions as recurring decimals

    a) $\frac{1}{3}$ b) $\frac{1}{30}$ c) $\frac{1}{60}$ d) $\frac{1}{300}$

2. Express the following fractions as recurring decimals

    a) $\frac{1}{11}$ b) $\frac{1}{22}$ c) $\frac{1}{33}$ d) $\frac{2}{11}$

3. Express the following fractions as recurring decimals

    a) $\frac{1}{999}$ b) $\frac{2}{999}$ c) $\frac{1}{111}$ d) $\frac{1}{110}$

4. a) Write down $\frac{1}{9}$ as a recurring decimal.

    b) Without using a calculator multiply your answer to (a) by 9.

    c) Multiply $\frac{1}{9}$ by 9 and compare with your answer to part (b).

    d) Consider the difference between 1 and $0.\dot{9}$; this may help explain the apparent paradox in part (c).

5. Express the following recurring decimals as fractions:

    a) $0.1111\ldots$ b) $0.010101\ldots$ c) $0.003\,003\,003\,\ldots$

6. Express each of the fractions $\frac{1}{7}, \frac{2}{7}, \frac{3}{7}, \frac{4}{7}, \frac{5}{7}$, and $\frac{6}{7}$ as a decimal. Do they all give recurring decimals?

    Can you find any pattern in the decimals you get?

With the help of your calculator find $\frac{1}{29}$ as a decimal correct to 11 decimal places.

The calculator gives $\frac{1}{29} = 0.034\,482\,8$ correct to 7 d.p.

(Clear display and enter 0.034 482, i.e. leave off the last decimal place so the number entered is *less* than $\frac{1}{29}$.)

Using the calculator, $1 - (29 \times 0.034\,482) = 0.000\,022$

(This number is 29 times the difference between $\frac{1}{29}$ and 0.034 482.)

Using the calculator $0.000\,022 \div 29 = 0.000\,000\,758\,62$

(This number is the difference between $\frac{1}{29}$ and 0.034 482.)

$\therefore \frac{1}{29} = 0.034\,482\,758\,62$ correct to 11 d.p.

Questions 7 and 8 require a calculator that gives 8 s.f. in the display and has scientific notation.

7. a) Use your calculator to write down the first six decimal places when $\frac{1}{17}$ is expressed as a decimal.

b) Multiply the answer to (a) by 17.

c) Subtract the answer to (b) from 1.

d) Divide the answer to (c) by 17.

e) Use the answers to (a) and (d) to give $\frac{1}{17}$ as a decimal *correct* to 10 d.p.

8. Use a method similar to that described in question 6 to find $\frac{1}{13}$ correct to 11 d.p.

IRRATIONAL NUMBERS

We know that there are numbers which cannot be written down exactly, e.g. π, $\sqrt{2}$. It was the Greek Pythagorean philosophers who first discovered these numbers and the discovery shattered their belief that everything in the universe was exactly expressible in numbers. The Pythagoreans called these numbers 'unutterable' but we now call them *irrational*.

An irrational number can be represented by a length but cannot be expressed as a fraction.

When the irrational numbers are included with the rational numbers, the combined set is called the set of *real numbers*.

The set of real numbers includes all the numbers that it is possible to represent on a number line:

Numbers involving square roots can often be simplified by expressing the product of two square roots as a single square root,

e.g.
$$\sqrt{3} \times \sqrt{2} = \sqrt{3 \times 2} = \sqrt{6}$$

Conversely, a single square root can sometimes be expressed as a product,

e.g.
$$\sqrt{12} = \sqrt{4 \times 3} = \sqrt{4} \times \sqrt{3} = 2\sqrt{3}$$

When these methods are used, a number that appears to be irrational may turn out to be rational,

e.g.
$$\sqrt{3} \times \sqrt{12} = \sqrt{36} = 6$$

and
$$\frac{\sqrt{8}}{\sqrt{2}} = \frac{\sqrt{4} \times \sqrt{2}}{\sqrt{2}} = \sqrt{4} = 2$$

Using the phrase *real numbers* suggests that there are numbers which are not real, and for interest we will have a brief look at these.

Consider the quadratic equation $x^2 + 4 = 0$.

Solving this equation gives $x^2 = -4$

$$x = \pm\sqrt{-4}$$

There is no real number which, when squared, gives -4 so this equation has roots which are not real. This opens up yet another set of numbers and if you continue to study mathematics you will meet these numbers and find that they do have practical applications in the real world.

EXERCISE 13d

In questions 1 to 9 state whether the given number or expression is rational or irrational. For each rational number, write down an equivalent fraction $\frac{a}{b}$, where a and b are positive integers with no common factors.

If the number is irrational, simplify it if possible.

1. a) 0.7   b) $\sqrt{2}$ c) 0.625

2. a) 0.333...   b) π c) 0.125

3. a) $0.\dot{6}$ b) $\sqrt{5}$ c) $\sqrt{\dfrac{9}{25}}$

4. a) $\sqrt{3}+1$ b) $\sqrt{2}-1$ c) $\sqrt{2}\times\sqrt{8}$

5. a) $\pi\sqrt{3}$ b) $(\sqrt{2})^4$ c) $\sqrt{2}-1.414$

6. a) $\sqrt{2}\times\sqrt{3}$ b) $(\sqrt{2})^3$ c) $\sqrt{3}\times\sqrt{3}$

7. a) $\sqrt{2}+\sqrt{7}$ b) $\sqrt{12.25}$ c) $\dfrac{\sqrt{6}}{\sqrt{2}}$

8. a) $\dfrac{\sqrt{12}}{\sqrt{3}}$ b) $\dfrac{\sqrt{12}}{\sqrt{4}}$ c) $\sqrt{6.25}$

9. a) $16^{-1/2}$ b) $9^{-1/2}$ c) $8^{-1/2}$

10. Consider the numbers $-4, \sqrt{5}, \pi, 0.5, -1.8, \frac{2}{7}, \sqrt{9}$. List those that are
a) integers   b) rational   c) irrational.
Arrange the given numbers in ascending order of size.

Simplify   a) $3\sqrt{8}+\sqrt{72}$ b) $\sqrt{27}-\sqrt{12}$

a) $3\sqrt{8}+\sqrt{72} = 3\sqrt{4\times2}+\sqrt{36\times2}$

$\qquad\qquad\quad = 3\times2\sqrt{2}+6\sqrt{2}$

$\qquad\qquad\quad = 6\sqrt{2}+6\sqrt{2}$

$\qquad\qquad\quad = 12\sqrt{2}$

b) $\sqrt{27}-\sqrt{12} = \sqrt{9\times3}-\sqrt{4\times3}$

$\qquad\qquad\quad = 3\sqrt{3}-2\sqrt{3}$

$\qquad\qquad\quad = \sqrt{3}$

Simplify

11. $3\sqrt{12}+\sqrt{27}$ **13.** $\sqrt{108}-\sqrt{75}$ **15.** $\sqrt{98}-\sqrt{50}$

12. $\sqrt{32}-\sqrt{18}$ **14.** $\sqrt{125}+\sqrt{45}$ **16.** $\sqrt{63}-\sqrt{28}$

Express in the form $a + k\sqrt{b}$.

a) $1 + \dfrac{2}{\sqrt{3}}$ b) $\dfrac{2}{2 - \sqrt{3}}$

a) $1 + \dfrac{2}{\sqrt{3}} = 1 + \dfrac{2 \times \sqrt{3}}{\sqrt{3} \times \sqrt{3}}$

$= 1 + \dfrac{2\sqrt{3}}{3}$

$= 1 + \dfrac{2}{3}\sqrt{3}$

b) $\dfrac{2}{2 - \sqrt{3}} = \dfrac{2 \times (2 + \sqrt{3})}{(2 - \sqrt{3})(2 + \sqrt{3})}$

(We needed to get rid of the square root in the denominator. Using the fact that $(a + b)(a - b) = a^2 - b^2$, we chose to multiply $(2 - \sqrt{3})$ by $(2 + \sqrt{3})$ to give $(2)^2 - (\sqrt{3})^2$.)

$= \dfrac{4 + 2\sqrt{3}}{(2)^2 - (\sqrt{3})^2}$

$= \dfrac{4 + 2\sqrt{3}}{4 - 3}$

$= 4 + 2\sqrt{3}$

Express in the form $a + k\sqrt{b}$.

17. $2 + \dfrac{1}{\sqrt{2}}$ **19.** $\dfrac{2}{\sqrt{2}} - 1$ **21.** $\dfrac{\sqrt{2}}{\sqrt{3}} + 1$

18. $3 + \dfrac{2}{\sqrt{3}}$ **20.** $\dfrac{5}{2\sqrt{2}} - 2$ **22.** $\dfrac{\sqrt{3}}{\sqrt{2}} - \dfrac{\sqrt{8}}{\sqrt{2}}$

23. $\dfrac{1}{1-\sqrt{2}}$ **25.** $\dfrac{1}{\sqrt{3}-1}$ **27.** $\dfrac{2}{1+2\sqrt{3}}$

24. $\dfrac{2}{2+\sqrt{2}}$ **26.** $\dfrac{5}{\sqrt{3}+2}$ **28.** $\dfrac{3}{3\sqrt{2}-1}$

Which of the following expressions are rational and which are irrational ? Justify your answers.

29. $2^0 + 2^{-1}$ **31.** $2^0 + 2^{-1/2}$ **33.** $5^0 + 5^{-1}$

30. $2^0 + 2^{-1} + 2^{-2}$ **32.** $3^1 + 3^{-1/2}$ **34.** $4^{1/2} + 4^{-1/2}$

HYPOTHESES AND COUNTER EXAMPLES

A *hypothesis* is a statement that is thought to be true. Some hypotheses can be *proved* to be true; others can be shown to be false.

'The sum of the angles of a triangle is equal to 180°' is a hypothesis that can be proved to be true but the hypothesis that 'all prime numbers are odd' can be proved to be false.

When a hypothesis is false it can frequently be proved to be so by giving a *counter example*, i.e. by giving an example that does not fit the hypothesis. For example, 2 is a prime number and it is an even number. So the hypothesis 'all prime numbers are odd' is false.

The number 2 is *counter* to the hypothesis (i.e. shows it to be false).

To prove that a hypothesis is true we can use any convincing argument (i.e. one that will convince other people). Consider, for example, the statement,

'The sum of three consecutive whole numbers is always divisible by 3.'

We can start by testing the statement with a few particular examples.

$2+3+4 = 9$ and 9 is divisible by 3

$8+9+10 = 27$ and 27 is divisible by 3

$36+37+38 = 111$ and $111 \div 3 = 17$, i.e. 111 is divisible by 3.

These examples lead us to believe that the statement is probably true; to prove that it is true whichever three consecutive numbers are chosen, we need to give a convincing general argument.

We can start by looking at the examples to see if we can find a pattern;
the second number is $1+$ the first number
and the third number is $2+$ the first number.

Now we can generalise:

The sum of any three consecutive whole numbers is

(first number) + (first number + 1) + (first number + 2)

If n is the first number, then this can be written as

$$n + n + 1 + n + 2 = 3n + 3$$

and $3n + 3$ can be divided exactly by 3 whatever the value of n.

An interesting form of argument starts by assuming that the hypothesis we want to prove is, in fact, false. We then argue a contradiction of this assumption. This is called *proof by contradiction* which we have already used in Book 4A, when we proved that a tangent to a circle is perpendicular to the radius through the point of contact. We will now prove by contradiction that $\sqrt{2}$ is an irrational number.

Assume that $\sqrt{2}$ is rational,

i.e. $\sqrt{2} = \dfrac{a}{b}$, where a and b are integers and have no common factors.

Squaring this gives $2 = \dfrac{a^2}{b^2}$, i.e. $2b^2 = a^2$ [1]

Hence a^2 is even and therefore a is even, i.e. $a = 2c$ where c is an integer.

Replacing a by $2c$ in [1] gives $2b^2 = (2c)^2$

i.e. $2b^2 = 4c^2$

so $b^2 = 2c^2$

Therefore b^2 is even, so b is even.

But a and b cannot both be even numbers if the original assumption (that there are no common factors) is correct, so we deduce that this assumption is wrong, i.e. $\sqrt{2}$ is not rational.

EXERCISE 13e

In this exercise each question states a hypothesis. If you believe that the hypothesis is false, give a counter example to support your conclusion. If you believe the hypothesis to be true, and can prove it, you might like to give a proof.

1. The square of a positive integer is always greater than the integer.

*2. The square root of a positive integer is always smaller than the integer.

*3. The product of two integers is always another integer.

*4. When one positive number is divided by another, the question is never an integer.

*5. The sum of two odd numbers is always even.

*6. Every number that is not divisible by 2 is prime.

*7. The sum of two irrational numbers is irrational.

*8. The product of two irrational numbers is always irrational.

*9. The square root of the product of two irrational numbers is always irrational.

*10. The cube of a number is always greater than its square.

*11. If a and b are two positive whole numbers then

a) $\sqrt{ab}$ is bigger than either a or b

b) $a + b < ab$

c) $a - b < \dfrac{a}{b}$

*12. The square of a number is always bigger than the number.

*13. The square root of a number is always smaller than the number.

*14. If the area of a square is A sq. units and the perimeter of the same square is P units then $A < P$.

*15. The length of any side of a triangle is less than the sum of the lengths of the other two.

*16. All positive whole numbers can be expressed as the sum of a selection from the numbers $1, 2, 4, 8, 16, \ldots$ without using any number more than once.

*17. If the opposite sides of a quadrilateral are parallel, the quadrilateral is a rectangle.

*18. If the diagonals of a quadrilateral are equal, the quadrilateral is a rectangle.

*19. The numbers in the sequence $u_n = 4n - 1$ are prime numbers.

*20. When a whole number is squared the last digit of the result is $1, 4, 5, 6$ or 9.

*21. When a whole number is cubed the last digit of the result can have any value.

*22. The sum of the exterior angles of a polygon is $360°$.

*23. If $a > b$ then $ac > bc$ for all values of c except $c = 0$.

*24. If a and b are positive integers such that $a > b$ then $a^b > b^a$.

*25. If a, b and c are positive integers $\dfrac{a}{c} < \dfrac{b}{c}$.

*26. In a triangle, one angle is always greater than the sum of the other two.

*27. For all a and b, $(a+b)^2 > a^2 + b^2$.

*28. The probability of scoring an even number when a dice is rolled is the same as the probability of scoring a number that is prime.

*29. If a triangle is inscribed in a square such that the vertices of the triangle lie on the sides of the square, the perimeter of the triangle is less than the perimeter of the square.

*30. If a triangle is inscribed in a square such that the vertices of the triangle lie on the sides of the square the area of the triangle is less than half the area of the square.

*31. The mean of a set of data is smaller than its median.

*32. For a right-angled triangle the area of the semicircle drawn on the longest side is equal to the sum of the areas of the semicircles drawn on the other two sides.

*33. In a quadrilateral, if the diagonals are at right angles the quadrilateral is a square.

MIXED EXERCISE

EXERCISE 13f

1. Find a formula for the nth term of the sequence $5, 12, 19, 26, 33, \ldots$ Draw a flow chart to work out the first seven terms of this sequence.

What is the 50th term of this sequence?

What is the smallest value of n for which $u_n > 500$?

2. Use a difference table to find the next two terms in the sequence
$$3, 5, 12, 28, 57, 103, \ldots$$

3. What name can we give to the sequence $3, 4, 7, 11, 18, 29, 47, \ldots$?
Give the next three terms.
Find the difference between the square of any number in the sequence and the product of the two numbers adjacent to the number you have squared. What do you notice?

4. Insert the numbers $1.6, -2, 2.5, -3, 2.501$ in the spaces below.

_____ < _____ < _____ < _____ < _____

5. Are the following statements true or false?
a) $\sqrt{16}$ is an integer   b) $\sqrt{16}$ is a real number
c) $\sqrt{16}$ is an irrational number   d) $\sqrt{16}$ is a prime number.

6. Look at the numbers $-6, 0.5, \frac{2}{5}, 3, \sqrt{5}, 1.25, -0.5$.
List those that are
a) prime numbers   b) integers   c) rational numbers.
Insert the given numbers in the spaces below.

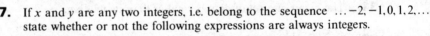

_____ < _____ < _____ < _____ < _____ < _____ < _____

7. If x and y are any two integers, i.e. belong to the sequence $\ldots -2, -1, 0, 1, 2, \ldots$ state whether or not the following expressions are always integers.
a) $x + y$ b) $x - y$ c) xy d) $x \div y$

8. 'If two prime numbers are added the result is always a prime number.'
Give a pair of prime numbers which shows that this statement is false.

9. If x and y are any two rational numbers, state whether or not the following expressions are always rational.

a) $x + y$ b) $(x - y)$ c) xy d) $x \div y$ e) $\sqrt{x}$

10. Goldbach's conjecture is 'every even number is the sum of two prime numbers'. Verify that Goldbach's conjecture is correct for
a) 8   b) 16   c) 28   d) 6

(This conjecture has been verified for all numbers up to at least 10 000 but its proof still eludes mathematicians!)

Here is a method for finding a square root of a number, correct to as many decimal places as you have patience for.

Find $\sqrt{17}$ correct to 3 d.p. using successive approximations.

(For an answer correct to 3 d.p., all working must be to 4 d.p.)

First estimate $\qquad \sqrt{17} \approx 4.1$

1. Next find $17 \div 4.1$: $\quad 17 \div 4.1 = 4.1463 \quad$ (to 4 d.p.)

$\qquad (\therefore \quad 4.1 < \sqrt{17} < 4.1463)$

2. Next find the mean of 4.1 and 4.1463

$$\tfrac{1}{2}(4.1 + 4.1463) = 4.1231$$

Use this as a better approximation for $\sqrt{17}$

Second estimate $\qquad \sqrt{17} \approx 4.1231$

(Now repeat the steps above using the second estimate.)

1. $\quad 17 \div 4.1231 = 4.1231 \quad$ (to 4 d.p. so step 2 is not needed)

i.e. to 4 d.p. $\quad (4.1231)^2 = 17$

$\qquad \therefore \quad \sqrt{17} = 4.123 \quad$ correct to 3 d.p.

Use the method illustrated in the worked example to find the square roots of the numbers in questions 11 to 13 giving your answers correct to 3 decimal places.

11. 20   **12.** 2.9   **13.** 0.5

14. Simplify:

a) $1 + \frac{1}{2}$ b) $1 + \dfrac{1}{2 + \frac{1}{2}}$ c) $1 + \dfrac{1}{2 + \dfrac{1}{2 + \frac{1}{2}}}$

15. Taking (a), (b) and (c) of question 14 as the first three terms in a sequence, write down the next two terms of the sequence and simplify them.

16. Using the answers to questions 14 and 15, you now have a sequence of 5 fractions. Square each of these fractions, giving your answer as a decimal to as many decimal places as your calculator permits. What do you think will happen if you continue the sequence of fractions?

(Note that these fractions are called *continued fractions*.)

14 STATISTICS AND PROBABILITY

HISTOGRAMS AND FREQUENCY POLYGONS

In Book 3A, Chapter 26, we considered histograms with equal width bars and some with varying width bars. We will now consider this topic again.

Suppose that we wish to draw a histogram to illustrate the following frequency table which shows the distribution of the weights of seventy sixteen-year-old girls.

Weight w (kg)	$32 \leqslant w < 34$	$34 \leqslant w < 40$	$40 \leqslant w < 44$	$44 \leqslant w < 48$	$48 \leqslant w < 52$	$52 \leqslant w < 60$	$60 \leqslant w < 70$
Frequency	1	9	10	12	17	12	9

Remember that for a histogram it is the *area* of a bar that gives the frequency for the group it represents. In this distribution the widths of the intervals vary, so the heights of the bars have to be adjusted to ensure that the area of each bar represents the frequency for the interval it covers.
The values for the heights of the bars will depend on what we choose as the unit for the widths of the intervals.

When each bar has been adjusted so that its area represents the frequency, the height of the bar is called the *adjusted frequency*, or the *relative frequency*, or the *frequency density*.

In this distribution, the interval that occurs most frequently is 4 kg; choosing this as our unit width, the height of each bar with this interval is the number given in the frequency table.
The width of the first group is half the unit width so the height of this bar is twice its frequency, i.e. 2. The heights of the bars for the remaining two groups are calculated in a similar way.

This becomes clearer if we add two more rows to the table, one for the width of the group and one for the height of the bar. Remember that 'width' × 'height' = frequency.

Weight w (kg)	$32 \leqslant w < 34$	$34 \leqslant w < 40$	$40 \leqslant w < 44$	$44 \leqslant w < 48$	$48 \leqslant w < 52$	$52 \leqslant w < 60$	$60 \leqslant w < 72$
Frequency	1	9	10	12	17	12	9
Width of bar	0.5	1.5	1	1	1	2	3
Height of bar	2	6	10	12	17	6	3

However we could equally well have chosen 1 kg as the unit width for the bars and this would give the following table.

Weight w (kg)	$32 \leqslant w < 34$	$34 \leqslant w < 40$	$40 \leqslant w < 44$	$44 \leqslant w < 48$	$48 \leqslant w < 52$	$52 \leqslant w < 60$	$60 \leqslant w < 72$
Frequency	1	9	10	12	17	12	9
Width of bar	2	6	4	4	4	8	12
Height of bar	0.5	1.5	2.5	3	4.25	1.5	0.75

The histogram obtained is given below.

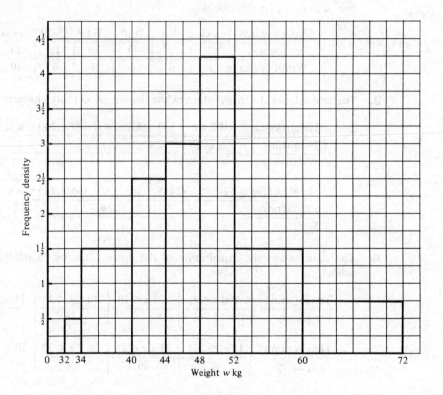

Notice that the vertical axis is labelled 'frequency density'. It could equally be labelled 'adjusted frequency' or 'relative frequency'. Note that to be able to get information from a histogram we need to know either the horizontal unit or the actual frequency represented by one of the bars. A histogram whose bars are of equal width will probably have its vertical scale labelled 'frequency'. In this case it is assumed that the width of a bar is the horizontal unit.

EXERCISE 14a

In questions 1 to 5 draw a histogram.

1. In this question the widths of the bars are also included in the table. The table gives the distribution of the marks of 100 pupils in an English examination.

Mark	0–29	30–39	40–49	50–59	60–99
Frequency	9	15	24	36	16
Width of bar	30	10	10	10	40

2. This table shows the distribution of the number of words per sentence on one page of a particular book.

No. of words	1–3	4–6	7–10	11–14	15–20	21–30
Frequency	2	7	11	16	18	13
Width of bar	3	3	4	4	6	10

3. The table shows the distribution of the heights of 65 fourteen-year-old boys.

Height h (cm)	$100 \leqslant h < 130$	$130 \leqslant h < 140$	$140 \leqslant h < 145$
Frequency	6	11	8
Width of bar	30		

Height h (cm)	$145 \leqslant h < 155$	$155 \leqslant h < 165$	$165 \leqslant h < 185$
Frequency	14	14	12
Width of bar			

4. The table shows the distribution of the times taken by 78 pupils to get to school.

Time t (min)	$0 \leqslant t < 5$	$5 \leqslant t < 10$	$10 \leqslant t < 15$	$15 \leqslant t < 18$
Frequency	6	1	18	9

Time t (min)	$18 \leqslant t < 21$	$21 \leqslant t < 26$	$26 \leqslant t < 30$	$30 \leqslant t < 40$
Frequency	12	19	9	4

5. The table gives the results of a survey, which was conducted in a region of France, to find the areas of 185 farms.

Area A (hta)	$0 \leqslant A < 4$	$4 \leqslant A < 8$	$8 \leqslant A < 12$	$12 \leqslant A < 17$
Frequency	34	22	38	30

Area A (hta)	$17 \leqslant A < 24$	$24 \leqslant A < 28$	$28 \leqslant A < 32$	$32 \leqslant A < 42$
Frequency	28	13	10	10

6. a) A horticulturalist measures the heights of plants of a new variety, and obtains the following results for 100 plants.

Height h (cm)	$20 \leqslant h < 25$	$25 \leqslant h < 27$	$27 \leqslant h < 28$	$28 \leqslant h < 30$
Number of plants	5	36	39	20

Draw a histogram to represent this data.

b) The histogram below shows the distribution of the heights of the plants of the same variety grown by a different horticulturalist.

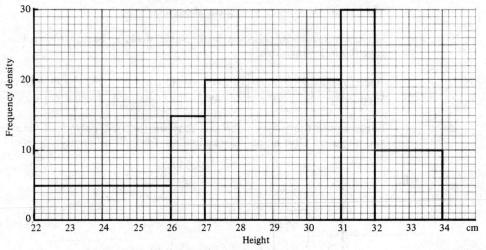

There are 20 plants in this sample whose heights are at least 32 cm but less than 34 cm. How many plants are there
  i) with heights at least 31 cm but less than 32 cm ?
  ii) with heights at least 27 cm but less than 31 cm ?
  iii) in the sample ?

7. The polygon below shows the distribution of the ages of passengers alighting from buses at Camberley Crescent during the course of one week.

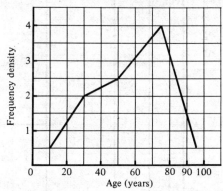

Copy this frequency polygon on squared paper and use it to complete the following table.

(Sketch in the bars first and fill in the third line of the table before you attempt to complete the fourth line.)

Age n (years)	$0 \leqslant n < 20$	$20 \leqslant n < 40$	$40 \leqslant n < 60$	$60 \leqslant n < 90$	$90 \leqslant n < 100$
Frequency density	0.5				
Width of bar	20				
Frequency	10				

How many passengers were there altogether ?

Similar information collected in the same week, at Bramberdown bus stop, gave the following table.

Age n (years)	$0 \leqslant n < 20$	$20 \leqslant n < 40$	$40 \leqslant n < 60$	$60 \leqslant n < 90$	$90 \leqslant n < 100$
Frequency	60	85	40	30	0

Superimpose the polygon for this data on the first polygon. Compare the two polygons. Give a possible explanation for their differences.

8.

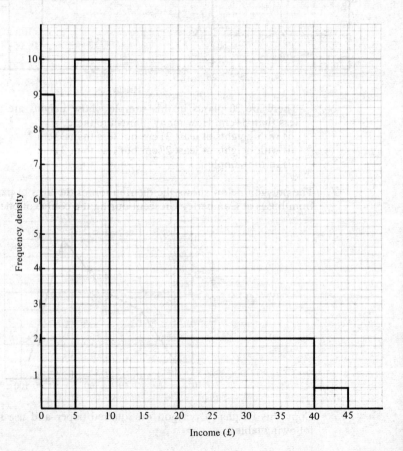

In a survey, a number of pupils were asked how much money (in £s) they received each week. Each pupil ticked one of the following responses.

0 up to but not including 2
2 up to but not including 5
5 up to but not including 10
10 up to but not including 20
20 up to but not including 40
40 up to but not including 45

Exactly 50 pupils ticked the '5 up to but not including 10' response.

The histogram shows the results of the survey.

a) Calculate the number of pupils who took part in the survey.

b) By taking the mid-interval values find an estimate for the mean weekly income.

9. The table shows the distribution of the working life of the fluorescent tubes used in a department store.

Life of tube x (hours)	$0 \leqslant x < 100$	$100 \leqslant x < 200$	$200 \leqslant x < 300$
Number of tubes f	95	230	350

Life of tube x (hours)	$300 \leqslant x < 400$	$400 \leqslant x < 600$
Number of tubes f	550	420

a) What is the range of this distribution ?

b) Using mid-interval values, find an estimate for the mean of the distribution.

c) Find the frequency density for each interval and hence draw a histogram to represent this distribution, labelling both axes clearly.

10. The distribution of the ages of the 103 staff in a large comprehensive school are given in the table.

Age (in years)	22–24	25–29	30–39	40–49	50–59	60–69
Frequency	9	10	42	32	7	3
Frequency density	3			3.2		

a) i) Copy and complete the table of frequency densities.
   ii) On graph paper, draw a histogram to illustrate the age distribution of the comprehensive school staff.

In a nearby private school the staff has the following age distribution.

Age (in years)	25–29	30–39	40–49	50–69
Percentage of staff	5	26	44	25

b) Write down two comparisons about the age distributions of the staff at the two schools.

11. Sixty boxes of Conference pears were examined and the number of damaged pears in each box was recorded, with the following results.

Number of damaged pears	0-3	4-7	8-11	12-15	16-18
Frequency	29	15	9	5	2
Cumulative frequency	29	44			

Copy and complete this table for the distribution of damaged pears per box. Hence draw the cumulative frequency curve and use it to find

a) the median   b) the quartiles   c) the interquartile range,

for this distribution.

12. One hundred boxes of Comice pears were examined and the number of damaged pears in each box was recorded with the following results.

Number of damaged pears	0-3	4-7	8-11	12-15	16-18
Frequency	35	25	16	12	12

Draw the cumulative frequency curve for this data and use it to find the median and interquartile range.

Compare the median and interquartile range for this data with the median and interquartile range you obtained in question 10.

QUESTIONNAIRES

Most of the statistics we have used so far have been obtained by observation, e.g. the heights and weights of people or the marks obtained in some school tests. Apart from observation the most common way of obtaining statistics is by the use of a questionnaire. Government questionnaires are forms designed by statisticians and completed by the general public, e.g. birth certificates or census forms; but anyone can compile a questionnaire to yield useful information by following a few simple rules.

1. The form should be as concise as possible and there should be the minimum number of questions necessary to obtain the required information.

2. The questions should be simple and unambiguous in their possible interpretation.

3. Questions likely to arouse strong feelings, or attract inaccurate answers, should be avoided.

4. The form should be as attractive as possible to the eye. Hence the need for an appealing layout and clear type.

5. When asking for confidential information in a voluntary enquiry, the person's name and address should not be put on the form unless it is essential.

6. If you compile a questionnaire, try it out on a few people first and be prepared to change it. You will almost certainly find that some of your questions are ambiguous or open to misinterpretation.

Given below is part of a questionnaire sent to a random selection of customers of Barclays Bank. The object of the questionnaire is to find out where the service to the customer needs improving and how this can be achieved.

CASH DISPENSERS

Q12.   *Does the branch that you visit most often have a cash dispenser ?*

Yes ☐ 1   No ☐ 2   Go to Q18

Q13.   *Approximately how often do you use the cash dispenser at the branch you visit most often ?*

A couple of times per week or more ☐ 1

Around once per week ☐ 2

Around once per fortnight ☐ 3

Around once per month ☐ 4

Around once every 3 months or less ☐ 5

Q14.   *Thinking about the branch you visit most often, have you used the cash dispenser in the last 2 months ?*

Yes ☐ 1   No ☐ 2   Go to Q18

Q15.   *Was the cash dispenser working ?*

Yes ☐ 1   No ☐ 2   Go to Q17

Q16.   *Were you able to obtain the service you required (e.g. balance, amount of cash required) ?*

Yes ☐ 1   No ☐ 2

Q17.   *Which comment below best describes your views on the <u>reliability</u> of the cash dispenser(s) at the branch you visit most often ?*

The cash dispenser(s) are often out of order or out of cash even in the week ☐ 1

The cash dispenser(s) are often out of order or out of cash during busy periods/weekends ☐ 2

The cash dispenser(s) are normally working including weekends ☐ 3

The cash dispenser(s) always allow me to get money when I need to ☐ 4

Don't know/no experience ☐ 5

GENERAL

Q42. *Please state whether you agree or disagree with the following statements*

	Agree strongly	Agree slightly	Neither agree nor disagree	Disagree slightly	Disagree strongly
The bank always keep me well informed about charges and I know where I stand	a ☐ 1	☐ 2	☐ 3	☐ 4	☐ 5
The mail sent by the bank is important and relevant	b ☐ 1	☐ 2	☐ 3	☐ 4	☐ 5
The bank does everything it can to make clear the range and extent of its products and services	c ☐ 1	☐ 2	☐ 3	☐ 4	☐ 5
Opening hours are very flexible and completely meet my needs	d ☐ 1	☐ 2	☐ 3	☐ 4	☐ 5
Whenever my branch is open I can get the service I need	e ☐ 1	☐ 2	☐ 3	☐ 4	☐ 5
Charges are fair	f ☐ 1	☐ 2	☐ 3	☐ 4	☐ 5
I can always discuss detailed financial matters in complete privacy at my branch	g ☐ 1	☐ 2	☐ 3	☐ 4	☐ 5
My branch is bright, pleasant and well set out	h ☐ 1	☐ 2	☐ 3	☐ 4	☐ 5
My branch hardly ever makes any mistakes	i ☐ 1	☐ 2	☐ 3	☐ 4	☐ 5
Cheques are always cleared within 3 or 4 days	j ☐ 1	☐ 2	☐ 3	☐ 4	☐ 5
Letters I receive are always well written and helpful	k ☐ 1	☐ 2	☐ 3	☐ 4	☐ 5
I can easily see my branch manager whenever I want	l ☐ 1	☐ 2	☐ 3	☐ 4	☐ 5
I would recommend the branch I visit most often to a friend	m ☐ 1	☐ 2	☐ 3	☐ 4	☐ 5

The extracts from the bank questionnaire include six questions regarding Cash Dispensers and thirteen general questions. Notice that the questions can all be answered quickly and simply by using ticks.

The first batch of questions seek the answers of fact, while the general questions tend to reflect opinions.

To what extent do you think these questions satisfy the rules given earlier?

EXERCISE 14b

For questions 1 to 8 refer to the questionnaire given in the text.

1. What is the effect of answering 'no' to question 12?

2. Do you think the possible answers have been placed in order of priority by the designer of the questionnaire?

3. Why do you think the questions refer to the *branch* you visit most often?

4. What is question 17 trying to find out? Which answer would the bank like to see?

5. Are the questions in the General Section framed to help the bank to get all the answers it would like to have in a single column?

6. Do you think that some of the parts in the General Section should be more critical? For example, 'My branch always seems to be making mistakes'.

7. As far as you can judge from the sample given, do you think that the information returned to the bank will be useful? Should it help them to improve their service?

8. Many customers who receive such questionnaires do not return them. How would you interpret the attitude of these customers?

For each question from 9 to 15 design a short questionnaire that will help you to carry out the investigation.

*9. Study the use made of your school or local public library.

*10. Determine how most pupils travel to school. Find the time taken and the difficulties encountered.

*11. Assess whether or not pupils believe that the educational provision for them has been improved during the last five years.

*12. Determine whether some car owners (drivers) are more satisfied with their cars than others.

*13. Test the attitudes of the pupils in your school to school uniform.

*14. Survey the local litter problem with a view to improving the environment.

*15. Determine whether or not motorists prefer a car propelled by a diesel engine rather than one propelled by a petrol engine, and find the reasons for the preference.

*16. Choose topics that you would like to know more about, or problems that you would like to help to solve, and construct questionnaires that will give you the information that will help you to achieve these aims.

STANDARD DEVIATION

In Book 4A we investigated ways in which the spread or dispersion of a set of data could be measured. One measurement used was the *range*, but this is not particularly useful since it can be distorted by one or more extreme values. A much better method is to find the upper and lower *quartiles*, but even this is not entirely satisfactory. A far more sophisticated measure of dispersion is the *standard deviation*; this has the advantage that it uses all the values and is the most generally quoted measure of dispersion. We want to make use of all the differences between the given values and the mean, but because some of these are negative, we use the squares of the differences. If we have n values, $x_1, x_2, x_3, \ldots x_n$ and if $\bar{x}$ is the mean, then the standard deviation, or s.d., is given by

$$\text{s.d.} = \sqrt{\frac{(x_1 - \bar{x})^2 + (x_2 - \bar{x})^2 + \ldots + (x_n - \bar{x})^2}{n}}$$

and is measured in the same unit as the original data. Its calculation is best illustrated by a simple example.

To find the standard deviation of $12, 2, 8, 10, 3, 5$ and 9, we first find the mean. Then we calculate the square of the difference between each number and the mean. It is easier to follow what is going on if the data is set out in a table.

x	$x - \bar{x}$	$(x - \bar{x})^2$
12	5	25
2	−5	25
8	1	1
10	3	9
3	−4	16
5	−2	4
9	2	4
Total 49		84

The mean, $\bar{x}$, is $49/7 = 7$;   s.d. $= \sqrt{84 \div 7} = 3.46$ (to 3 s.f.)

Note that we must total the first column and find $\bar{x}$ before the second column can be filled in.

For data given in a frequency table the value of $(x-\bar{x})^2$ has to be multiplied by the frequency of x. For grouped data, the halfway value of the group is used for x (in the same way as it is when calculating the mean) to give an approximate value for the standard deviation. A worked example is given in the following exercise.

For large quantities of data, the calculation of a standard deviation is tedious. However, most scientific calculators are capable of calculating the mean and the standard deviation. If you have one, it is well worth the effort to learn how to use it, but you will probably need to consult the manual and follow the instructions carefully. Many computer programs (often included in a database) also enable you to find both the mean and the standard deviation.

EXERCISE 14c

1. Find the mean and standard deviation for each of the following sets of data;
   a) the marks, out of 20, that Chris scored in five tests: 3, 5, 9, 12, 14
   b) the heights, in centimetres, of some geraniums: 56, 72, 49, 24, 85
   c) the masses of four letters: 16 g, 38 g, 27.5 g, 56.7 g
   d) sales figures at a department store, in thousands of pounds, for the four quarters of last year: 431, 448, 453, 473.

2. The lengths, in centimetres, of a sample of 10 leaves from my lime tree were
   8.6, 7.4, 9.3, 10.2, 7.6, 11.4, 8.9, 9.2, 8.5, 10.6
   Find the standard deviation for these lengths.

3. The data given below shows the fat content, in grams per 100 g, for ten different varieties of biscuit.
   25.8, 24.6, 21.9, 28.1, 21.9, 25.3, 29.2, 20.1, 15.6, 21.2
   Calculate the mean and standard deviation for the fat content of these biscuits.

4. The annual salaries of the directors of Eduwell PLC are £60 000, £60 000, £60 000, £60 000, £75 000, £75 000, £80 000 and £150 000.
   Calculate the mean and standard deviation for the annual salary of the Board of Directors of Eduwell PLC.
   (You may find it easier to work in thousands of pounds, e.g. £60 k.)

Twenty beans were planted in a tray. The table shows the distribution of the heights of the resulting plants three weeks later.

Height h (cm)	$1 \leqslant h < 4$	$4 \leqslant h < 7$	$7 \leqslant h < 10$	$10 \leqslant h < 13$
Frequency f	2	5	10	3

Find the standard deviation for these heights.

Height h (cm)	f	Halfway value x	fx	$x - \bar{x}$	$(x - \bar{x})^2$	$f(x - \bar{x})^2$
$1 \leqslant h < 4$	2	2.5	5	−5.1	26.01	52.02
$4 \leqslant h < 7$	5	5.5	27.5	−2.1	4.41	22.05
$7 \leqslant h < 10$	10	8.5	85	0.9	0.81	8.1
$10 \leqslant h < 13$	3	11.5	34.5	3.9	15.21	45.63
Total	20		152			127.8

$$\bar{x} = \frac{152}{20} = 7.6$$

$$\text{s.d.} = \sqrt{\frac{f(x_1 - \bar{x})^2 + f(x_2 - \bar{x})^2 \ldots}{n}}$$

$$= \sqrt{\frac{127.8}{20}} = \sqrt{6.39} = 2.53$$

5. Twenty boxes of apples were examined and the number of damaged apples in each box was recorded. Copy and complete the table given below and hence calculate the mean and standard deviation for this distribution.

No. of damaged apples	Frequency f	Halfway value x	fx	$x - \bar{x}$	$f(x - \bar{x})^2$
0–4	12	2	24		
5–9	4				
10–14	3				
15–19	1				
	20				

6. The masses, to the nearest gram, of the potatoes in a bag were recorded and are given in the table.

Mass (grams)	Frequency f	Halfway value x	fx	$x - \bar{x}$	$f(x - \bar{x})^2$
118–126	9	122	1098		
127–135	12				
136–144	26				
145–153	25				
154–162	15				
163–171	9				
172–180	4				

Copy and complete this table. Hence calculate the mean and standard deviation for this distribution.

7. The table shows the distribution of the times taken by 50 children to complete an obstacle race.

Time t (sec)	$0 \leqslant t < 40$	$40 \leqslant t < 50$	$50 \leqslant t < 60$	$60 \leqslant t < 70$
Frequency	12	21	6	11

Calculate the standard deviation for these times.

THE NORMAL DISTRIBUTION

Most of the histograms and frequency polygons we have drawn so far have been skewed to one side or the other, and in each case the mean, median and mode have all been different. Two skewed frequency polygons are given below. The negatively skewed polygon shows the distribution of the marks in a basic arithmetic test for the pupils entering Trim School while the positively skewed polygon shows the distribution of the weekly pay at a local factory.

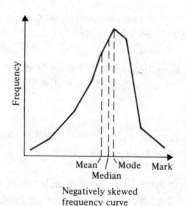

Negatively skewed
frequency curve

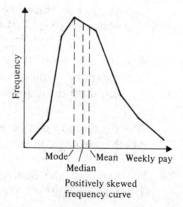

Positively skewed
frequency curve

One particular theoretical distribution is extremely important. It is called the *normal distribution* and when it arises the mean, the median and the mode all have the same value. Many continuous quantities that occur naturally, such as heights and weights, approximate very closely to the normal distribution, i.e. for these naturally occurring quantities, this distribution is the *norm*.

This histogram shows the important characteristics of a normal distribution.

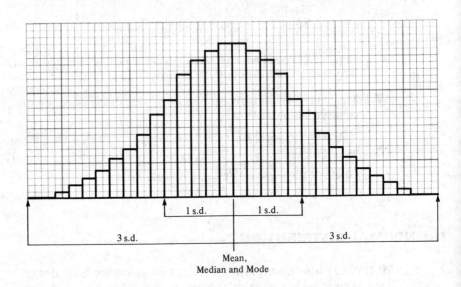

Mean,
Median and Mode

Notice that

1. it has a 'bell' shape

2. it is symmetrical about the mean, the median and the mode

3. about two thirds (67%) of the distribution lies within one standard deviation (1 s.d.) of the mean on either side.

4. virtually all of the distribution lies within 3 standard deviations of the mean on either side; i.e. the range of the distribution is about 6 standard deviations.

Any distribution can be judged against these four characteristics to determine whether or not it approximates to a normal distribution.

For example, the histogram opposite illustrates the heights of 300 pupils. The mean height is 157 cm and the standard deviation is 7.3 cm.

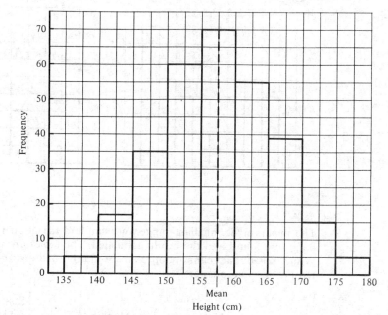

Marking the mean height on the horizontal scale, we see that the histogram is approximately symmetrical about the mean height.

The range of the distribution is (180–135) cm, i.e. 45 cm. Six standard deviations is 6 × 7.3 cm, i.e. 43.8 cm and this is almost the same as the range of the distribution. The percentage of the distribution that lies within one standard deviation from the mean, i.e. in the range 150.2 cm to 164.8 cm, is about 63 %.

It is therefore reasonable to conclude that these heights approximate to a normal distribution.

EXERCISE 14d

1. Which of these histograms cannot represent a normal distribution ? Give brief reasons for your answers.

a)

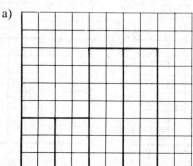

b)

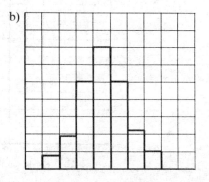

c) 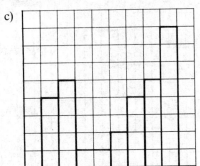   d)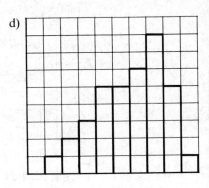

2. The mean, mode, median, range and standard deviation for various sets of data were found and the results tabulated. The tables are reproduced below. Which sets of data cannot approximate to a normal distribution ? Give brief reasons for your answers.

	Mean	Mode	Median	Range	Standard deviation
a)	62.8	54.1	55.2	124.8	12.4
b)	12.1	11.9	12.3	8.2	3.9
c)	25.4	24.9	25.2	16.1	2.6
d)	42.2	58.4	49.5	58.3	15.2
e)	142	126	130	150	28

3. Each of these histograms illustrates a distribution whose mean value is 28.5 cm and whose standard deviation is 8.8 cm.
Which of them is approximately a normal distribution ?

a) 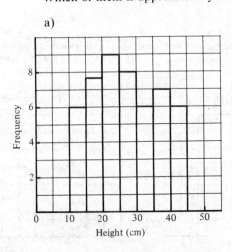   b)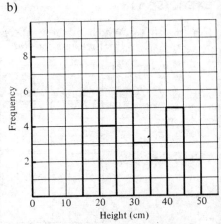

c)

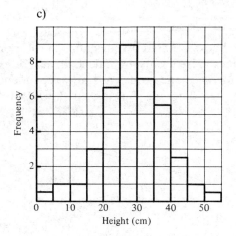

d)

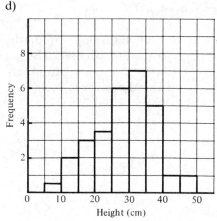

4. The first table shows the number of times that the various numbers of heads should theoretically be obtained when 6 coins are tossed together 64 times. The second table shows the number of heads that were obtained when six coins were tossed together 64 times.

Number of heads	0	1	2	3	4	5	6
Theoretical frequency	1	6	15	20	15	6	1

Number of heads	0	1	2	3	4	5	6
Experimental frequency	0	4	18	22	14	4	2

Draw histograms to illustrate each set of data. Use a calculator in statistics mode to find out the mean number of heads and the standard deviation for the theoretical distribution and for the experimental results. Use these, together with the shapes of the two histograms, to compare the two distributions, giving reasons for any conclusions you draw. Do you think that either distribution approximates to a normal distribution ?

5. Ken has only a very small plot in which to grow potatoes and wants to choose the variety that will give the best crop. He takes his wife Wendy with him to help decide on the variety of seed potato he will buy. After much discussion they decide to choose between two varieties, which are:

Winchester which, according to the details given, should yield potatoes with a mean weight of 202 g and a standard deviation of 31.4 g.

King Harold, which should yield a mean weight of 198 g and a standard deviation of 39.7 g.

Assume that the weights of the potatoes for each variety are normally distributed.

Wendy advises him to buy Winchester seed potatoes. Does she give the best advice ? Justify your answer.

PROBABILITY

Tree diagrams   In previous books we used tree diagrams to solve problems involving two events. Sometimes these events are independent. For example, when two coins are tossed, the way one coin lands is independent of the way the other coin lands. A tree diagram showing all the possibilities is given below.

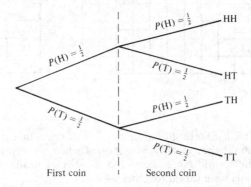

On other occasions the second event is dependent on what happens first. Suppose, for example, that a bag contains 3 red discs and 2 yellow discs. If a disc is now removed and not returned to the bag, and a second disc is then removed, the probability that the second disc will be red (or yellow) will depend on the colour of the first disc withdrawn. The probability tree for this problem is given below.

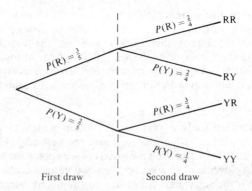

Remember that in both cases we multiply probabilities when we follow a path along the branches of the tree, but we add probabilities at the ends of several paths. In the example given above, the probability of selecting 2 red discs is $\frac{3}{5} \times \frac{2}{4} = \frac{3}{10}$ (taking the top path only) and the probability of selecting 1 red disc and 1 yellow disc is $\frac{3}{5} \times \frac{2}{4} + \frac{2}{5} \times \frac{3}{4} = \frac{3}{5}$ (both of the middle paths are acceptable).

EXERCISE 14e

1. When the car park at Brinsons empties at the end of the day the probability that a car turns left at the first junction is $\frac{3}{4}$ and that a car turns left at its next junction is $\frac{2}{5}$. A car leaves the car park. What is the probability that
   a) it turns right and then right again
   b) it makes one left turn and one right turn at the first two junctions it encounters.

2. The probability that a GCSE candidate from Potterton School obtains Level 8 or better is $\frac{3}{5}$ in English, $\frac{1}{2}$ in mathematics and $\frac{3}{8}$ in physics.
   a) Copy the tree diagram and write the missing probabilities on it.

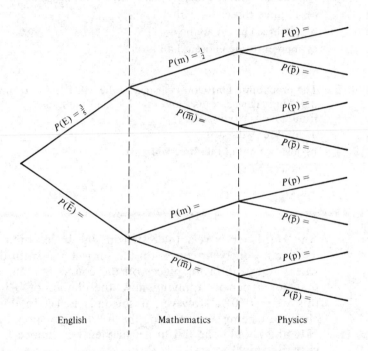

P(E) means 'the probability of obtaining a Level 8 or better in English,' P($\overline{\text{E}}$) means 'the probability of having a grade lower than Level 8 in English,' and so on.

   b) Use your probability tree to find the probability that a candidate chosen at random from Potterton School will
      i) obtain at least Level 8 in all three subjects
      ii) be graded lower than Level 8 in all three subjects
      iii) obtain at least Level 8 in exactly two of these subjects.

   c) Last year 160 pupils in the fifth year were entered for the GCSE exams in these three subjects. How many of these pupils were expected to obtain at least Level 8 in two or more of these subjects ?

3. When the school bus arrives at Bracknel Lane, 5 boys and 6 girls are waiting to board it. They get on in random order.

a) What is the probability that a girl gets on first ?

b) If the first pupil to get on the bus is a girl what is the probability the next one on is also a girl ?

Find the probability that

c) one of the first two pupils to board the bus is a boy and one is a girl

d) the first three to board are all girls.

4. Three pupils are to be selected at random from the school athletics team which consists of 8 girls and 6 boys. Those selected are to go on a five day residential training course. What is the probability that

a) all three chosen are girls

b) all three chosen are boys

c) more girls are chosen than boys ?

5. The probability that Don's car passes the MOT test next time is $\frac{4}{5}$, that Mag's car passes is $\frac{5}{7}$ and that Joe's car passes is $\frac{1}{2}$.
Find the probability that

a) all three will pass

b) just two out of the three will pass

c) no car passes ?

Ann Hardwick is very interested in fine bone china and wants to attend a one-year course on the subject at Swarbridge College where competition for places on the course is high. She is told that, for a person applying now, the chance of being selected this year is 60%. However, if she fails to get in this year, her chance of being accepted for the following year is increased to 75% and should she fail to get in then her chance for the third year rises to 90%.

a) Draw a tree diagram for this information.

b) Calculate the probability that Ann will be offered a place   i) next year   ii) the year after next.

c) 400 people have applied for the course this year. How many of this year's applicants   i) will be accepted for this year
ii) will be able to follow the course the year after next
iii) fail to be selected for any one of the next three courses ?

d) What is the chance that an applicant this year will get on the course either this year, next year or the year after ?

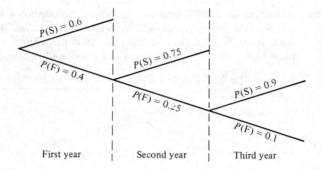

First year | Second year | Third year

$P(S)$ means 'the probability of getting on a course' and $P(F)$ means 'the probability of failing to get on a course'.

b) i) $P($ Ann gets on the course next year$)$
$= P($ she fails to get on this year$) \times$
$P($ she gets on next year$)$

$= 0.4 \times 0.75 = 0.3$

ii) $P($ Ann gets on the course the year after next$)$

$= 0.4 \times 0.25 \times 0.1 = 0.01$

c) i) Number likely to get on course this year

$= 400 \times P($ getting on course this year$)$

$= 400 \times 0.6 = 240$

ii) Number likely to get on the year after next

$= 400 \times 0.4 \times 0.25 \times 0.9 = 36$

iii) Number failing to get on a course this year, next year or the year after

$= 400 \times 0.4 \times 0.25 \times 0.1 = 4$

d) $P($ getting on one of the three courses$)$

$= 0.6 + 0.4 \times 0.75 + 0.4 \times 0.25 \times 0.9 = 0.99$

(or $1 - 0.4 \times 0.25 \times 0.1 = 0.99$)

6. A student at the Moneywise School of Accountancy has a 70% chance of passing an accountancy examination at the first attempt. Each time a student retakes an examination, the student's chance of passing is reduced by 10%, i.e. there is a 60% chance of passing after one failure, and so on.

a) Copy the tree diagram given below and fill in the missing probabilities.

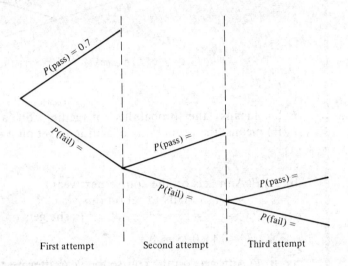

First attempt   Second attempt   Third attempt

b) Calculate the probability that a Moneywise student chosen at random will pass
   i) at the second attempt
   ii) at the third attempt.

c) Out of 100 Moneywise students chosen at random how many should pass
   i) at the first attempt
   ii) at the second attempt
   iii) at the third attempt ?

d) What is the chance that a student chosen at random will pass at either the first or the second or the third attempt ?

7. Andy is not a very good navigator. When he enters a small town, the probability that he gets lost and cannot find the correct road to continue his journey, is 0.2. When he enters a large town, the probability that he does not find the correct exit road is 0.25. He starts on a journey that passes through two small towns followed by one large town. Draw a tree diagram to represent this information and use it to find the probability that

a) he reaches the second small town and leaves it on the correct road

b) he reaches the large town but fails to find the correct exit road.

8. Helen and Tim play a game by tossing two coins together. Helen plays first and the first to get two heads wins.

  a) For one turn in any game, what is the chance

      i) of getting two heads, $P(W)$

      ii) of not getting two heads, $P(\overline{W})$?

  b) Copy the tree diagram and fill in the missing probabilities

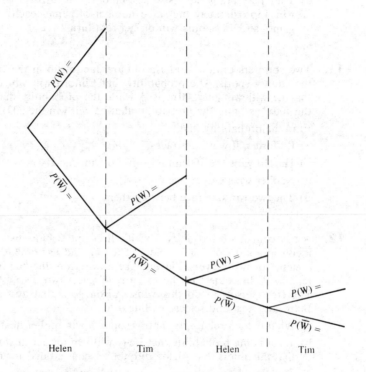

  c) What is the probability that

      i) Tim wins on his first turn

      ii) Helen wins on her second turn ?

  d) They play the game 256 times. How many of these is Tim likely to have won by the time each player has had two turns ?

  e) Is this a fair game ? Who has the better chance of winning ? Suppose Tim plays first in the second game, Helen plays first in the third game, Tim in the fourth and so on. Would you consider it to be a fair game then ?

9. Repeat parts (b), (c) and (d) of question 8 using three coins; three heads to give a win.

10. Amjun and Sabina play a game with a dice. The game is won by rolling a 6.

a) What is the probability that a 6 is scored when the dice is rolled ?

b) Amjun goes first. Draw a tree diagram to show the probabilities after each player has had up to two turns.

c) What is the probability that
i) Sabina wins on her first turn
ii) Amjun wins either on his first turn or on his second turn ?

d) They play the game 500 times, taking it in turns to go first. Should they win approximately the same number of games each ? About how many games should Sabina win on her first turn ?

11. Two sprinters Linford and Harold are due to run in the 100 m and 200 m in the county sports. The probability that Linford will win the 100 m is $\frac{1}{5}$ and that he will win the 200 m is $\frac{3}{10}$ while the probability that Harold will win the 100 m is $\frac{1}{4}$ and the probability that he will win the 200 m is $\frac{1}{7}$.

Find the probability that

a) Linford will win both races.

b) Harold wins the 100 m and Linford wins the 200 m.

c) Neither wins either race.

d) The two win one race between them.

12. A bag contains 8 red discs, 5 white discs and 3 blue discs. All the discs are identical apart from their colour. The bag and its contents are to be used in a game for two players. Players take a disc from the bag in turn and do not replace it; the object of the game is to select two discs of the same colour. The first person to do this wins. Alison goes first and selects a red disc. Betty goes next and selects a white disc.

a) What is the probability that Alison will win on her next turn ?

b) What is the probability that Betty will win on her next turn ? (Remember that this infers that Alison did not select a red disc for her second turn.)

c) Explain why your answer to part (a) implies that this is not a fair game.

d) They decide to change the rules to make it fairer. Betty will make her second selection before Alison. Repeat parts (a) and (b). Is the game any fairer now ?

PROBABILITY USING CIRCLE DIAGRAMS

Some probability questions are best solved in diagrammatic form by using intersecting circles drawn within a rectangle (the diagrams are called Venn diagrams). The following exercise begins with a worked example.

(Reminder: some questions can also be solved using a possibility space. This method was considered in Book 2A, Chapter 2.)

EXERCISE 14f

In a class of 28 students, each has a dog or a cat or both. If 20 keep a dog and 7 of these also have a cat, show this information on a diagram. Hence find the probability that a student chosen at random has

a) a dog   b) a cat only   c) just one of these pets.

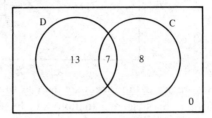

(Since some students have both a dog and a cat we draw two intersecting circles.)

We label one circle D to denote dogs and the other circle C for cats.

Since 7 keep both a cat and a dog we place 7 in the overlapping region. This leaves $20 - 7$, i.e. 13 in the 'dog only' region and $28 - 20$, i.e. 8 in the 'cat only' region. There are no students outside the circles but within the rectangle, since every student has at least one pet.

a) $P(\text{a dog}) = \frac{20}{28} = \frac{5}{7}$

b) $P(\text{a cat only}) = \frac{8}{28} = \frac{2}{7}$

c) $P(\text{a dog or a cat but not both}) = \dfrac{13 + 8}{28} = \frac{21}{28} = \frac{3}{4}$

1. The diagram shows the ways of coming to school used by the sixth formers at Brimpton School.

A represents the number walking
B represents the number coming by bus
C represents the number coming by car

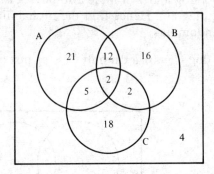

a) How many sixth formers are there at Brimpton School ?

b) Give a possible explanation for the four sixth formers who are not included within any circle.

c) What is the probability that a pupil chosen at random
   i) uses exactly one way of getting to school
   ii) uses more than one way of getting to school
   iii) does not use a car ?

2. In a certain group of students some are in one or more of the school athletics, rugby and cricket teams. The diagram shows these numbers; in A are those in the athletics team, in R are those in the rugby team and in C are those in the cricket team.

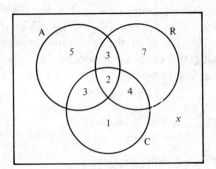

If there are 30 students in the group, what is the value of x ?

What is the probability that a pupil chosen at random is in

a) the rugby team   b) exactly one team

c) more than one team   d) the athletics team ?

3. There are 30 pupils in a class, all of whom have a computer C, or a CD player P, or both. The probability that any given pupil has a computer and a CD player is $\frac{4}{15}$, while the probability that a pupil selected at random has a CD player is $\frac{3}{5}$. How many pupils have a CD player but not a computer ?

4. A questionnaire on 'Holiday Transport' given to 60 people produced the following facts: 40 had used a car, 28 had used an aeroplane, 16 had used a train, 18 had used both a car and an aeroplane, 5 had used both a car and a train, 4 had used a train only, 20 had used a car only and 6 had not been on holiday. Draw a diagram of three intersecting circles within a rectangle and write x in the space representing all three modes of transport.

a) Find the value of x.

b) What is the probability that a person selected from this group
  i) went on holiday but did not use a car
  ii) went on holiday and used more than one form of transport ?

MIXED EXERCISE

EXERCISE 14g

1. A darts player keeps a record of his scores over a period of 160 visits to the dartboard. The table shows the distribution of these scores.

Score	0–20	21–40	41–60	61–80	81–100	101–120	121–140	141–160	161–180
Frequency	3	7	9	21	22	34	34	22	8
Score	⩽20	⩽40	⩽60	⩽80	⩽100	⩽120	⩽140	⩽160	⩽180
Cumulative frequency			19	40	62	96			

Copy and complete the table and hence find

a) the number of times he scored more than 140

b) the number of times he scored less than 161

c) the probability that he scores more than 100.

d) Draw the cumulative frequency curve for the above data and use it to estimate
  i) the median score
  ii) the upper and lower quartiles
  iii) the interquartile range.

2. The table is based on a batsman's scores in one season. Copy and complete the table to show the cumulative frequencies.

Score	0–24	25–49	50–74	75–99	100–149	150–199	200–300
Frequency	5	4	21	12	8	3	2
Score	⩽24	⩽49	⩽74	⩽99	⩽149	⩽199	⩽300
Cumulative frequency							

a) How many innings did he play ?

b) How many centuries did he score ?

c) In how many innings did he score 50 or more ?

Draw a cumulative frequency polygon for this data and use it to estimate

d) his median score

e) the interquartile range.

What is the probability that on his next visit to the crease the batsman scores 50 or more ?

3. The table shows the masses of 50 adults at the beginning and end of a weightwatching programme.

Mass (stones)		6–8	9–11	12–14	15–17	18–20	21–23	24–26
Number of people	At beginning	1	3	8	20	12	4	2
	At end	1	7	20	14	8	0	0

a) Find   i) the mean mass   ii) the modal mass   iii) the median mass
at the beginning and at the end of the course.

b) Draw a frequency polygon to show the mass distribution
   i) at the beginning of the course
   ii) at the end of the course.

c) Compare the two distributions. The standard deviation of the masses at the end of the programme was 2.94. Would you expect the standard deviation at the beginning of the programme to have been higher than, lower than, or equal to, 2.94 ?

4. This frequency table shows the results of asking the members of a Women's Institute to count the number of items in their handbags.

Number of items	0–4	5–9	10–14	15–19	20–24	25–27
Frequency	1	4	9	15	8	3

a) Find the mean and modal group for this data.

b) Make a cumulative frequency table for this distribution and use it to draw a cumulative frequency curve.

c) Use your cumulative frequency curve to estimate the median and interquartile range.

d) Calculate the standard deviation for the number of items in the ladies' bags.

e) What is the probability that one of these handbags chosen at random will contain
   i) fewer than 10 items
   ii) more than 19 items ?

f) When the items in the bags of 30 teenage girls were counted it was found that the mean number of items was 10.2 and the standard deviation was 3.5. Compare the number of items in the bags of the ladies from the W.I with those of the teenagers.

5. A bag contains 5 white discs and 5 black discs. Two players draw discs from the bag one at a time in turns and do not replace them. Andy goes first and draws a white disc. Beth follows and draws a black disc.

   a) What is the probability that

      i) Andy draws a white disc on his second turn

      ii) Andy fails to draw a white disc on his second turn but Beth draws a black disc on her second turn

      iii) after three dips into the bag Andy has two discs of the same colour ?

   b) What is Beth's chance of drawing a black disc if she has her second go before Andy has his second go ?

6. During the winter of 2002 the probability that it will snow on any day is $\frac{1}{10}$. In 2012, because of possible climatic changes, the probability that it will snow on any day will reduce to $\frac{1}{15}$.

   a) Calculate the probability that it will snow on any three consecutive days in the winter of 2002.

   b) Calculate the probability that it will not snow on 1st, 2nd or 3rd of January 2012.

   c) Calculate the probability that it will snow on Christmas Day 2002 but will not snow on Christmas Day 2012.

   d) Assuming that each winter consists of 90 days, on how many days in total, in the winters of 2002 and 2012, can snow be expected to fall ?

7. When I go to the local music store the probability that I can buy any particular CD I want is $\frac{2}{5}$, but if I go to the department store in nearby Tadchester the probability is $\frac{5}{6}$. I want to buy two particular CDs. What is the probability that

   a) I can get them both locally

   b) I fail to get either locally but get both at Tadchester

   c) I fail to get either CD locally or at Tadchester

   d) I get one CD locally and the other at Tadchester ?

8. During the month of August the probability that it will rain on any given day in my home region is $\frac{1}{8}$ and the probability that it will rain at my favourite holiday resort in Spain is $\frac{1}{15}$. I decide to go to the holiday resort for 10 days.

   a) What is the probability that

      i) I enjoy 10 rain-free days

      ii) it rains every day

      iii) it did not rain at home on any of the days I was away ?

   b) Is it true to say that I have almost twice the chance of 10 rain-free days if I go to Spain than if I stay at home ?

9. The Multiflex Manufacturing Company selects its staff by using a series of tests. All prospective employees must sit a basic numeracy test before they are allowed to sit Tests A and B. The chance of passing the numeracy test is 65%; the chance of passing Test A is 70%, the chance of passing Test B is 50% and the chance of passing both Test A and Test B is 35%. Copy and complete the diagram to show the different percentages in the various categories.

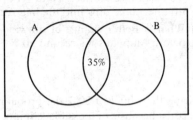

This year 2000 people have applied for jobs with the company. How many of these would you expect

a) to be eliminated by the basic numeracy test

b) to go on to sit Tests A and B

c) to pass Test A

d) to pass both Test A and Test B

e) to fail Test A and Test B

f) to pass Test A but fail Test B

g) to pass Test B but fail Test A ?

10. The frequency table gives the distribution of the ages of 225 trees in a wood.

Age t (years)	$0 < t \leqslant 25$	$25 < t \leqslant 50$	$50 < t \leqslant 100$	$100 < t \leqslant 150$	$150 < t \leqslant 200$	$200 < t \leqslant 300$
Frequency	30	40	55	46	37	17

Find the frequency density for each bar width and hence draw, on the same diagram, a frequency polygon and histogram to represent this data.

11. Tim Harvey breeds Cavalier King Charles spaniels. At present he has 3 ruby puppies, 5 tricolours and 4 black and tan puppies. When he opens the pen door they are likely to come out in random order.

a) What is the probability that the first one out is
   i) a tricolour   ii) a black and tan ?

b) If the first one out is a ruby, what is the probability that the next one out will also be a ruby ?

Find the probability that

c) one of the first two puppies out is a ruby and one is a black and tan

d) the first three puppies out are all tricolours

e) one of the first three puppies out is a ruby, one is a tricolour and one is a black and tan

f) the first three out are all of the same colour ?

15 SINE AND COSINE FORMULAE

SINES OF OBTUSE ANGLES

In earlier work we have used sines of acute angles. Now, with the help of a calculator, we shall investigate the sines of angles from $90°$ to $180°$.

EXERCISE 15a

1. a) Copy the following table.

x	0	15	30	45	60	75	90
$\sin x°$							

x	105	120	135	150	165	180
$\sin x°$						

Complete the table, using a calculator to find $\sin x°$ for each angle in the table, correcting the value to 2 d.p.

b) Using scales of 1 cm for 15 units on the horizontal axis and 1 cm for 0.2 on the vertical axis, plot these points on a graph and draw a smooth curve through the points.

c) This curve has a line of symmetry. About which value of x is the curve symmetrical?

d) From your graph, find the two angles for which i) $\sin x° = 0.8$ ii) $\sin x° = 0.6$ iii) $\sin x° = 0.4$. Find, in each case, a relationship between the two angles.

2. Use a calculator to complete the following statements.

a) $\sin 30° = \boxed{}$, $\quad \sin 150° = \boxed{}$, $\quad 150° = \boxed{} - 30°$

b) $\sin 40° = \boxed{}$, $\quad \sin 140° = \boxed{}$, $\quad 140° = \boxed{} - 40°$

c) $\sin 72° = \boxed{}$, $\quad \sin 108° = \boxed{}$, $\quad 108° = \boxed{} - 72°$

These results suggest that, if two angles are supplementary (i.e. add up to $180°$), their sines are the same, i.e.

$$\sin x° = \sin(180° - x°)$$

335

EXERCISE 15b

Find $\sin x°$.

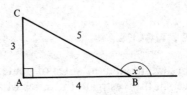

$$\sin x° = \sin(180° - x°)$$

$$= \sin A\widehat{B}C$$

$$= \frac{3}{5}$$

In questions 1 to 6, find $\sin x°$.

1.

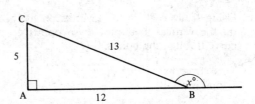

2.

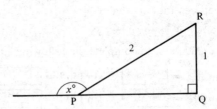

3.

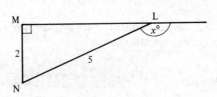

4.

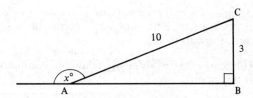

5.

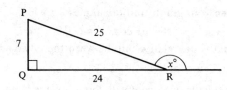

6.

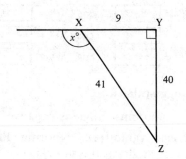

In questions 7 to 12, $x°$ is an acute angle. Find x.

7. $\sin x° = \sin 165°$ **10.** $\sin x° = \sin 100°$

8. $\sin x° = \sin 140°$ **11.** $\sin x° = \sin 175°$

9. $\sin x° = \sin 152°$ **12.** $\sin x° = \sin 91°$

COSINES OF OBTUSE ANGLES

EXERCISE 15c

1. a) Copy and complete the following table, using a calculator to find $\cos x°$ for each angle in the table, correcting the value to 2 d.p.

x	0	15	30	45	60	75	90
$\cos x°$							

x	105	120	135	150	165	180
$\cos x°$						

b) Using scales of 1 cm for 15 units on the horizontal axis and 1 cm for 0.2 on the vertical axis, plot these points on a graph and draw a smooth curve through them.

c) This curve has a point of rotational symmetry. What is the value of x at this point ?

d) What do you notice about the sign of cosines of obtuse angles ?

e) From your graph find the angles for which
   i) $\cos x° = 0.8$　ii) $\cos x° = -0.8$
   What is the relationship between these two angles ?

2. Use a calculator to complete the following statements.

a) $\cos 30° = \boxed{}$, $\cos 150° = \boxed{}$, $150° = \boxed{} - 30°$

b) $\cos 50° = \boxed{}$, $\cos 130° = \boxed{}$, $130° = \boxed{} - 50°$

c) $\cos 84° = \boxed{}$, $\cos\ 96° = \boxed{}$, $96° = \boxed{} - 84°$

These results suggest that

1. the cosine of an obtuse angle is negative
2. the numerical value (i.e. ignoring the sign) of the cosines of supplementary angles is the same, i.e.

$$\cos x° = -\cos(180° - x°)$$

EXERCISE 15d

Find $\cos x°$.

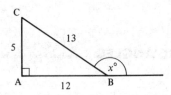

$$\cos x° = -\cos(180° - x°)$$

$$= -\cos A\widehat{B}C$$

$$= -\frac{12}{13}$$

In questions 1 to 4, find $\cos x°$.

1.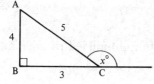

3.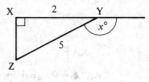

2.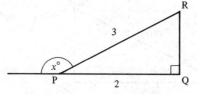

4.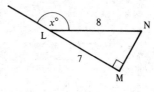

5. Find $\widehat{A}$ if   a) $\cos A = -\cos 20°$ b) $\cos A = -\cos 50°$.

TRIGONOMETRIC RATIOS AS FRACTIONS

For an angle A in a right-angled triangle, if one of $\sin A$, $\cos A$ or $\tan A$ is given as a fraction, we can draw a right-angled triangle and mark in the lengths of two sides.

For example, if $\sin A = \dfrac{3}{5}$, this triangle can be drawn.

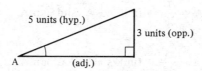

Then, using Pythagoras' Theorem, the length of the third side can be calculated. In this case it is of length 4 units.

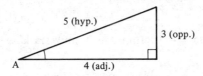

Now the cosine of angle A can be written down as a fraction,

i.e. $\cos A = \dfrac{4}{5}$

Similarly $\tan A = \dfrac{3}{4}$

EXERCISE 15e

If $\cos P = \dfrac{12}{13}$, draw a suitable right-angled triangle and hence find $\sin P$ and $\tan P$.

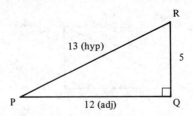

$$QR = 5 \quad (\text{Pythag. th., or recognising a 5, 12, 13 triangle.})$$

Therefore $\qquad\qquad\qquad \sin P = \dfrac{5}{13}$

and $\qquad\qquad\qquad\qquad \tan P = \dfrac{5}{12}$

---

1. If $\sin A = \dfrac{7}{25}$ find $\cos A$ and $\tan A$.

2. If $\cos A = \dfrac{5}{13}$ find $\sin A$ and $\tan A$.

3. If $\tan P = \dfrac{3}{4}$ find $\sin P$ and $\cos P$.

4. If $\cos D = \dfrac{3}{5}$ find $\tan D$ and $\sin D$.

5. If $\sin X = \dfrac{9}{41}$ find $\cos X$ and $\tan X$.

6. If $\tan A = 1$ find $\sin A$ and $\cos A$.

(Remember that $1 = \dfrac{1}{1}$ and leave the square root in your answer.)

7. ABC is an equilateral triangle of
side 2 units. D is the midpoint of
AC.

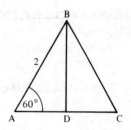

a) Show that $AD = 1$ unit
and $BD = \sqrt{3}$ units.

b) Find the value in square root
form of
i) $\sin 60°$ ii) $\cos 60°$
iii) $\tan 60°$.

c) Find in square root form the
value of
i) $\sin 30°$ ii) $\cos 30°$
iii) $\tan 30°$.

8. In $\triangle ABC$, $AB = BC = 1$ unit
and $A\widehat{B}C = 90°$.

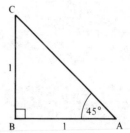

a) Show that $CA = \sqrt{2}$ units.

b) Find in square root form, the
value of
i) $\sin 45°$ ii) $\cos 45°$
iii) $\tan 45°$.

9. If $\sin A = \dfrac{12}{13}$ find $2\sin A \cos A$ expressing your result as a decimal.
Find $\widehat{A}$ and hence $\sin 2A$. What conclusion can you draw?

10. If $\cos A = \dfrac{4}{5}$ find $\cos^2 A - \sin^2 A$ expressing your result as a decimal.
Find $\widehat{A}$ and hence $\cos 2A$. What conclusion can you draw?

11. If $\sin X = \dfrac{x}{y}$ find $\cos^2 X + \sin^2 X$.

12. If $\sin A = \dfrac{11}{61}$ find $\dfrac{2\tan A}{1 - \tan^2 A}$.

13. If $\tan A = \frac{2}{5}$
a) Find   i) $\sin^2 A$ ii) $\cos^2 A$ iii) $1 + \tan^2 A$ iv) $1 - \cos^2 A$.
b) Comment on the answers to parts (i) and (iv).
c) Comment on the answers to parts (ii) and (iii).
d) If, instead, $\tan A = \frac{3}{7}$, do you find the same relationships in (b) and (c)?

TRIGONOMETRIC RATIOS OF 30°, 45° AND 60°

As we have seen from questions 7 and 8 in the last exercise, it is possible to give the trig ratios of 30°, 45° and 60° in an exact form.

It is useful to gather the results together in a table.

	sin	cos	tan
30°	$\frac{1}{2}$	$\frac{\sqrt{3}}{2}$	$\frac{1}{\sqrt{3}}$
45°	$\frac{1}{\sqrt{2}}$	$\frac{1}{\sqrt{2}}$	1
60°	$\frac{\sqrt{3}}{2}$	$\frac{1}{2}$	$\sqrt{3}$

EXERCISE 15f

1. If $\sin A = \dfrac{1}{2}$ and $\widehat{A} < 90°$ find $\cos A$.

Hence find, in square root form, the value of
a) $2 \sin A \cos A$ b) $2 \cos^2 A - 1$

2. Use the table given in the text to write down the values of $\sin 30°$, $\cos 30°$, $\sin 60°$ and $\cos 60°$.

a) Hence find, in square root form, the value of
  i) $\sin 30° \cos 60° + \cos 30° \sin 60°$
  ii) $\sin 60° \cos 30° - \cos 60° \sin 30°$
b) What angle has a sine equal in value to your answer to part (a)(i)?
c) What angle has a sine equal in value to your answer to part (a)(ii)?

MIXED QUESTIONS

EXERCISE 15g

1. Write down, as a fraction,
  a) $\cos x°$ b) $\sin x°$

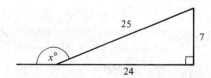

2. Find two angles each with a sine of 0.5

3. If $\cos 59° = 0.515$ what is $\cos 121°$?

4. Find an obtuse angle whose cosine is equal to $-\cos 72°$.

5. If $\sin x° = \frac{4}{5}$, find as a fraction
   a) $\sin(180° - x°)$ b) $\cos x°$ c) $\cos(180° - x°)$

6. Use your calculator to make a table of values of $\sin x°$ for values of x from 0 to 720 at intervals of 45.

Taking scales of 1 cm to 90 units on the x-axis and 1 cm to 1 unit on the y-axis, use the table of values, together with the knowledge of the shape drawn for $y = \sin x°$ in Exercise 15a, to draw the graph of $y = \sin x°$ for 0 to 720.

7. Follow the sequence of steps in question 6 to draw the graph of $y = \cos x°$ for 0 to 720.

TRIANGLE NOTATION

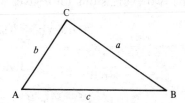

In a triangle ABC, the sides can be referred to as AB, BC and CA. It is convenient, however, to use a single letter to denote the number of units in the length of a side and the standard notation uses

   a for the side opposite to angle A
   b for the side opposite to angle B
   c for the side opposite to angle C.

In this triangle, for example,

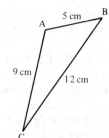

$a = 12$
$b = 9$
$c = 5$

$$\sin x = \sin(180 - x).$$

THE SINE RULE

Consider a triangle ABC in which there is no right angle.

If a line is drawn from C, perpendicular to AB, the original triangle is divided into two right-angled triangles ADC and BDC as shown.

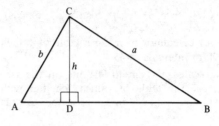

In △ADC $\qquad\qquad \sin A = \dfrac{h}{b} \;\Rightarrow\; h = b \sin A$

In △BDC $\qquad\qquad \sin B = \dfrac{h}{a} \;\Rightarrow\; h = a \sin B$

Equating the two expressions for h gives

$$a \sin B = b \sin A$$

Hence $\qquad \dfrac{a}{\sin A} = \dfrac{b}{\sin B} \qquad$ (dividing both sides by $\sin A \sin B$)

Now if we were to divide △ABC into two right-angled triangles by drawing the perpendicular from B to AC the similar result would be

$$\frac{b}{\sin B} = \frac{c}{\sin C}$$

Combining the two results gives

$$\frac{a}{\sin A} = \frac{b}{\sin B} = \frac{c}{\sin C}$$

This result is called the *sine rule* and it enables us to find angles and sides of triangles which are *not* right-angled.

It is made up of three equal fractions, but only two of them can be used at a time. When using the sine rule we choose the two fractions in which three quantities are known and only one is unknown.

In all the following exercises, unless a different instruction is given express angles correct to 1 d.p. and lengths to 3 s.f.

EXERCISE 15h

In $\triangle ABC$, $AC = 3\,\text{cm}$, $\widehat{B} = 40\,^\circ$ and $\widehat{A} = 65\,^\circ$.
Find the length of BC.

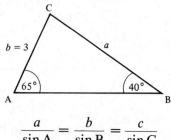

$$\frac{a}{\sin A} = \frac{b}{\sin B} = \frac{c}{\sin C}$$

(The four quantities involved are a, b, $\widehat{A}$ and $\widehat{B}$ so we use the first two fractions in the sine rule.)

$$\frac{a}{\sin 65\,^\circ} = \frac{3}{\sin 40\,^\circ}$$

$$a = \frac{3\sin 65\,^\circ}{\sin 40\,^\circ}$$

$$= \frac{3 \times 0.9063}{0.6428}$$

$$= 4.2297$$

Therefore BC $= 4.23\,\text{cm}$ correct to 3 s.f.

1. In $\triangle ABC$, $AB = 7\,\text{cm}$, $\widehat{A} = 32\,^\circ$ and $\widehat{C} = 49\,^\circ$. Find BC.

2. In $\triangle PQR$, $\widehat{Q} = 56\,^\circ$, $\widehat{R} = 72\,^\circ$ and $PR = 11.3\,\text{cm}$. Find PQ.

3. In $\triangle XYZ$, $\widehat{X} = 28\,^\circ$, $YZ = 4.9\,\text{cm}$ and $\widehat{Y} = 69\,^\circ$. Find XZ.

4. In $\triangle ABC$, $BC = 8.3\,\text{cm}$, $\widehat{A} = 61\,^\circ$ and $\widehat{C} = 58\,^\circ$. Find AB.

5. In $\triangle LMN$, $LM = 17.7\,\text{cm}$, $\widehat{N} = 73\,^\circ$ and $\widehat{L} = 52\,^\circ$. Find MN.

6. In $\triangle PQR$, $\widehat{P} = 54\,^\circ$, $\widehat{Q} = 83\,^\circ$ and $QR = 7.9\,\text{cm}$. Find PR.

7. In $\triangle ABC$, $BC = 161\,\text{cm}$, $\widehat{A} = 41\,^\circ$ and $\widehat{B} = 76\,^\circ$. Find AC.

The sine rule can be used when one angle is obtuse.

In $\triangle ABC$, $AB = 6 \text{ cm}$, $\widehat{B} = 25°$ and $\widehat{C} = 110°$. Find AC.

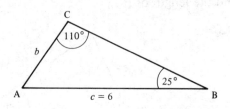

From the sine rule $\quad \dfrac{a}{\sin A} = \boxed{\dfrac{b}{\sin B} = \dfrac{c}{\sin C}}$

$$\frac{b}{\sin 25°} = \frac{6}{\sin 110°}$$

$$b = \frac{6 \sin 25°}{\sin 110°}$$

$$= \frac{6 \times 0.4226}{0.9397}$$

$$= 2.6983$$

Therefore $AC = 2.70 \text{ cm}$ correct to 3 s.f.

8. In $\triangle ABC$, $\widehat{A} = 124°$, $\widehat{B} = 31°$ and $AC = 41 \text{ cm}$. Find BC.

9. In $\triangle PQR$, $\widehat{Q} = 43°$, $\widehat{R} = 106°$ and $PQ = 7.9 \text{ cm}$. Find PR.

10. In $\triangle LMN$, $LM = 831 \text{ cm}$, $\widehat{L} = 27°$ and $\widehat{N} = 114°$. Find MN.

11. In $\triangle DEF$, $EF = 51 \text{ cm}$, $\widehat{D} = 52°$ and $\widehat{F} = 98°$. Find DE.

12. In $\triangle ABC$, $AC = 62.7 \text{ cm}$, $\widehat{B} = 122°$ and $\widehat{C} = 35°$. Find AB.

13. In $\triangle PQR$, $\widehat{Q} = 25°$, $PQ = 8 \text{ cm}$ and $\widehat{R} = 37°$. Find PR.

Sometimes the third angle of a triangle must be found before two suitable fractions can be selected from the sine rule.

In $\triangle ABC$, $AC = 4\,cm$, $\widehat{A} = 35°$ and $\widehat{C} = 70°$. Find BC.

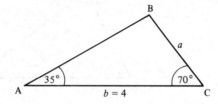

(The two sides involved are a and b so we must use $\widehat{A}$ and $\widehat{B}$ in the sine rule.)

First find $\widehat{B}$

$$\widehat{B} = 180° - 35° - 70° = 75°$$

From the sine rule $\boxed{\dfrac{a}{\sin A} = \dfrac{b}{\sin B}} = \dfrac{c}{\sin C}$

$$\frac{a}{\sin 35°} = \frac{4}{\sin 75°}$$

$$a = \frac{4\sin 35°}{\sin 75°}$$

$$= \frac{4 \times 0.5736}{0.9659}$$

$$= 2.3754$$

Therefore $BC = 2.38\,cm$ correct to 3 s.f.

14. In $\triangle ABC$, $\widehat{B} = 81°$, $\widehat{C} = 63°$ and $BC = 13\,cm$. Find AB.

15. In $\triangle PQR$, $PQ = 15.3\,cm$, $\widehat{P} = 106°$ and $\widehat{Q} = 21°$. Find QR.

16. In $\triangle LMN$, $LN = 108\,cm$, $\widehat{L} = 59°$ and $\widehat{N} = 44°$. Find LM.

17. In $\triangle PQR$, $\widehat{P} = 61°$, $\widehat{R} = 102°$ and $PR = 67\,cm$. Find PQ.

The sine rule can be used twice if the lengths of two sides are required.

In $\triangle ABC$, $BC = 71$ cm, $\widehat{A} = 62°$ and $\widehat{B} = 54°$. Find AB and AC.

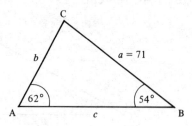

(Because $\widehat{A}$, $\widehat{B}$ and a are given we will first find b.)

From the sine rule $\qquad \dfrac{b}{\sin B} = \dfrac{a}{\sin A}$

$$\frac{b}{\sin 54°} = \frac{71}{\sin 62°}$$

$$b = \frac{71 \sin 54°}{\sin 62°} = \frac{71 \times 0.8090}{0.8829} = 65.05$$

Therefore $AC = 65.1$ cm correct to 3 s.f.

(Now to find c we need $\widehat{C}$.)

$$\widehat{C} = 180° - 62° - 54° = 64°$$

From the sine rule $\qquad \dfrac{c}{\sin C} = \dfrac{a}{\sin A}$

$$\frac{c}{\sin 64°} = \frac{71}{\sin 62°}$$

$$c = \frac{71 \sin 64°}{\sin 62°} = \frac{71 \times 0.8988}{0.8829} = 72.27$$

Therefore $AB = 72.3$ cm correct to 3 s.f.

(Note that, to find c we equate $\dfrac{c}{\sin C}$ to $\dfrac{a}{\sin A}$ and not to $\dfrac{b}{\sin B}$. This is because a is given in the question, whereas b was calculated in the first section, and its value might not be correct.)

18. In △PQR, $\widehat{P} = 61°$, $\widehat{Q} = 54°$ and PR = 7 cm. Find QR and PQ.

19. In △ABC, AB = 13 cm, $\widehat{B} = 40°$ and $\widehat{C} = 67°$. Find BC and CA.

20. In △PQR, $r = 191$, $\widehat{P} = 37°$ and $\widehat{Q} = 64°$. Find p and q.

21. If $\widehat{A} = 49°$, $\widehat{C} = 82°$ and $b = 27$, find a and c in △ABC.

Complete the following table, which refers to a triangle ABC.

	AB	BC	AC	$\widehat{A}$	$\widehat{B}$	$\widehat{C}$
22.		19 cm			53°	76°
23.			146 cm	72°		69°
24.	81 cm			37°	59°	
25.			97 cm		48°	61°
26.	12 cm			54°	102°	
27.			9.9 cm	26°		121°

28.

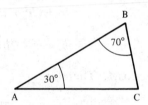

a) Given that BC = 6 cm, find AB

b) Given that AC = 11 cm, find BC.

THE COSINE RULE

It is not always possible to use the sine rule to find the unknown facts about a triangle. For instance, if the three sides of △ABC are given, but no angles are known, it is impossible to select two equal fractions from the sine rule so that only one unknown quantity is involved.

$$\frac{a}{\text{unknown}} = \frac{b}{\text{unknown}} = \frac{c}{\text{unknown}}$$

For cases like this, where the sine rule fails, we need a different formula.

Consider a triangle ABC divided into two right-angled triangles by a line BD, perpendicular to AC. Let the length of AD be x so that $DC = b - x$.

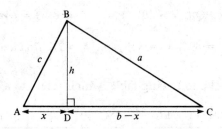

Using Pythagoras' Theorem in triangles ABD and CBD gives

$$c^2 = h^2 + x^2$$

and $\qquad\qquad a^2 = h^2 + (b - x)^2$

$$= h^2 + b^2 - 2bx + x^2$$

$$= b^2 + (h^2 + x^2) - 2bx$$

$$= b^2 + c^2 - 2bx$$

In $\triangle ABD$, $x = c \cos A$. Therefore

$$a^2 = b^2 + c^2 - 2bc \cos A$$

This result is called the *cosine rule*.

If we were to draw a line from A perpendicular to BC, or from C perpendicular to AB, similar equations would be obtained, i.e.

$$b^2 = c^2 + a^2 - 2ac \cos B$$

$$c^2 = a^2 + b^2 - 2ab \cos C$$

Note that, in each version of the cosine rule, the side on the left and the angle on the right have the same letter.

When using the cosine rule it is a good idea to put brackets round the term containing the angle

i.e. $\qquad\qquad a^2 = b^2 + c^2 - (2bc \cos A)$

EXERCISE 15i

In a triangle ABC, AB $= 6$ cm, BC $= 7$ cm and $\widehat{B} = 60°$. Find AC.

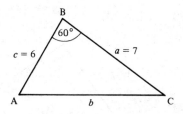

(The unknown side is b, and $\widehat{B}$ is known, so we use the version of the cosine rule that starts with b^2.)

$$b^2 = c^2 + a^2 - (2ca \cos B)$$
$$= 6^2 + 7^2 - (2 \times 6 \times 7 \cos 60°)$$
$$= 36 + 49 - (84 \times 0.5)$$
$$= 85 - 42 = 43$$
$$\Rightarrow \qquad b = \sqrt{43} = 6.557$$

Therefore AC $= 6.56$ cm correct to 3 s.f.

The lengths of the sides of each triangle are measured in centimetres.

1. In $\triangle$ABC, $\widehat{A} = 54°$, $b = 7$ and $c = 5$. Find a.

2. In $\triangle$ABC, $a = 4$, $b = 11$ and $\widehat{C} = 33°$. Find c.

3. In $\triangle$PQR, PQ $= 5$ cm, QR $= 8$ cm and $\widehat{Q} = 68°$. Find PR.

4. In $\triangle$LMN, LM $= 26$ cm, $\widehat{M} = 45°$ and MN $= 17$ cm. Find LN.

5. In $\triangle$PQR, $\widehat{Q} = 51°$, $p = 9$ and $r = 5$. Find q.

6. In $\triangle$ABC, $c = 12$, $b = 13$ and $\widehat{A} = 69°$. Find a.

7. In $\triangle$LMN, $\widehat{L} = 37.6°$, $m = 21.7$ and $n = 13.8$. Find l.

8. In $\triangle$DEF, EF $= 12.4$ cm, DF $= 9.7$ cm and $\widehat{F} = 58.6°$. Find DE.

9. In $\triangle$PQR, PR $= 8.9$ cm, PQ $= 11.2$ cm and $\widehat{P} = 47.1°$. Find QR.

If the given angle is obtuse its cosine is negative and extra care is needed in using the cosine rule; brackets are even more helpful in this case.

Triangle ABC is such that BC = 11 cm, AC = 8 cm and $\widehat{C} = 130°$. Find AB.

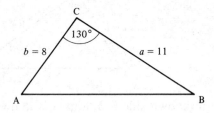

Using the cosine rule

$$c^2 = a^2 + b^2 - (2ab \cos C)$$
$$= 11^2 + 8^2 - (2 \times 11 \times 8 \cos 130°)$$
$$= 121 + 64 - (176 \times [-0.6428])$$
$$= 185 + 113.13$$
$$= 298.13$$
$$\Rightarrow \qquad c = \sqrt{298.13}$$
$$= 17.27$$

Therefore   AB = 17.3 cm   correct to 3 s.f.

10. In $\triangle$ABC, AB = 8 cm, AC = 11 cm and $\widehat{A}$ = 113°. Find BC.

11. In $\triangle$PQR, QR = 14 cm, PR = 10 cm and $\widehat{R}$ = 128°. Find PQ.

12. In $\triangle$LMN, LM = 35 cm, MN = 21 cm and $\widehat{M}$ = 97°. Find LN.

13. In $\triangle$ABC, a = 19, b = 12 and $\widehat{C}$ = 136°. Find c.

14. In $\triangle$PQR, q = 2.4, r = 3.7 and $\widehat{P}$ = 100°. Find p.

15. In $\triangle$DEF, d = 9, f = 12 and $\widehat{E}$ = 106°. Find e.

16. In $\triangle$XYZ, XY = 47 cm, XZ = 81 cm and $\widehat{X}$ = 94°. Find YZ.

17. In $\triangle$ABC, AC = 6.4 cm, BC = 3.9 cm and $\widehat{C}$ = 121°. Find AB.

The cosine rule can be used to find an unknown angle when three sides of a triangle are given.

In $\triangle ABC$, $AB = 5$ cm, $BC = 6$ cm and $CA = 8$ cm. Find
a) the smallest angle   b) the largest angle,   in the triangle.

a)

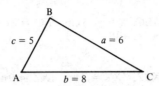

(The smallest angle is opposite to the shortest side, so we are looking for $\widehat{C}$ and will use the cosine rule starting with c^2.)

$$c^2 = a^2 + b^2 - (2ab\cos C)$$
$$5^2 = 6^2 + 8^2 - (2 \times 6 \times 8 \cos C)$$
$$25 = 36 + 64 - (96\cos C)$$

$96\cos C + 25 = 100$ (adding $96\cos C$ to each side)

$96\cos C = 75$ (subtracting 25 from each side)

$$\cos C = \frac{75}{96} = 0.7813$$

Therefore $\widehat{C} = 38.6°$ to 1 d.p.

b) (The largest angle is opposite to the longest side, so we are looking for $\widehat{B}$ and will use the cosine rule starting with b^2.)

$$b^2 = c^2 + a^2 - (2ca\cos B)$$
$$8^2 = 5^2 + 6^2 - (2 \times 5 \times 6 \cos B)$$
$$64 = 25 + 36 - (60\cos B)$$

$60\cos B = 61 - 64 = -3$

$$\cos B = \frac{-3}{60} = -0.05$$

(Because $\cos B$ is negative $\widehat{B}$ must be an obtuse angle.)

Therefore $\widehat{B} = 92.9°$ to 1 d.p.

18. In △ABC, AB = 8 cm, BC = 4 cm and AC = 5 cm. Find $\widehat{A}$.

19. In △PQR, PQ = 4 cm, QR = 2 cm and PR = 5 cm. Find $\widehat{Q}$.

20. In △LMN, LM = 8 cm, MN = 5 cm and LN = 6 cm. Find $\widehat{N}$.

21. In △ABC, AB = 3 cm, BC = 2 cm and AC = 4 cm. Find the smallest angle in △ABC.

22. In △XYZ, XY = 7 cm, XZ = 9 cm and YZ = 5 cm. Find the largest angle in △XYZ.

23. In △DEF, DE = 2.1 cm, EF = 3.6 cm and DF = 2.7 cm. Find the middle-sized angle in △DEF.

24.

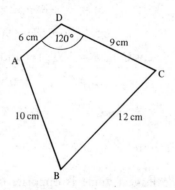

Use the information given in the diagram to find

a) the length of AC   b) $\widehat{ABC}$

25. In △ABC, AB = 5.2 cm, $\widehat{A}$ = 32° and BC = 2.9 cm.

a) Use the sine rule to find the value for sin C and show that the two possible values for $\widehat{C}$ are 71.8° and 108.2°.

b) Draw sketches of △ABC (make AC the base) to show that for each of the values of $\widehat{C}$ you found in part (a) it is possible to draw a triangle. For each triangle
   i) write down the value for $\widehat{B}$
   ii) find the length of AC.

   (The triangle as defined in this question is *ambiguous*, as it is possible to construct two different triangles with the given measurements.)

THE AMBIGUOUS CASE

In question 25 of the last exercise we saw that it is sometimes possible to draw two triangles when two sides and a non-included angle are given. It must not be thought that it is *always* possible to draw two triangles when this data is given. The questions in the next exercise will help you to understand this.

EXERCISE 15j

In this exercise the data refers to triangle ABC and uses standard notation. All lengths are measured in centimetres.

1. Show that two different triangles are possible given that $a = 12$, $c = 16$ and $\widehat{A} = 35°$.

2. Show that it is impossible to draw a triangle which $a = 8$, $b = 12$ and $\widehat{A} = 48°$.

3. Is it possible to draw a triangle in which $a = 8.4$, $b = 16.8$ and $\widehat{A} = 30°$? Give a reason for your answer.

4. Is it possible to draw a triangle in which $a = 21$, $b = 26$ and $\widehat{B} = 35°$? Justify your answer.

5. How many triangles can be drawn when $a = 12.5$, $b = 8$ and $\widehat{A} = 44°$.

6. Find the unknown angles and side of the triangle in which $a = 4.2$, $b = 5.42$ and $\widehat{A} = 42°$.

From the questions in the previous exercise it is possible to deduce the feasibility of drawing a triangle ABC when a, b and $\widehat{A}$ are given. These conditions are given here for interest.

1. If $a < b \sin A$ there is no solution.

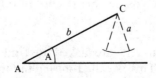

2. If $a = b \sin A$ there is one solution and $\hat{B} = 90°$.

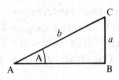

3. If $a > b \sin A$ and $a < b$ there are two solutions.

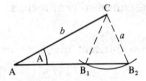

4. If $a > b \sin A$ and $a > b$ there is one solution.

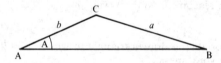

MIXED QUESTIONS

If three independent facts are given about the sides and/or angles of a triangle and we are asked to find one or more of the unknown quantities, we must first decide whether to use the sine rule or the cosine rule.

The sine rule is the easier to work out so it is chosen whenever possible and that is when the given information includes a side and the angle opposite to it (remember that, if the two angles are given the third angle is also known). The cosine rule is chosen only when the sine rule cannot be used.

In some questions we are asked to find *all* the remaining information about a triangle. This is called *solving* the triangle.

EXERCISE 15k

In a triangle LMN, LM = 9 cm, MN = 11 cm and $\widehat{M}$ = 70°.
Find LN.

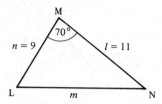

(As we are not given an angle and the side opposite to it, the
sine rule cannot be used so we use the cosine rule.)

$$m^2 = l^2 + n^2 - (2ln \cos M)$$
$$= 11^2 + 9^2 - (2 \times 11 \times 9 \cos 70°)$$
$$= 121 + 81 - (198 \times 0.3420)$$
$$= 202 - 67.72 = 134.28$$
$$\Rightarrow \qquad m = \sqrt{134.28} = 11.59$$

Therefore LN = 11.6 cm correct to 3 s.f.

Fill in the blank spaces in the table.

	a	b	c	$\widehat{A}$	$\widehat{B}$	$\widehat{C}$
1.	11.7			39°	66°	
2.		128	86	63°		
3.			65		79°	55°
4.	16.3	12.7				106°
5.		263			47°	74°
6.	14			53°	82°	
7.			17.8	107°		35°
8.		16	23	81°		
9.	13.2		19.6		120°	
10.		22.6			50°	83°

Solve $\triangle PQR$ given that $PQ = 11\,\text{cm}$, $\widehat{R} = 82°$ and $P = 47°$.

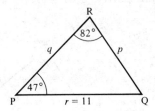

(We are given r and $\widehat{R}$ so we can use the sine rule to find p.)

From the sine rule $\qquad \dfrac{p}{\sin P} = \dfrac{r}{\sin R}$

$$\dfrac{p}{\sin 47°} = \dfrac{11}{\sin 82°}$$

$$p = \dfrac{11\sin 47°}{\sin 82°}$$

$$= \dfrac{11 \times 0.7314}{0.9903} = 8.124$$

Therefore $QR = 8.12\,\text{cm}$ correct to 3 s.f.

(Now to find q we need $\widehat{Q}$ in order to use the sine rule.)

$$\widehat{Q} = 180° - 47° - 82° = 51°$$

From the sine rule $\qquad \dfrac{q}{\sin Q} = \dfrac{r}{\sin R}$

$$\dfrac{q}{\sin 51°} = \dfrac{11}{\sin 82°}$$

$$q = \dfrac{11\sin 51°}{\sin 82°}$$

$$= \dfrac{11 \times 0.7771}{0.9903} = 8.632$$

Therefore $PR = 8.63\,\text{cm}$ correct to 3 s.f.

(All sides and angles have now been found, so the triangle has been solved.)

11. Solve $\triangle ABC$ given that $a = 8.4$, $\widehat{A} = 52°$, $\widehat{B} = 74°$.

12. Solve $\triangle PQR$ given that $p = 12.6$, $q = 7.4$, $r = 16.3$.

13. Solve $\triangle LMN$ given that $m = 15$, $n = 18$, $\widehat{L} = 64°$.

14. Solve $\triangle DEF$ given that $d = 27$, $e = 19$, $f = 34$.

THE AREA OF A TRIANGLE

We already know that the area, A, of a triangle can be found by multiplying half the base, b, by the perpendicular height, h, i.e.

$$A = \tfrac{1}{2}bh$$

In some cases, however, the perpendicular height is not given, so an alternative formula is needed.

Consider a triangle ABC in which the lengths of BC and CA, and the angle C, are known.

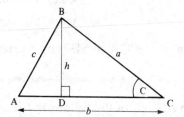

The line BD, drawn from B perpendicular to AC, is a perpendicular height of the triangle. Therefore the area of the triangle is $\tfrac{1}{2}bh$.

But, in triangle BDC, $\sin C = \dfrac{h}{a}$ i.e. $h = a\sin C$

Therefore the area of the triangle is $\tfrac{1}{2}ba\sin C$

i.e. $$A = \tfrac{1}{2}ab\sin C$$

Alternatively we could draw perpendicular heights from A or from C, giving similar expressions for the area,

i.e. $A = \tfrac{1}{2}bc\sin A$ and $A = \tfrac{1}{2}ac\sin B$

Note that in each of the these expressions for the area, two sides and the included angle are involved, i.e. in general

Area $= \tfrac{1}{2} \times$ product of two sides $\times$ sine of included angle

EXERCISE 15I

Find the area of △PQR if $\widehat{P} = 120°$, PQ = 132 cm and PR = 95 cm.

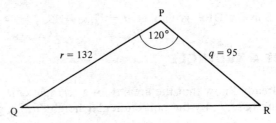

(r and q are given, and $\widehat{P}$ is the included angle.)

$$A = \tfrac{1}{2}qr\sin P$$
$$= \tfrac{1}{2} \times 95 \times 132 \times \sin 120°$$
$$= \tfrac{1}{2} \times 95 \times 132 \times 0.8660$$
$$= 5429$$

The area of △PQR = 5430 cm² correct to 3 s.f.

Find the area of each of the following triangles.

1. △ABC; AC = 11.6 cm, BC = 14.2 cm, $\widehat{C} = 80°$

2. △PQR; $p = 217$, $q = 196$, $\widehat{R} = 117°$

3. △XYZ; XY = 81 cm, XZ = 69 cm, $\widehat{X} = 69°$

4. △LMN; $m = 29.3$, $n = 40.6$, $\widehat{L} = 74°$

5. △ABC; $a = 18.1$, $c = 14.2$, $\widehat{B} = 101°$

6. △PQR; PQ = 234 cm, PR = 196 cm, $\widehat{P} = 84°$

7. △XYZ; $x = 9$, $z = 10$, $\widehat{Y} = 52°$

8. △ABC; AC = 3.7 m, AB = 4.1 m, $\widehat{A} = 116°$

9. △DEF; EF = 72 cm, DF = 58 cm, $\widehat{F} = 76°$

10. △PQR; $q = 20.3$, $p = 16.7$, $\widehat{R} = 61°$

In triangle ABC, AB = 15 cm, $\widehat{A} = 60°$ and $\widehat{B} = 81°$. Find
a) BC   b) the area of $\triangle ABC$.

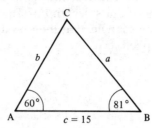

a) (In order to use the sine rule to find a we need $\widehat{C}$.)

$$\widehat{C} = 180° - 60° - 81° = 39°$$

From the sine rule, $\boxed{\dfrac{a}{\sin A}} = \dfrac{b}{\sin B} = \boxed{\dfrac{c}{\sin C}}$

$$\frac{a}{\sin 60°} = \frac{15}{\sin 39°}$$

$$a = \frac{15 \sin 60°}{\sin 39°}$$

$$= \frac{15 \times 0.8660}{0.6293} = 20.64$$

Therefore BC = 20.6 cm correct to 3 s.f.

b) (We know two sides, a and c, and the included angle is $\widehat{B}$.)

$$A = \tfrac{1}{2}ac \sin B$$

$$= \tfrac{1}{2} \times 20.64 \times 15 \sin 81°$$

$$= \tfrac{1}{2} \times 20.64 \times 15 \times 0.9877 = 152.8$$

Therefore the area of $\triangle ABC$ is 153 cm² correct to 3 s.f.

11. In $\triangle ABC$, BC = 7 cm, AC = 8 cm, AB = 10 cm. Find $\widehat{C}$ and the area of the triangle.

12. $\triangle PQR$ is such that PQ = 11.7 cm, $\widehat{Q} = 49°$ and $\widehat{R} = 63°$. Find PR and the area of $\triangle PQR$.

13. In $\triangle LMN$, LM = 16 cm, MN = 19 cm and the area is 114.5 cm². Find $\widehat{M}$ and LN.

14. The area of $\triangle ABC$ is 27.3 cm². If BC = 12.8 cm and $\widehat{C} = 107°$ find AC.

PROBLEMS

In many problems a description of a situation is given which can be illustrated by a diagram. Our aim is to find, in this diagram, a triangle in which three facts about sides and/or angles are known. A second diagram, showing only this triangle, can then be drawn and the appropriate rules of trigonometry applied to it.

EXERCISE 15m

From a port P a ship Q is 20 km away on a bearing of 125° and a ship R is 35 km away on a bearing of 050°. Find the distance between the two ships.

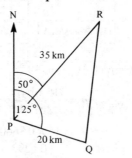 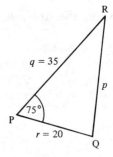

(PQR is a suitable triangle since PR and PQ are known and $Q\hat{P}R$ can be found.)

$$Q\hat{P}R = 125° - 50° = 75°$$

(The distance between the ships is QR, so we must calculate p in $\triangle PQR$.)

In $\triangle PQR$, using the cosine rule gives

$$p^2 = q^2 + r^2 - (2qr\cos P)$$
$$= 35^2 + 20^2 - (2 \times 35 \times 20 \times \cos 75°)$$
$$= 1225 + 400 - (1400 \times 0.2588)$$
$$= 1625 - 362.3 = 1262.7$$
$$\Rightarrow \qquad p = 35.53$$

Therefore the distance between the ships is 35.5 km correct to 3 s.f.

In a quadrilateral ABCD, AB = 5 cm, BC = 6 cm, CD = 7 cm, $\widehat{ABC} = 120°$ and $\widehat{ACD} = 90°$. Find

a) the length of the diagonal AC   b) the area of △ABC

c) the area of △ADC   d) the area of the quadrilateral.

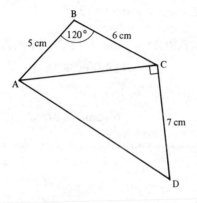

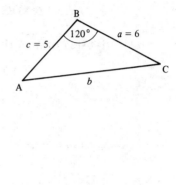

a) In △ABC, using the cosine rule gives

$$b^2 = c^2 + a^2 - (2ca \cos B)$$

$$= 5^2 + 6^2 - (2 \times 5 \times 6 \cos 120°)$$

$$= 25 + 36 - (60 \times [-0.5])$$

$$= 61 + 30$$

$$= 91$$

$$\Rightarrow \qquad b = \sqrt{91}$$

$$= 9.539$$

Therefore AC = 9.54 cm correct to 3 s.f.

b) For △ABC, $A = \frac{1}{2}ac \sin B$

$$= \frac{1}{2} \times 5 \times 6 \times \sin 120°$$

$$= 15 \times 0.8660$$

$$= 12.99$$

Area △ABC = 13.0 cm² correct to 3 s.f.

c) ($\triangle$ADC is a right-angled triangle, so we use $\frac{1}{2}$ base $\times$ perpendicular height for its area.)

$$A = \tfrac{1}{2}bh$$

$$= \tfrac{1}{2} \times AC \times CD$$

$$= \tfrac{1}{2} \times 9.539 \times 7$$

$$= 33.38$$

Area $\triangle$ADC $= 33.4\,\text{cm}^2$ correct to 3 s.f.

d) Area of quadrilateral ABCD $=$ area $\triangle$ABC $+$ area $\triangle$ADC

$$= 12.99\,\text{cm}^2 + 33.38\,\text{cm}^2$$

$$= 46.37\,\text{cm}^2$$

$$= 46.4\,\text{cm}^2$$ correct to 3 s.f.

1. Starting from a point A, an aeroplane flies for 40 km on a bearing of 169°
to B, and then for 65 km on a bearing of 057° to C. Find the distance
between A and C.

2.

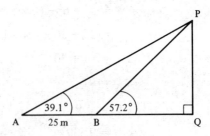

From two points A and B, on level ground, the angles of elevation of the top
of a radio aerial PQ are found to be 39.1° and 57.2°. If the distance between
A and B is 25 m, find

a) $A\widehat{P}B$

b) the height of the radio aerial.

3. A children's slide has a flight of steps of length 2.7 m and the length of the
straight slide is 4.2 m. If the distance from the bottom of the steps to the
bottom of the slide is 4.9 m find, to the nearest degree, the angle between the
steps and the slide.

4.

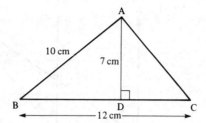

Using the information given in the diagram

a) find the area of $\triangle ABC$

b) use the formula   area $\triangle ABC = \frac{1}{2}ac \sin B$ to find $\widehat{B}$

c) find AC.

5. A helicopter leaves a heliport A and flies 2.4 km on a bearing of 154° to a checkpoint B. It then flies due east to its base C. If the bearing of C from A is 112° find the distances AC and BC. The helicopter flies at a constant speed throughout and takes 5 minutes to fly from A to C. Find its speed.

6. P, Q and R are three points on level ground. From Q, P is 60 m away on a bearing of 325° and R is 94 m away on a bearing of 040°.

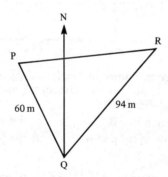

a) Find $\cos Q$.

b) Using the cosine rule, or otherwise, find the distance between P and R.

7. ABCD is a quadrilateral in which AB = 4.1 cm, BC = 3.7 cm, CD = 5.3 cm, $\widehat{ABC} = 66°$ and $\widehat{ADC} = 51°$. Find

a) the length of the diagonal AC

b) $\widehat{CAD}$

c) the area of quadrilateral ABCD, considering it as split into two triangles by the diagonal AC.

8.

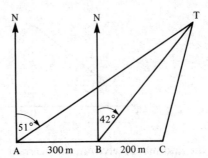

The diagram shows three survey points, A, B and C, which are on an east–west line on level ground. From point A the bearing of the foot of a tower T is 051°, while from B the bearing of the tower is 042°. Find

a) $T\widehat{A}B$ and $A\widehat{T}B$ b) AT   c) CT.

9.

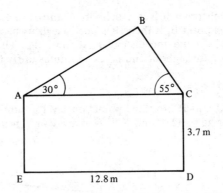

The diagram shows the end wall of a bungalow. The roof has one face inclined at 30° to the horizontal and the other inclined at 55° to the horizontal. Find

a) the length of AB   b) the length of BC
c) the area of the end wall   d) the height of B above ED.

10. In a quadrilateral ABCD, DC is of length 3 cm, the length of the diagonal BD is 10 cm, $B\widehat{A}D = 30°$, $B\widehat{D}A = 45°$ and $B\widehat{D}C = 60°$. Calculate
a) the length of (i) AB (ii) BC   b) the area of the quadrilateral.

11. The points A, B and C are on the circumference of a circle with centre O and radius 10 cm. The lengths of the chords AB and BC are 8 cm and 3 cm respectively. Calculate

a) $A\widehat{O}B$ b) $B\widehat{O}C$ c) the length of the chord AC
d) the area of quadrilateral ABCO.

(Remember that OA = OB = OC = 10 cm.)

12.

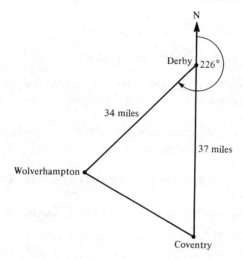

The diagram represents the positions of Derby, Coventry and Wolverhampton.
Coventry is 37 miles due south of Derby.
Wolverhampton is 34 miles from Derby on a bearing of 226°.

a) Calculate the distance and bearing of Wolverhampton from Coventry.

b) How far is Wolverhampton

    i) north of Coventry   ii) west of Derby ?

MIXED EXERCISES

EXERCISE 15n

1. If $\cos A = \frac{5}{13}$ and $\widehat{A}$ is acute, find $\sin A$ and $\tan A$.

2. Find two angles between $0°$ and $180°$ for which the sine is 0.3667 (a calculator may be used).

3. If $\cos P = 0.43$ find, without using a calculator, $\cos(180° - P)$.

4. In $\triangle ABC$, $BC = 161\,\text{cm}$, $\widehat{B} = 109°$ and $\widehat{A} = 51°$. Find AC.

5. A triangle PQR is such that $QR = 7.6\,\text{cm}$, $PQ = 5.9\,\text{cm}$ and $\widehat{Q} = 107°$. Find PR.

6. Find the area of $\triangle ABC$ if $AB = 8.2\,\text{cm}$, $BC = 11.3\,\text{cm}$ and $\widehat{B} = 125°$.

7. A boat sails $11\,\text{km}$ from a harbour on a bearing of $220°$. It then sails $15\,\text{km}$ on a bearing of $340°$. How far is the boat from the harbour ?

EXERCISE 15p

1. If $\sin P = \sin 37°$ and $\widehat{P}$ is obtuse, find $\widehat{P}$.

2. $\cos x° = 0.123$ and $\cos y° = -0.123$. If $x°$ is acute and $y°$ is obtuse find y in terms of x.

3. If $\widehat{A}$ is an acute angle, complete the following statements.
   a) $\cos(180° - A) = \dots$ b) $\sin(180° - A) = \dots$ c) $-\cos A = \dots$

4. In $\triangle PQR$, $\widehat{Q} = 61°$, $PR = 14.7\,\text{cm}$ and $\widehat{R} = 84°$. Find PQ.

5. Find the lengths of AB and BC in $\triangle ABC$ if $AC = 7.3\,\text{cm}$, $\widehat{A} = 49°$ and $\widehat{C} = 78°$.

6. In $\triangle LMN$, $MN = 14.2\,\text{cm}$, $LN = 17.3\,\text{cm}$ and $LM = 11.8\,\text{cm}$. Find
   a) the smallest angle   b) the largest angle,   in the triangle.

7. A flower bed in a park is in the form of a quadrilateral ABCD in which $AB = 4\,\text{m}$, $\widehat{B} = 90°$, $BC = 6.2\,\text{m}$, $CD = 7.3\,\text{m}$ and $DA = 5\,\text{m}$. Find
   a) the angle $A\widehat{D}C$ b) the area of the flower bed
   c) the amount of mulch needed to cover the bed evenly to a depth of 8 cm.

16 FUNCTIONS

DEFINITIONS AND NOTATION

Consider the straight line given by the equation $y = 6 - 2x$. To find the y-coordinate on this line when $x = -3$,

$$y = 6 - 2(-3) = 6 + 6 = 12$$

Similarly, if the nth term of a sequence is $n^2 + 2$, then the sixth term is $6^2 + 2$ i.e. 38.

In both of the above cases we start with one number, apply a rule, and get another number.

A rule that changes one number into another number is called a *function*. The function 'halve' can be illustrated by this flow chart.

The letter f is used to represent a function. The *result* of applying a function to x is written $f(x)$. (We read this 'f of x'.)

Hence, when f is the function 'halve' we write $f(x) = \frac{1}{2}x$.
Similarly, if $f(x) = x^2$, then the function is 'square'.

Also, if $f(x) = 2x - 5$, then $f(3)$ means the result of applying f to the number 3,

i.e. $$f(3) = 2(3) - 5 = 1$$

The set of numbers that we put into a function is called the *domain* of the function.

The set of numbers that result from using the function is called the *range* of the function.

EXERCISE 16a

1. Describe the given functions in words

a) $f(x) = 2x$ b) $f(x) = x + 2$ c) $f(x) = \dfrac{1}{x}$ d) $f(x) = x^3$

2. Draw a flow chart to illustrate the functions

a) $f(x) = 3x + 1$ b) $f(x) = 2 - 2x$ c) $f(x) = x^2 - 1$ d) $f(x) = \dfrac{1}{1+x}$

If $f(x) = \frac{1}{2}x^2 - 4$ find $f(-2)$.

$$f(x) = \tfrac{1}{2}x^2 - 4$$

$$\therefore \qquad\qquad f(-2) = \tfrac{1}{2}(-2)^2 - 4$$

$$= \tfrac{1}{2}(4) - 4$$

$$= -2$$

---

3. Given that $f(x) = 2x - 1$ find
a) $f(0)$ b) $f(4)$ c) $f(-1)$ d) $f(-5)$

4. If $f(x) = 3 - 4x$ find
a) $f(0)$ b) $f(1)$ c) $f(-1)$ d) $f(-\frac{1}{2})$

5. If $f(x) = (1-x)^2$ find
a) $f(1)$ b) $f(0)$ c) $f(-1)$ d) $f(-2)$

6. If $f(x) = x^2 - 2x + 3$ find
a) $f(4)$ b) $f(0)$ c) $f(3)$ d) $f(-1)$

7. The function f is defined by $f(x) = \dfrac{3}{1+x}, x \neq -1$. Find

a) $f(2)$ b) $f(-2)$ c) $f(0)$ d) $f(-4)$

8. The function f is defined by $f(x) = 2x - \dfrac{4}{x}, x \neq 0$. Find

a) $f(2)$ b) $f(4)$ c) $f(-1)$ d) $f(-8)$
Explain why this function cannot be applied to zero.

If $f(x) = x^2 - 4$ find the values of x for which $f(x) = 5$.

$$f(x) = x^2 - 4$$

If $f(x) = 5$ then
$$x^2 - 4 = 5$$
$$x^2 = 9$$
$$x = \pm\sqrt{9}$$

$x = 3$ or $x = -3$.

In each question from 9 to 17 find the value(s) of x for which the given function has the given value.

9. $f(x) = 5x - 4$, $f(x) = 2$

10. $f(x) = \dfrac{1}{x}$, $f(x) = 5$

11. $f(x) = 3 - x$, $f(x) = -4$

12. $f(x) = 2x + 1$, $f(x) = -9$

13. $f(x) = x^2$, $f(x) = 9$

14. $f(x) = \dfrac{1}{x^2}$, $f(x) = 1$

15. $f(x) = x^2 - 2x$, $f(x) = 3$

16. $f(x) = x + \dfrac{1}{x}$, $f(x) = 2$

17. $f(x) = (x + 1)(x - 2)$, $f(x) = 0$

18. If $f(x) = x^2 + x - 6$, find
a) $f(1)$ b) $f(-1)$
c) the values of x for which $f(x) = 0$.

19. If $f(x) = x^2 - 2x - 15$, find
a) $f(2)$ b) $f(-2)$
c) the values of x for which
   i) $f(x) = 0$ ii) $f(x) = 9$

20. Given that $f(x) = x^3 - 8$ find

a) $f(0)$ b) $f(1)$

c) the value of x for which $f(x) = 0$

d) the value of x for which $f(x) = 1$.

21. Find the value of k if $f(3) = 3$ where

a) $f(x) = kx - 1$ b) $f(x) = x^2 - k$.

22. The function f is defined by $f(x) = kx^2 - 5$

a) If $k = 2$, find   i) $f(-3)$ ii) $f(1)$

b) If $f(4) = 11$, find k.

23. The function f is defined by $f(x) = x^2 + x - 4$.

a) Find $f(0)$, $f(1)$ and $f(2)$.

b) Is $f(x)$ increasing or decreasing in value as x increases in value from zero ?

c) *Estimate* the value of x, greater than zero, for which $f(x) = 0$.

24. The function f is defined by $f(x) = 6 - x$.

a) Find $f(-2)$, $f(0)$ and $f(4)$.

b) Is $f(x)$ increasing or decreasing in value as x increases in value ?

c) Give the value of x for which $f(x) = 0$.

d) Give the range of values of x for which $f(x)$ is negative.

25. Given that $f(x) = x^2 + 2$

a) Find $f(0)$, $f(2)$, $f(4)$, $f(10)$.

b) Is $f(x)$ increasing or decreasing in value as x increases in value from zero ?

c) Find $f(0)$, $f(-1)$, $f(-3)$, $f(-10)$.

d) What is the least possible value for $f(x)$?

GRAPHICAL REPRESENTATION

Consider the function $f(x) = 4x - 2$ for all values of x.

If we write $y = f(x)$ then the equation $y = 4x - 2$ can be used to give a graphical representation of $f(x)$.

Now $y = 4x - 2$ is the equation of a straight line with gradient 4 and y intercept -2.

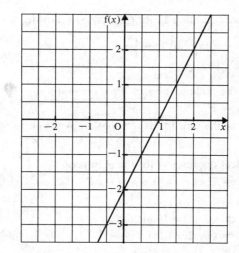

The vertical axis can be labelled either $f(x)$ or y, since $y = f(x)$. A graphical representation like this gives a picture of how $f(x)$ changes in value as the value of x varies.

In this case the graph shows that, as x increases in value the corresponding values of $f(x)$ also increase.

EXERCISE 16b

Draw a sketch graph to represent each of the following functions.

1. $f(x) = 2x$

2. $f(x) = x + 1$

3. $f(x) = x^2$

4. $f(x) = \dfrac{1}{x}, \quad x \neq 0$

5. $f(x) = x^3$

6. $f(x) = 1 - x$

7. $f(x) = 1 - x^2$

8. $f(x) = \dfrac{2}{x^2}, \quad x \neq 0$

9. $f(x) = (x - 1)(x - 2)$

10. $f(x) = x^3 + 2$

11. On the same set of axes draw a sketch graph of
   a) $y = x$ b) $y = x + 1$ c) $y = x - 2$
   Give the transformation that maps the graph of (a) to the graph of (b).

12. On the same set of axes draw a sketch graph of
   a) $y = x^2$ b) $y = x^2 + 1$ c) $y = x^2 - 2$
   Give the transformation that maps the graph of (a) to the graph of (c).

13. Repeat question 12 for each of the following, for $x > 0$.

   a) $y = \dfrac{1}{x}$ b) $y = \dfrac{1}{x} + 1$ c) $y = \dfrac{1}{x} - 1$

14. On the same set of axes draw the graph of
   a) $y = x^2$ b) $y = -x^2$
   Name the transformation that maps the curve for (a) to the curve for (b).

15. Repeat question 14 for the graphs of
   a) $y = x - 1$ b) $y = 1 - x$

16. Repeat question 14 for the graphs of
   a) $y = x^2 + 2$ b) $y = -x^2 - 2$

17. On the same set of axes draw the graphs of
   a) $y = x^2$ b) $y = (x - 2)^2$ c) $y = (x + 3)^2$
   How can you use the graph of $y = x^2$ to sketch the graph of $y = (x - a)^2$?

18. On the same set of axes draw the graphs of
   a) $y = x^3 - 1$ b) $y = 1 - x^3$
   c) $y = (x - 1)^3 - 1$ d) $y = 1 - (x - 1)^3$

TRANSFORMATIONS OF GRAPHS

The previous exercise has shown that if the graph of $y = f(x)$ is given we can obtain sketches of the graphs of several related equations. These are now considered in greater detail.

THE GRAPH OF $y = f(x) + k$

Consider the curves whose equations are

$$y = f(x) \quad \text{and} \quad y = f(x) + k$$

where k is a number.

Questions 11 to 13 of the last exercise show that the curve $y = f(x) + k$ is a translation, parallel to the y-axis, of the curve $y = f(x)$.

If k is positive the translation is k units upwards and if k is negative the translation is k units downwards.

This fact can be very useful when sketching curves. For example, to sketch the curve $y = x^3 - 4$, we can start with the known shape and position of $y = x^3$ and then move it 4 units downwards.

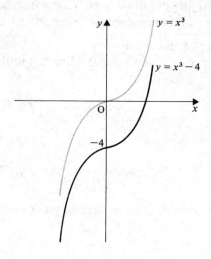

THE GRAPH OF $y = -f(x)$

Questions 14 to 16 of the last exercise show that the curve $y = -f(x)$ is the reflection in the x-axis of the curve $y = f(x)$.

Hence to sketch the curve $y = -\dfrac{1}{x}$, we can start with the known curve $y = \dfrac{1}{x}$ and reflect it in the x-axis.

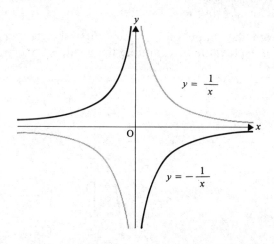

THE GRAPH OF $y = f(x - a)$

Question 17 of the last exercise shows that the curve $y = f(x - a)$ is given by translating the graph of $y = f(x)$ a distance a in the positive direction of the x-axis. If a is negative the graph moves to the left.

Hence to sketch the graph of $y = (x + 3)^2$ i.e. $y = [x - (-3)]^2$, we start by sketching $y = x^2$ and then sliding it 3 units to the left.

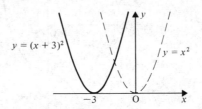

Similarly, if $y = x^3$, we can sketch $y = (x - 2)^3$ as shown below.

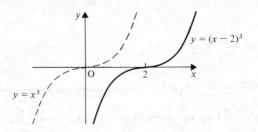

THE GRAPHS OF $y = kf(x)$ AND $y = f(tx)$, $t > 1$

We sketch the graph of $y = kf(x)$ by stretching the graph of $y = f(x)$ by a factor of k in the y direction.

To sketch the graph of $y = 2x^3$, first sketch the graph of $y = x^3$ and then, for each value of x, double the y value.

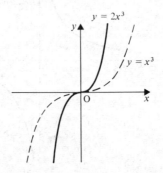

For $t > 1$, we sketch the graph of $y = f(tx)$ by reducing the width of the graph of $y = f(x)$ to $\dfrac{1}{t}$ of its original width.

To sketch the graph of $y = (3x)^2$, first sketch the graph of $y = x^2$ and reduce the width of it to $\frac{1}{3}$ of its original width.

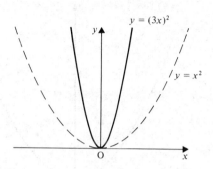

THE GRAPH OF $y = f(-x)$

If
$$f(x) = x^2 - 3x + 2 \qquad [= (x-2)(x-1)]$$

then
$$f(-x) = (-x)^2 - 3(-x) + 2$$
$$= x^2 + 3x + 2 \qquad [= (x+2)(x+1)].$$

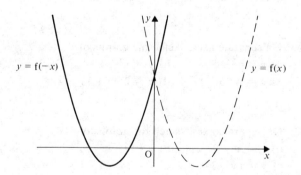

The sketch shows that $y = f(-x)$ is the reflection of $y = f(x)$ in the y-axis.

In general we sketch the graph of $y = f(-x)$ by reflecting the graph of $y = f(x)$ in the y-axis.

EXERCISE 16c

1. Sketch the graph of $y = x^2$, which is given below, four times. Use these, one at a time, to sketch the graph of
   a) $y = x^2 - 3$ b) $y = (x-1)^2$
   c) $y = 2 - x^2$ d) $y = 2x^2$

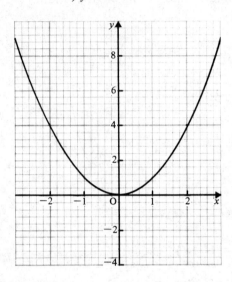

2. Sketch, on separate diagrams, the graphs of
   a) $y = 2x$ b) $y = 2x - 1$
   c) $y = 1 - 2x$ d) $y = 3(1 - 2x)$

3. On separate axes, sketch the graphs of
   a) $y = x^2 + 5$ b) $y = x^2 - 4$
   c) $y = 4 - x^2$ d) $y = 2(x^2 + 5)$

4. On separate axes, sketch the graphs of
   a) $y = x^2 - 9$ b) $y = 9 - x^2$
   c) $y = (x - 3)^2$ d) $y = (x - 3)^2 + 3$

5. Sketch, on separate axes, the graphs of
   a) $y = x^3$ b) $y = -x^3$
   c) $y = 8 - x^3$ d) $y = (x + 1)^3$
   e) $y = x^3 + 3$ f) $y = \frac{1}{2}x^3$

6. This is a sketch of the graph of $f(x) = 2^x$.

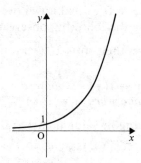

Copy this sketch and, on the same diagram, sketch the graph of
a) $f(x) = -2^x$ b) $f(x) = 1 - 2^x$

7.

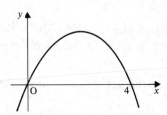

This is a sketch of the graph of $f(x) = 4x - x^2$.
Draw this sketch several times larger and, on the same diagram, sketch the graph of
a) $f(x) = x^2 - 4x$ b) $f(x) = x^2 - 4x - 4$ c) $f(x) = 4(2x) - (2x)^2$

8.

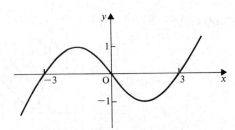

The sketch shows the graph of $y = f(x)$.
On separate diagrams draw sketches of
a) $y = -f(x)$ b) $y = f(-x)$ c) $y = f(x + 3)$
d) $y = f(x - 3)$ e) $y = f(3x)$ f) $y = 2f(x)$

THE RECIPROCAL OF A FUNCTION

If the graph of $y = f(x)$ is known, we can deduce the shape of the curve $y = 1/f(x)$ using the following observations.

If $f(x)$ is positive, then so is $1/f(x)$; and if $f(x)$ is negative, $1/f(x)$ is also negative, i.e.

when the curve $y = f(x)$ is above the x-axis, the curve $y = 1/f(x)$ is also above the x-axis, and when $y = f(x)$ is below the x-axis, so is $y = 1/f(x)$.

If $f(x)$ is increasing in value then $1/f(x)$ is decreasing in value, i.e.

when the curve $y = f(x)$ is going up, the curve $y = 1/f(x)$ is going down.

In the same way, when $f(x)$ is decreasing, $1/f(x)$ is increasing in value, i.e.

when the curve $y = f(x)$ is going down, the curve $y = 1/f(x)$ is going up.

When the value of $f(x)$ is large, the value of $1/f(x)$ is small, i.e.

when the y-coordinates on the curve $y = f(x)$ are large, the curve $y = 1/f(x)$ is close to the x-axis.

When the value of $f(x)$ is small, the value of $1/f(x)$ is large, i.e.

when $y = f(x)$ is close to the x-axis, the y-coordinates on $y = 1/f(x)$ are large.

In particular, at the values of x where $f(x)$ is zero, $1/f(x)$ does not have a value, i.e.

where the curve $y = f(x)$ cuts the x-axis, there is a break in the curve $y = 1/f(x)$.

When $f(x) = \pm 1$, $1/f(x) = \pm 1$, i.e.

the curves $y = f(x)$ and $y = 1/f(x)$ intersect at points where $y = 1$ and $y = -1$.

All these observations are illustrated on this diagram which shows the familiar graphs of $y = x$ and $y = \dfrac{1}{x}$.

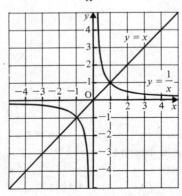

EXERCISE 16d

Access to a graphics calculator or computer, although not essential, will enable you to check your results.

1. Sketch the graph of $f(x) = x^2$. On the same axes, sketch the graph of $\dfrac{1}{f(x)}$,

   i.e. $y = \dfrac{1}{x^2}$.

2. Repeat question 1 for the functions given by $f(x) = x^3$ and $f(x) = x^4$.

3. The sketch shows the graph of $f(x) = x - 2$. Copy it and, on the same axes sketch the graph of

   $y = \dfrac{1}{f(x)}$.

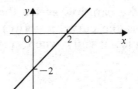

4. The sketch shows part of the graph of $f(x) = 2x - x^2$. Copy it and, on the same axes, sketch the graph of

   $y = \dfrac{1}{f(x)}$.

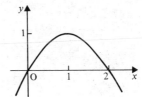

QUADRATIC FUNCTIONS

Any function of the form given by $f(x) = ax^2 + bx + c$ is called a quadratic function.

From Book 4A, chapter 5, we know that the graph of a quadratic function has a distinctive shape, called a parabola.

If a is positive, the parabola has a lowest point (called its vertex), so the quadratic function has a least value, but it has no greatest value.

If a is negative, the parabola has a highest point (also called its vertex), so the quadratic function has a greatest value, but it has no least value.

All these parabolas have a line of symmetry which is a vertical line through the vertex.

FINDING THE GREATEST OR LEAST VALUE

We can find the greatest, or least, value of any quadratic function without plotting an accurate graph.

If a quadratic function factorises, we can find its line of symmetry and hence find the greatest or least value at the turning point.

For example, suppose we wish to find the greatest (or least) value of the function given by $f(x) = 8 - 2x - x^2$.

Factorising, $f(x) = 8 - 2x - x^2 = (4+x)(2-x)$

We can now sketch the curve $y = f(x)$. The coefficient of x^2 is negative, so the curve $y = f(x)$ has a greatest value. The curve crosses the x-axis (i.e. $y = 0$) where $x = -4$ and where $x = 2$.

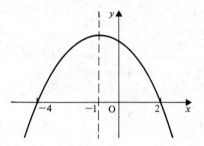

The curve has a line of symmetry that cuts the x-axis midway between $x = -4$ and $x = 2$ i.e. where $x = -1$. Therefore the greatest value of $f(x)$ occurs when $x = -1$, i.e. the greatest value of $f(x)$ is $f(-1)$.

Greatest value is $8 - 2(-1) - (-1)^2 = 8 + 2 - 1 = 9$

Another way to find the greatest or least value of a quadratic function is to use the method of completing the square.

Suppose, for example, that $f(x) = x^2 - 3x - 1$

We can change $x^2 - 3x$ into a perfect square by adding $\frac{9}{4}$,

i.e. $x^2 - 3x + \frac{9}{4} = (x - \frac{3}{2})^2$

Therefore we can rewrite $x^2 - 3x - 1$ as $(x^2 - 3x + \frac{9}{4}) - 1 - \frac{9}{4}$

$$= (x - \frac{3}{2})^2 - \frac{13}{4}$$

Notice that we add $\frac{9}{4}$ to $x^2 - x$ to make a perfect square, but to keep $f(x)$ unaltered we need to *subtract* $\frac{9}{4}$ from the number term.

Therefore

$$f(x) = (x - \tfrac{3}{2})^2 - \tfrac{13}{4}$$

Because it is a square, the value of $(x - \tfrac{3}{2})^2$ is always greater than or equal to zero.

i.e. whatever value x has, $f(x) \geqslant \tfrac{-13}{4}$

and $f(x) = \tfrac{-13}{4}$ when $(x - \tfrac{3}{2})^2 = 0$ i.e. when $x = \tfrac{3}{2}$

Hence $f(x)$ has a least value of $\tfrac{-13}{4}$, and this least value occurs when $x = \tfrac{3}{2}$.

Note that this method *must* be used if you are asked to *prove* that a quadratic function has a greatest/least value. (The graphical method assumes the existence of a greatest/least value.)

EXERCISE 16e

1. If $f(x) = (1 - 4x)^2$, explain why $f(x) \geqslant 0$ for all values of x.

2. If $f(x) = (x - 1)^2 - 4$, explain why $f(x) \geqslant -4$ for all values of x.

3. a) If $f(x) = (2x - 1)^2 + 6$, explain why $f(x) \geqslant 6$ for all values of x.
   b) For what value of x does $f(x)$ have its least value?
   c) Find the least value of $f(x)$.

4. a) If $f(x) = 5 - (x + 1)^2$, explain why $f(x) \leqslant 5$ for all values of x.
   b) For what value of x does $f(x)$ have its greatest value?
   c) Find the greatest value of $f(x)$.

5. a) If $f(x) = 25 - (2 - 3x)^2$, does $f(x)$ have a greatest or a least value?
   b) Find this greatest (or least) value and the value of x for which it occurs.

6. a) Explain how you know that $f(x)$ has a least value, given that
   $f(x) = (x - 2)^2 - 25$
   b) Find the least value and the value of x for which it occurs.
   c) Sketch the curve with equation $y = f(x)$.

7. State whether $f(x)$ has a greatest or a least value. Find this value and the value of x at which it occurs when $f(x)$ is
   a) $(x - 1)(x + 5)$ b) $(3 + x)(1 - x)$ c) $(x - 2)(x - 4)$
   d) $(x - 7)$ e) $(x + 2)^2$ f) $(1 - 2x)(x + 2)$

Express in the form $p(x+q)^2+r$

a) $2x^2 - 6x + 5$ b) $5 - 4x - x^2$

Find the greatest value of the function $f(x) = 5 - 4x - x^2$

a) $2x^2 - 6x + 5$

(We start by taking out a factor of 2 from the x^2 and x terms.)

$$2x^2 - 6x + 5 = 2(x^2 - 3x) + 5$$
$$= 2(x^2 - 3x + \tfrac{9}{4}) + 5 - \tfrac{9}{2}$$

(Notice that $\tfrac{9}{4}$ was added inside the bracket to make that a perfect square but, because the bracket is doubled, we have to subtract $2 \times \tfrac{9}{4}$, i.e. $\tfrac{9}{2}$, from the number term.)

$$\therefore \qquad 2x^2 - 6x + 5 = 2(x - \tfrac{3}{2})^2 + \tfrac{1}{2}$$

(Notice that $p = 2$, $q = -\tfrac{3}{2}$ and $r = \tfrac{1}{2}$.)

b) $5 - 4x - x^2$

(In order to complete the square the x^2 term must be positive, so we take out the factor -1 from the x^2 and x terms.)

$$5 - 4x - x^2 = 5 - (4x + x^2)$$
$$= 5 - (x^2 + 4x)$$
$$= 5 - (x^2 + 4x + 4) + 4$$
$$= 9 - (x + 2)^2$$

(This function is now in the form $9 - (0 \text{ or a +ve number})$ so it has a greatest value of 9 (which occurs when $x = -2$).)

8. Given that $f(x) = x^2 - 8x + 7$
   a) write $f(x)$ in the form $(x+b)^2 + c$
   b) for what value of x does $f(x)$ have a least value ?
   c) find this least value.

9. a) Given that $f(x) = 4x^2 + 12x - 5$ write $f(x)$ in the form $(ax+b)^2 + c$.
   b) For what value of x does $f(x)$ have its least value ?
   c) Find this least value.

10. Express each function in the form $p(x+q)^2 + r$.
    a) $x^2 - 3x + 3$ b) $x^2 + 3x + 3$ c) $x^2 - 3x - 3$
    d) $2x^2 + 4x + 7$ e) $2x^2 - 4x - 7$ f) $2 + x - x^2$
    g) $3 + 2x - x^2$ h) $3 - 2x - x^2$ i) $5 + 6x - 2x^2$

11. Use your results from question 9 to give the greatest/least value of each function and the value of x at which it occurs. Sketch the graph of each function.

12. The function, f, is given by $f(x) = x^2 + 5x + 9$.
a) Show that $f(x)$ has a least value and find it.
b) Sketch the curve $y = f(x)$.
c) Use your sketch to explain why there are no values of x for which $f(x) = 0$.

13. The function, f, is given by $f(x) = 4x - x^2 - 6$.
a) Show that $f(x)$ has a greatest value and find it.
b) Sketch the curve $y = f(x)$.
c) Use your sketch to explain why there are no values of x for which $f(x) = 0$.

TRIGONOMETRIC FUNCTIONS

We first met sines, cosines and tangents, when dealing with angles in right-angled triangles and so tend to think of these trigonometric ratios in relation to acute angles only. However, $\sin x°$ has a value for any value of x and so has $\cos x°$. Use your calculator to find, say, $\sin 240°$, $\cos 315°$.

EXERCISE 16f

1. Copy and complete the following table, using a calculator to find $\sin x°$ correct to 2 d.p. for each value of x.

x	0	15	30	45	60	75	90	105	120
$\sin x°$	0	0.26							

x	135	150	165	180	195	210	225	240
$\sin x°$								

x	255	270	285	300	315	330	345	360
$\sin x°$								

2. Use the values you obtained in your table for question 1 to draw the graph of $y = \sin x°$.

3. Make another table, using the same values of x as given in question 1, for values of $\cos x°$ correct to 2 d.p., i.e.

x	0	15	30	...	345	360
$\cos x°$	1	0.97				

4.   Use the values in the table in question 3 to draw the graph of $y = \cos x°$.
Use the same ranges and scales for the x and y axes as in question 2.

THE GRAPH OF f(x) = sinx °

The graph drawn for question 2 in the last exercise should look like this,
which is the graph for the function $f(x) = \sin x°$.

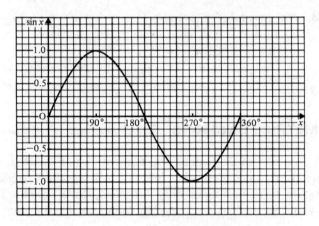

The curve has a distinctive shape: it is called a *sine wave.*

THE GRAPH OF f(x) = cosx °

The graph drawn for question 4 in the last exercise should look like this,
which is the graph for the function $f(x) = \cos x°$.

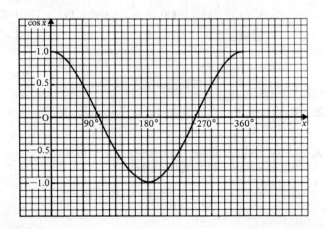

Notice that the cosine curve looks quite different from the sine curve for the domain $0 \leqslant x \leqslant 360$.

However, if both curves are drawn for a larger domain, the relationship between the curves becomes obvious. Questions 6 and 7 in the next exercise explore this relationship further.

EXERCISE 16g

1. a) Draw a sketch of the curve $y = \sin x°$ for $0 \leqslant x \leqslant 360$.
b) On the same diagram sketch the curve $y = -\sin x°$.
c) On the same diagram sketch the curve $y = 1 + \sin x°$.

2. a) Draw a sketch of the curve $y = \cos x°$ for $0 \leqslant x \leqslant 360$.
b) On the same diagram sketch the curves
   i) $y = 1 + \cos x°$ ii) $y = -\cos x°$

3. a) Draw a sketch of the curve $f(x) = \sin x°$ for $0 \leqslant x \leqslant 360$.
b) From your sketch, find the values of x for which $f(x) = 0$.
c) On the same axes draw a line to show how the value(s) of x can be found for which $f(x) = 0.4$.

4. a) Draw a sketch of the curve $f(x) = \cos x°$ for $0 \leqslant x \leqslant 360$.
b) For what values of x is $f(x) = 0$?
c) On the same axes draw lines to show how the values of x can be found for which   i) $f(x) = 0.5$ ii) $f(x) = -0.8$.

5. For the domain $0 \leqslant x \leqslant 360$, give the range of
a) $f(x) = \sin x°$ b) $f(x) = \cos x°$

6. Draw the graph of $y = \sin x°$ for $0 \leqslant x \leqslant 720$ using the following steps.
a) Make a table of values of $\sin x°$ for values of x from 0 to 720 at intervals. of 30 units. Use a calculator and give values of $\sin x°$ correct to 2 d.p.
b) Draw the y-axis on the left-hand side of a sheet of graph paper and scale it from -1 to 1 using 2 cm to 0.5 units. Draw in the x-axis and scale it from 0 to 720 using 1 cm to 60 units.
c) Plot the points given in the table made for (a) and draw a smooth curve through them.

7. Draw the graph of $y = \cos x°$ for $0 \leqslant x \leqslant 720$ using the same sequence of steps as in question 6.
Compare the graphs of $y = \sin x°$ and $y = \cos x°$. What do you notice?

8. For values of x between 0 and 360, sketch on the same diagram the graphs of
a) $y = \sin x°$ b) $y = \sin(x + 30)°$ c) $y = \sin(x + 90)°$

9. For values of x between 0 and 360, sketch on the same diagram the graphs of
a) $y = \cos x°$ b) $y = \cos(x + 45)°$ c) $y = \cos(x + 90)°$

You will need access to a graphics calculator or a computer with graph drawing software for questions 10 to 12. If you can print out the results, do so and keep them.

10. Set the range to $-360 \leqslant x \leqslant 360$ and $-2 \leqslant y \leqslant 2$.
a) Draw the graph of $y = \sin x°$ and then superimpose the graph of $y = \sin 2x°$.
b) Describe the transformation that transforms the first curve to the second.
c) Clear the screen and repeat (a) and (b) for $y = \sin x°$ and $y = \sin 3x°$.
d) *Without drawing the graphs*, describe the transformation that transforms the curve $y = \sin x°$ to the curve $y = \sin \frac{1}{2}x°$.

11. a) Set the range to $0 \leqslant x \leqslant 1080$ and draw the graph of $y = \sin x°$.
b) What is the range of values of $\sin x°$?
c) *Sketch* the graph of $y = \sin x°$ for $-360 \leqslant x \leqslant 4 \times 360$.

12. Repeat question 10 for $y = \cos x°$.

13. Sketch the graph of $f(x) = \sin x°$ for $0 \leqslant x \leqslant 360$, and use it to sketch the graph of $y = \dfrac{1}{\sin x°}$.

THE SINE AND COSINE FUNCTIONS

The last exercise shows that $f(x) = \sin x°$ is never greater than 1 and never less than -1,

i.e.   for all values of x, $-1 \leqslant \sin x° \leqslant 1$.

Note also that the curve repeats at intervals of 360 units.

The function $f(x) = \cos x°$ has the same properties. In fact, if the curve $y = \sin x°$ is translated 90 units to the left, we get the curve $y = \cos x°$.

THE GRAPH OF $y = \tan x^\circ$

The graph that results from plotting values of $\tan x^\circ$ against x in the range $0 \leqslant x \leqslant 360$, is given below.

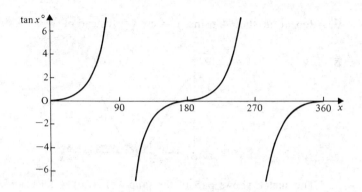

This shows that the function given by $y = \tan x^\circ$ has properties that are quite different from those of the sine and cosine functions. The main differences are;

$\tan x^\circ$ has no greatest or least value;

the graph of $y = \tan x^\circ$ does have a repeating pattern, but it repeats at intervals of 180 units;

the graph has 'breaks' or 'discontinuities' in it which occur when $x = 90$ and every step of 180 units from there along the x-axis.

(If you find $\tan 89^\circ$, $\tan 89.9^\circ$, $\tan 89.99^\circ$, etc. on your calculator you get larger and larger values. When you find $\tan 90^\circ$ the calculator display reads 'error'. Why do you think this is so?)

EXERCISE 16h

1. Sketch the graph of $y = \tan x^\circ$ for $0 \leqslant x \leqslant 360$ and use it to sketch, on the same axes, the graph of
   a) $y = \tan(x + 90)^\circ$ b) $y = \tan(x - 90)^\circ$.
   What does the graph of $y = \tan(x + 180)^\circ$ look like?

2. Use the graph of $y = \tan x^\circ$ to sketch the graph of
   a) $y = \tan x^\circ + 2$ b) $y = \tan x^\circ - 2$.

3. Sketch the graph of $y = \dfrac{1}{\tan x^\circ}$ for $0 \leqslant x \leqslant 360$.

4. Sketch the curves $y = 1 + \sin x°$ and $y = \tan x°$ for $0 \leqslant x \leqslant 360$. Hence give the number of values of x from 0 to 360 inclusive for which $1 + \sin x° = \tan x°$.

If you have access to a computer or graphics calculator, find these values, each correct to the nearest degree.

5. Repeat question 4, using $y = \cos x°$ instead of $y = 1 + \sin x°$.

6.

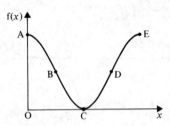

The sketch shows part of the graph of $f(x) = 1 + \cos x°$. Write down the coordinates of the points marked on the curve.

7. a)

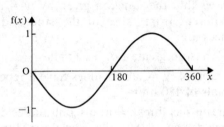

b)

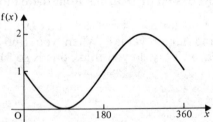

c)

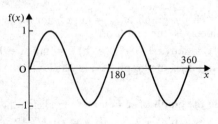

Each of the curves given above was found by transforming the graph of $f(x) = \sin x°$. In each case suggest a possible transformation and give the equation of the transformed curve.

8. a)

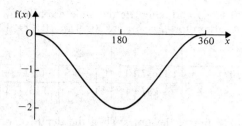

b)

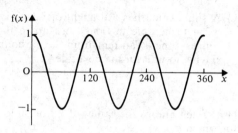

c)

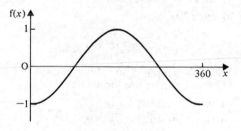

Each of the curves given above was found by transforming the graph of $f(x) = \cos x°$. In each case suggest a possible transformation and give the equation of the transformed curve.

9. The depth of water, d metres, in a harbour, t hours after noon, is given by $d = 4 + \cos 30t°$ and is illustrated in the sketch below.

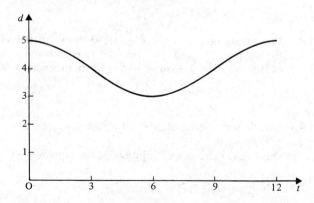

a) Copy and complete the table given below and use it to draw an accurate graph for $d = 4 + \cos 30t°$ for $0 \leqslant t \leqslant 12$.

t	0	1	2	3	4	5	6	7	8	9	10	11	12
$\cos 30t°$	1	0.87	0.5	0	−0.5	−0.87	−1	−0.87	−0.5	0			
$4 + \cos 30t°$	5	4.87	4.5	4	3.5	3.13	3	3.13	3.5				

b) Estimate the times when the depth of water in the harbour is less than 3.5 m.

c) A ship, which has a draught of 3.2 m (i.e. it requires water to a depth of 3.2 m to be able to float), ties up in the harbour at noon. What is the longest time it can remain in the harbour without becoming stranded and having to wait for the next tide ?

10. Use sketch graphs for values of x from 0 to 360 to find the *exact* values of x for which

a) $\sin x° = -\sin x°$

b) $\cos x° = -\cos x°$

11. Use sketch graphs for values of x from 0 to 360 to determine how many values of x there are for which

a) $\sin x° = \sin 2x°$

b) $\sin x° = \sin 3x°$

12. Use sketch graphs for $0 \leqslant x \leqslant 180$ to find approximate values of x for which

a) $\sin x° = \sin(x - 90)°$

b) $\cos x° = \cos(x - 90)°$.

Use your calculator, together with 'trial and improvement' methods to give your answers to parts (a) and (b) correct to the nearest integer.

13. For values of x between 0 and 180 draw, on the same axes, sketch graphs for $y = \sin x°$ and $y = \tan x° - 1$. Hence show that there is one solution of the equation $1 + \sin x° = \tan x°$ between $x = 60$ and $x = 70$.

14. Sketch the graphs of $y = \sin x°$ and $y = 2 - \dfrac{x}{30}$ for $0 \leqslant x \leqslant 90$. Hence show that there is one solution of the equation $60 - x = 30 \sin x°$ between $x = 30$ and $x = 50$.

15. Sketch the graphs of $y = \cos x°$ and $y = \dfrac{x}{6}$ for $0 \leqslant x \leqslant 90$. Hence show that there is one solution of the equation $x = 6 \cos x°$ between 0 and 20.

    a) If x_n is an approximate root of the equation, then x_{n+1} is a better approximation, where $x_{n+1} = 6 \cos x_n°$. Use this iteration formula, with $x_1 = 5$, to find x correct to 2 decimal places.

    b) If the values of x are not restricted to those between 0 and 90, how many solutions does the equation have ?

16. Sketch the graph of $y = 5 \sin x°$ for $0 \leqslant x \leqslant 180$. On the same set of axes, sketch the graph of $x - 10y - 20 = 0$. Hence show that the equation $x - 50 \sin x° - 20 = 0$ has a solution between $x = 60$ and $x = 70$.
Draw an accurate plot of the graphs for $63 \leqslant x \leqslant 68$ at intervals of 1 unit to find this root correct to the nearest whole number.

17. a) What graphs need to be drawn to solve graphically the equation $50 \cos x° = x - 20$?

    b) What equation can be solved by finding the value of x at the point of intersection of the graphs $y = \sin x°$ and $y = 1 - \frac{1}{50}x$?

18. a) What graphs could you draw to solve graphically the equation $30 \sin x° = 20 - 2x$.

    b) The x-coordinates of the points of intersection of the graphs $y = 14 \tan x°$ and $y = (x-1)^2$ are found. Write down the equation that has these values of x as roots.

19. Sketch the graphs of $y = \tan x°$ and $y = \frac{1}{10}x - 2$ for $0 \leqslant x \leqslant 90$. Hence show that two values of x satisfy the equation $10 \tan x° = x - 20$. Show that the larger value of x that satisfies this equation lies between 75 and 85.

20. Copy and complete the table to give values of $\sin x° + \cos x°$ for values of x from 0 to 360. Give each value correct to 2 d.p.

x	0	15	30	45	...	330	345	360
$\sin x°$	0		0.5				−0.26	0
$\cos x°$	1		0.87				0.97	1
$\sin x° + \cos x°$	1		1.37				0.71	1

Hence draw the graph of $f(x) = \sin x° + \cos x°$ for values of x from 0 to 360. Use your graph to find   a) the least value   b) the greatest value, of $f(x)$ within the given range.

21.

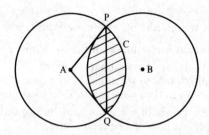

a) Two circles, centres A and B, each of radius r cm, intersect at P and Q. If $\hat{PAQ} = x°$ find an expression for
 i) the area of the sector APCQ
 ii) the area of triangle APQ
 iii) the area of the minor segment PQC.

b) Hence show that the area common to both circles is

$$r^2\left(\frac{\pi x}{180} - \sin x°\right)$$

c) Show that, if the common area is equal to one-half the area of either circle, then

$$\frac{\pi x}{180} - \sin x° = \frac{\pi}{2}$$

d) Sketch the graphs of $y = \sin x°$ and $y = \frac{\pi}{180}(x - 90)$ for values of x in the range $90 \leqslant x \leqslant 180$. Hence show that the equation

$$\frac{\pi x}{180} - \sin x° = \frac{\pi}{2}$$

has a root between 130 and 140.

e) If x_n is an approximate root of the above equation, then x_{n+1} is a better approximation,

where $$x_{n+1} = 90 + \frac{180}{\pi}\sin x_n°.$$

Use this iteration with $x_1 = 130$ to find x correct to the nearest whole number.

17 REVISION AND PROBLEM SOLVING EXERCISES

The exercises in this chapter are organised into four sections, one section for each of Attainment Targets 2, 3, 4 and 5. The last exercise in each section applies the knowledge to problems and investigations suitable for Attainment Target 1.

NUMBER

The first two exercises revise the knowledge required for levels 7 to 10 of Attainment Target 2.

EXERCISE 17a

Do not use a calculator for this exercise.

1. Find the prime factors of 1800. Hence find
   a) the values of x, y and z for which $1800 = 2^x \times 3^y \times 5^z$
   b) the smallest integer that 1800 can be multiplied by to make the result a perfect square.

2. Find the prime factors of 676. Hence find the square root of 676.

3. Evaluate   a) $2.5 \div 0.05$ b) $\dfrac{0.12 \times 0.03}{0.4}$

4. A box contains 96 cubes. Is it possible to build a solid cuboid using all these cubes so that each edge is at least 2 cubes long? Give reasons for your answer.

5. The mass of magnesium in one test tube is 3.5×10^{-6} grams and the mass of magnesium in another test tube is 7.4×10^{-8} grams.
Which of these masses is greater?

6. Evaluate   a) $25^{1/2}$ b) 5^{-3} c) $\sqrt[3]{8}$

7. Find x if $36^x = \frac{1}{6}$.

8. a) Evaluate s where $s = \dfrac{v^2 - u^2}{2a}$ and $v = 0.8$, $u = -1.2$ and $a = -2$.

b) Find the number of pieces of tape, each $\frac{5}{8}$ inch long, that can be cut from $2\frac{1}{2}$ feet of tape.

9. A council purchases 153 books at a cost of £9.99 each for use by 24 libraries. Each library contributes an equal amount towards the cost.
Find, roughly, how much each library pays.

10. Which of the following numbers are rational ?

a) $\sqrt{8}$ b) $\dfrac{\sqrt{8}}{\sqrt{2}}$ c) $\sqrt{81}$ d) $(\sqrt{8})(\sqrt{2})$ e) 3.14   f) $\frac{22}{7}$ g) π

11. Simplify   a) $\sqrt{2} + \sqrt{8}$ b) $\sqrt{3} \times \sqrt{12}$ c) $\dfrac{1}{\sqrt{2}}$

12. When Anna does her shopping, she calculates a rough value for the bill by rounding *up* the price of each article to the nearest 50 p. She buys 20 items and, from her estimate, knows that her bill will be £30.50 or less.
What is the least that her bill could be ?

13. A bank uses electronic scales to weigh coins. The scales show the weight in grams correct to one decimal place. Explain why these scales show the weight of one coin as 9.1 grams and the weight of 100 identical coins as 907.2 grams.

EXERCISE 17b

1. An advertisement in a magazine offered computer programs sold direct from the USA. The price quoted for a disk of games was $35. The exchange rate at the time was £1 = $1.78.
What was the price of the disk in sterling ?

2. The mass of a decaying radioactive element is measured as 400 grams. It loses 10 % of its mass each year. What will the mass be after 4 years ?

3. The time allowed for cleaning one office was increased from 10 minutes to $12\frac{1}{2}$ minutes. The number of cleaners employed was increased in the same ratio. If 40 cleaners are employed after the increase, how many extra cleaners were taken on ?

4. Express   a) $\frac{1}{7}$ as a decimal   b) $0.\dot{2}\dot{7}$ as a fraction.

5. To the nearest cubic centimetre, the volume of a cuboid box is 240 cm³. The height of the box, to the nearest centimetre, is 12 cm.
Find, correct to 3 s.f. the upper and lower bounds of the area of the base of the box.

6. Find the value of $\dfrac{\sqrt{2.87} + 3.25}{5.09 \times 1.7^2}$ giving your answers correct to 3 s.f.

7. Find the highest integral value of n for which $3^n < 10^7$.

8. A statistician is using the formula $v = ns^2$. The value of n has a maximum error of 1 % and the value of s has a maximum error of 5 %.
Find the largest possible error in the calculated value of v.

9. In a training session, David did two time trials for the 100 m sprint. On the first trial his time was recorded as 12.74 seconds and on the second trial his time was recorded as 13.03 seconds. Find
a) David's average speed for the first trial in km/h
b) David's average speed for the two runs combined in km/h.
c) What information do you need to be able to give the degree of accuracy of your answers to (a) and (b) ?

10. Light travels at 3.00×10^8 m/s. Calculate the time it takes light to travel a distance of 7.45×10^6 km.

11. After two successive increases of 10 %, the cost of a rail journey was £ 59.29. What was the cost before the first increase ?

12. When $\frac{1}{23}$ is expressed as a decimal, the calculator display shows 0.043 478 2. Is this an exact value or has it been rounded up or rounded down ?

EXERCISE 17c

The problems in this exercise are relevant to Attainment Target 1. A dagger indicates a longer problem.

1. Using at most four numbers, each of which must be either 2 or 3, and the ordinary rules of addition, subtraction and multiplication, it is possible to make other numbers.
For example, $1 = 3 - 2$ and $10 = (3 \times 3) + 3 - 2$
a) Show that there are other ways of making 10.
b) Find as many ways as possible of making the numbers 6, 7 and 8.
c) Investigate the assertion that any number can be made.

2. Investigate the truth or otherwise of the following statements.
a) The product of three consecutive positive integers is divisible by 2.
b) The sum of three consecutive positive integers is divisible by 2.
c) $\sqrt{3}$ is an irrational number.

3. Rose designs a new game that requires four cubes to fit tightly in a sleeve with two open ends as shown in the diagram.

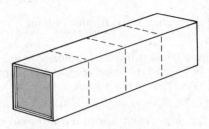

The sleeve is to be made by one manufacturer and the cubes by another. The cubes are ordered to have an edge of 25 mm and the sleeve to have internal measurements of 100 mm by 25 mm by 25 mm, all measurements being given to the nearest millimetre.

When Rose gets the first cubes and sleeves, she finds that when she tries to fit four cubes into the sleeve, the fourth cube will not go in.

a) Explain what the problem could be.

b) What other problems could have occurred ?

c) What can Rose do to avoid such problems in future ?

4. The value of an integer$_{\text{modulo 4}}$, is defined as the remainder when that integer is divided by 4,

e.g. $27_{\text{modulo 4}} = 3$ since $27 \div 4$ gives a remainder 3.

a) What are the values that a modulo 4 number can have ?

b) Copy and complete these tables for modulo 4 numbers.

+	0	1	2	3
0				
1				
2				
3				

×	0	1	2	3
0				
1				
2				
3				

c) If a number, a, can be added to another number b so that $a + b = b$ then a is called the identity number under addition. Similarly, if a number c exists so that $c \times b = b$, c is called the identity under multiplication.

Show that there is an identity modulo 4 number for addition and for multiplication.

d) The inverse of a number under addition is defined as follows.
(number) + (its inverse) = Identity under addition.
Show that each modulo 4 number has an inverse under addition.

e) The inverse of a number under multiplication is defined in a similar way to the inverse under addition.
Which modulo 4 numbers have an inverse under multiplication and which do not ?

f) Investigate modulo 6 numbers.

g) Give some examples of modulo arithmetic used in everyday life.

5. Here is a method for finding rational approximations for $\sqrt{2}$.

Step 1. Start with a fraction that is roughly equal to $\sqrt{2}$.

Step 2. Find the fraction which, when multiplied by the first one, gives 2.

Step 3. Find the mean of the two fractions – this is a better approximation for $\sqrt{2}$.

a) Start with $\frac{7}{5}$ as the first approximation. Find the better approximation. Use your calculator to find the number of decimal places to which it is accurate.

b) Now use the fraction found in (a) as the first approximation to find an even better approximation.

c) Adapt the method for finding a rational approximation for $\sqrt{5}$

d) Explain why the method works.

†6. Here is a method for finding successively better rational approximations for $1 + \sqrt{2}$.

Start with $2 + \frac{1}{2}$ as the first approximation.

The next approximation is $2 + \dfrac{1}{2 + \frac{1}{2}}$

and the next approximation is $2 + \dfrac{1}{2 + \dfrac{1}{2 + \frac{1}{2}}}$

a) Continue the pattern to find the next two approximations and evaluate them as decimals. To how many decimal places are they accurate ?

b) The pattern can be continued indefinitely, and patterns of this type are called continued fractions. Use reference books to find other continued fractions.

c) Find the irrational number for which $1 + \dfrac{1}{1 + \dfrac{1}{1 + \dfrac{1}{1 + \cdots}}}$

can be used to find approximations.

d) Use reference books to find other methods for finding rational approximations for square roots. Give a brief description of any that you find.

ALGEBRA

The first two exercises in this section revise the knowledge required for Levels 7 to 10 of Attainment Target 3.

EXERCISE 17d

1. Find the positive solution of the equation $x^2 + 4x = 3$ by

a) *trial and improvement*, giving the answer correct to 1 decimal place

b) using an iteration formula, giving the answer correct to 2 decimal places

c) calculation, giving the answer in the form $a\sqrt{b} + c$.

2. Find the largest integer that satisfies the inequality

   a) $3(x-1) < 2x + 5$ b) $x^2 \leqslant 10$ c) $x^2 < x + 1$

3. Factorise   a) $3a^2b - 6ab^2$ b) $6x^2 - x - 35$.

4. Simplify   a) $\dfrac{x^2 + 3x}{2x^2 + 2x - 12}$ b) $\dfrac{x^2y^3}{xy^4}$ c) $\left(\dfrac{1}{a^4}\right)^{-1/2}$

   d) $3 - \dfrac{2x+3}{x-5}$ e) $\dfrac{1}{2x+1} - \dfrac{3}{x-2}$

5. The first four terms of a sequence are

$$\tfrac{1}{2}, \quad \tfrac{1}{2} + \tfrac{1}{4}, \quad \tfrac{1}{2} + \tfrac{1}{4} + \tfrac{1}{8}, \quad \tfrac{1}{2} + \tfrac{1}{4} + \tfrac{1}{8} + \tfrac{1}{16}$$

   a) Simplify these terms and find an expression for the nth term.

   b) Find the value to which the nth term converges.

6. a) Make t the subject of the formula $v = \tfrac{1}{2}gt^2$.

   b) The area of a circle is given by $A = \pi r^2$ and the circumference is given by $C = 2\pi r$. Find a formula for the area of a circle in terms of the circumference.

7. Find the values of x and y for which $2x - 3y = 5$ and $x = 2y + 8$.

8. A contractor estimates that he can refit a shop in 5 days if he employs 8 people on the job.

   a) If he finds that he can spare only 5 employees for the job, how many days will the refit take ?

   b) If the owner of the shop wants the job done in 3 days, how many people will need to be used on the job ?

9. a) This flow chart can be used to find the integer nearest to, but less than, the cube root of 143.

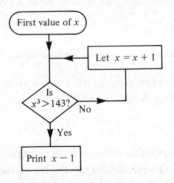

   i) If the first value of x is 4 what will the printout be ?

   ii) If the first value of x is 10, what goes wrong ?

b) This flow chart will solve an equation. What is the equation and how accurate is the answer ?

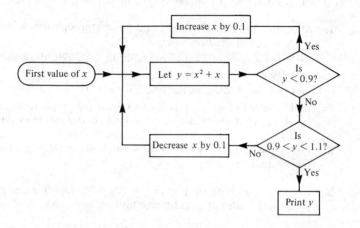

10. a) Write down the positive square root of $169x^{10}$.

b) To what power must x be raised to give $\dfrac{1}{x^4}$?

11. In an experiment different objects are allowed to sink in a tank of liquid. The acceleration, $a\,\text{m/s}^2$, of an object is inversely proportional to the square of the time, t seconds, taken to reach the bottom.

a) If a concrete brick takes 1.6 s to reach the bottom, and the acceleration is calculated as $2\,\text{m/s}^2$, find the relationship between a and t.

b) A small stone takes 0.8 s to reach the bottom. What is its acceleration ?

c) A wooden block never reaches the bottom. What is its acceleration ?

12. A garden path is 36 m long. The path can be paved by laying paving stones, x cm long, end to end without cutting any stones. It can also be paved in the same way using paving stones that are 24 cm shorter, but 5 more paving stones are needed.

a) Write down an expression in terms of x for the number of longer paving stones needed to pave the path.

b) Write down an expression in terms of x for the number of shorter paving stones needed to pave the path.

c) Form an equation in x and solve it to find the number of longer paving stones needed.

13. a) Arrange $x^2 - 7x + 2$ in the form $(x - a)^2 - b$.

b) Hence find the least value of $x^2 - 7x + 2$.

c) Sketch the graph of $y = x^2 - 7x + 2$.

EXERCISE 17e

You will need some A4 sheets of graph paper for this exercise.

1. a) A line has a gradient of 4 and passes through the point $(1, -2)$. Find the equation of the line.

b) Using a scale of 1 cm to one unit on each axis, draw the line for values of x from -2 to 2.

c) Find the gradient of the line $2y - x = 1$.

d) Using the same axes as for (b) draw the graph representing $2y - x = 1$. Hence find the values of x and y where the two lines intersect.

2. Using the graphs drawn for question 1, show the region which satisfies all the inequalities $2y - x \leqslant 1$, $x > 0.5$, $y > 4x - 6$.

3. a) Draw the graph of $y = (x - 1)(2x + 3)$ for values of x between -2 and 2 using scales of 2 cm for one unit on both axes.

b) Complete the table for values of y when $y = \dfrac{1}{x^2}$.

x	-2	-1.5	-1	-0.5	0.5	1	1.5
y		0.44					

c) Write down the values of x at the points of intersection of the two graphs and the equation for which these values are solutions.

4. The graph shows the velocity of a car on a road between two sets of traffic lights.

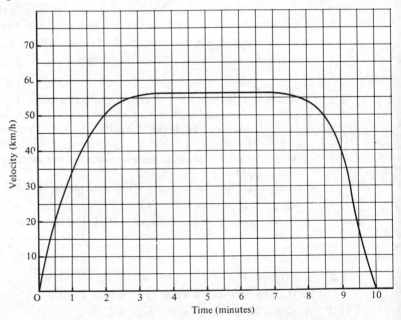

a) For how long did the car maintain a steady speed ?

b) Estimate the acceleration of the car 2 minutes after leaving the first set of lights.

c) What is the distance between the two sets of lights ?

5. a) The diagram shows the graph of $y = x^2$. Copy or trace the diagram and on it draw the graphs of $y = x^2 - 1$ and $y = 1 - x^2$.

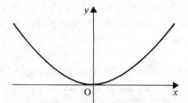

b) Sketch the graph of $y = x^3$. On the same set of axes sketch the graphs of $y = -x^3$, $y = 2 - x^3$ and $y = (x - 2)^3$.

6. An open box is made by cutting a square from each corner of a rectangular sheet of card measuring 12 cm by 16 cm.

a) If the length of the side of each square removed is x cm, draw a diagram showing the net for the box. What is the upper limit for the value of x ?

b) If the area of the base of the box is A cm², show that
$$A = 4(6-x)(8-x)$$
Hence find the size of the squares removed if the area of the base of the box is 96 cm².

c) If the volume of the box is V cm³, write down a formula for V in terms of x.

d) Draw the graph of V plotted against x for values of x from 0 to 6 and values of y from 0 to 200. Hence find the largest volume that the box can have.

7. The following table gives the results of an experiment.

p	12	15	25	30	50
v	5.1	3.9	2.4	2.1	1.2

a) Which of the following statements is most likely to be true ?

v varies as p; v varies inversely as p; v varies as p^2; v varies as $\dfrac{1}{\sqrt{p}}$.

b) By choosing the most appropriate relationship between v and p, estimate the value of v when $p = 35$.

8. A coach leaves London at midday taking a group to an exhibition that is 100 miles away. It travels at a steady 24 m.p.h. for the first 8 miles and then at a steady 70 m.p.h. for the next 50 miles. It stops at a service station for 30 minutes and then completes the journey at a steady speed of 65 m.p.h.

a) Using a scale of 1 cm for 5 miles and 1 cm for 10 minutes, draw a graph to illustrate the journey.

b) At what time did the coach reach its destination ?

c) A car sets off from the exhibition centre at 1.30 p.m. and travels non-stop to London at a steady 70 m.p.h. Draw a graph illustrating the car's journey on the same set of axes.

d) When did the car meet the coach ?

9. In each part sketch the graph required to illustrate the situation.

a) The speed of a ski jumper against time, from the start of the slope to stopping at the end of the jump.

b) The depth of water against time when water is poured at a steady rate into a goldfish bowl which is spherical in shape.

c) The cost of a telephone call against time.

10. The table shows the value of a sum of money invested in a 'Growth' bond at various intervals from the time of investment.

Initial investment	Value after 1 year	Value after 2 years	Value after 3 years	Value after 4 years	Value after 5 years
£ 5000	£ 5400	£ 5832	£ 6299	£ 6802	£ 7347

a) Illustrate these values on a graph.

b) Find the percentage increase in the value of the investment each year.

c) What is the rate of growth of the initial investment ?

EXERCISE 17f

The problems in this exercise are relevant to Attainment Target 1. Those marked with a dagger are longer problems.

1. If the sum of the digits in a number is divisible by three then the number itself is also divisible by three. Why does this work ?

a) Start with any two digit number, $10a + b$, where a and b are each less than 10. What you have to show is that if $a + b$ is divisible by three then so is $10a + b$.

b) Extend your argument to a number of any size.

c) Explain why the similar test for divisibility by 9 works.

2. A Fibonacci sequence is one where the nth term is the sum of the two previous terms.

a) If the first two terms of a Fibonacci sequence are $1, 2$, write down the next five terms.

b) Write down the value, correct to four decimal places of the first 8 terms of the sequence whose nth term is $\dfrac{u_n}{u_{n+1}}$, where u_n is the nth term of the sequence given in (a).

c) Repeat (a) and (b) with some other Fibonacci sequences. What do you notice ?

3. Find an expression for the value of the nth term of the sequence
$$9^2, \quad 99^2, \quad 999^2, \quad 9999^2, \quad \dots$$

4. a) Write down three different numbers less than 10. Using all three digits form all the possible three figure numbers.

b) Find the sum, x, of the list of three figure numbers formed in (a), then find the sum, y, of the three numbers you started with. Find the value of $x \div y$.

c) Repeat (a) and (b) with three different numbers. Investigate your results.

5. If the number $abcde$ is multiplied by 4, the result is $edcba$. Find $abcde$.

6. The operation $*$ on any two real numbers p and q is defined by
$$p * q = 2p + 2q$$

a) Find the value of $4 * 3$.

b) If $p = 3$, $q = -5$ and $r = 1.3$, find $(p * q) * r$.

c) Explain why for all real values of p, q and r,
$$(p * q) * r \neq p * (q * r)$$
unless $p = r$.

d) If the operation $p * q$ is redefined as $p * q = p \div q$, give an example of values of p, q and r for which $(p * q) * r = p * (q * r)$. What is the condition for values of p, q and r if the relationship given in (c) is to be true ?

7. The operation $\bullet$ is defined on real numbers a and b by
$$a \bullet b = a^2 - b^2$$

a) Find the value of $3 \bullet 2$.

b) If $a = 4$, $b = -1$ and $c = 2$ find the value of
i) $a \bullet b - b \bullet c$ ii) $(a \bullet b) \bullet c$.

c) Explain why brackets are needed in $(a \bullet b) \bullet c$.

d) Prove that in general, $a \bullet b \neq b \bullet a$.

† 8. To do this question you will need to have worked through both question 6 and 7 above and question 4 from Exercise 17c.

A set of numbers is a group under an operation on two of the numbers if the following conditions are satisfied:

(1) the operation always results in a number in the set,

(2) one of the numbers is an identity for the operation,

(3) each number has an inverse under the operation,

(4) the operation is such that if a, b and c are numbers in the set,

$$a * (b * c) = (a * b) * c.$$

a) Investigate whether the set of numbers modulo 4 is a group under the operation $p * q$, where   i) $p * q = p + q$ ii) $p * q = p \times q$.

b) Repeat part (a) with modulo 7 numbers.

c) Investigate whether the set of integers (positive and negative whole numbers including zero) is a group under the ordinary operation of
i) addition   ii) subtraction   iii) multiplication   iv) division.

d) Determine whether all the rational numbers form a group under any of the ordinary operations of arithmetic as given in part (c).

† 9. A sequence is generated using the formula $u_{n+1} = \dfrac{2u_n - 1}{1 - u_n}$.

a) Write down the first 5 terms when   i) $u_1 = 5$ ii) $u_1 = 1$.

b) Which one of the sequences generated in (a) converges ?

c) Find the equation which can be solved by a sequence generated from the given formula. Use the equation to explain your answers to (a) and (b).

† 10. The first two terms of a Fibonacci sequence are $u_1 = x$ and $u_2 = y$.

a) Write down, in terms of x and y, the first ten terms of the sequence.

b) Another sequence is defined by $s_n = u_1 + u_2 + u_3 + \ldots + u_n$. Write down the terms s_1 to s_{10}.

c) Show that $s_6 = au_5$ and $s_{10} = bu_7$ and give the values of a and b.

d) Predict a value of m and a value of n for which $s_m = cu_n$ and test your prediction. If you have predicted correctly, give the value of c.

e) Predict further values of m, n and c. If you can write a simple computer program, do so to test your predictions.

SHAPE AND SPACE

The first two exercises in this section revise the knowledge needed for Levels 7 to 10 of Attainment Target 4.

EXERCISE 17g

1. The following diagrams are not drawn to scale. Determine whether the two figures are similar. Give reasons for your decision.

a)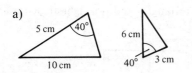

b)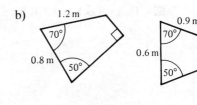

c)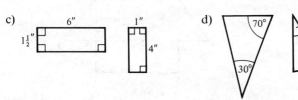

d)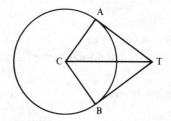

2. A cylindrical can has a radius r cm and its height is h cm.
   a) Find the volume of the can when $r = 2.5$ and $h = 6.8$.
   b) A can with radius 2.8 cm has a capacity of 33 cl. What is the height of the can ?
   c) Which of the following formulae is dimensionally correct for the surface area of a closed can ?
   $$\textbf{A}\ A = \pi r^2 h \quad \textbf{B}\ A = 2\pi r^2 + h \quad \textbf{C}\ A = \pi r + h \quad \textbf{D}\ A = 2\pi r^2 + 2\pi rh$$

3. The diagram shows a drive band which goes round a flywheel (the circle, centre C, and a pin T).

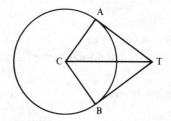

The radius of the wheel is 6 inches and T is 10 inches from the centre of the wheel. Find
   a) the length of the drive band that is not in contact with the wheel
   b) the angle ACT
   c) the length of the band that is in contact with the wheel.

4. The coordinates of four vertices of a cuboid are $(-2, 0, 0)$, $(2, 0, 0)$, $(2, 4, 0)$ and $(2, 4, 3)$. Find
   a) the coordinates of the other vertices
   b) the length of the longest diagonal of the cuboid.

5. This net is formed of three rectangles and two right-angled triangles.

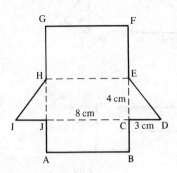

a) Name the solid formed by the net and sketch it.

b) Find the surface area of the solid.

c) Find the volume of the solid.

d) Calculate the length of AE   i) on the net   ii) in the solid.

e) A fly crawls on the surface of the solid from G to C. What is the shortest distance that the fly can crawl ?

6. Two tankers, X and Y are 4 km apart and X is due east of Y. The master of a ferry finds that the bearing of X from the ferry is 320° and the bearing of Y from the ferry is 290°. How far is the ferry from the tanker X ?

7. If $\sin x° = 1$, find the values of x in the range $0 \leqslant x \leqslant 720$.

8. $\mathbf{M} = \begin{pmatrix} 1 & -1 \\ 1 & 1 \end{pmatrix}$. Find

a) $\mathbf{M}^2$

b) integers n and m for which $\mathbf{M}^n = m\mathbf{I}$ where $\mathbf{I}$ is the identity matrix.

9. The diagram shows a 1:5 scale model of a car.

a) The model is 70 cm long. How long is the car ?

b) The surface area of glass on the model is 1020 cm². What is the area of glass on the car ?

c) The volume of the boot on the car is 1.3 m³. What is the volume of the boot on the model ?

10.

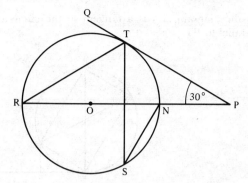

In the diagram, PQ is a tangent to the circle whose centre is O.

Find the size of

a) $T\widehat{O}P$.   b) $T\widehat{S}N$.   c) $R\widehat{S}T$.

11. The diagram shows a square-based pyramid. E is vertically above F, the centre of the base; AB $= 8$ cm and EF $= 10$ cm.

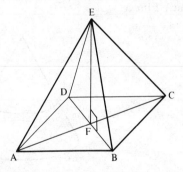

a) Find the length of EC.

b) Find the angle between edge EC and the base ABCD.

c) Find the angle between the face ECB and the base ABCD.

12. ABCDEF is a regular hexagon with each side 2 cm in length.

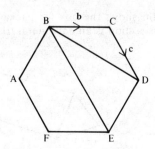

a) Show that $B\widehat{D}E = 90°$.

b) Show that $BD = 2\sqrt{3}$ cm.

c) Explain why $\overrightarrow{ED} = \mathbf{b} - \mathbf{c}$.

13. In the diagram, TA is a tangent to the circle and TB is a diameter. DF is parallel to BT.

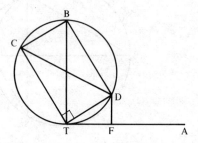

a) Show that △CDT is similar to △TDF.

b) Show that triangles BTD and CTD are congruent.

14. This candle is to be cut in half so that each half has the same weight (i.e. volume). Find *x*.

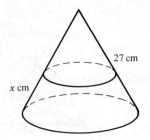

EXERCISE 17h

1. The diagram shows the box for packaging a bar of chocolate. It is a prism whose cross-section is an equilateral triangle.

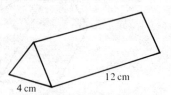

a) Sketch the cross-section and find the height of the box.

b) Sketch a net for the box and hence find its surface area.

2. At t hours after 6 a.m. the depth of water, h metres, at the end of a pier is given by $h = 8 - 3\sin(29t)°$.

a) Plot values of h against values of t at unit intervals from 0 to 12. Use a scale of 1 cm for 1 unit on both axes.

b) When was high tide and when was low tide ?

c) A passenger liner can tie up at the end of the pier provided there is at least 10 m of water. For how long can the liner tie up ?

3. When turning right at a junction, the recommended procedure is first to move as far to the right as possible while staying on the correct side of the road and then wait until it is safe to turn.

The diagram below shows an articulated lorry, L, 3 m wide and 20 m long which is about to turn right. The lorry is loaded with steel girders which project 5 m beyond the rear axle, PQ, of the lorry.

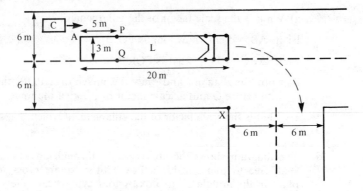

a) The lorry turns right in such a way that its rear wheels, P and Q, turn in quadrants of circles, centre X, starting level with the corner X. Make a scale drawing, using a scale of 1:100, showing the road layout, the starting position of the rear wheels of the lorry, and the position, A, of the end of the nearside girder. Mark P_1, Q_1 and A_1 the initial positions of P, Q and A.

b) Plot different positions of P, Q and A as XQP turns about X, 10° at a time. A_1 is the initial position of A and A_{10} will show the position of A when turning right is complete.
Use your drawing to estimate how close the end of the nearside girder gets to the edge of the road.

c) The driver of a car, C sees the back end of the lorry swinging towards him. The car is 2 m wide. Will the driver of the car need to take evasive action to avoid being hit by the lorry ?

4. The coordinates of the vertices of a triangle are $(2, 0)$, $(-3, -1)$, $(1, 4)$. Draw the triangle and label it A.

a) Draw the image of A when it is rotated 90° clockwise about the origin and then enlarged by a factor 3, centre the origin. Label the image B.

b) Find the matrix which defines the inverse of the transformation that maps A to B.

5. In this diagram, △PQR is an enlargement of △ABC.

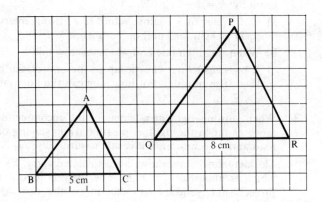

a) What is the scale factor of the enlargement ?

b) If AB = 5 cm, how long is PQ ?

c) If $A\widehat{B}C = 53°$, what is $P\widehat{Q}R$?

d) Copy the diagram and draw the image of △PQR under an enlargement with centre Q and a scale factor of $\frac{1}{2}$. Label the image XYZ.

e) What is the scale factor of the enlargement which maps △ABC to △XYZ ?

6. The diagram shows the cross section through an assembly of a cylindrical shaft free to rotate inside a box with a square cross section. It is kept in place in the middle of the box by four cylindrical rollers, one in each corner of the box. (Only one of these rollers is shown.)

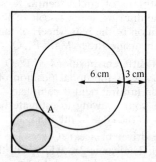

In the diagram, the radius of the circle in the centre is 6 cm and the sides of the box are 18 cm long.

a) Make a full size copy of the diagram but leave out the small circle.

b) Now add the small circle to the diagram, showing all necessary construction lines.

c) What is the diameter of this circle ?

7. a) On the same set of axes, sketch the graphs $y = 1 + \cos x°$ and $y = 1 - \dfrac{x}{300}$, for values of x in the range $-180 \leqslant x \leqslant 180$.

b) How many solutions does the equation $x + 300 \cos x° = 0$ have ?

c) By plotting a suitable section of the graph, find the largest solution to the equation.

EXERCISE 17i

The problems in this exercise are relevant to Attainment Target 1. Those marked with a dagger are longer problems.

1. A corridor is 1 m wide and 3 m high.

a) A heavy pipe is slid along the floor. What is the longest pipe that will go round the corner ?

b) What is the longest thin rod, light enough to be picked up and manoeuvered at any angle, that will go round the corner ?

2. This diagram is the net for a dice. The number of dots on pairs of opposite faces add up to seven.

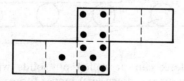

a) Copy and complete the net.

b) Draw a different net for the same dice.

3. This is a classic puzzle. Sketch or describe the one solid that will pass, with no space to spare, through each of the three holes drawn below.

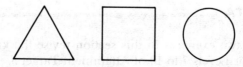

4. a) i) Prove that the square of any odd number greater than 1 can be expressed as the sum of 2 consecutive numbers.

   ii) There is a connection between the three numbers in part (i) and the three sides of certain right-angled triangles. Explain this.

b) Prove that twice the square of any number greater than 1 is the sum of either two consecutive even numbers or two consecutive odd numbers. Find a geometric relationship between twice the original number and the two final numbers.

5. Prove that the circle drawn on the hypotenuse of a right-angled triangle as diameter, passes through the opposite vertex of the triangle.

6. The numbers in this matrix form a magic square, i.e. the sum of the elements in any row, column or diagonal is the same.

$$\begin{pmatrix} 2 & 7 & 6 \\ 9 & 5 & 1 \\ 4 & 3 & 8 \end{pmatrix}$$

a) Find the square of the matrix. Describe the pattern the entries form.

b) Investigate the squares of other 3×3 matrices whose entries form a magic square.

†7. Pythagoras' theorem states that the area of the square drawn on the hypotenuse of a right-angled triangle is equal to the sum of the areas of the squares drawn on the other two sides of the triangle. Investigate other similar shapes drawn on the sides of right-angled triangles.

†8. A plank can be rolled on cylinders. As the plank is pushed forward, the cylinder emerging at the back can be taken to the front.

a) The plank can be rolled on solids with other cross-sections without moving up and down as it moves forward. One such cross-section has the shape of a 50p coin. Investigate why this works.

b) Find some other cross-section shapes which will achieve the same result.

c) What are the practical difficulties of making a wheel in the shape of a 50p coin ?

HANDLING DATA

The first two exercises in this section revise the knowledge and techniques needed for Levels 7 to 10 of Attainment Target 5.

EXERCISE 17j

1. Peter suspected that a dice he owned was biased so he rolled it many times. The results are in this table.

Score	1	2	3	4	5	6
Frequency	54	75	120	180	94	78

a) How many times did he roll the dice ?

b) Using the figures in the table, what is the probability that the next roll of his dice will score   i) 6   ii) either 3 or 4 ?

2. To start a game of darts, a player has to hit a 'double' and is allowed three attempts at each turn. The probability that Joe will be successful with his first dart is 20 %. The probability that he will be successful with his second dart is 30 % and the probability that he will be successful with his third dart is 40 %.

a) What is the probability that Joe will not hit a double with his first dart ?

b) What is the probability that Joe will not hit a double with any of his first three darts ?

3. An ordinary unbiased dice is rolled.

a) If the dice is rolled three times, what is the probability that a six is scored each time ?

b) If the dice is rolled twice, what is the probability that
   i) just one six is scored
   ii) a 'double' is scored (i.e. the same number is scored with each roll) ?

c) If the dice is rolled 3000 times, how many of these rolls is likely to result in a six ?

4. Three cards are dealt, one after the other, from an ordinary pack of 52 playing cards.

a) What is the probability that the first card is a spade ?

b) What is the probability that the first two cards are spades ?

c) What is the probability that all three cards are aces ?

5. Jamie runs a sideshow at a school fête that involves taking a straw from a cup. A prize is won if the straw has a black end. There are two cups, a yellow cup holding 60 straws of which 5 have black ends and a red cup holding 54 straws of which 8 have black ends. The straw is put back into the cup it was taken from. Joanna has a go.

a) What is the probability that she chooses the yellow cup ?

b) If she chooses the red cup, what is the probability that she wins a prize ?

c) What is the probability that she wins a prize ?

d) If she does win a prize, what is the probability that she chose the red cup ?

e) Jamie estimates that about 500 people will have a try. How many prizes should he provide ?

6. This planning network shows the time, in minutes, needed to machine the parts required for a plug.

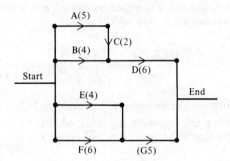

a) If at least four machines are available, how long does the activity take to complete ?

b) If only two machines are available, how long does the job take ?

7. A market gardener has to replant his apple orchard. He has room for at most 200 trees. He decides to plant a mixture of cooking apple trees and eating apple trees, with at least 50 eating and at least 10 cooking apple trees. He also decides that he wants at least twice as many eating as cooking apple trees. An eating apple tree yields a crop of 200 kg and a cooking apple tree yields 300 kg.

a) If x is the number of cooking apple trees and y is the number of eating apple trees, write down as many inequalities concerning x and y as you can.

b) Illustrate these inequalities on a graph, shading the region where all of them are satisfied.

c) If the total yield of the trees is P kg, write down an equation connecting P, x and y. Hence find the number of each variety of tree he should buy to maximise the yield.

8. The activities involved when two people close up a market stall for the day, and the time taken for each activity are given in the table.

Activity	Time required (minutes)	Activities to be done previously
A Bank money	10	D
B Pack goods in boxes	8	
C Load boxes in van	5	B
D Count money	5	
E Remove placards	3	
F Put placards in van	1	E
G Collect rubbish	4	B
H Bin rubbish	1	G
I Clean stall	5	B, C, E, F, G

Use a critical path diagram (planning network) to find the minimum time needed to do this job.

EXERCISE 17k

1. This table shows the distribution of the heights of a batch of tomato plants three weeks after the seeds were planted.

Height (h cm)	$0 \leqslant h < 5$	$5 \leqslant h < 10$	$10 \leqslant h < 15$	$15 \leqslant h < 20$	$20 \leqslant h < 25$	25–
Frequency	20	4	15	36	25	0

a) How many seeds were sown ?

b) What could be a reason for the high frequency in the $0 \leqslant h < 5$ group ?

c) Draw a frequency polygon to illustrate the information.

d) A second batch of tomato seeds of a different variety were planted and the heights of the resulting plants were measured after three weeks. The information is illustrated in this frequency polygon.

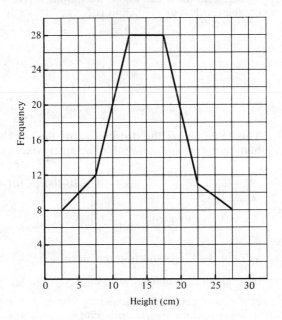

Compare the distribution of the heights of the two batches of plants.

2. Use the frequency table given in question 1 for the first batch of tomatoes, and the frequency polygon given for the second batch, to construct cumulative frequency tables for the given data. Hence draw the corresponding cumulative frequency curves and use them to find the median and interquartile range for each batch of tomatoes.

Compare the interquartile ranges for the two batches.

3. This table shows the maximum speed and the fuel consumption in m.p.g. at a steady speed of 56 m.p.h. for some cars.

Maximum speed (m.p.h.)	99	121	137	119	132	134	112	135	106	139
Fuel consumption at steady 56 m.p.h. (m.p.g.)	55.4	44.1	47.9	42.8	35.3	36.7	41.5	29.6	52.3	25.4

a) Plot a scatter diagram to illustrate the relationship between the maximum speed of a car and the fuel consumption at a steady 56 m.p.h.

b) The fuel economy of one car appears to be out of line with the general pattern. What is the maximum speed of this car ?

c) Draw a line of best fit and use it to predict the fuel consumption at 56 m.p.h. for a car whose maximum speed is 145 m.p.h. How reliable do you think your prediction is ?

4. This table shows the distribution of the weekly wages paid to employees, both part-time and full-time, of a supermarket chain.

Wages	£1–50	£51–100	£101–150	£151–200	£201–400
Frequency	150	0	85	150	5
Cumulative frequency					

a) Give the range and find the mean wage.

b) Copy and complete the table.

c) Draw a cumulative frequency curve and use it to estimate the median wage and the interquartile range.

d) Give a possible reason for the large number in the first group.

e) If you were the owner of the supermarket chain and wanted to give a figure for the spread of the weekly wages of employees, would you choose the range or the interquartile range ? Give a reason for your choice.

f) If you wanted to give as fair a figure as possible for the average weekly wage of employees, would you choose the mean or the median ? Give reasons for your choice.

g) If you were free to work out an average in any way you chose, what could you do to give a fair idea of average wages ?

5. One hundred apples were weighed and their weights, to the nearest gram and in order of size, are given in this list.

45	46	46	47	49	51	52	54	60	67	70	78	80	85	85	88	90	92	95	97
97	100	102	103	103	105	106	107	107	108	108	109	109	109	110	111	112	112	113	114
115	116	116	116	117	117	118	118	118	119	119	119	119	120	120	120	120	121	121	122
123	124	125	125	127	129	130	131	132	132	133	134	135	137	137	139	140	145	147	150
155	160	168	170	172	180	195	198	200	210	220	225	230	239	250	267	270	276	286	291

a) Copy and complete the following frequency table.

Weight (w grams)	$40 \leqslant w < 80$	$80 \leqslant w < 100$	$100 \leqslant w < 120$	$120 \leqslant w < 140$	$140 \leqslant w < 200$	$200 \leqslant w < 300$
Half-way value	60					
Frequency	12					

b) Draw a histogram to illustrate the data.

c) Use halfway values to find the mean weight. Explain why the result is an estimate.

6. Joanne did a survey in which she asked pupils in her school how much money they received each week, including pocket money and earnings. This histogram shows the results of this survey.

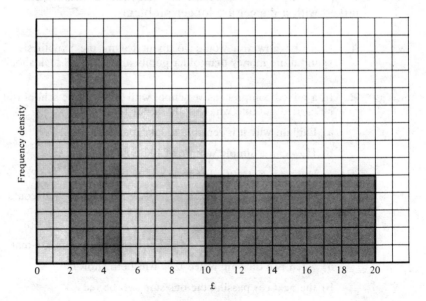

If 36 pupils said they had less than £2 a week, how many pupils were asked in the survey?

7. This table shows the distribution of weights of 100 'Golden Wonder' marrows.

Weight (w kg)	$0 \leqslant w < 1$	$1 \leqslant w < 2$	$2 \leqslant w < 3$	$3 \leqslant w < 4$	$4 \leqslant w < 5$
Frequency	10	15	35	24	16

a) Find the mean weight and the standard deviation.

b) A similar analysis of 100 'Green Giant' marrows showed that their mean weight was 2.49 kg and their standard deviation was 1.39 kg. Which variety showed the greater variability of weights ?

c) If you had to choose which of these varieties to grow in an attempt to win the heaviest marrow competition, which would you select and why ? Assume that the weights for each variety have a normal distribution.

8. Jason is doing a survey on the use made of the school canteen.

a) Write three suitable questions for a questionnaire.

b) Jason cannot ask everyone in the school. Suggest ways in which he could try to get a representative sample of students.

EXERCISE 17I

The questions in this exercise are relevant to Attainment Target 1. Those marked with a dagger are longer problems.

1. Describe how you would go about testing the hypothesis, 'Younger pupils spend more money than older pupils in the school tuck shop'.

2. In a mixed comprehensive school with 2000 on the school roll, a survey is to be carried out into what pupils eat for lunch.

a) Explain why it is sensible to take a sample.

b) How can a simple sample of 100 pupils be chosen ?

c) How can a stratified sample of 100 pupils be chosen ?

d) Write down three multiple response questions that could be part of the questionnaire.

3. Explain how you would find a figure for the probability that

a) when two dice are rolled they will both show 6

b) the next car passing the bus stop will be red

c) the newsagent will sell 50 copies of the *Sun* tomorrow

d) you will be studying some mathematics in two years time.

†**4.** The tables give details for the maximum speed, acceleration and fuel economy (in m.p.g.) for a selection of petrol and diesel engine cars.

Petrol engines

Max. speed (m.p.h.)	99	121	137	119	132	134	112	135	106	139
Seconds to reach 62.5 m.p.h. from 0	16.0	9.5	8.0	10.9	9.2	9.8	13.5	8.5	16.5	8.5
Fuel economy (m.p.g.) Simulated urban driving	32.8	25.7	28.5	24.8	19.3	20.0	23.3	27.7	31.7	27.2
At 56 m.p.h.	55.4	44.1	47.9	42.8	35.3	36.7	41.5	49.6	52.3	49.6
At 75 m.p.h.	42.6	34.9	38.2	34.0	28.2	30.1	32.5	39.2	40.9	39.2

Diesel engines

Max. speed (m.p.h.)	95	104	107	100	108	101	112	94	109	93
Seconds to reach 62.5 m.p.h. from 0	18.5	14.5	13.5	17.9	15.1	19.0	14.0	20.0	14.5	19.5
Fuel economy (m.p.g.) Simulated urban driving	40.9	39.8	39.8	30.4	32.8	35.8	32.1	42.2	42.2	40.9
At 56 m.p.h.	67.3	54.3	58.9	53.3	51.4	54.3	51.4	64.2	61.4	64.2
At 75 m.p.h.	47.1	39.8	42.8	40.9	39.8	40.4	39.2	47.1	44.8	44.5

a) Use this information to decide whether or not the following statements are sensible.

   i) Diesel engines give more miles per gallon than petrol engines.

   ii) If I intend to do a lot of urban driving there is a far greater incentive to buy a car with a diesel engine than one with a petrol engine.

   iii) Cars with petrol engines have better acceleration and higher top speeds than cars with diesel engines.

   iv) At 75 m.p.h. diesel engines have little advantage over petrol engines in terms of fuel economy.

   v) Fuel economy for cars with diesel engines travelling at 75 m.p.h. shows little variability.

   vi) The faster a car with a petrol engine is driven the poorer the fuel economy.

b) Collect what other information you need and then give a considere response to the following statement.

   The cost of running a car with a diesel engine is considerably cheaper for urban driving than a car with a petrol engine.

†**5.** It is often said that it is possible to detect an author's style of writing.

a) List some features of prose that can be compared using statistics.

b) Compare a piece of prose written in the nineteenth century with a piece of prose written in the second half of the twentieth century.

c) Is there any evidence to suggest that the two pieces of prose given below are written by different people ?

i) *Concetta knocked at the door at half past seven. The morning was as bright and cloudless as all the mornings were. Barbara jumped up, looked from one window at the mountains, from the other at the sea; all seemed to be well with them. All was well with her too, this morning. Seated at the mirror, she did not so much as think of the big monkey in the far obscure corner of the room. A bathing dress and a bath-gown, sandals, a hand-kerchief round her head, and she was ready. Sleep had left no recollection of last night's boredom. She ran downstairs.*

ii) *The moon burnt for a moment through the clouded sky and silvered the rails and the steps of the fire-escape, showed the huddle of chimney pots above him, and dimmed the light in the top room. It travelled between the clouds with the swiftness of a car, and the whole globe heeled over with it. The Assistant Commissioner clutched the rail and lowered his head, attacked again by dizziness. Every attack was followed by a great fear, not the fear of death, but the fear of enforced retirement, a fear which he fought with his efficiency, his hesitations which conserved his energy, and his meticulousness. With that chill at his brain he mounted the last steps.*

ANSWERS

CHAPTER 1

Exercise 1a   Page 2

No answers are provided for this exercise because there is more than one way to write out an acceptable solution. Also some of the criticisms of the given solutions are in the category of 'bad practice' and the perception of bad practice varies from one individual to another.

Exercise 1b   Page 8

This exercise provides examples for discussion.

CHAPTER 2

Test 2A   Page 11

1. 82   **2.** 14   **3.** 32   **4.** 645   **5.** 1677   **6.** 43   **7.** 1791   **8.** 66   **9.** 48

Test 2B   Page 11

1. -5 **3.** 10   **5.** -12 **7.** -2 **9.** -10 **11.** 22   **13.** 6   **15.** -5 **17.** -8
2. -12 **4.** -3 **6.** -2 **8.** 9   **10.** 7   **12.** 6   **14.** -4 **16.** -18 **18.** 11

Test 2C   Page 12

1. 2   **3.** 7   **5.** 14   **7.** 6   **9.** 30   **11.** 100   **13.** $2 \times 3 \times 5$ **15.** $2 \times 3^2 \times 5^2 \times 7$
2. 4   **4.** 7   **6.** 8   **8.** 12   **10.** 60   **12.** 120   **14.** $2^2 \times 3^3$

Exercise 2a   Page 13

1. 111   **4.** 2820   **7.** 68   **10.** 3   **13.** 752   **16.** 51459 **19.** 27   **22.** 504
2. 217   **5.** 72   **8.** 2271   **11.** 6   **14.** 1518   **17.** 19   **20.** 126   **23.** 120
3. 1144   **6.** 12   **9.** 80   **12.** 13   **15.** 1782   **18.** 31   **21.** 30   **24.** 60

Exercise 2b   Page 13

1. 5   **4.** 15   **7.** -2 **10.** 48   **13.** 15   **16.** 6   **19.** 2   **22.** -12
2. 1   **5.** 8   **8.** -7 **11.** 16   **14.** 30   **17.** 19   **20.** 5   **23.** 0
3. -10 **6.** 3   **9.** -4 **12.** 2   **15.** -2 **18.** -8 **21.** 4   **24.** 16

Exercise 2c   Page 14

1. 6
2. 4
3. 5
4. 12
5. 18
6. 12
7. 15
8. 6
9. 30
10. 20
11. 24
12. 42

13. i) 6   ii) 216
14. i) 12   ii) 864
15. i) 1   ii) 140
16. i) 9   ii) 630
17. $2^3 \times 3$
18. $2^3 \times 3^2$
19. $2^2 \times 3 \times 7^2$
20. $2^2 \times 3 \times 5^2$
21. $2^2 \times 3 \times 11$
22. $2 \times 3 \times 13$
23. $2 \times 3^2 \times 13$
24. $2^3 \times 3^2 \times 5^2$

25. $2^2 \times 3^2 \times 5^2$; 30
26. $2^2 \times 7^2$; 14
27. $2^6 \times 7^2$; 56
28. $3^2 \times 13^2$; 39
29. 3×5^2; 3
30. 2×3^4; 2
31. $2^2 \times 3 \times 5$; 15
32. $2^4 \times 3^2 \times 7 \times 11$; 77
33. a) 60 mins   b) 9828 s
34. a) 24 cm   b) 61
35. 126 m

Test 2D   Page 16

1. $1\frac{1}{12}$
2. $\frac{1}{4}$
3. $\frac{7}{20}$
4. $1\frac{7}{8}$
5. $1\frac{17}{35}$
6. $\frac{9}{35}$
7. $3\frac{3}{4}$
8. $1\frac{21}{40}$
9. $\frac{65}{108}$
10. $\frac{16}{39}$
11. $\frac{4}{5}$
12. $2\frac{1}{20}$
13. $\frac{13}{22}$
14. $16\frac{2}{3}$
15. $3\frac{7}{16}$

Exercise 2d   Page 17

1. $1\frac{5}{24}$
2. $4\frac{26}{35}$
3. $\frac{3}{20}$
4. $1\frac{1}{6}$
5. $\frac{3}{5}$
6. 5
7. $\frac{9}{77}$
8. $\frac{25}{48}$
9. $\frac{5}{36}$
10. $\frac{9}{20}$
11. $1\frac{4}{5}$
12. $\frac{17}{30}$
13. $-\frac{1}{6}$
14. $\frac{3}{5}$
15. $\frac{13}{20}$
16. $\frac{15}{16}$
17. 62
18. $12\frac{3}{8}$
19. $3\frac{1}{3}$
20. $1\frac{1}{2}$
21. $75\frac{3}{5}$
22. $\frac{3}{5}$
23. $2\frac{14}{65}$
24. $\frac{1}{128}$

Test 2E   Page 18

1. 0.3
2. 1.23
3. 4.21
4. −1.39
5. 0.72
6. 0.017
7. 0.45
8. 0.016
9. 50
10. 0.3
11. 4
12. 40

Test 2F   Page 18

1. 0.47
2. 9400
3. 1 120 000
4. 17.8
5. 0.0705
6. 2.8
7. 0.2572
8. 5.033
9. 0.232

Exercise 2e   Page 19

1. 60
2. 0.0054
3. 0.064
4. 0.79
5. 1.423
6. 800
7. 1.44
8. −3.4
9. 12.58
10. 0.125
11. −0.73
12. 0.458
13. 1
14. 4
15. 1
16. 50
17. 0.0675
18. 0.9

Exercise 2f   Page 20

1. 20
2. 5
3. 1.2
4. 4
5. 2
6. 3
7. 0.5
8. 0.03
9. 4
10. 3
11. 500
12. 1000
13. 12
14. 10
15. 1

Exercise 2g   Page 23

1. −143
2. 0.001 92
3. 3.50
4. 2.51
5. 4270
6. 0.214
7. a) 0.8   b) 0.688
   d) i) 0.652   ii) 3.13
8. 0.384
9. a) 0.111...
   b) 0.$\dot{1}$
   c) 0.5
10. a) 0.$\dot{1}$42 85$\dot{7}$
    b) 0.1$\dot{8}$
    c) 0.8$\dot{3}$
    d) 0.2$\dot{3}$
11. $\frac{2}{9}$

12. $\frac{1}{3}$
13. $\frac{10}{3}$
14. $\frac{1}{90}$
15. $\frac{1}{30}$
16. $\frac{10}{9}$
17. $\frac{1}{99}$
18. $\frac{1}{33}$
19. $\frac{10}{99}$
20. b) e.g. 0.076 923 08 to 8 d.p.
    c) No. Multiply the answer to (a) by 13.
    d) Multiply 0.174 825 1 by 143: this gives a number less than 25 so it has been rounded down.

21. 0.026, 0.053, 0.25, 0.52, 2.07
22. $\frac{1}{2}$, 0.555, $\frac{2}{3}$, 0.67
23. 0.037, $\frac{1}{20}$, $\frac{4}{15}$, 0.295, 0.542
24. −3, $\frac{3}{8}$, 2.7, 3.8
25. $-2\frac{2}{3}$, −1.63, $1\frac{2}{3}$, 2.25
26. If the calculator rounds down and then uses this rounded down value for the next calculation, the result will be less than the true value.

Exercise 2h   Page 26

1. 2×10^{11}
2. 1×10^5
3. 2×10^6
4. 5.04×10^6
5. 2.8×10^{-2}
6. 4.9992×10^6
7. 16.6
8. 0.966
9. 0.335

10. 7200.81
11. 5830
12. 73.6
13. 4.67×10^{-11}
14. 6.25
15. 1 15.2
    2 5.29
    3 1.13
    4 3.72

    5 1.74
    6 3.44
    7 0.460
    8 0.0382
    9 3.89
    10 3.28
16. 1.49×10^{-10}
17. 2.23×10^{-3} g
18. a) 15 minutes   b) 2.123×10^8 km

Test 2G   Page 27

1. a) 24%   b) 29%
   c) 175%   d) 1.5%
2. a) $\frac{21}{50}$ b) $\frac{7}{25}$
   c) $\frac{1}{40}$ d) $1\frac{1}{5}$

3. a) 0.12   b) 1.15
   c) 6.4   d) 0.45
4. £57
5. 34 m³

6. 400
7. 288 m²
8. $\frac{3}{5}$
9. 65%

Test 2H   Page 27

1. 300 g
2. 4.4 lb
3. 20% decrease
4. 5 p
5. 800

Exercise 2i   Page 28

1. a) $\frac{3}{10}$ b) $\frac{41}{50}$
   c) $1\frac{3}{10}$ d) $1\frac{1}{4}$

2. a) 93%   b) 9.5%
   c) 37.5%   d) 46.7%

3. a) 0.54   b) 2.6
   c) 1.38   d) 0.364

4. 28%, $\frac{2}{7}$, 0.3, $\frac{1}{3}$
5. $\frac{4}{7}$, 55%, 0.48, $\frac{5}{11}$
6. a) £2.20   b) 700 g
7. a) £9   b) 35 miles
8. a) $8\frac{1}{8}$ (exactly) or 8.13 m
   to 3 s.f.
   b) £54.60

9. a) 48 litres   b) 0.6 m
10. a) $\frac{4}{13}$ b) 30.8%
11. 40%
12. 38
13. 57.7%
14. 2849
15. 4%

Exercise 2j   Page 30

Answers are given exact, or corrected to the nearest penny, cm, etc. depending on the context of the question.

1. a) £88   b) £92
   c) £86
2. a) £139.50   b) £105
   c) £131.25
3. a) 25%   b) 20%
   c) 10%   d) $12\frac{1}{2}$%
4. £11 200
5. £42.30
6. £4.30

7. 2.70 m (2.63 m is the
   calculated answer but dress
   material is usually sold in
   10 cm units)
8. Loss of 11.1%
9. £100 000
10. 37.5%
11. 162 cm
12. 25%

13. 70
14. £1400
15. 460 g
16. 660 tons
17. £150
18. £850.67
19. a) 5%   b) 5%
20. £48.49

Exercise 2k   Page 33

1. £420

2. £240

3. a) £78
   b) the piano and the ring
4. a) £525   b) £252

5. a) £251.40   b) £243.78
6. £2103; about £40 (£40.44)
7. About £160 (£158.71)

Test 2I   Page 34 —————————————————————————————————

1. 2 : 3   **3.** 2.5 km   **5.** £ 28, £ 8   **7.** 30 cm

2. 1 : 3.5   **4.** 2 : 5   **6.** 6 m, 18 m, 24 m

Exercise 2I   Page 35 —————————————————————————————————

1. 16 : 3   **8.** 1 : 50   **15.** 1 : 40 000
2. 15 : 2   **9.** 1 : 10 000   **16.** 2.6 km
3. 2 : 4 : 7   **10.** 1 : 200 000   **17.** £ 20, £ 25
4. 1 : 1.75   **11.** 1 : 2500   **18.** £ 14, £ 21, £ 21
5. 1 : 3.125   **12.** 1 : 24   **19.** 5 cm
6. 1 : 4000   **13.** 1 : 500   **20.** 1 : 4
7. 4 : 7   **14.** 6 cm

Exercise 2m   Page 37 —————————————————————————————————

1. 54 litres   **5.** £ 9.60 per m² is cheaper,   **9.** 2400 sq ft/gallon
2. 16 mm (some patterns say   £ 8.75/sq yd ≈ £ 10.25/m²   **10.** About 200 miles
  'use $\frac{5}{8}''$ or 15 mm')   **6.** a) 2   b) 1.5 ha   **11.** 1600 m²
3. 1.8 m   The answers to questions 7–9 are
4. Apples sold loose (1 kg for   approximate.
  98 p is about 45 p per lb)   **7.** a) 22 m/s   b) 28.8 km/h
                                     8. a) 25 m.p.h.   b) 112 km/h

Exercise 2n   Page 38 —————————————————————————————————

1. a) 14.3 cm³   **4.** 2614.4   **6.** £ 900
  b) 70   **5.** a) 5, 7   b) 9, 12, 15   **7.** a) 9.1×10^{10} km
2. £ 297.50   c) 1, 4, 5, 12, 15   b) 1 : 0.494
3. 215   d) 1, 4, 9   c) 167 hours

Exercise 2p   Page 39 —————————————————————————————————

1. $3^2 \times 7^2$, 21   **3.** 19 full glasses with some left   **5.** £ 114 000
                                        over.   **6.** 1 : 192 000
2. £ 510   **4.** $\frac{11}{100}$ **7.** 0.8 fl. oz.

Exercise 2q   Page 40 —————————————————————————————————

1. a) 36   b) 24   **3.** £ 12.50, £ 15, £ 22.50   **5.** $3\frac{5}{6}$
  c) 3   **6.** £ 186.67
2. £ 14 675   **4.** £ 575.13   **7.** 3.39

Exercise 2r   Page 40 —————————————————————————————————

1. C   **3.** D   **5.** A   **7.** A   **9.** A   **11.** C
2. B   **4.** B   **6.** B   **8.** B   **10.** C   **12.** B

CHAPTER 3

Exercise 3a   Page 42

1. $5x^2 - 2x - 3$
2. $6x^2$
3. x^3
4. $3x$
5. $x^2 - 3x$
6. $-a + 3b + c$
7. $42xy$
8. $x^2 - x$
9. x^3
10. x
11. $6x - 8$

12. $6a + 4b + 8$
13. $10x - 1$
14. $x^2 - 4x - 8$
15. $ac - ab$
16. $12 + 9x - 4x^2$
17. $x^2 + 7x + 12$
18. $x^2 + x - 12$
19. $x^2 - 25$
20. $x^2 - 10x + 25$
21. $2x^2 - 5x - 12$
22. $ac - bc - ad + bd$

23. $4x^2 + 20x + 25$
24. $1 + x - 6x^2$
25. $x^2 - xy - 2y^2$
26. $6 - x - x^2$
27. $4x + 9$
28. $a^2 + b^2$
29. $4x^2 - 4x - 8$
30. $2x^2 + 4x + 10$
31. $4x - x^2$
32. $-12x^2 + 42x - 18$

Exercise 3b   Page 43

1. $2(x - 2)$
2. $3(2a - 3c)$
3. $2x(x - 3)$
4. $6(2a + 3b - 4c)$
5. $xy(x + y)$
6. $x(x - 1)$

7. $4(x + 5y)$
8. $9xy(x + 2y)$
9. $(a + b)(x + 2y)$
10. $(p - r)(q + s)$
11. $(2m - p)(n - q)$
12. $(x^2 + 1)(x + 1)$

13. $(v - 3)(4u + 3)$
14. $(a - 2x)(b - 2y)$
15. $(ax - y)(x + a)$
16. $(a - 2c)(b - 3d)$

Exercise 3c   Page 44

1. $(x + 4)(x + 8)$
2. $(x - 3)(x - 4)$
3. $(x - 3)(x + 3)$
4. $(x - 3)^2$
5. $(a - 7)^2$
6. $(y + 9)(y - 2)$
7. $(x + 5)(x - 3)$
8. $(x - 11)(x + 7)$
9. $(x + 6)(x + 5)$
10. $x(x - 9)$
11. $3(x + 1)^2$
12. $4(x + 3)(x - 1)$
13. $9(y - 2)(y + 2)$
14. $5(y - 1)(y - 7)$
15. $6x(2x - 3)$
16. $2(b - 5)(b - 2)$

17. $8(x + 3)(x - 2)$
18. $3(x + 4)(x - 4)$
19. $(2x + 1)(x + 3)$
20. $(3x - 1)(x + 4)$
21. $(3x - 2)(3x + 2)$
22. $(3x + 1)(2x + 3)$
23. $(3x - 5)(4x - 3)$
24. $(5x - 2)(x + 1)$
25. $(2x + 3)(2x - 1)$
26. $(6x - 5)(2x - 3)$
27. $(12x - 5)(x - 3)$
28. $(5x - 3)(5x + 3)$
29. $x(x - 25)$
30. $(5 - x)(5 + x)$
31. $(x - 5)^2$
32. $(x - 25)(x - 1)$

33. $(x + 5)(x + 5a)$
34. $(1 - 4x)(1 + 3x)$
35. $5(2x - 3)(x - 1)$
36. $5(x + 5)^2$
37. $(101 + 99)(101 - 99)$
$= 200 \times 2 = 400$
38. $(2x - 3)(2x + 3)$.
$391 = 20^2 - 3^2 = 23 \times 17$
39. $3(x - 4)(x + 4)$.
$252 = 3(10^2 - 4^2)$
$= 3 \times 3 \times 2 \times 2 \times 7$
40. $k = 6.24$
41. 57.2
42. $30^2 - 1^2 = 29 \times 31$

Exercise 3d   Page 46

1. 11
2. 45
3. 72
4. 3
5. -6

6. 12
7. $3\frac{1}{3}$
8. not possible
9. $-\frac{1}{6}$
10. 2

11. 7
12. not possible
13. a) ± 13 b) ± 3
14. a) 18   b) 2
c) -9
15. $\pm \frac{6}{5}$

Exercise 3e   Page 47

1. 32
2. 1
3. 10
4. 27
5. $\frac{1}{25}$
6. $\frac{1}{9}$
7. 18
8. $1\frac{2}{3}$
9. 2^6

10. 5^3
11. 4^0
12. 2^{-2}
13. a^7
14. a^3
15. a^{10}
16. a^3
17. $a^5 + a^2$
18. $7a$

19. a^7
20. 1
21. a^{-10}
22. 6
23. 2
24. 5
25. $\frac{3}{2}$
26. $\frac{3}{2}$
27. 3

28. x
29. 1
30. $x^{1/4}$
31. $x^{1/2} + x^{1/3}$
32. $18x^6$
33. x^2
34. $x^{1/2}$
35. x^2
36. x

37. $a^{1/2} \times b^{1/3}$
38. $x^{1/4}$
39. x^2
40. 4
41. 4
42. 6
43. 2
44. 3
45. 3

Exercise 3f   Page 49

1. 8
2. 27
3. 1
4. $\frac{1}{2}$
5. 25
6. 81
7. $\frac{3}{2}$
8. 100

9. $\frac{1}{10\,000}$
10. x^2
11. $x^{3/2} + x^{1/2}$
12. x
13. x
14. x^2
15. x^{-2}
16. $x^{1/2}$

17. $x^{1/2}$
18. $x^{3/2}$
19. a) 6×10^{10} b) 1.5×10^2
    c) 3.02×10^6 d) 2.98×10^6
20. a) 3.84×10^{-7} b) 1.5×10
    c) 2.56×10^{-3} d) 2.24×10^{-3}

Exercise 3g   Page 50

1. 2
2. $1\frac{2}{3}$
3. 5
4. 1
5. $\frac{3}{4}$

6. 1
7. 3
8. -8
9. $\frac{3}{2}$
10. 2

11. -3
12. $5\frac{1}{2}$
13. 4
14. 12
15. $34\frac{1}{2}°$, $69°$, $76\frac{1}{2}°$

Exercise 3h   Page 51

1. $x = 2, y = 1$
2. $x = -1, y = 4$
3. $x = 2, y = -3$
4. $x = 0, y = -1$
5. $x = 12, y = 5$
6. $x = -4, y = -24$
7. $x = 8, y = 3$
8. $x = 3, y = 1$

9. $x = 9, y = -6$
10. $x = 1, y = -2$
11. $x = 4, y = 1$
12. $x = -7, y = 3$
13. $x = 4\frac{1}{2}, y = 1\frac{1}{2}$
14. $x = -1, y = 1$
15. $x = 6, y = 1$
16. $x = 2, y = 1$

17. $x = -2, y = 4$
18. $x = 3, y = -2$
19. 6, 19
20. 27
21. length 17 cm, width 9 cm
22. 10 p

Exercise 3i   Page 54

1. $x = 2$ or $x = -3$
2. $x = 0$ or $x = 4$
3. $x = 1$ or $x = 5$
4. $x = -\frac{1}{4}$ or $x = \frac{6}{7}$
5. 4 or 3
6. ± 5
7. 0 or 6

8. 2 or -3
9. 7
10. 0 or -3
11. -2 or 4
12. 5 or 2
13. ± 1
14. $1\frac{1}{2}$ or $-2\frac{1}{2}$

15. 1 or 2
16. -1 or $\frac{1}{2}$
17. 3.83 or -1.83
18. $\frac{1}{2}$ or -1
19. -0.38 or -2.62
20. 1.18 or -0.85
21. 2.56 or -1.56

22. 3.64 or −0.14

23. 1.45 or −3.45

24. −0.29 or −1.71

25. 3.30 or −0.30

26. 1.43 or 0.23

27. 1.16 or −5.16

28. 1.62 or −0.62

29. ±4.47

30. 3.19 or 0.31

31. −5.16 or 1.16

32. 1.59 or −1.26

33. a) It is not possible to go beyond $(x-1)^2 = -4$ because $\sqrt{-4}$ is not real.

b) $x = \dfrac{2 \pm \sqrt{-16}}{2}$ and $\sqrt{-16}$ cannot be found.

34. a) i) not soluble by either method
   ii) not soluble

b) No, because $7^2 - (4 \times 1 \times 15)$ is negative

c) $b^2 - 4ac$ must be positive or zero

35. a) $p^2 - 12 \geqslant 0$

b) $25 - 4c \geqslant 0$

c) $q^2 - 4pr \geqslant 0$

d) $b^2 - 4ac \geqslant 0$

Exercise 3j   Page 58

1. a) $x = \pm1.38$
b) $x = -1.58$
c) $x = \pm2.14$
d) $x = \pm2.65$
e) $x = \pm1.68$
f) $x = 1.47$
g) $x = -2.08$
h) no solution
i) $x = \pm0.287$

2. ±2

3. $p = -10, q = 25$

4. $x^2 - 5x + 6 = 0$

5. 2.70 m

6. 4

7. 4 and 5 or −3 and −2

8. 9 or −8

9. a) $\dfrac{90}{x}$ hours

b) $\dfrac{90}{x+5}$ hours

c) $\dfrac{90}{x} - \dfrac{90}{x+5} = \dfrac{1}{4}$; 40

10. 30 mph

11. 8

Exercise 3k   Page 59

1. $\dfrac{xy}{10}$

2. $\dfrac{5}{3}$

3. $\dfrac{1}{ab}$

4. $\dfrac{b}{a}$

5. $\dfrac{8p}{qr}$

6. $\dfrac{12}{c}$

7. $\dfrac{3}{4}$

8. $\dfrac{9}{10}$

9. $3(x-1)$

10. $\dfrac{x}{2}$

11. $\dfrac{2}{x}$

12. −1

13. $\dfrac{x-2}{x+2}$

14. $\dfrac{x-2}{x-1}$

15. $\dfrac{x+3}{x-2}$

16. $\dfrac{x+3}{3}$

17. $\dfrac{a+b}{a-b}$

18. $\dfrac{x-4}{x-5}$

19. $-\dfrac{x+1}{2}$

20. $\dfrac{4}{9}$

21. 2

22. $\dfrac{1}{(x+a)^2}$

23. $\dfrac{(x+3)(x-4)}{(x-3)(x+4)}$

24. $\dfrac{(a+b)^2}{a^2+b^2}$

Exercise 3l   Page 60

1. $\dfrac{11x}{15}$

2. $\dfrac{3x+1}{21}$

3. $\dfrac{7x-1}{12}$

4. $\dfrac{19x-19}{10} = \dfrac{19(x-1)}{10}$

5. $\dfrac{x+3}{12}$

6. $\dfrac{2+x^2}{2x}$

7. $\dfrac{11}{2x}$

8. $\dfrac{-5}{(x+2)(x-3)}$

9. $\dfrac{26-3x}{20}$

10. $1\frac{4}{11}$

11. -5

12. $2\frac{4}{7}$

13. 2

14. 81

15. 1 or 6

16. 2

17. 4. -2

18. a) $\dfrac{5x+y}{x^2-y^2}$ b) $\dfrac{a^2-b^2+4}{2(a-b)}$

19. a) 11   b) $\frac{1}{15}$

20. a) 9 or 1   b) $\frac{1}{2}$

21. a) $\dfrac{1}{1-x}$ b) $\dfrac{1}{y-x}$

Exercise 3m   Page 62

1. $x = 1, y = 2$
   or $x = 2, y = 1$
2. $x = 3, y = -1$
   or $x = 1, y = -3$
3. $x = 2, y = 2$
   or $x = 1\frac{1}{2}, y = 2\frac{1}{2}$
4. $x = 4, y = -2$
   or $x = -\frac{8}{3}, y = \frac{14}{3}$
5. $x = 0, y = 3$
   or $x = 3, y = 0$
6. $x = 3, y = 4$
   or $x = 4, y = 3$
7. $x = -2, y = 6$
   or $x = 2\frac{1}{2}, y = -3$

8. $x = 0, y = -3$
   or $x = 2, y = 1$
9. $x = 4, y = 4$
   or $x = 0, y = 0$
10. $x = 2, y = 4$
   or $x = 12, y = \frac{2}{3}$
11. $x = 2, y = 3$
   or $x = 3, y = 2$
12. $x = 5, y = 1$
   or $x = -7, y = -5$
13. $x = 1, y = -1$
   or $x = \frac{17}{13}, y = \frac{-7}{13}$
14. $x = 1, y = 1$
   or $x = 5, y = -5$

15. $x = 3, y = 2$
   or $x = -\frac{3}{2}, y = -4$
16. $x = -1, y = 2$
   or $x = 7\frac{1}{2}, y = -1\frac{2}{5}$
17. $x = 1, y = -2$
   or $x = -\frac{1}{3}, y = -2\frac{8}{9}$
18. $x = 3, y = 2$
   or $x = \frac{5}{4}, y = 3\frac{3}{4}$
19. $x = 3, y = 1$
   or $x = -1, y = 5$
20. $x = 3, y = -2$
   or $x = 1, y = 2$

Exercise 3n   Page 65

1. a) $\dfrac{18a^2}{bc}$ b) $\dfrac{2c}{b}$
   c) $\dfrac{b+2c}{6a}$
2. $6 - 3x$

3. a) 5 or 0
   b) $\frac{1}{4}$
4. $\dfrac{5}{(x-2)(x+3)}$

5. a) 1   b) 2   c) $\frac{1}{64}$
6. 1.81 or -3.31
7. $\dfrac{x+4}{x+2}$

Exercise 3p   Page 65

1. ± 9
2. a) x^5 b) x^{-1} or $\frac{1}{x}$
   c) x^6

3. $x = 5, y = 3\frac{1}{2}$
4. a) $(x+2)(x-3)$
   b) $(x^2+1)(x-1)$

5. $\dfrac{14x-26}{15}$ or $\dfrac{2(7x-13)}{15}$
6. -6 or 7
7. $25 - 8a \geqslant 0$

Exercise 3q   Page 66

1. $\frac{1}{3}$ or 3
2. a) $4(x-2)(x+2)$
   b) $4x(x-4)$
   c) $(4x-1)(x-1)$

3. $-3\frac{4}{5}$
4. a) 4
   b) $\frac{1}{8}$
   c) 64

5. $x = -5, y = -4$
6. 5.83 or 0.17
7. 3

CHAPTER 4

Exercise 4a   Page 69

1. 483 cm²
2. 69.7 cm²
3. 56 cm²
4. 96 cm²
5. 216 cm²
6. 24 cm²
7. 38.5 cm²
8. 32.5 cm²
9. 226 cm²
10. 2120 cm²
11. 9.02 cm²
12. 86.6 cm²
13. a) approximately 210 cm²,
   216 cm², 2025 cm²
   b) 68.9π cm², 72π cm²,
   675π cm²
14. a) 101 cm² i.e. 32π cm²
   b) 3.27 cm² i.e. $\dfrac{25\pi}{24}$ cm²

15. 603 cm² (192π),
   1010 cm² (320π)
16. a) i) 29.4 cm by 21.6 cm
   ii) 0.294 m by 0.216 m
   b) i) 635.0 cm²   ii) 635 cm²
17. 188 cm² (60π), 8 cm
18. 2.82 cm
19. 2.44 cm
20. a) i) 25.1 cm   ii) 13.7 cm²
   iii) 78.5 %
   b) e.g.

21. a) 95 hectares
   b) 0.95 km²
22. a) 33.7 °   b) 3.15 m
   c) 1.05 m   d) 1.65 m²
23. a) 85.8 cm²   b) 114 cm²
   c) 75.2 %
24. a) 75 m²   b) 175 m²
   c) 80 m
25. 67.7 mm
26. a) 4630 cm²   b) 253 cm
   c) £ 3.70   d) 61 p
27. 400 cm²

Exercise 4b   Page 76

1. 1470 cm³, any number over
   681
2. 720 cm³
3. 121 cm³
4. 14 100 cm³
5. a) 3.4 cm³   b) 3400 mm³
6. 251 ml
7. 6$\frac{2}{3}$ cm
8. 4.30 cm
9. a) 25 cm   b) 1250 cm²
   c) 900 cm²   d) 7800 cm²
   e) 45 000 cm³
10. 20.5 cm
11. 27 cm
12. 20.4 mm

13. 3.04 cm
14. 579 cm³
15. a) 12 cm³   b) 55.8 cm³
   c) 48 cm³
16. a) 402 ft² (128π)
   b) 37.4 m²   c) 34.2 m³
17. 6.93 cm
18. a) 9π cm³   b) 3π cm³
   c) 20π cm³
19. 1.5 cm
20. a) $\frac{80}{9}$ cm   b) $\frac{8}{3}$
21. a) i) 3850 cm³   ii) 3.85 litres
   b) 0.223 m²

22. a) i) 216 cm³   ii) 72 cm³
   iii) 144 cm³
   b) i) 216 cm²   ii) 116 cm²
23. a) 25.0 cm   b) 50 cm
   c) 26.6 °   d) 1490 cm²
24. a) 11 m²   b) 2.5 m
   c) 15 m²   d) 66 m³
   e) 24 m²   f) 0.48 m³
25. 740 g/sec, 800 cm³/sec, 36π sec
26. a) 9 cm
   b) i) 18 cm × 36 cm   ii) 8
   iii) 18   iv) 20 cm
   v) 21.5 % wasted in each
   layer
27. 8.25 cm

Exercise 4c   Page 83

1. a) length   b) area   c) volume
   d) length   e) volume   f) area
2. a) length   b) volume   c) area
3. e.g.   a) cm   b) cm²   c) cm³
   d) cm³   e) cm   f) cm²
4. a) area   b) volume   c) area
   d) length   e) volume   f) area
5. c) area ≠ length   d) volume ≠ area + volume   e) volume ≠ length + area   f) length ≠ volume/length
6. C

Exercise 4d   Page 85

1. a) 46 499   b) 45 500
2. 1450
3. 550 and 649

4. a) 2049 millions
     b) 1950 millions
5. a) £ 47.49   b) £ 42.50

6. £ 754 999 and £ 745 000
7. 2049 and 1950
8. 999

9.

Number	Correct to nearest	Smallest possible value	Largest possible value
4560	10	4555	4564
1800	100	1750	1849
5000	1000	4500	5499
80 000	10 000	75 000	84 999
30 000	1000	29 500	30 499
66 700	100	66 650	66 749
4500	100	4450	4549
4000	1000	3500	4499

Exercise 4e   Page 87

1. Nearly 9.65 cm, 9.55 cm
2. Nearly 5.65 cm, 5.55 cm
3. Nearly 31.5 cm, 30.5 cm
4. Nearly 8250 mm, 8150 mm

5. Nearly 126.5 m, 125.5 m
6. Nearly 50.5 kg, 49.5 kg
7. Nearly 350 miles, 250 miles
8. Nearly 8.355 m/s, 8345 m/s

9. $3.5 \leqslant l < 4.5$
10. $2.5 \leqslant D < 3.5$
11. $165.5 \leqslant h < 166.5$
12. $0.488 < D < 0.512$

Exercise 4f   Page 88

1. a) just less than 10.5 cm
     b) 9.5 cm
     c) just less than 110.25 cm^2
     d) 90.25 cm^2
2. a) Upper limits: just less
       than 20.5 cm and 15.5 cm
       Lower limits: 19.5 cm and
       14.5 cm
     b) just less than 317.75 cm^2,
       282.75 cm^2
3. just less than 20.5 cm^3
     i.e. 8615.125 cm^3,
     19.5 cm i.e. 7414.875 cm^3
4. a) £ 1377.38   b) £ 106.27
5. just less than 68.25, 52.25
6. just less than 169, 121
7. just less than $\frac{4}{3}\pi \times 12.5^3$,
     $\frac{4}{3}\pi \times 11.5^3$
8. just less than 22.75, 21.25
9. just less than 86.625, 39.375
10. just less than 14, 13
11. just less than 45π, 43π
12. just less than 306.25π,
      272.25π

13. just less than $\dfrac{12.5^2}{10.5}$, $\dfrac{11.5^2}{9.5}$
14. just less than 16, just above 4
15. i) just less than 11.45, 10.95
      ii) just less than 7.2, just
        above 6.8
      iii) just less than 8.265, 7.425
16. 8.14, 7.99
17. a) 11.5, 16.5   b) 1.5, 6.5
      c) 30, 63   d) 1.25, 2.625
18. a) 5.5, 10.2   b) 5.16, 23.12
      c) $5\frac{2}{3}$, $\dfrac{4.3}{3.4}$ d) 19.93, 57.8
      i.e. 1.264
19. a) 4.5 cm, 5.5 cm
      b) 121.5 cm^2, 181.5 cm^2
      c) 91.125 cm^3, 166.375 cm^3
20. a) 5.1 cm, 12.6 cm, 13.52 cm
        i) 31.22 cm   ii) 32.13 cm^2
      b) i) 4.07 %   ii) 7.1%
21. a) i) 1 %   b) 4.04 m
      c) 3663 cm to the nearest cm
      d) i) 1 %   ii) 2.01 %
22. 2.39 %

23. 873 mm × 485 mm
24. the exact amount
25. a) £ 5.10   b) 95
26. a) 0.7 % too big
      b) percentage error is
        $(0.12l + 0.1w)/(l + w)$
        and this cannot be
        evaluated unless $l : w$ is
        known
27. 150 g butter, 60 g sugar,
      210 g flour
28. 21 %
29. a) 130 °F   b) 38 °C
      c) 60 °C   d) 130 °F
30. 200 miles
31. a) i) 150 cm^2 ii) 1700 cm^2
      b) i) 4 cm   ii) 28 cm
32. a) i) 30 m.p.g.   ii) 36 m.p.g.
        iii) 56 m.p.g.
      b) i) 9 l/100 km
        ii) 7 l/100 km
        iii) 5.6 l/100 km

Exercise 4g   Page 94

1. C   **2.** A   **3.** C   **4.** B   **5.** D   **6.** B   **7.** A   **8.** A

CHAPTER 5

Note that where questions require reasons, the main steps in the arguments are given: they are *not* full answers but may help if you are stuck.

Exercise 5a   Page 98

1. a) 25
b)

p	q	x
3	4	5
5	12	13
7	24	25

c) 250 mm
2. $p = 74°, q = 68°, r = 38°$
3. a) $x = 108°$
b) $y = 45°, z = 67.5°$
c) $p = 120°, q = 60°,$
  $r = 30°$
4. a) $\triangle$AEB ⦀ $\triangle$CDB
  equiangular (⦀ means 'is
  similar to')
b) $\triangle$ABD ≡ $\triangle$ACD r.h.s.

c) $\triangle$ABF ≡ $\triangle$BAC s.a.s. and
  $\triangle$AGF ≡ $\triangle$BGC a.a.s.
d) ABC ⦀ $\triangle$ADB ⦀ $\triangle$BCD
  equiangular
e) $\triangle$ABF ≡ $\triangle$DCE a.a.s. or
  s.a.s. or s.s.s. and
  $\triangle$BGC ⦀ $\triangle$FGD ⦀ $\triangle$DCE
  a.a.a.
f) $\triangle$LMR ⦀ $\triangle$PQR a.a.a.
5. a) $1:2.5 = 2:5$
b) 0.72 cm   c) 25:4
6. $\triangle$AMB ≡ $\triangle$ALC (s.a.s.)
  $\Rightarrow \triangle$BLN ≡ $\triangle$CNM (a.a.s.)
  where N is the intersection
  of LC and
  BM $\Rightarrow$ B$\hat{\text{L}}$C = B$\hat{\text{M}}$C
7. 36°

8. a) 15 cm   b) 16 cm^2
9. a) In $\triangle$BCX, $\hat{\text{B}} = \hat{\text{C}} = 60°$
  $\therefore \hat{\text{X}} = 60°$.
  Similarly $\hat{\text{Y}} = \hat{\text{Z}} = 60°$
b) 24 cm
10. a) A$\hat{\text{F}}$E = A$\hat{\text{B}}$E
  (opp ∠'s ‖gram)
  = B$\hat{\text{D}}$C
  (alt ∠'s);
  F$\hat{\text{A}}$G = A$\hat{\text{D}}$B
  = D$\hat{\text{B}}$C;
  $\triangle$AFC ⦀ $\triangle$BDC
b) a.a.s.
c) 1:4
d) 1:8

Exercise 5b   Page 103

1. $x = 70°$
2. $p = 90°, q = 56°, r = 34°$
3. $x = 41°, y = 27°, z = 112°$
4. $x = 39°, y = 51°, w = 78°$
5. $p = 30°, q = 120°, r = 30°$
6. $x = 20°, y = 50°, z = 110°$
7. $e = 48.5°, f = 71°, g = 60.5°$
8. $p = 36°, q = 24°, r = 78°$
9. $p = 35°, q = 35°, r = 75°$

10. $x = 60°, y = 90°$
11. A$\hat{\text{B}}$C = 90°, so AC is a
  diameter, $\therefore$ A$\hat{\text{D}}$C = 90°
12. A$\hat{\text{O}}$B = 120° (2$\hat{\text{C}}$)
  $\therefore$ A$\hat{\text{O}}$D = 60°,
  OA = OD $\Rightarrow$ O$\hat{\text{A}}$D = O$\hat{\text{D}}$A
  = 60°
13. 25°
14. 5 cm

15. a) $\triangle$AEC ⦀ $\triangle$DBE (a.a.a)
b) $\dfrac{\text{AE}}{\text{ED}} = \dfrac{\text{CE}}{\text{EB}}$ c) 12 cm

16. A$\hat{\text{C}}$B = A$\hat{\text{B}}$C (isos $\triangle$)
  = angle between tangent
  at A and AB $\Rightarrow$ alternate
  angles equal

17. $\triangle$RMP ⦀ $\triangle$QMS

Exercise 5c   Page 108

These answers have been calculated. Your answers should be within +0.1 or −0.1 of the given answer.

1. 5 cm
2. 6.2 cm
3. 7 cm

4. 10 cm
5. 5.8 cm

6. 10.4 cm
7. c) The radius is 4 cm

436   *ST(P) Mathematics 5A*

Exercise 5d   Page 110

1.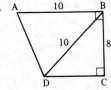
a) 6 cm   b) 64 cm²

2.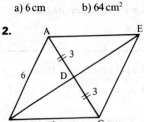
a) a rhombus (diagonals bisect at rt ∠'s)
b) 10.4 cm   c) 31.2 cm²

3.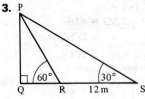
a) In △PRS, $\widehat{P} = 30°$,
$\widehat{R} = 120°, \widehat{S} = 30°$
b) 12 m   c) 10.4 m

4.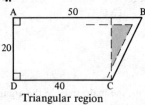
Triangular region

5.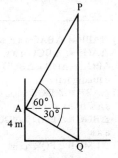
a) $\widehat{A} = 90°, \widehat{P} = 30°$,
$\widehat{Q} = 60°$
b) 8 m   c) 16 m

6.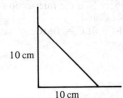

7.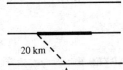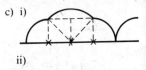

8. a) Straight line parallel to the given line.
b)
c) i)
ii)

9. Square of side 12 cm

Exercise 5e   Page 111

1. a) i) PQ as 9.2 cm and QR as 7.6 cm
ii) PQ as 11.5 cm and QR as 9.5 cm
b) 68 m   c) 57.6 m
d) 1 cm to 10 m is easier than 1 cm to 8 m as multiplication and division by 10 is easier than by 8.
1 cm to 5 m is easier than 1 cm to 8 m as it is easier to multiply and divide by 5 than by 8.

2. a) 0.5 km   b) 72 cm
c) 21 km

3. a) about 25 km

b) about 55 km
c) about 50 km
(By the nature of the problem, those answers can only be approximate: any attempt to be more accurate is ridiculous!)

4. a) a bit more than 5 miles
b) about 12½ miles
c) about 8 miles.

5. a) 10 km   b) 1.25 %
c) 20 km   d) 5 km
Choose a scale that involves straightforward calculations, i.e. $1 : 10^n$ or $1 : 5 \times 10^n$ or $1 : 2 \times 10^n$ and then select

from these the scale that gives the largest practical drawing.

6. a) 4.06 cm calculated correct to 3 s.f.
b) 4.21 cm calculated correct to 3 s.f.; 3.7 % (2 s.f.)
c) A difference less than 0.1 cm means that your drawing is as accurate as you can expect without using expensive drawing equipment. A difference greater than 0.1 cm probably indicates an error.

Exercise 5f   Page 114

These answers are calculated. You can consider your drawings accurate if your answers are within the given tolerances.

1. b) 22.8 cm, 25 m, 13.2 m:
all $\pm$ 0.1 m
c) area AEFD = 126.9 m^2,
area EBCF = 133.1 m^2:
$\pm$ 0.5 m^2; 126.9 : 133,1
$\approx$ 25 : 26

2. a) Q is nearest to P on
calculated distance, (64 m).
However a small error in
the drawing will give
another answer – all three
gates are **about** 65 m
walking distance from P.
c) 5170 m^2 correct to 3 s.f.:
$\pm$ 200 m^2

3. b) 9.5 m ($\pm$ 0.2 m)

4. a) 479 m: $\pm$ 1 m, 12 600 m^2;
$\pm$ 100 m^2
b)

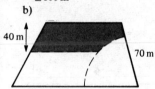

5. a) 20.4 m; $\pm$ 0.1 m
b) 500 m^3; exact

6. a) 118°
b) 7.73 km: $\pm$ 0.1 km

7. 36.4 km; $\pm$ 0.7 km

8. 38.1 nautical miles: $\pm$ 0.7;
320° $\pm$ 1°

9. a) A$\widehat{B}$C = 100°,
B$\widehat{C}$D = 142°,
A$\widehat{D}$C = 70°
b) 290°
d) 76.3 m $\pm$ 1.5 m
e) 100° $\pm$ 1°; 330.5° $\pm$ 1°

10. a)

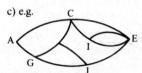

c) 964 m $\pm$ 20 m; 296° $\pm$ 1°

11.

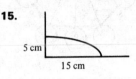

5.7 km to 12.1 km

12. b) 41.1 m   c) 80 m

13. b) 27.5 km

14. a) Circle radius
i) 6 cm, centre A
ii) 12 cm, centre D
iii) 3 cm, centre D
c) Circles centre midpoint of
AD, radii 6 cm and 9 cm.

15.

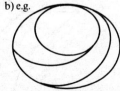

16. c) 3.2 m   d) No

CHAPTER 6

Exercise 6a   Page 120

1. b) No
c) (i), (iii), (iv) and (v) are
traversable

2. a)

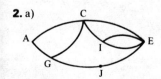

b) Yes. E.g. road inspector,
postman

c) e.g.

C
A   E
I
G
J

d) ACGJEI (2 possible
routes); ACIEJC (2
possible routes); AGCIEJ
(2 possible routes);
AGJECI (1 route);
AGJEIC (2 possible
routes)

e) AGCIEJ

3. a) No; yes, from B or C
b) e.g.

4. There must not be more
than 2 points at which an
odd number of roads meet.

Exercise 6b Page 123

1. a)

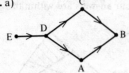

b) Not enough information to answer this.

2.

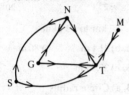

3.

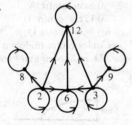

4. W.E.

	2	3	4	12
2	1	0	0	0
3	0	1	0	0
4	1	0	1	0
12	1	1	1	1

qu. 2.

	G	S	N	T	M
G	0	0	1	1	0
S	0	0	1	1	0
N	1	1	0	1	0
T	1	1	1	0	1
M	0	0	0	1	0

qu. 3.

	2	3	6	8	9	12
2	1	0	1	1	0	1
3	0	1	1	0	1	1
6	0	0	1	0	0	1
8	0	0	0	1	0	0
9	0	0	0	0	1	0
12	0	0	0	0	0	1

5. BD, BC, CD

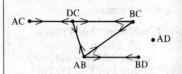

6. e.g. 'is less than'

Exercise 6c Page 126

1. a) Yes
b) 15 mins, CE
c) e.g.

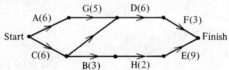

2. a) A: E
B: A, E, G
C: F, G
D: A, B, C, E, F, G
E, F, G: none

b)

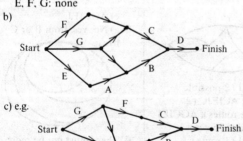

c) e.g.

Start

Exact form depends on time taken by each activity.

3. a)

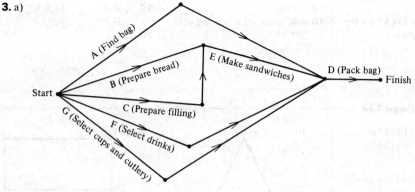

b)

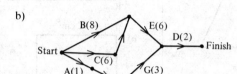

16 mins

c)

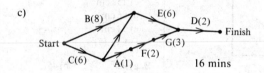

16 mins

d) No advantage
   In (b) 2nd and third persons, 8 or 10 mins
   In (c) 2nd person, 2 or 4 mins

4. a)

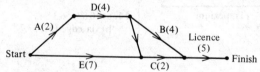

b) 15 weeks: A, D, B, Ministry

CHAPTER 7

Exercise 7a   Page 129

1. 62.3°
2. 43.4°
3. 4.57 cm
4. 7.71 cm
5. 25.8°
6. 4.69 cm

7. $\widehat{Q} = 55.8°$, $\widehat{R} = 34.2°$
8. $YZ = 4.06$ cm, $\widehat{Y} = 52.0°$
9. $\widehat{B} = 36°$, $AC = 2.53$ cm
10. $\widehat{N} = 48.6°$, $\widehat{L} = 41.4°$
11. $AC = 6$, $A\widehat{C}B = 45°$

12. 94.2 m
13. a) 54°
    b) 5.51 cm
    c) 110 cm^2
14. 6.71 cm
15. 82.8°

16. a) 6.5 m
   b) 45.2° (or 134.8° for the obtuse angle)

17. 5.77 m
18. 6.40 miles on a bearing 231.3°

19. a) 36.9°   b) 26.6°
   c) 63.4°
20. 25.7 m

Exercise 7b   Page 132

1. a) 10 m   b) 21.5 m
   c) 36.9°   d) 15.6°
   e) 528 m²

2. a) 10 m   b) 13.4 m
   c) 14.4 m   d) 22.6°

3. a) 13.0 cm   b) 45°
   c) 49.1°

4. a) 21.2 m   b) 27.9°
   c) 22.6 m   d) 70.6°

5. a) 3.20 cm   b) 51.3°
   c) 38.7°   d) 32.7°

6. a)

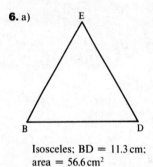

Isosceles; BD = 11.3 cm; area = 56.6 cm²

b)

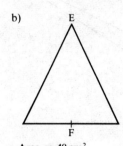

Area = 40 cm²

7. a) PQ = 3 cm
   b) P

Square; area = 9 cm²

c)

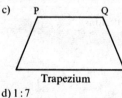

Trapezium

d) 1 : 7

8. a)

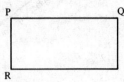

Area = 32 cm²

b)

Area = 24 cm²
   c) 152 cm²
   d) 96 cm³
   e) 24 cm³
   f) Cut (a)

9. a) 45°   b) 45°
   c) 5.66 in   d) 35.3°

10. a) 26.6°
   b) 26.6°
   c) 7.81 cm
   d) 21°

11. a) 10.8″, 56.3°
   b) via edge BC, 33.7°

Exercise 7c   Page 140

1. a)

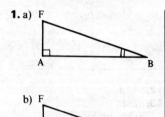

b)

c)

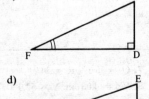

d)

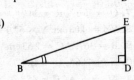

e)

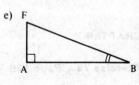

f)

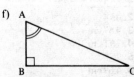

2. a)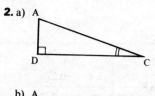

b)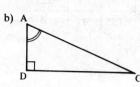

c)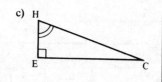

d)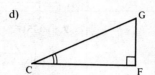

e)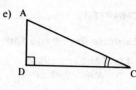

f)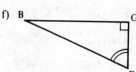

3. a)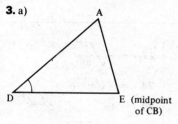

E (midpoint of CB)

b)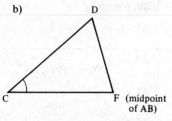

F (midpoint of AB)

c)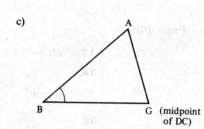

G (midpoint of DC)

d)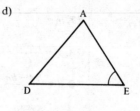

4. a) 14.1 m   b) 12.2 m
c) 54.7 °   d) 11.2 m
e)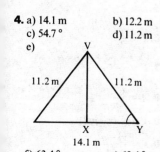

f) 63.4 °   g) 63.4 °

5. a) AF = 5 cm, FC = 23.9 cm
b)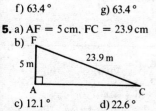

c) 12.1 °   d) 22.6 °

6. a) i) 3 m   ii) 2.60 m
b)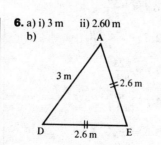

d) 54.7 °, 70.5 °, 2.45 m
   (allow ±2 % for drawing)
7. a) 26.2 °
b) 47.3 °
c) 49.4 °
d) 59.0 °
8. a) 7.48 units
b) 15.5 °

9. a) 107.5 m, 152 m
b) i) 249 m   ii) 272 m
c) i) from the midpoint of a
     side of the base, e.g. P
   ii) from a corner of the
     base e.g. A
10. a) 5 m, 9.43 m
b) 36.9 °, 18.5 °
11. 54.7 °

CHAPTER 8

Exercise 8a   Page 146

1. a) 8.2   b) 7.5
   c) 0.006

2. a) 462   b) 3.5

3. a) $7\frac{1}{2}$ b) -10

4. a) 25 °C   b) 59 °F

5. a) 14   b) 20
   c) 12

6.

x	-3	-2	1.5	-1	-0.25
y	-53	-14.5	-4.75	1	12.0

7. a) 0.751   b) 3.97

c) $\pi\left(\sqrt{\dfrac{l+r}{g}} - \sqrt{\dfrac{l}{g}}\right)$

d) -3.9%

8. a) 0   b) -17 c) -24

9. a) 4.2   b) $2.\dot{3}$ c) -4.5

Exercise 8b   Page 148

1. $\dfrac{c}{a+b}$

2. $\dfrac{c-b}{a}$

3. $\dfrac{c}{a+b}$

4. $\dfrac{c}{a+1}$

5. $\dfrac{c}{b-1}$

6. $\dfrac{b-a}{c}$

7. $\dfrac{c-2a}{a}$

8. $\dfrac{ab}{a+b}$

9. $\dfrac{bc-a}{2}$

10. $\dfrac{a+b}{b-a}$

11. $\dfrac{c}{a+b}$

12. $\dfrac{ab+a-b}{a+b}$

13. 0   (If $a \neq b$)

14. 1

15. $u = v - at$

16. $h = \dfrac{A - 2\pi r^2}{2\pi r}$

17. $m = \dfrac{y-k}{x-h}$

18. $a = \dfrac{v-u}{t}$

19. $a = \dfrac{2A - bh}{h}$

20. $l = \dfrac{S - 4a^2}{4a}$

21. $d = \dfrac{l-a}{n-1}$

22. $n = \dfrac{l-a+d}{d}$

23. $t = \dfrac{2S}{u+v}$

24. $f = \dfrac{uv}{u+v}$

25. $u = \pm\sqrt{v^2 + 2as}$

26. $g = \dfrac{\pi^2 l}{T^2}$

27. $r = \pm\sqrt{\dfrac{V}{\pi h}}$

28. $c = \pm\sqrt{a^2 - b^2}$

29. $t = 4a^2$

30. $r = \pm\sqrt{q^2 - p^2}$

31. $t = (a-h)^2$

32. $a = \pm\sqrt{\dfrac{r}{3-p^2}}$

33. $b = \dfrac{A}{c+d}$

34. $h = \dfrac{\pi r^2 - A}{\pi r}$

35. $v = 2 - \dfrac{3s}{t}$

36. $x = \dfrac{yz}{2z - y}$

37. $F = \dfrac{12}{6-n}$

38. $A = \dfrac{C^2}{4\pi}$

39. $V = \frac{1}{2}Ar - \pi r^3$

40. $s = \dfrac{v^2 - u^2}{2a}$

Exercise 8c   Page 150

1. a) $T = a + b + c$
   b) $a = T - b - c$

2. $C = 6p + 8q$

3. $y = 20(N+1)$

4. a) $x - 6$
   b) $P = 6(x - 6)$

5. $T = N(S - C)$

6. $A = \dfrac{xy}{10\,000}$

7. a) 25
   b) $x = 4 + 3(n-1)$
      or $x = 1 + 3n$

8. a) $AB = 30 - 2x$,
$BC = 40 - 2x$
b) $V = x(30 - 2x)(40 - 2x)$
or $V = 4x(15 - x)(20 - x)$

9. a) $A = x(300 - x)$
b) 120 m by 180 m

10. a) $(x^2 - 5)\,\text{cm}^2$
b) $(x^3 - 5x)\,\text{cm}^3$ c) 5

11. a) $\dfrac{144}{x^2}$ b) 5.66 cm

12. 10
13. 3
14. a) $12x\,^\circ$

b) Hour hand $(60 + x)^\circ$.
minute hand: $12x\,^\circ$

c) $\frac{60}{11}$

15. $5x + y = (x + y) + 4x$.
Both $(x + y)$ and $4x$ are
divisible by 4.

Exercise 8d   Page 152

1. $x \geqslant 2$
2. $x < 2$
3. $x \geqslant \frac{1}{5}$
4. $x > 1\frac{2}{3}$
5. $1 < x < 5$
6. $x < -2\frac{1}{4}$
7. $8\frac{1}{2} < x < 11\frac{1}{2}$
8. $-7 < x < 2$
9. $-5 \leqslant x \leqslant 1$
10. $x < 3\frac{1}{2}, 3$
11. $-2 < x < \frac{1}{2}, -1, 0$
12. $x > 9, 10$
13. $2x + y \geqslant 5, x > 0$ and $y > 0$
14. For example $(2, 3)$, $(1, 1)$, $(-10, -12)$

15. For example $(10, 1)$, $(3, -2)$, $(3\frac{3}{4}, \frac{1}{4})$

16. a) $x \geqslant 2, x \leqslant 2$ so $x = 2$ only
b) $x > 2, x < 2$ so there are no values of x

17. a)
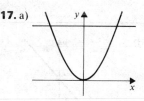

b) 4, -4
c) $-4 < x < 4$

18. a) $x \leqslant -7, x \geqslant 7$
b) $-1 < x < 1$
c) $x < 0, x > 3$

19. a) $(x - 3)(x - 2)$
b)
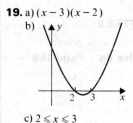

c) $2 \leqslant x \leqslant 3$

20. a) $x \leqslant -2, x \geqslant 5$
b) $-1 < x < 6$

Exercise 8e   Page 154

1. a) $x + 3 > 2x, x < 3$
b) 2, 1
2. a) $a > 2m, m > s + 4$
b) 15, 7, 2 or 1; 14, 6, 1; 15, 6, 1; 13, 6, 1
3. a) $(15x + 20y)$ pence
b) $3x + 4y \leqslant 40, x \geqslant 0$, $y \geqslant 0, x \leqslant 13, y \leqslant 10$

c) 0, 1, 2, 3 or 4
d) $x = 5, y = 2$
or $x = 1, y = 5$

4. a) $C = 6x + 2\frac{1}{2}y$
b) $12x + 5y \leqslant 200, x \geqslant 0$,
$y \geqslant 0, x \leqslant 16, y \leqslant 40$
c) 9 hardbacks, 14 paperbacks

5. a) 5 bottles   b) $C = x + 6y$
c) $x + 6y = 30; x \geqslant 0, y \geqslant 0$,
$x \leqslant 30, y \leqslant 5$
d) $x = 30, y = 5$
6. a) $P = x + 2y$
b) $x > 3y$
c) $x + 2y \geqslant 22$
d) 5 desks and 11 tables

Exercise 8f   Page 155

1. $\dfrac{x + y}{1000}\,\text{kg}$

2. a) 4   b) 25
c) 144   d) 4

3. $x > -\frac{2}{3}$

4. $p = \sqrt{\dfrac{A}{\pi} - 3q^2}$

5. a) $b = \dfrac{2a}{3}$ b) $\dfrac{b}{a} = \dfrac{2}{3}$

6. $-\frac{3}{2} < x < \frac{3}{2}$

Exercise 8g   Page 156

1. -4
2. ± 2.85

3. a) $1\frac{1}{3}$
b) 4
c) 4

4. $h = \dfrac{A}{2\pi r + a}$
5. $\frac{1}{2}x + 2y \leqslant 70$
6. $-3 \leqslant x \leqslant 5$

Exercise 8h   Page 156

1. $x = \dfrac{5p + 3q}{p + q}$

2. $10x + y$

3. -2

4. a) $-1, 1\frac{1}{2}$
   b) Roughly $1\frac{1}{2}$

5. $y = \dfrac{ab^2}{z^2}$

6. $h = \dfrac{\pm\sqrt{A^2 - \pi^2 r^4}}{\pi r}$

CHAPTER 9

Exercise 9a   Page 158

1. a) 5, 2   b) $\frac{2}{3}, \frac{1}{5}$
   c) $\frac{1}{2}, 2$ d) $-\frac{1}{2}, 2$

2. B
3. C
4. B
5. B
6. A
7. a)

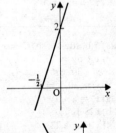

b)

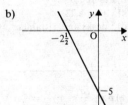

c)

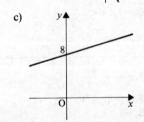

d)

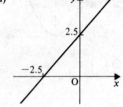

e)

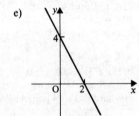

f)

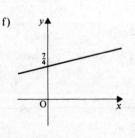

8. a) Yes   b) No

9. a) $y = 2x + 3$
   b) $y = -3x + 4$
   c) $y = \frac{1}{2}x - 2$
     or $x - 2y - 4 = 0$
   d) $y = -\frac{2}{3}x + \frac{1}{3}$
     or $2x + 3y - 1 = 0$
10. a) 3   b) -3
   c) 18
11. a) 0   b) 1
   c) -2
12. $a = 0, b = 8, c = 0$
13. a) $\frac{1}{2}$ b) 7
   c) $-\frac{1}{3}$ d) $\frac{3}{4}$
14. a) A(1, 0), B(4, 6)
   b) 2   c) -2
   d) $y = 2x - 2$
15. a) A($-4, -1$), B(4, -3)
   b) $-\frac{1}{4}$ c) -2
   d) $y = -\frac{1}{4}x - 2$

16.

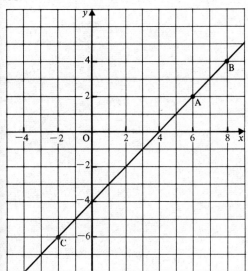

gradient is 1
y intercept is -4
$y = x - 4$

17.

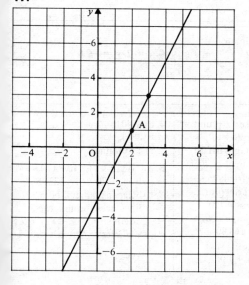

18.

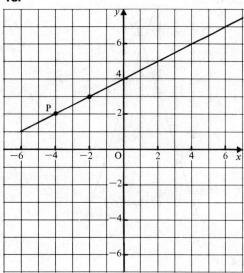

19. a) $y = 3x + 2$
b) $y = \frac{1}{2}x + \frac{5}{2}$
c) $y = -2x + 10$
d) $y = -\frac{3}{4}x - \frac{23}{4}$

20. a) $y = \frac{1}{2}x + 2$
b) $y = -\frac{1}{3}x - \frac{4}{3}$
c) $y = \frac{5}{2}x + 3$
d) $y = \frac{2}{5}x - \frac{19}{5}$

21. a) Yes
b) Yes
c) No
d) No

22. a) i) A$(3, 0)$ (ii) B$(0, 4)$
b) $-\frac{4}{3}$
c) 5 units
d) 6 sq units

23. a) 3   c) $y = -3x + 9$

b)
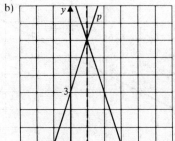

24. a) $-\frac{1}{2}$ c) $\frac{1}{2}$, C(0, −1)

b)   d) $y = \frac{1}{2}x - 1$

                                                 e) 12 sq units

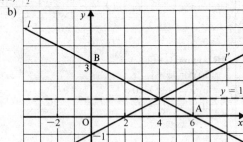

Exercise 9b   Page 165

Note that values read from a graph can only be approximate.
1. $x = 2.6, y = 2.3$ **3.** $x = 3.1, y = -2.2$ **4.** $x = 2, y = -2.8$
2. $x = 2.2, y = 4.5$

Exercise 9c   Page 166

1. a) £76
b) 6500
c) £12
d) gradient $= \frac{88}{24\,000} = 0.0037$.
The gradient gives the
cost of one kilowatt hour.

2. a) £37.50
b) 760
c) 1000
d) Tariff A   Gradient $= \frac{55}{1000}$
$= 0.055$, i.e. electricity costs

£0.055 per unit i.e. 5.5 p/unit.
Vertical intercept is 10
i.e. standing charge is £10
Tariff B   Gradient $= \frac{40}{1000}$
$= 0.04$, i.e. electricity costs
£0.04 per unit i.e. 4 p/unit.
Vertical intercept is 25
i.e. standing charge is £25
3. a) £20   b) £64.80
c) 1143
d) 0.07, 7 p ∴ cost is 7 p
per unit.

4. a) 3740 lb
b) 886 kg
c) 1.53 tonnes

5. a) i) $12   ii) £17.13
iii) £10.70   iv) $22.75
b) Steeper gradient, both
lines pass through the
origin.
c) £1.73 less

Exercise 9d   Page 170

1.
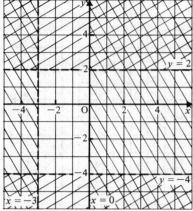

3.
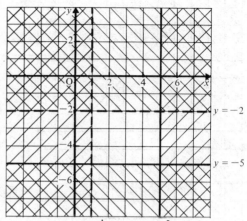

2.
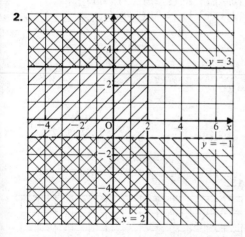

4.
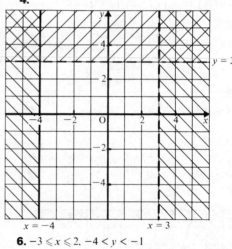

5. $-2 \leqslant x \leqslant 4, y \leqslant 2$

6. $-3 \leqslant x \leqslant 2, -4 < y < -1$

7.
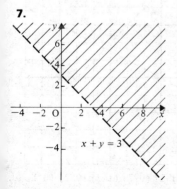

8.
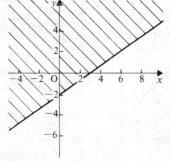

9.
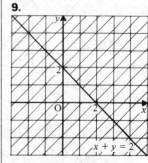

$(0, 0), (2, 0), (0, 2)$

10.

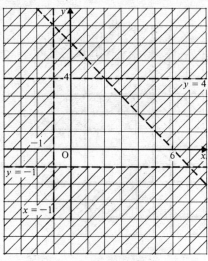

$(-1, -1), (7, -1), (2, 4), (-1, 4)$

12.

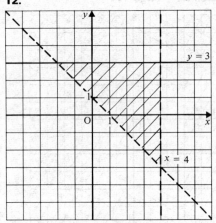

$(-1, 3), (0, 3), (1, 3), (2, 3), (3, 3)$
$(0, 2), (1, 2), (2, 2), (3, 2), (1, 1)$
$(2, 1), (3, 1), (2, 0), (3, 0), (3, -1)$

11.

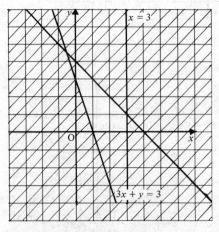

$(1, 0), (3, 0), (3, 1), (0, 4), (0, 3)$

13.

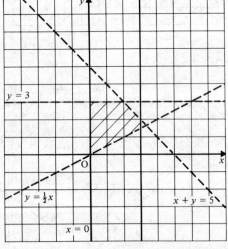

$(0, 4), (0, 3), (1, 3), (0, 2), (1, 2), (2, 2), (0, 1), (1,$

14.

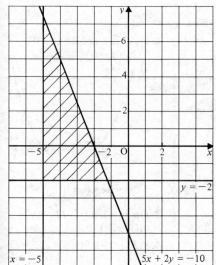

$(-5, -2 \to 7), (-4, -2 \to 5), (-3, -2 \to 2),$
$(-2, -2), (-2, -1), (-2, 0)$

15. $y \geqslant -1.5, x \leqslant 3\frac{1}{2}, x - y \leqslant -3$

16. $y > -4, 2x - y < -2$ or $y > 2x - 2, x + y \leqslant 4$

17. a) $x + y \leqslant 3, y \geqslant 0,$
  $x - 2y \leqslant -6$
  b) $y \leqslant 5, y \geqslant 0, x + y \geqslant 3,$
  $x - 2y \leqslant -6$
  c) $y \leqslant 5, x + y \geqslant 3,$
  $x - 2y \geqslant -6$
  d) $y \geqslant 0, y \leqslant 5, x - 2y \leqslant -6$

18. a) $x \leqslant 3, x + y \geqslant 5,$
  $3x - 2y + 6 \leqslant 0$
  b) $x \geqslant 0, y \geqslant 0, x + y \leqslant 5,$
  $x \leqslant 3, 3x - 2y \geqslant 6$
  c) $y \geqslant -5, x \leqslant 0,$
  $3x - 2y + 6 \leqslant 0$
  d) $3x - 2y + 6 \leqslant 0, y \geqslant -5,$
  $x + y \leqslant 5$

19. a) greatest, 6, at $(3, 3)$
  least, 0, at $(0, 0)$
  b) greatest, 9, at $(3, 3)$
  least, 0, at $(0, 0)$

20. a) greatest, 3, at $(1, 2)$
  least, -2, at $(-2, 0)$
  b) greatest, 4, at $(1, 2)$
  least, -4, at $(-2, 0)$

21. a) $(30, 500), (100, 200),$
  $(55, 500), (175, 200)$
  b) i) $(175, 200)$
  ii) $(100, 200)$

Exercise 9e   Page 177

1. a) and b)

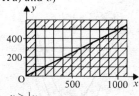

$y \geqslant \frac{1}{2}x$
c) $P = \frac{1}{100}(2x + 3y)$
d) 1000 plain, 500 fancy: £35

2. a) $100 \leqslant x + y \leqslant 200,$
  $y \leqslant \frac{1}{2}x, x > 0, y \geqslant 0$

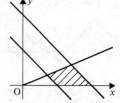

b) $40x + 25y$; 67 cans and 33 tetrapaks

3. 18

4. a) $0 \leqslant x \leqslant 10, 0 \leqslant y \leqslant 20,$
  $x + y \leqslant 15$

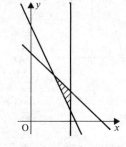

b) $2x + y \geqslant 21$
c) 11
d) 6 lorries and 9 vans

5. 12 brand A drives and 12 brand B drives

6. b)

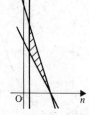

c) 10 chocolate and 70 plain
7. b) $y \leqslant 50x - x^2$

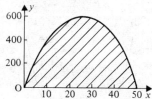

c) 25 grams; e.g. stronger mixture not absorbed as well
d) 15 grams
e) $0 < x < 30$

CHAPTER 10

Exercise 10a   Page 182

1. a)

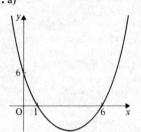

b)

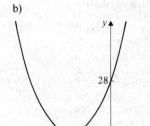

c)

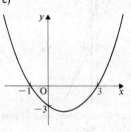

d)

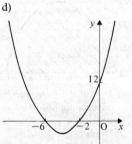

e)

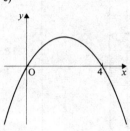

f)

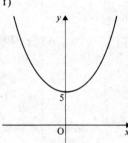

g)

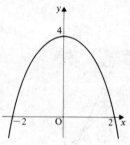

h)

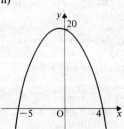

2. a) $A(0,6)$, $B(2,0)$, $C(3,0)$
b) $2x + y - 6 = 0$
c)

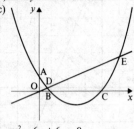

$x^2 - 6x + 6 = 0$

3. a) $p = -1$, $q = -20$
b) $(0, -20)$

4. a) $A(-3,0)$, $B(0,9)$
b)

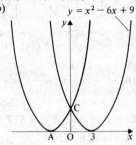

5.

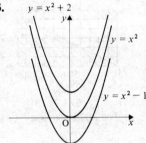

6.

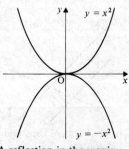

A reflection in the x-axis.

7.

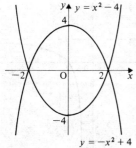

A reflection in the *x*-axis.

8. a) A($-3,0$), B($0,9$), C($3,0$)
b)

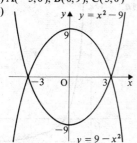

9. a)

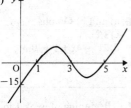

b)

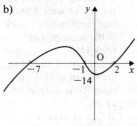

c)

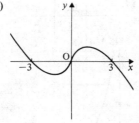

d)

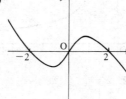

e)

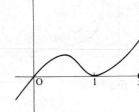

10. A($-3,0$), B($4,0$)

11. $a = 0, b = -16$

12.

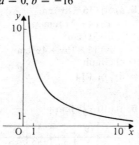

13.

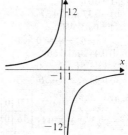

14. C
15. C
16. B
17. D
18. a)

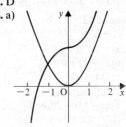

b) -1
c) $x^2 = x^3 + 2$
d) exact if -1 used as estimate
e) There are no other roots

19. c) 3; $-2, 0.3, 1.5$

20. There is only one root which is 0.75 to 2 s.f.

Exercise 10b   Page 189

1. a) -2.76
b) 1.38 and 3.62
c) -3.25, when *x* is 2.5
d) 0.68 and 4.30

2. a) 4.04
b) 6, when $x = -1$

c) -3.45 and 1.45

3. a) -3.24 and 1.24
b) -3.24 and 1.24
c) -2.73 and 0.73
d) -4.74 and 2.74
e) -4.43 and 2.32

4.

x	-1	0	2
$3x^2 - 3x - 2$	4	-2	4

a) -0.46 and 1.46
b) -0.88 and 1.88
c) -1.30 and 2.30

5. a) −6.31
   b) −0.37 and 4.37
   c) −0.83, 4.83,
      $x^2 - 4x - 4 = 0$
   d) 0.44 and 4.56
      $x^2 - 5x + 2 = 0$
   e) $0.44 < x < 4.56$

6. a)

x	−1	0	4
$4(x^3 - x^2 - 6x)$	16	0	96

   b) Graph
   c) 3.1 (only value)
   d) For all values of x
      above 3.1
   e) $4x^3 - 4x^2 - 19x - 20 = 0$

7. a) −3.42   b) 3.27
   c) −2.71

8. a) −3.3, 0.5, 2.8
   b) $x^3 - 9x + 4 = 0$
   c) One root

9. a) 2.2 and 10.8
   b) $x^2 - 13x + 20 = 0$
   c) $2.2 \leqslant x \leqslant 10.8$
   d) Because we cannot find a
      value of y when $x = 0$

10. a) 1.51
   b) 0.23 and 8.77
   c) $x^2 - 9x + 2 = 0$

11.

x	0.5	1
$\dfrac{1}{x^2}$	4	1

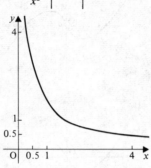

12.

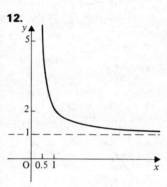

13.

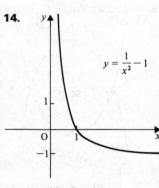

14.

$$y = \frac{1}{x^2} - 1$$

15. a) and b) Graphs
   c) 1.71
   d) $2x^2 - 4x + 1 = 0$

Exercise 10c   Page 197

1. a) £10 250 when 3500
      switchboards are produced
   b) 300 (approx)
   c) More than 1440 but less
      than 5560

2. a) 57.2 m
   b) 1.44 s and 5.56 s
   c) 3.5 s
   d) 0 m

3.

x	20	40	70
A	2000	2400	0

   a) 13.2 m or 56.8 m
   b) Max. area 2450 m² when
      $x = 35$ m
   c) 1568 m²
   d) 2352 m²

4. b)

x	2	2.3
C	16	21.2

   c) Graph   d) 3.16 ft
   e) $2.75 \leqslant x < 3$

5. a) i) $(16 - 8x)$ cm
      ii) $(4 - 2x)$ cm
      iii) $3x^2$ cm²
      iv) $16 - 16x + 4x^2$ cm²
   c) Graph
   d) $\frac{8}{7}$ or 1.14

6. a) $(10 - \frac{1}{2}x)$ cm
   c)

x	0	2	4	6
C	0	36	128	252

x	8	10	12	14
C	384	500	576	588

x	16	18	20
C	512	324	0

   d) Graph   e) 114 cm³
   f) 8.3 and 17.4
   g) 592 cm² when $x = 13.3$

7. a) Beginning of week 1 to
      the end of week 3 and
      from beginning of week 7
      to the early part of
      week 11
   b) Beginning of week 4 to
      the end of week 6 and
      from the middle of week
      11 on.
   c) i) End of week 6
      ii) Early in week 11
   d) Probably a fall in price
   e) False

8. a) 4 a.m.   b) 3 hours
   c) 40 °C   d) 1.1 °C
   e) About 2 p.m.
   f) Peter's temperature
      appears to fall fairly
      steadily

Exercise 10d   Page 203

1. a) after 4 s   b) 5 m/s
   c) 2.5 m/s   d) 10 m/s
   e) −10 m/s   f) −4.8 m/s
   g) quadratic
      $(d = 20t - 5t^2)$

2. a)

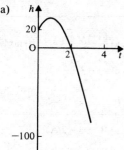

b) i) 10 m/s   ii) −40 m/s
c) 22.5 m
d) 2 s

3.

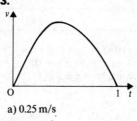

a) 0.25 m/s
b) 0.6 m/s²
c) 0.5 s
d) 0.2 m

4. a) At the beginning of the
      race.
   b) 200 m.p.h.
   c) 1 minute
   d) 75 m.p.h.
   e) 2.8 miles.

5. a) 24 m/s²
   b) 17 m/s
   c) 3.3 min
   d) $15\frac{3}{4}$ km
   e) 13 km

Exercise 10e   Page 206

1. He is
   a) accelerating from rest
   b) running at a constant
      speed
   c) accelerating as he runs
      towards the winning post.

2. a) He accelerates from rest
      until he attains his steady
      running speed
   b) He runs at a steady speed
   c) He increases his speed
      until he is running 'flat
      out' at the end.

3. B

4. C

5. C

6.

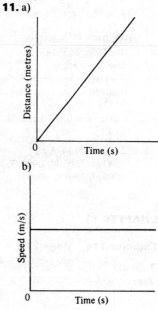

7.

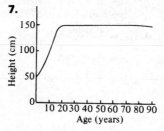

8.

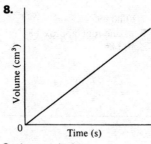

9. a) true   b) false   c) true

10.

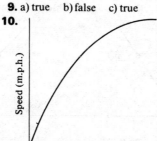

11. a)

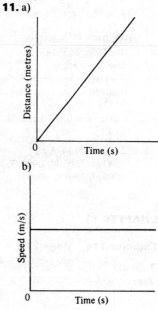

b)

12.

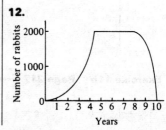

13. a) 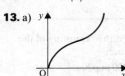 b) 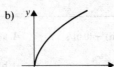 c) 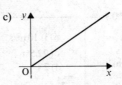 d)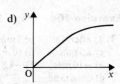

Exercise 10f   Page 212

1. a) 1, 1.5, 1.71, 1.83, 1.89; 2
   b) 2, −10, −298, −266 410, −2.13 × 10^{11}

2. a) 0.43   b) no limit
3. 1 a): $x^2 - 5x + 6 = 0$
   2 a): $3x^2 + x - 1 = 0$

4. a) $\dfrac{(1 - \sqrt{3})}{2}$ b) no limit
   c) $\dfrac{(1 - \sqrt{3})}{2}$

Exercise 10g   Page 214

1. a) $u_{n+1} = \dfrac{1}{u_n^2 + 2}$

   b) $u_{n+1} = \dfrac{1}{u_n^2 + 2}$

2. b) $u_{n+1} = \dfrac{5 - u_n^2}{7}$

   c) 0.5, 0.678 571, 0.648 506, 0.654 206, 0.653 145
   The sequence is converging to a limit between 0.6542... and 0.6531... One root of the equation is 0.65 correct to 2 s.f.

3. a) 2, 3.5, 2.857 14, 3.05, 2.983 61, 3.005 49, 2.998 17, 3.000 61, 2.9998, 3.000 07; 3

   b) 0, −1.5, −0.857 143, −1.05, −0.983 607, −1.005 49, −0.998 172, −1.000 61, −0.999 797, −1.000 07; −1
   c) The equation is $x^2 - 2x - 3 = 0$ which has two roots, i.e. 3 and −1.

4. a) $x = \dfrac{x^2 - 9}{2}$,
   $x = \pm\sqrt{2x + 9}$,
   $x = \dfrac{2x + 9}{x}$
   b) $x = \sqrt{2x + 9}$ and
   $x = \dfrac{2x + 9}{x}$; 4.16
   c) larger
5. a) one root, approx 1.8
   b) 1.86

6. a) $B = 5 - 2/A$,
   i.e. $u_{n+1} = 5 - \dfrac{2}{u_n}$

   b) 4, 4.5 (if 4 is taken as A)

   d) 5 decimal places, change line 50

   e) $x^2 - x - 1 = 0$

   f) Depending on the operating system, the computer will hang or return an error message because the numbers rapidly get huge. E.g. insert a line 45: IF ABS (A − B) > 100 THEN PRINT "DIVERGES": GOTO 80

CHAPTER 11

Exercise 11a   Page 216

1. b), c)
2. a)   b)   c) 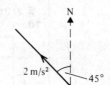   d)

Exercise 11b   Page 217

1. $a = \begin{pmatrix} 3 \\ 4 \end{pmatrix}$, $b = \begin{pmatrix} -4 \\ -3 \end{pmatrix}$, $c = \begin{pmatrix} 0 \\ -3 \end{pmatrix}$, $d = \begin{pmatrix} 2 \\ -3 \end{pmatrix}$

2. a)   b)   c)   d)   e)

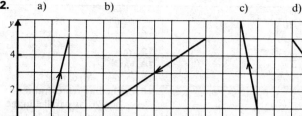

3. $\overrightarrow{AB} = \begin{pmatrix} 3 \\ 6 \end{pmatrix}$, $\overrightarrow{BA} = \begin{pmatrix} -3 \\ -6 \end{pmatrix}$, $\overrightarrow{AC} = \begin{pmatrix} 1 \\ -3 \end{pmatrix}$

4. a) B(2, −2), C(3, 3)

b) $\begin{pmatrix} 1 \\ 5 \end{pmatrix}$

5. (−4, 5)

6.

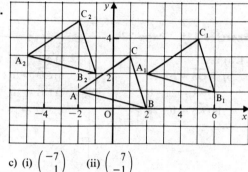

c) (i) $\begin{pmatrix} -7 \\ 1 \end{pmatrix}$ (ii) $\begin{pmatrix} 7 \\ -1 \end{pmatrix}$

Exercise 11c   Page 219

1. a) $a = \begin{pmatrix} -1 \\ 2 \end{pmatrix}$, $b = \begin{pmatrix} 1 \\ 2 \end{pmatrix}$,

$c = \begin{pmatrix} -2 \\ 1 \end{pmatrix}$, $d = \begin{pmatrix} 2 \\ 1 \end{pmatrix}$,

$e = \begin{pmatrix} 4 \\ 2 \end{pmatrix}$, $f = \begin{pmatrix} -1\frac{1}{2} \\ 3 \end{pmatrix}$,

$g = \begin{pmatrix} 4 \\ -2 \end{pmatrix}$, $h = \begin{pmatrix} 3 \\ 6 \end{pmatrix}$

b) $g = -2c$, $h = 3b$,
$f = 1\frac{1}{2}a$, $e = 2d$

2. a) $a = \begin{pmatrix} 3 \\ 0 \end{pmatrix}$, $b = \begin{pmatrix} 3 \\ 4 \end{pmatrix}$,

$c = \begin{pmatrix} 3 \\ 4 \end{pmatrix}$, $d = \begin{pmatrix} 0 \\ 6 \end{pmatrix}$,

$e = \begin{pmatrix} -3 \\ 4 \end{pmatrix}$, $f = \begin{pmatrix} 6 \\ 0 \end{pmatrix}$,

$g = \begin{pmatrix} -3 \\ -4 \end{pmatrix}$

b) $f = 2a$, $b = c = -g$

3. b) $\overrightarrow{AC} = \begin{pmatrix} 4 \\ 3 \end{pmatrix} = \frac{1}{3}a$,

$\overrightarrow{CB} = \begin{pmatrix} 8 \\ 6 \end{pmatrix} = \frac{2}{3}a$,

c) $\overrightarrow{BA} = -a$
$\overrightarrow{CA} = -\frac{1}{3}a$,
$\overrightarrow{BC} = -\frac{2}{3}a$

4. a) 3 : 1
b) 3 : 4
c) 1 : 4

5. a) 2 : 1
b) 3 : 2
c) 3 : 1

6. $\overrightarrow{AD} = \begin{pmatrix} -4 \\ 4 \end{pmatrix}$ D is (−5, 4)

7. $\frac{5}{3}a$

Exercise 11d   Page 221

1. $|a| = |b| = |c| = |d| = 2.24$,
$|e| = |g| = 4.47$,
$|f| = 3.35$, $|h| = 6.71$

2. $|a| = 3$,
$|b| = |c| = |e| = |g| = 5$,
$|d| = |f| = 6$

Exercise 11e   Page 223

4. $\begin{pmatrix} 3 \\ 6 \end{pmatrix}$

5. $\begin{pmatrix} 3 \\ 6 \end{pmatrix}$

6. $\begin{pmatrix} 9 \\ -2 \end{pmatrix}$

7. $\begin{pmatrix} 1 \\ -1 \end{pmatrix}$

8. $\begin{pmatrix} 10 \\ -3 \end{pmatrix}$

9. $\begin{pmatrix} 2 \\ 7 \end{pmatrix}$

10. $\begin{pmatrix} -2 \\ -7 \end{pmatrix}$

11. $\begin{pmatrix} 1 \\ -1 \end{pmatrix}$

12. $\begin{pmatrix} -9 \\ 2 \end{pmatrix}$

13. Yes

14. No

15. c) Yes   d) 6; no

16. c) The line representing $2a + 2b$ is parallel to the line representing $a + b$ and is twice its length

Exercise 11f   Page 224

1. a) Yes
   b) i) $\overrightarrow{QS} = b - a$,
      ii) $\overrightarrow{SR} = 2a - b$,
      iii) $\overrightarrow{RS} = b - 2a$

2. a) $\overrightarrow{AB} = q - p$
   b) $\overrightarrow{CD} = \frac{1}{2}q$
   c) $\overrightarrow{DB} = \frac{1}{2}q$
   d) $\overrightarrow{AD} = \frac{1}{2}q - p$

3. a) Trapezium
   b) i) $\overrightarrow{BC} = a - b$,
      ii) $\overrightarrow{BD} = a - 2b$,
      iii) $\overrightarrow{AC} = a + b$

4. $\overrightarrow{BC} = \begin{pmatrix} -7 \\ 2 \end{pmatrix}$, $\overrightarrow{CB} = \begin{pmatrix} 7 \\ -2 \end{pmatrix}$

5. $h = 2, k = 3$

Exercise 11g   Page 226

1. a) $\overrightarrow{AP} = \frac{1}{2}b$
   b) $\overrightarrow{AQ} = \frac{1}{2}c$
   c) $\overrightarrow{BC} = c - b$
   d) $\overrightarrow{PQ} = \frac{1}{2}c - \frac{1}{2}b$
   e) $\overrightarrow{PQ} = \frac{1}{2}\overrightarrow{BC}$
   f) $PQ = \frac{1}{2}BC$

2. a) $\overrightarrow{OP} = \frac{1}{2}a$
   b) $\overrightarrow{AB} = b - a$
   c) $\overrightarrow{AQ} = \frac{1}{2}(b - a)$
   d) $\overrightarrow{PQ} = \frac{1}{2}b$
   e) $\overrightarrow{SR} = \frac{1}{2}b$
   g) Parallelogram

3. a) $\overrightarrow{BD} = b - a$
   b) $\overrightarrow{BP} = \frac{1}{3}(b - a)$
   c) $\overrightarrow{BQ} = \frac{2}{3}(b - a)$
   d) $\overrightarrow{AP} = \frac{2}{3}a + \frac{1}{3}b$
   e) $\overrightarrow{CQ} = \frac{2}{3}a + \frac{1}{3}b$

4. a) $\overrightarrow{AB} = b$
   b) $\overrightarrow{AP} = \frac{2}{3}b$
   c) $\overrightarrow{OP} = a + \frac{2}{3}b$
   d) $\overrightarrow{OR} = \frac{1}{2}b$
   e) $\overrightarrow{CQ} = \frac{3}{4}a$
   f) $\overrightarrow{RQ} = \frac{3}{4}a + \frac{1}{2}b$
   g) $\overrightarrow{RQ} = \frac{3}{4}\overrightarrow{OP}$
   h) $RQ : OP = 3 : 4$

5. a) A, B and C lie in a straight line
   b) Parallelogram
   c) Trapezium   d) ECBF

6. a) $\overrightarrow{BP} = 6a - 2b$
   b) $\overrightarrow{BQ} = 3a - b$
   c) $\overrightarrow{BP} = 2\overrightarrow{BQ}$
   d) $1 : 2$

7. a) $3r - q$ b) $\frac{3}{2}r - \frac{1}{2}q$
   c) $\frac{3}{2}r + \frac{1}{2}q$ d) $3r$
   e) i) parallelogram,
      ii) trapezium

Exercise 11h   Page 230

1. $\begin{pmatrix} 3\frac{1}{2} \\ 5 \end{pmatrix}$, 23 sq. units

2. a) $\begin{pmatrix} -1\frac{1}{2} \\ 6\frac{1}{2} \end{pmatrix}$ b) $\begin{pmatrix} 1\frac{1}{2} \\ 2\frac{1}{2} \end{pmatrix}$

   c) $\begin{pmatrix} -3 \\ 4 \end{pmatrix}$

3. a) $\begin{pmatrix} 5 \\ 6 \end{pmatrix}$ b) $\begin{pmatrix} 2 \\ 1\frac{1}{2} \end{pmatrix}$ c) $\begin{pmatrix} 2 \\ 3 \end{pmatrix}$

4. a) $(-7, \ 7)$
   b) $(-2, \ 3)$
   c) $(-3, \ 1)$ i.e. B
   d) 7 sq. units

5. a) $\overrightarrow{OC} = b - a$, $\overrightarrow{OD} = -a$,
$\overrightarrow{OE} = -b$, $\overrightarrow{OF} = a - b$

b) i) $\overrightarrow{AB} = b - a$,
ii) $\overrightarrow{BC} = -a$,
iii) $\overrightarrow{CD} = -b$,
iv) $\overrightarrow{DE} = a - b$
v) $\overrightarrow{EF} = a$
vi) $\overrightarrow{FA} = b$

6. $\overrightarrow{OA} = 3x - y$,
$\overrightarrow{OB} = -x - y$,
$\overrightarrow{OC} = -2x + 4y$

7. a) $\overrightarrow{BA} = a - b$
b) $\overrightarrow{AB} = b - a$
c) $\overrightarrow{BC} = \frac{1}{2}(a - b)$
d) $\overrightarrow{AC} = \frac{1}{2}(b - a)$
e) $\overrightarrow{OC} = \frac{1}{2}a + \frac{1}{2}b$; Yes

8. a) $\overrightarrow{AC} = y - x$
b) $\overrightarrow{AD} = \frac{1}{3}(y - x)$
c) $\overrightarrow{CA} = x - y$
d) $\overrightarrow{CD} = \frac{2}{3}(x - y)$
e) $\overrightarrow{BD} = \frac{2}{3}x + \frac{1}{3}y$

9. a) $\overrightarrow{AB} = b - a$
b) $\overrightarrow{BA} = (a - b)$
c) $\overrightarrow{AC} = \frac{1}{4}(b - a)$
d) $\overrightarrow{BC} = \frac{3}{4}(a - b)$
e) $\overrightarrow{OC} = \frac{3}{4}a + \frac{1}{4}b$
f) $\overrightarrow{OD} = \frac{1}{2}a + \frac{1}{6}b$
g) $\overrightarrow{DC} = \frac{1}{4}a + \frac{1}{12}b$

10. a) $\overrightarrow{PQ} = q - p$
b) $\overrightarrow{PR} = k(q - p)$
c) $\overrightarrow{RQ} = (l - k)q + (k - l)p$
d) $\overrightarrow{OR} = kq + (l - k)p$

Exercise 11i   Page 235

1. 86.3°

2.
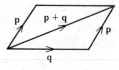

3. a)
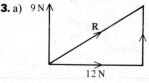

b) 15 N

4. a)
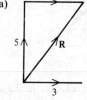

b) 59.0°

5. 65.4 km/h *from* 276.5°

6. 10 N

7. a) 63.4° to downstream bank
b) 60° to upstream bank
c) 1.52 m/s

Exercise 11j   Page 237

1. $h = -4, k = 5$
2. $h = 7, k = -6$
3. $h = 6, k = 12$
4. $h = 5, k = 7$
5. $h = 5, k = 6$
6. $h = \frac{1}{2}, k = -\frac{5}{6}$
7. $h = 2, k = 1$
8. $h = \frac{7}{5}, k = 1$
9. $h = 2, k = \frac{1}{2}$
10. $k = 2$
11. $k = -28$
12. $k = 4$
13. $k = \pm 6$
14. $k = 6$ or -4
15. $k = 5$ or -1

16. $k = 2$ or $\frac{1}{5}$

17. a) $\overrightarrow{OD} = k(\frac{2}{3}a + \frac{1}{3}b)$,
$\overrightarrow{BD} = \frac{2}{3}ka + (\frac{1}{3}k - 1)b$
b) 3
c) $OC:CD = 1:2$

18. a) $\overrightarrow{BD} = ka - \frac{1}{4}b$
b) $k = \frac{1}{2}$ c) $\dfrac{BD}{OC} = \frac{1}{2}$

19. a) $\overrightarrow{RQ} = hp$
b) $\overrightarrow{PR} = r - p$
c) $\overrightarrow{PQ} = (h - 1)p + r$
d) $\overrightarrow{PS} = k(r - p)$
e) $\overrightarrow{OS} = (l - k)p + kv$

f) $h = \dfrac{1}{k}$
g) $h = 2, k = \frac{1}{2}$

20. a) $\overrightarrow{PQ} = q - p$
b) $\overrightarrow{PM} = \frac{1}{3}(q - p)$
c) $\overrightarrow{OM} = \frac{2}{3}p + \frac{1}{3}q$
d) $\overrightarrow{ON} = \frac{1}{2}p$
e) $\overrightarrow{QN} = \frac{1}{2}p - q$
f) $\overrightarrow{QL} = h(\frac{1}{2}p - q)$
g) $\overrightarrow{OL} = \frac{1}{2}hp + (1 - h)q$
h) $\overrightarrow{OL} = k(\frac{2}{3}p + \frac{1}{3}q)$
i) $h = \frac{4}{5}, k = \frac{3}{5}$

Exercise 11k   Page 242

1. a) $6a + 8j$ c) $i - j$ e) $-7i - 4j$ g) $6i - 2j$ i) $6i + 15j$
   b) $2i + 5j$ d) $7i + 4j$ f) $5i + 9j$ h) $i - 11j$

2. a)   b)   c)

   d)   e)    f)

   g)   h)

   i)   j) $|a| = \sqrt{34}$, $|b| = 5$, $|c| = 2$

3. $2i + 4j,\ -3i + 9j,\ -6i - 4j$

4. a) $5i + 4j,\ -5i + j,\ i - 3j$
   b) $\overrightarrow{PQ} = -10i - 3j$,
      $\overrightarrow{QR} = 6i - 4j$,
      $\overrightarrow{RQ} = -6i + 4j$

   c) $2\frac{1}{2}i,\ -2i - j$
   d) $\overrightarrow{PS} = 3i - 2j,\ \overrightarrow{QS} = 13i + j$
   e) $\overrightarrow{PS} = \frac{1}{2}\overrightarrow{QR},\ \dfrac{PS}{QR} = \frac{1}{2}$

5. a) $2i + 4j,\ (2, 4)$
   b) $i + 2j$
   c) $\overrightarrow{EC} = 2i + 1\frac{1}{2}j = \frac{1}{2}\overrightarrow{OA}$

Exercise 11l   Page 244

1. a) $\overrightarrow{OR} = \frac{4}{5}p,\ \overrightarrow{RP} = \frac{1}{5}p$,
      $\overrightarrow{PQ} = q - p$
   b) $\overrightarrow{PS} = \frac{1}{5}(q - p),\ \overrightarrow{RS} = \frac{1}{5}q$
   c) RS is parallel to OQ and
      $RS = \frac{1}{5}OQ$
   d) trapezium   e) 120 cm^2

2. a) $\overrightarrow{AD} = 2b - 2a$
   b) $\overrightarrow{BE} = 2b - 4a$
   c) $\overrightarrow{EG} = 3a$
   d) $\overrightarrow{HG} = 2b - 2a$
   e) $\overrightarrow{HG} = 2\overrightarrow{FE}$
   f) rhombus

3. a) $\overrightarrow{OD} = 2c,\ \overrightarrow{AD} = 2c - a$
   b) $b = \frac{1}{2}a + c$
   c) $k = \frac{3}{2}$

4. a) $(-1,\ 10)$
   b) $h = 3,\ k = -2$

5. $A(2,\ -1),\ B(5,\ 3),$
   $C(3,\ 8),\ D(0,\ 4)$ 23 sq. units

CHAPTER 12

Exercise 12a   Page 247

1.

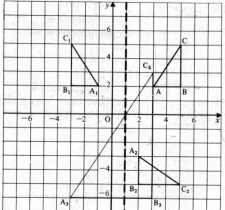

3.

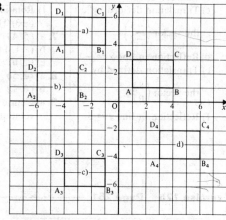

e) Translation defined by $\begin{pmatrix} -7 \\ 8 \end{pmatrix}$

f) Translation defined by $\begin{pmatrix} 7 \\ 1 \end{pmatrix}$

2.

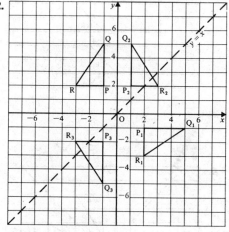

d) Rotation of 180° about O
e) Rotation of 90° anticlockwise about O

4.

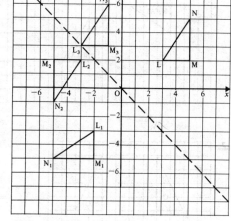

△LMN

5. a) Rotation of 90° clockwise about O
   b) Reflection in the line $x = -1$

c) Translation defined by the vector $\begin{pmatrix} -8 \\ 6 \end{pmatrix}$

d) 90° anticlockwise

6. a) Translation defined by

the vector $\begin{pmatrix} -6 \\ 0 \end{pmatrix}$

b) Rotation of 180° about O

c) Translation defined by

the vector $\begin{pmatrix} -5 \\ -2 \end{pmatrix}$

d) Reflection in line $x = -2$

e) Translation defined by

the vector $\begin{pmatrix} 8 \\ 0 \end{pmatrix}$

f) Reflection in line $x = 5$

g) Translation defined by

the vector $\begin{pmatrix} 6 \\ 0 \end{pmatrix}$

h) Reflection in line $x = -2$

i) Rotation of 180° about $(-3, 0)$

7. a) $(5, 4)$

b) $(-1, 1)$

c) $(2, 0)$

8. a) $(2, 5)$

b) $(0, 1)$

9. a) Centre E, angle of rotation 90° clockwise

b) Line EB

c) Centre midpoint of EB, angle of rotation 180°

10. a) AB = BC = PB = BQ, AC = PQ

b) 60° clockwise

c) 60° clockwise, 60°

d) 105°

e) 6 cm

11. a) $(2, -5)$; 90° anticlockwise

b) Equidistant from A and A′, B and B′, C and C′

Exercise 12b   Page 251

1.
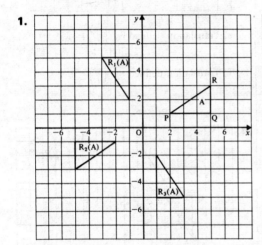

3.
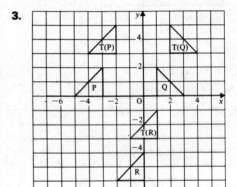

2.
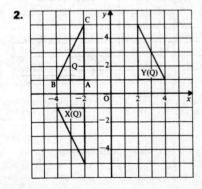

4.
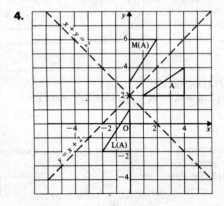

5.

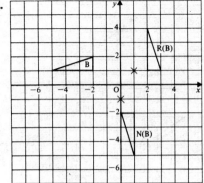

Exercise 12c   Page 253

1.

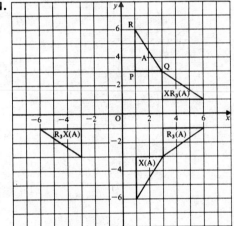

e) Reflection in line $y = -x$

2.

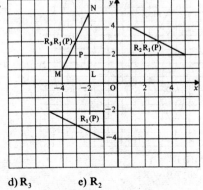

d) R_3 e) R_2

3.

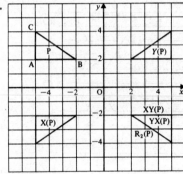

f) Yes

g) Yes

h) Rotation of 180° about O, i.e. R_2

4.

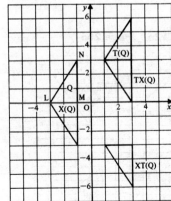

e) Translation defined by the vector $\begin{pmatrix} 4 \\ -3 \end{pmatrix}$

f) Translation defined by the vector $\begin{pmatrix} 0 \\ 6 \end{pmatrix}$

Exercise 12d   Page 254

1.

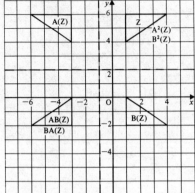

b) Rotation of $180°$ about O; AB = BA

2.

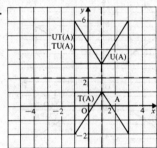

b) Yes
c) Yes

3.

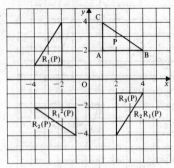

a) $R_1^2 = R_2$, $R_2R_1 = R_3$
b) $R_3^2 = R_2$, $R_2R_3 = R_1$, $R_3R_2 = R_1$

Exercise 12e   Page 255

1.

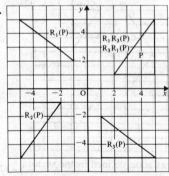

a) $R_1R_2 = R_3R_1 = I$
b) $R_2^2 = I R_2R_3 = R_1$, $R_1R_2 = R_3$

2.

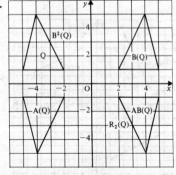

b) i) $B^2 = I$
   ii) $AB = R_2$

3.

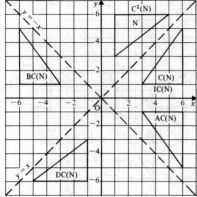

b) i) $DC = R_2$
ii) $C^2 = I$
iii) $AC = R_3$
iv) $BC = R_1$
v) $IC = C$

4.

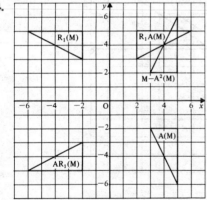

b) i) $A^2 = I$
ii) $AR_1 = D$
iii) $R_1A = C$
c) False

5.

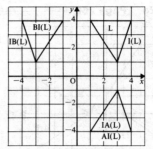

b) $AI = A$, $BI = B$, $IA = A$, $IB = B$

6. a)

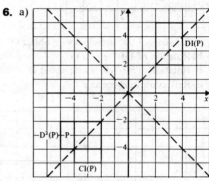

b) $CI = C$, $DI = D$, $D^2 = I$

7. a)

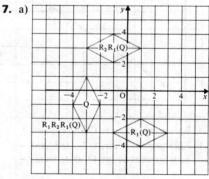

b) $R_2R_1 = R_3$, $R_1R_2R_1 = I$
c) True

Exercise 12f   Page 258

1. a) $\begin{pmatrix} 12 & 6 \\ 8 & 4 \end{pmatrix}$ b) (16)

c) Not possible   d) $\begin{pmatrix} 10 \\ 6 \end{pmatrix}$

e) Not possible   f) Not possible

g) Not possible   h) $\begin{pmatrix} 16 & -7 \\ 0 & 9 \end{pmatrix}$

i) $(12\ 14\ 8)$ j) $\begin{pmatrix} 3 \\ 2 \end{pmatrix}$

k) $\begin{pmatrix} 4 & -1 \\ 0 & 3 \end{pmatrix}$ l) $\begin{pmatrix} 1 & 0 \\ 0 & 1 \end{pmatrix}$

2. $a = 1$ $b = 2$
3. $x = 2$ $y = 1$
4. $p = 2$, $q = 8$, $r = 0$
5. $\begin{pmatrix} 1 & 1 \\ 1 & 2 \end{pmatrix}$

464   *ST(P) Mathematics 5A*

Exercise 12g   Page 260

1.

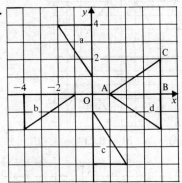

a) Rotation of 90° anticlockwise about O
b) Rotation of 180° about O
c) Rotation of 90° clockwise about O
d) Reflection in the *x* axis

2.

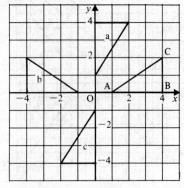

a) Reflection in the line $y = x$
b) Reflection in the *y* axis
c) Reflection in the line $y = -x$

3.

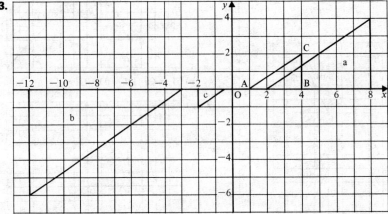

a) Enlargement centre O, scale factor 2
b) Enlargement centre O, scale factor -3
c) Enlargement centre O, scale factor $-\frac{1}{2}$

4.

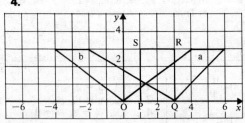

5.

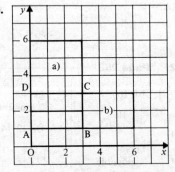

Exercise 12h   Page 263

1. 4   **4.** 6   **7.** 7
2. 1   **5.** −2   **8.** 1
3. −2   **6.** 2   **9.** 0

10. a)

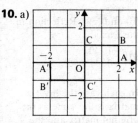

b) 2, 2   c) 1   d) 1

11. a)

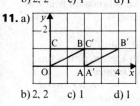

b) 2, 2   c) 1   d) 1

12. a)

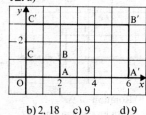

b) 2, 18   c) 9   d) 9

13. a)

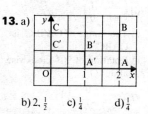

b) 2, $\frac{1}{2}$ c) $\frac{1}{4}$ d) $\frac{1}{4}$

14. a)

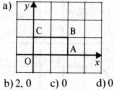

b) 2, 0   c) 0   d) 0

15. a)

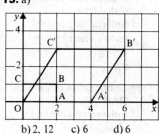

b) 2, 12   c) 6   d) 6

In questions 10 to 15, the area scale factor (c) is equal to the determinant (d).

Exercise 12i   Page 265

1. Rotation of 90°
anticlockwise about O

2. (0, 0), (0, 1), (−1, 1),
(−2, 1)

3. Rotation of 180° about O

4. Enlargement centre O,
scale factor $2\frac{1}{2}$

5. (0, 0), (0, 1), (3, 1), (2, 1)

6. The square becomes a line
segment

7. 1. 1   2. 1   3. 1
    4. $\frac{25}{4}$ 5. 1   6. 0
8. a) A line segment   b) 0, 0
    c) 0
9. a) 5, 5   b) 30
10. a) 6   b) 18

Exercise 12j   Page 266

1. Rotation of 60°
anticlockwise about (1, 1)
2. Reflection in the *x* axis
3. An enlargement centre O,
scale factor $\frac{1}{2}$
4. Translation defined by
$\begin{pmatrix} -2 \\ -3 \end{pmatrix}$
5. Rotation of 180° about O

6.

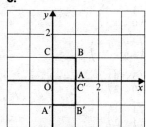

b) Rotation of 90° clockwise
about O
c) Rotation of 90°
anticlockwise about O
d) $\begin{pmatrix} 0 & -1 \\ 1 & 0 \end{pmatrix}$
e) The image of OA′B′C′ is
OABC
f) Rotation of 90°
anticlockwise about O

7.

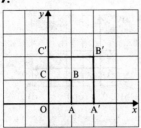

b) Enlargement centre O, scale factor 2
c) Enlargement centre O, scale factor $\frac{1}{2}$
d) $\begin{pmatrix} \frac{1}{2} & 0 \\ 0 & \frac{1}{2} \end{pmatrix}$
e) The image of OA′B′C′ is OABC
f) Enlargement centre O, scale factor $\frac{1}{2}$

8.

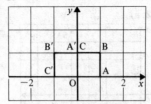

b) Rotation of 90° anticlockwise about O
c) Rotation of 90° clockwise about O
d) $\begin{pmatrix} 0 & 1 \\ -1 & 0 \end{pmatrix}$
e) The image of OA′B′C′ is OABC
f) Rotation of 90° clockwise about O
g) Yes; $\begin{pmatrix} 0 & 1 \\ -1 & 0 \end{pmatrix}$

9. (b) and (c)   Reflection in the line $y = x$
d) $\begin{pmatrix} 0 & -1 \\ -1 & 0 \end{pmatrix}$

10. (b) and (c)   Reflection in the y axis
d) $\begin{pmatrix} -1 & 0 \\ 0 & 1 \end{pmatrix}$

11. In each case the inverse matrix is the same as the original matrix and the transformation is its own inverse.

12. i) and ii)
a) The image is a line segment
b) There is no inverse transformation

Exercise 12k   Page 267 ——————————————————————————————

A shorter method using the inverse matrix is given here but it demands a degree of sophistication which not all pupils can command.

$$\begin{pmatrix} a & b \\ c & d \end{pmatrix} \begin{pmatrix} 2 & 3 \\ 1 & 4 \end{pmatrix} = \begin{pmatrix} 5 & 10 \\ 3 & 12 \end{pmatrix} \quad [1]$$

The inverse of $\begin{pmatrix} 2 & 3 \\ 1 & 4 \end{pmatrix}$ is $\frac{1}{5}\begin{pmatrix} 4 & -3 \\ -1 & 2 \end{pmatrix}$

Post multiply both sides of [1]

$$\begin{pmatrix} a & b \\ c & d \end{pmatrix} \left[\begin{pmatrix} 2 & 3 \\ 1 & 4 \end{pmatrix} \times \frac{1}{5}\begin{pmatrix} 4 & -3 \\ -1 & 2 \end{pmatrix}\right] = \begin{pmatrix} 5 & 10 \\ 3 & 12 \end{pmatrix} \times \frac{1}{5}\begin{pmatrix} 4 & -3 \\ -1 & 2 \end{pmatrix}$$

$$\begin{pmatrix} a & b \\ c & d \end{pmatrix} = \begin{pmatrix} 2 & 1 \\ 0 & 3 \end{pmatrix}$$

1. $\begin{pmatrix} 1 & 0 \\ 0 & 2 \end{pmatrix}$

2. $\begin{pmatrix} 1 & 2 \\ 2 & 0 \end{pmatrix}$

3. $\begin{pmatrix} 3 & 0 \\ 1 & 1 \end{pmatrix}$

4. $\begin{pmatrix} 1 & -1 \\ 0 & 5 \end{pmatrix}$

5. $\begin{pmatrix} 1 & -4 \\ 0 & 3 \end{pmatrix}$

6. $\begin{pmatrix} 9 & -4 \\ -2 & 1 \end{pmatrix}$

7. $\begin{pmatrix} 3 & 0 \\ 0 & 2 \end{pmatrix}$

8. $\begin{pmatrix} 1 & 1 \\ 1 & 2 \end{pmatrix}$

9. $\begin{pmatrix} 1 & 0 \\ 0 & -1 \end{pmatrix}$

10. $\begin{pmatrix} 0 & 1 \\ -1 & 0 \end{pmatrix}$

11. $\begin{pmatrix} 0 & -1 \\ 1 & 0 \end{pmatrix}$

12. $\begin{pmatrix} 0 & 1 \\ 1 & 0 \end{pmatrix}$

Exercise 12I   Page 270

1. a) P gives a reflection in the x-axis. Q a rotation of $90°$ clockwise about O.

c) Reflection in the line $y = -x$

d) $R = \begin{pmatrix} 0 & -1 \\ -1 & 0 \end{pmatrix}$ $S = \begin{pmatrix} 0 & 1 \\ 1 & 0 \end{pmatrix}$

e) $A_3B_3C_3D_3$

f) $A_4B_4C_4D_4$

g) (b) and (e) are the same. If we used P on $A_2B_2C_2D_2$ we would get (f).

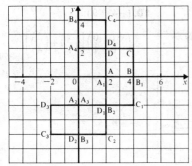

2. a)

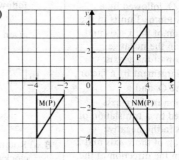

b) M is a rotation of $180°$ about O.
   NM is a reflection in the x-axis.

c) $L = \begin{pmatrix} 1 & 0 \\ 0 & -1 \end{pmatrix}$

d) $L(P) = NM(P)$, L is a reflection in the x-axis.

e) Yes.

3. a) $\begin{pmatrix} 0 & -1 \\ 1 & 0 \end{pmatrix}$ b) $\begin{pmatrix} 1 & 0 \\ 0 & -1 \end{pmatrix}$ c) $\begin{pmatrix} 0 & -1 \\ -1 & 0 \end{pmatrix}$

d) $R = QP$

4. a) $\begin{pmatrix} -y \\ x \end{pmatrix}$. Rotation $90°$ anticlockwise about O.

b) $\begin{pmatrix} 1 & 0 \\ 0 & 1 \end{pmatrix}$.

Exercise 12m   Page 273

1.

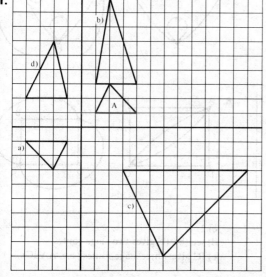

2. a) Rotation of $180°$ about O (or equivalent).

b) Stretch by factor 3 in direction of y-axis.

c) Enlargement by factor 3, centre O, followed by reflection in x-axis.

d) Reflection in y-axis followed by stretch factor 2 in direction of y-axis.

3.

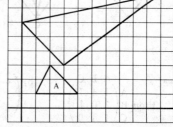

4. An enlargement by factor 2, centre O, followed by a translation of 3 units in the direction of the x-axis and 1 unit in the negative direction of the y-axis.

5. An enlargement by a factor $\frac{1}{2}$, centre O, and a reflection in the y-axis followed by a translation of 3 units in the negative direction of the x-axis and 2 units in the direction of the y-axis.

6. a) Rotation of 90° clockwise about O.

b) $\begin{pmatrix} 0 & 1 \\ -1 & 0 \end{pmatrix}\begin{pmatrix} x \\ y \end{pmatrix} = \begin{pmatrix} x' \\ y' \end{pmatrix}$

7. a) Reflection in the y-axis followed by a translation given by $\begin{pmatrix} 6 \\ -4 \end{pmatrix}$

b) $\begin{pmatrix} -1 & 0 \\ 0 & 1 \end{pmatrix}\begin{pmatrix} x \\ y \end{pmatrix} + \begin{pmatrix} 6 \\ -4 \end{pmatrix}$

$= \begin{pmatrix} x' \\ y' \end{pmatrix}$

8. a) Rotation of 90° clockwise about O and an enlargement by factor 2, centre O.

b) $\begin{pmatrix} 0 & 2 \\ -2 & 0 \end{pmatrix}\begin{pmatrix} x \\ y \end{pmatrix} = \begin{pmatrix} x' \\ y' \end{pmatrix}$

9. a) Reflection in the x-axis followed by a translation of 2 units in the direction of the y-axis

b) $\begin{pmatrix} 1 & 0 \\ 0 & -1 \end{pmatrix}\begin{pmatrix} x \\ y \end{pmatrix} + \begin{pmatrix} 0 \\ 2 \end{pmatrix}$

$= \begin{pmatrix} x' \\ y' \end{pmatrix}$

10. $(-4, \quad 9)$;

$\begin{pmatrix} -1 & 0 \\ 0 & 1 \end{pmatrix}\left[\begin{pmatrix} x \\ y \end{pmatrix} + \begin{pmatrix} 2 \\ 4 \end{pmatrix}\right]$

$= \begin{pmatrix} x' \\ y' \end{pmatrix}$

Exercise 12n   Page 275

1.
$$\text{From } \begin{array}{c} \\ A \\ B \end{array}\begin{array}{c} \text{To} \\ \begin{array}{cc} A & B \end{array} \\ \begin{pmatrix} 0 & 2 \\ 1 & 0 \end{pmatrix} \end{array}$$

2.
$$\text{From } \begin{array}{c} \\ A \\ B \\ C \end{array}\begin{array}{c} \text{To} \\ \begin{array}{ccc} A & B & C \end{array} \\ \begin{pmatrix} 0 & 2 & 1 \\ 2 & 0 & 1 \\ 1 & 1 & 0 \end{pmatrix} \end{array}$$

3.
$$\text{From } \begin{array}{c} \\ A \\ B \end{array}\begin{array}{c} \text{To} \\ \begin{array}{cc} A & B \end{array} \\ \begin{pmatrix} 2 & 1 \\ 1 & 2 \end{pmatrix} \end{array}$$

4.
$$\text{From } \begin{array}{c} \\ A \\ B \\ C \end{array}\begin{array}{c} \text{To} \\ \begin{array}{ccc} A & B & C \end{array} \\ \begin{pmatrix} 0 & 1 & 0 \\ 0 & 0 & 1 \\ 1 & 0 & 0 \end{pmatrix} \end{array}$$

5.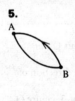

6.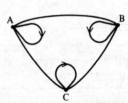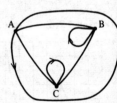

7.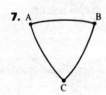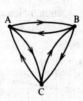

8.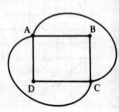

9. a)
$$\text{From } \begin{array}{c} \\ A \\ B \\ C \end{array}\begin{array}{c} \begin{array}{ccc} A & B & C \end{array} \\ \begin{pmatrix} 1 & 1 & 1 \\ 2 & 0 & 1 \\ 1 & 1 & 0 \end{pmatrix} \end{array}$$

b) $\begin{pmatrix} 4 & 3 & 2 \\ 3 & 3 & 2 \\ 3 & 1 & 2 \end{pmatrix}$

c) 2
d) see (b). R^2 gives two-stage routes
e) R^3 gives three-stage routes (e.g. AABC).

10. a)
$$R = \begin{pmatrix} 0 & 2 & 1 \\ 2 & 0 & 2 \\ 1 & 2 & 0 \end{pmatrix}$$
b)
$$R^2 = \begin{pmatrix} 5 & 2 & 4 \\ 2 & 8 & 2 \\ 4 & 2 & 5 \end{pmatrix}, \quad R^3 = \begin{pmatrix} 8 & 18 & 9 \\ 18 & 8 & 18 \\ 9 & 18 & 8 \end{pmatrix}$$
c) 4 routes

d) 9 routes (this includes routes such as ACBC.)

Exercise 12p   Page 277

1. a) 2
b) 5; Scale factor = 3

2. a) (9, 5)   b) (−1, 1)
c) (2, 1)

3. a) $\begin{pmatrix} 2 & -1 \\ -3\frac{1}{2} & 2 \end{pmatrix}$ b) (1, 2)

4. $\begin{pmatrix} y \\ x \end{pmatrix}$.   Reflection in the line $y = x$

5. a) $\begin{pmatrix} x \\ 3x + y \end{pmatrix}$
b) $(p, 4p)$
c) 4

Exercise 12q   Page 277

1. a) $\begin{pmatrix} 10 & -14 \\ 8 & -11 \end{pmatrix}$

b) $\begin{pmatrix} -3 & -2 \\ 4 & 2 \end{pmatrix}$

c) $\frac{1}{2}\begin{pmatrix} 2 & -2 \\ -5 & 6 \end{pmatrix}$

d) $\begin{pmatrix} 2 & 3 \\ 1 & 2 \end{pmatrix}$

e) $\begin{pmatrix} 46 & 16 \\ 40 & 14 \end{pmatrix}$

f) $\begin{pmatrix} 26 & -45 \\ -15 & 26 \end{pmatrix}$

g) $\begin{pmatrix} 12 & 4 \\ 10 & 4 \end{pmatrix}$

h) $\begin{pmatrix} 6 & -9 \\ -3 & 6 \end{pmatrix}$

2. a) $\begin{pmatrix} 0 & 2 \\ 2 & 0 \end{pmatrix}$

b) $\begin{pmatrix} 0 & 1 \\ 1 & 0 \end{pmatrix}$ i.e. **A**

c) **I**   d) **A**

e) **I**   f) **A**
g) −1   h) 1
i) **I**   j) **A**

3. $a = 23, b = -16$
$c = 19, d = -6$

4. a) $AB = \begin{pmatrix} 2 & 0 \\ 5 & k \end{pmatrix}$

$BA = \begin{pmatrix} 2 & 0 \\ 4 + 3k & k \end{pmatrix}$

b) $\frac{1}{3}$ c) $|B| = 0$

5. $\begin{pmatrix} 16 & -4 \\ -6 & 2 \end{pmatrix}$

Exercise 12r   Page 278

1. B   **2.** A   **3.** A   **4.** D   **5.** B   **6.** C

CHAPTER 13

Exercise 13a   Page 283

1. 19, 23
2. 48, −96
3. 36, 49
4. 1 + 3 + 5 + 7 + 9 + 11,
  1 + 3 + 5 + 7 + 9 + 11 + 13

5. $\frac{1}{81}$, $-\frac{1}{243}$
6. 42, 68
7. a) 3, 5, 7, 9
  b) 2, 4, 8, 16
  c) 0, 3, 8, 15

8. $u_n = 2n + 3$
9. $u_n = 3(n - 1)$
10. $u_n = 2^{n+1}$
11. $u_n = n(n + 2)$
12. $u_n = n^3$
13. $u_n = n^2 + 1$

14.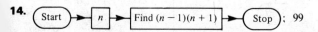
; 99

15. a)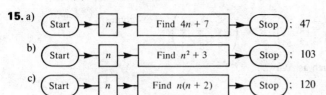

Start → n → Find $4n + 7$ → Stop ; 47

b) Start → n → Find $n^2 + 3$ → Stop ; 103

c) Start → n → Find $n(n + 2)$ → Stop ; 120

16. a) $(5, 26)$ b) $(10, 101)$
c) $(n, n^2 + 1)$

17. 0, 3, 8, 15, 24, 35

18. 2, 9, 20, 35, 54, 77

19.

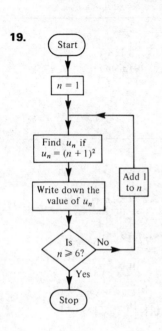

Start

$n = 1$

Find u_n if $u_n = (n + 1)^2$

Write down the value of u_n

Add 1 to n

Is $n \geqslant 6$?   No

Yes

Stop

20.

Start

$n = 1$

Find u_n if $u_n = \dfrac{n}{n + 1}$

Write down the value u_n

Add 1 to n

Is $n \geqslant 5$ No

Yes

Stop

21.

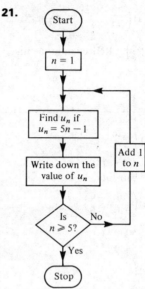

Start

$n = 1$

Find u_n if $u_n = 5n - 1$

Write down the value of u_n

Add 1 to n

Is $n \geqslant 5$?   No

Yes

Stop

22.

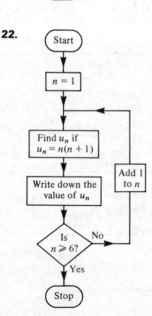

Start

$n = 1$

Find u_n if $u_n = n(n + 1)$

Write down the value of u_n

Add 1 to n

Is $n \geqslant 6$?   No

Yes

Stop

23. a) 6, 11, 16, 21, 26
b) i) $5n + 1$ ii) 151
c) 8, 12

24. a)   1 6 15 20 15 6 1
          1 7 21 35 35 21 7 1
        1 8 28 56 70 56 28 8 1
b) $u_1 = 1, u_2 = 2, u_3 = 4,$
   $u_5 = 8, .., u_9 = 256$
c) 2^{n-1}

25. a) 2 m
b) 20 m
c) $n(n + 1)$ m

26. a) The sum of the squares of
the first two is equal to
the square of the third.
b) Any one of $(9, 40, 41)$,
$(11, 60, 61)$, $(13, 84, 85)$...
There is a pattern to these
numbers:
the first numbers go
3, 5, 7, 9,...
and the second numbers go
4, 4 + 8, 4 + 8 + 12,
            4 + 8 + 12 + 16,....
and the third number in
each triple is the second
number +1

27. $\frac{1}{2}, \frac{1}{4}, \frac{1}{8}, \frac{1}{16}, \frac{1}{32}$. In theory the
bar will last for ever!

28. Each sequence ends in the
form... $x, x, 0$. The number x
is the highest common
factor of the integers that
start the sequence.

29. a) 1, 3, 6, 10, 15
b) 210
c) $\frac{1}{2}(n - 1)(n)$ or $\frac{n}{2}(n - 1)$
d) n e) 2, 3, 4, 5   f) 21

30. a) 1, 5, 14, 30, 55
b) 2870
c) $\frac{1}{6}(n - 1)n(2n - 1)$
d) n^2
e) 1, 4, 9, 16   f) 400

Exercise 13b   Page 288

1. 49, 70
2. 26, 37
3. 47, 73
4. 437, 683
5. 325, 540
6. 7, 29
7. e.g. multiply the previous term by 3; 81, 243, 729 or add 12 more than was previously added; 51, 87, 135.

8. e.g. multiply the previous term by 2; 24, 48, 96 or add 3 more than was previously added; 21, 33, 48.
9. e.g. add 2 more than was previously added; 10, 17, 26 or multiply previous term by 3 and subtract 1; 14, 41, 122.
10. $-241, -1265, -5361$;
$u_n - u_{n+1} = 4^{n-1}$;
$u_n = 100 - (4^0 + 4^1 + \ldots 4^{n-1})$

11. $\frac{5}{6}, \frac{6}{7}, \frac{7}{8}$; $u_n = \dfrac{n}{n+1}$
12. 126, 217, 344; $u_n = n^3 + 1$
13. 5.7, 6.8, 7.9;
$u_n = 1.3 + (n-1) \times 1.1$
14. 16, -32, 64; $u_n = (-2)^{n-1}$
15. $\frac{7}{9}, \frac{4}{5}, \frac{9}{11}$; $u_n = \dfrac{n+1}{n+3}$
16. 121 should be changed to 122.

17. The completed arrangement of numbers is:

8		10		13		20		34		58		95		148		220
	2		3		7		14		24		37		53		72	
		1		4		7		10		13		16		19		
			3		3		3		3		3		3			

18. a) 146   b) 99   c) 335
19. 22, 27
20. $u_n = 5n - 3$
21. 14, 84, 204, 374, 594
22. 14 84 204 374 594 864 1184
70 120 170 220 270 320
50 50 50 50 → 50
$27 \times 32 = 864, \ 32 \times 37 = 1184$

23. 9, 19, 29, 39, 49
24. $u_n = (5n-3)(5n+2)$
25. a) 2, 9, 21, 38, 60
b) 2, $\frac{9}{2}$, 7, $\frac{19}{2}$, 12
c) $u_n = \frac{1}{2}(5n-1)$
d) $u_n = \dfrac{n}{2}(5n-1)$
26. yes, 1
27. yes, 1
28. no
29. yes, 4.236…
30. no
31. yes, 3.162…, i.e. $\sqrt{10}$
32. a) 1, 3, 4, 7, 11, 18
b) 2, 3, 5, 8, 13, 21
c) 3, 4, 7, 11, 18, 29

33. 2, 1, 3, 4, 7
Apart from the first term, the numbers in the original sequence arise again.
1, 2, 3, 5, 8,… Yes

34. a) 1, 1, 2, 3, 5, 8, 13, 21   b) $\frac{1}{1}, \frac{1}{2}, \frac{2}{3}, \frac{3}{5}, \frac{5}{8}, \frac{8}{13}, \frac{13}{21}, \frac{21}{34}, \frac{34}{55}, \frac{55}{89}$
c) 1, 0.5, 0.6667, 0.6, 0.625, 0.6154, 0.6190, 0.6176, 0.6181, 0.6180
The nth term is converging to a value that lies between consecutive terms.

Exercise 13c   Page 293

1. a) $0.\dot{3}$ b) $0.0\dot{3}$
c) $0.01\dot{6}$ d) $0.00\dot{3}$

2. a) $0.\dot{0}\dot{9}$ b) $0.04\dot{5}$
c) $0.0\dot{3}$ d) $0.1\dot{8}$

3. a) $0.00\dot{1}$ b) $0.00\dot{2}$
c) $0.00\dot{9}$ d) 0.009

4. a) $0.\dot{1}$ b) $0.\dot{9}$

c) $\frac{1}{9} \times 9 = 1$, but $\frac{1}{9} = 0.1111…$
and $0.111… \times 9 = 0.999…$
so $0.999… = 1$ (?)
d) $1 - 0.999… = 0.000…$
($0.\dot{9}$ has no 'end' so $0.0000…$ has no 'end')
∴ $1 - 0.\dot{9} = 0$, ie $0.\dot{9}$ is equal to 1!
5. a) $\frac{1}{9}$ b) $\frac{1}{99}$ c) $\frac{1}{333}$

6. Yes, $\frac{1}{7} = 0.142\,857\,142…$
$\frac{2}{7} = 0.285\,714\,285…$
$\frac{3}{7} = 0.428\,571\,428…$
$\frac{4}{7} = 0.571\,428\,571…$
$\frac{5}{7} = 0.714\,285\,714…$
$\frac{6}{7} = 0.857\,142\,857…$

The same 6 integers appear in each cycle.

7. a) 0.058 823
  b) 0.999 991
  c) 0.000 009
  d) 0.000 000 529 41

  e) 0.058 823 529 4
8. a) 0.076 923
  b) 0.999 999
  c) 0.000 001

  d) 0.000 000 076 923
  e) 0.076 923 076 92

Exercise 13d   Page 295

1. a) $\frac{7}{10}$ b) irrational   c) $\frac{5}{8}$
2. a) $\frac{1}{3}$ b) irrational   c) $\frac{1}{8}$
3. a) $\frac{2}{3}$ b) irrational   c) $\frac{3}{5}$

4. a) irrational   b) irrational
  c) 4
5. a) irrational   b) $\frac{4}{1}$
  c) irrational
6. a) irrational
  b) irrational, $2\sqrt{2}$
  c) 3

7. a) irrational   b) $\frac{7}{2}$
  c) irrational, $\sqrt{3}$
8. a) $\frac{2}{1}$
  b) irrational, $\sqrt{3}$
  c) $\frac{5}{2}$

9. a) $\frac{1}{4}$ b) $\frac{1}{3}$
  c) irrational, $\dfrac{1}{2\sqrt{2}}$

10. a) -4, $\sqrt{9}$
  b) -4, 0.5, -1.8, $\frac{2}{7}$, $\sqrt{9}$
  c) $\sqrt{5}$, π; -4, 1.8, $\frac{2}{7}$, 0.5,
      $\sqrt{5}$, $\sqrt{9}$, π
11. a) $9\sqrt{3}$
12. $\sqrt{2}$
13. $\sqrt{3}$
14. $8\sqrt{5}$
15. $2\sqrt{2}$
16. $\sqrt{7}$

17. $2 + \frac{1}{2}\sqrt{2}$
18. $3 + \frac{2}{3}\sqrt{3}$

19. $-1 + \sqrt{2}$
20. $-2 + \frac{5}{4}\sqrt{2}$
21. $1 + \frac{1}{3}\sqrt{6}$
22. $-2 + \frac{1}{2}\sqrt{6}$

23. $-1 - \sqrt{2}$
24. $2 - \sqrt{2}$
25. $\frac{1}{2} + \frac{1}{2}\sqrt{3}$
26. $10 - 5\sqrt{3}$
27. $-\frac{2}{11} + \frac{4}{11}\sqrt{3}$
28. $\frac{3}{17} + \frac{9}{17}\sqrt{2}$
29. rational, $\frac{3}{2}$
30. rational, $\frac{7}{4}$
31. irrational, $2 + \frac{1}{2}\sqrt{2}$
32. irrational, $3 + \frac{1}{3}\sqrt{3}$
33. rational, $\frac{6}{5}$
34. rational, $\frac{5}{2}$

Exercise 13f   Page 301

1. $5 + 7(n-1)$ or $7n - 2$

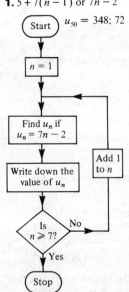
$u_{50} = 348$; 72

2. 170, 262
3. A Fibonacci sequence;
  76, 123, 199; the result is
  always 5.
4. $-3 < -2 < 1.6 < 2.5 < 2.501$
5. a) true   b) true
  c) false   d) false
6. a) 3   b) -6, 3
  c) -6, 0.5, $\frac{2}{3}$, 3, 1.25, -0.5
  $-6 < -0.5 < \frac{2}{3} < 0.5 < 1.25 < \sqrt{5} < 3$
7. a) yes
  b) yes
  c) yes
  d) no, e.g. $4 \div 3$
8. $5 + 3$, and an infinite
  number of other possibilities.
9. a) yes   b) yes
  c) yes   d) yes
  e) no
10. a) $5 + 3$ b) $13 + 3$
  c) $23 + 5$

d) $3 + 3$: if you assumed that
  the prime numbers had to
  be different you read
  more into the statement
  than was there: be careful.

11. 4.472

12. 1.703

13. 0.707

14. a) $1\frac{1}{2}$ b) $1\frac{2}{5}$ c) $1\frac{5}{12}$

15. a) $1 + \dfrac{1}{2 + \dfrac{1}{2 + \dfrac{1}{2 + \frac{1}{2}}}} = 1\frac{12}{29}$

  b) $1 + \dfrac{1}{2 + \dfrac{1}{2 + \dfrac{1}{2 + \frac{1}{2}}}} = 1\frac{29}{70}$

16. 2.25, 1.96, 2.006 944, 1.998 810, 2.000 204

The square of the fraction appears to be getting closer to 2, hence the fraction is getting closer to $\sqrt{2}$.

CHAPTER 14

Exercise 14a   **Page 306**

1.

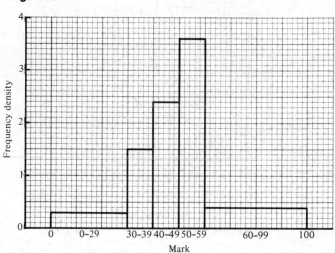

2.

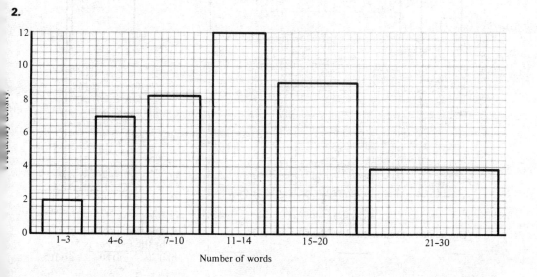

3.

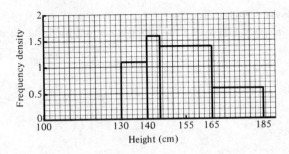

4.

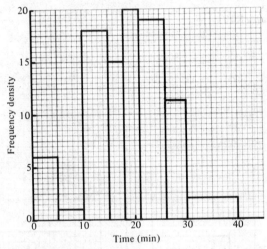

The frequency represented by the first bar is 6

5.

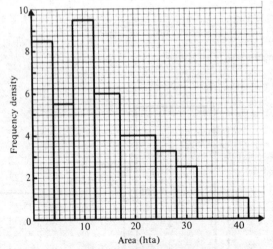

The frequency represented by the first bar is 34

6. a)

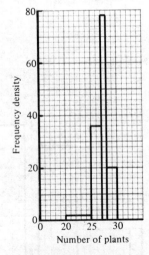

The frequency represented
by the first bar is 5
b) i) 30   ii) 80   iii) 165

7.

Age, n years	$0 \leqslant n < 20$	$20 \leqslant n < 40$	$40 \leqslant n < 60$	$60 \leqslant n < 90$	$90 \leqslant n < 100$
Frequency density	0.5	2	2.5	4	0.5
Frequency	10	40	50	120	5

225 passengers.

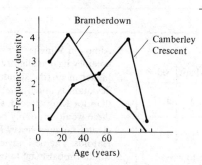

There is a much higher average age at Camberley Crescent than at Bramberdown and the age range is larger. The former is near living accommodation for older people e.g. an old peoples' home.

8. a) 195   b) £ 13.87

9. a) 600   b) 322
Frequency densities in order are 0.95, 2.3, 3.5, 5.5, 2.1

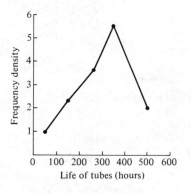

10. a) The frequency densities in order are 3, 2, 4.2, 3.2, 0.7, 0.3

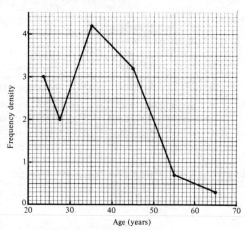

b) The staff in the private school
  i) are on the whole older
  ii) have a smaller range.

11. Cumulative frequencies are 29, 44, 53, 58, 60
a) 3.1
b) $Q_1 = 1.1$, $Q_3 = 7.25$
c) 6.15

12. 5, 9.1
The median and inter-quartile range for the Comice pears are larger than for the Conference pears.

Exercise 14b   Page 313

1. You don't have to answer questions 13 to 17

2. Probably

3. That is where they wish to highlight any problems.

4. The cash dispenser(s) always allow me to get money when I need to.

5. Yes — and it is the easiest one to use since it is the nearest to the questions.

The remaining questions are intended for discussion at a local level.

Exercise 14c   Page 315

1. a) 8.6, 4.13
 b) 57.2, 20.8
 c) 34.6, 15.0
 d) 451, 15.0

2. 9.17, 1.16
3. 23.4, 3.84
4. $\bar{x} = £77\,500$; s.d. $= £28.504$

5. 5.25, 4.55
6. 146.1, 13.7
7. 15.8

Exercise 14d   Page 319

1. b); it is symmetrical and roughly bell-shaped.
2. a) No; mean, mode and median differ too much
 b) No; range well below $6 \times$ s.d.
 c) Could be
 d) No; mean, mode and median differ too much.
 e) Could be

3. (b)

4.

	Mean	s.d.
Theoretical distribution	3	1.22
Experimental results	3.03	1.13

Both approximate to a normal distribution.

5. Although Winchester potatoes have a slightly higher mean, the standard deviation is much smaller than for King Harold, so these would probably be a greater range of heavy King Harolds. The best advice would probably be to buy King Harolds.

Exercise 14e   Page 323

1. a) $\frac{3}{20}$ b) $\frac{11}{20}$

2. a)

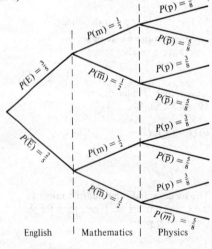

English | Mathematics | Physics

 b) i) $\frac{9}{80}$ ii) $\frac{1}{8}$ iii) $\frac{3}{8}$
 c) 78

3. a) $\frac{6}{11}$ b) $\frac{1}{2}$
 c) $\frac{6}{11}$ d) $\frac{4}{33}$

4. a) $\frac{2}{13}$ b) $\frac{5}{91}$ c) $\frac{8}{13}$

5. a) $\frac{2}{7}$ b) $\frac{33}{70}$ c) $\frac{1}{35}$

6. a)

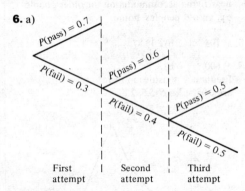

First attempt | Second attempt | Third attempt

 b) i) 0.18   ii) 0.06
 c) i) 700   ii) 180   iii) 60   d) 0.94
7. a) 0.64   b) 0.16
8. a) i) $P(\text{W}) = \frac{1}{4}$ ii) $P(\text{N}) = \frac{3}{4}$
 b)

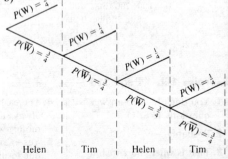

Helen | Tim | Helen | Tim

 c) i) $\frac{3}{16}$ ii) $\frac{9}{64}$ d) 75   e) No; Helen; yes.

9.

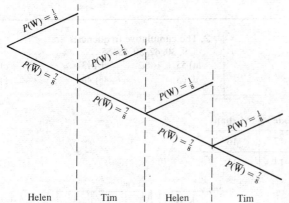

Helen | Tim | Helen | Tim

c) i) $\frac{7}{8} \times \frac{7}{8} \times \frac{7}{8} \times \frac{1}{8} = \frac{343}{4096}$

ii) $\frac{7}{8} \times \frac{7}{8} \times \frac{1}{8} = \frac{49}{512}$

d) About 49. Helen still has the better chance of winning, but it is not as great as when two coins were tossed. If they alternate who starts each game, it is a fair game.

10. a) $\frac{1}{6}$

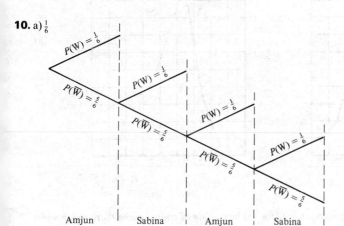

Amjun | Sabina | Amjun | Sabina

c) i) $\frac{5}{6} \times \frac{1}{6} = \frac{5}{36}$

ii) $\frac{1}{6} + \frac{5}{6} \times \frac{5}{6} \times \frac{1}{6} = \frac{61}{216}$

d) yes, 76

11. a) $\frac{3}{50}$ b) $\frac{3}{40}$ c) $\frac{429}{1400}$ d) $\frac{692}{1400} = \frac{173}{350}$

12. a) $\frac{1}{2}$ b) $\frac{12}{91}$

c) If Alison does not win with her second selection she still has a chance of winning, i.e. her total chance is greater than 0.5.
The game is therefore unfair.

d) (a) $\frac{9}{26}$ (b) $\frac{2}{7}$
The game is fairer but Alison is still more likely to win after they have selected two discs each.

Exercise 14f   **Page 329**

1. a) 80
b) cycle
c) i) $\frac{59}{80}$ ii) $\frac{21}{80}$ iii) $\frac{53}{80}$

2. $x = 5$
a) $\frac{7}{30}$ b) $\frac{13}{30}$
c) $\frac{2}{5}$ d) $\frac{13}{30}$

3. 10

4. a) 3
b) i) $\frac{7}{27}$ ii) $\frac{1}{2}$

Exercise 14g   Page 331

1. Cumulative frequency values are
3, 10, 19, 40, 62, 96, 130, 152, 160

2. The cumulative frequencies are
5, 9, 30, 42, 50, 53, 55

a) 55   b) 13   c) 46

d) 65   e) 46   f) $\frac{46}{55}$

3. a)

	Mean	Mode	Median
At beginning	16.5	15–17	16
At end	14.3	12–14	13

b)

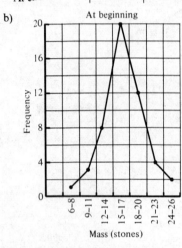

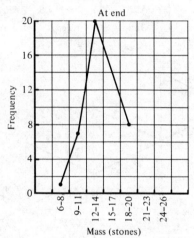

c) Both distributions skewed negatively. s.d. higher at beginning of course, since there was a wider spread of masses.

4. a) 16.3, 15–19

b)

Number of items	0–4	5–9	10–14	15–19	20–24	25–29
Frequency	1	4	9	15	8	3
Cumulative frequency	1	5	14	29	37	40

c) Median = 16; Q_1 = 12, Q_3 = 19.2
Inter-quartile range = 7.2

d) 5.76

e) i) $\frac{5}{40} = \frac{1}{8}$ ii) $\frac{11}{40}$

f) The ladies have an average about
16.3 – 10.2 i.e. 6.1 more items in their
handbags than teenage girls.
Since the standard deviation for the
ladies is 5.76 compared with 3.5 for the
teenage girls, there is a far greater
spread in the number of items in the
handbags of the ladies than those of
teenagers.

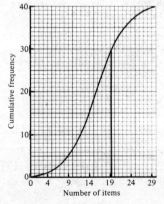

5. a) i) $\frac{1}{2}$ ii) $\frac{3}{7}$ iii) 1
b) $\frac{1}{2}$

6. a) $\frac{1}{1000}$
b) $\frac{2744}{3375}$ (0.813)
c) $\frac{7}{75}$ (0.093)   d) 15

7. a) $\frac{4}{25}$ b) $\frac{1}{4}$
c) $\frac{1}{100}$ d) $\frac{2}{3}$

8. a) i) $\left(\frac{14}{15}\right)^{10}$ ii) $\left(\frac{1}{15}\right)^{10}$
iii) $\left(\frac{7}{8}\right)^{10}$
b) yes

9. a) 700   b) 1300
c) 910   d) 1105
e) 195   f) 455
g) 195

10.

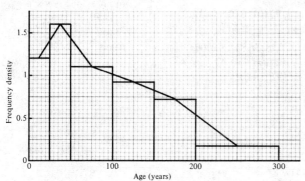

11. a) i) $\frac{5}{12}$ ii) $\frac{1}{3}$ b) $\frac{2}{11}$
c) $\frac{2}{11}$ d) $\frac{1}{22}$
e) $\frac{3}{11}$ f) $\frac{2}{55}$

CHAPTER 15

Exercise 15a   Page 335

1. b)

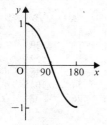

c) $x = 90°$
d) i) 53°, 127°,   ii) 37°, 143°,
iii) 24°, 156°
The sum of each pair
is 180°

2. a) sin 30° = 0.5,
sin 150° = 0.5,
150° = 180° − 30°
b) sin 40° = 0.6428,
sin 140° = 0.6428,
140° = 180° − 40°
c) sin 72° = 0.9511,
sin 108° = 0.9511,
108° = 180° − 72°

Exercise 15b   Page 336

1. $\frac{5}{13}$ **3.** $\frac{2}{5}$ **5.** $\frac{7}{25}$ **7.** 15°   **9.** 28°   **11.** 5°
2. $\frac{1}{2}$ **4.** $\frac{3}{10}$ **6.** $\frac{40}{41}$ **8.** 40°   **10.** 80°   **12.** 89°

Exercise 15c   Page 337

1. b)

c) 90°
d) they are negative
e) i) 37°,   ii) 143°
They are supplementary
(add up to 180°)

2. a) cos 30° = 0.8660
cos 150° = −0.8660
150° = 180° − −30°
b) cos 50° = 0.6428
cos 130° = −0.6428
130° = 180° − 50°
c) cos 84° = 0.1045
cos 96° = −0.1045
96° = 180° − 84°

Exercise 15d   Page 338

1. $-\frac{3}{5}$ **2.** $-\frac{2}{3}$ **3.** $-\frac{2}{5}$ **4.** $-\frac{7}{8}$ **5.** a) $\widehat{A} = 160°$ b) $\widehat{A} = 130°$

Exercise 15e   Page 340

1. $\cos A = \frac{24}{25}$, $\tan A = \frac{7}{24}$
2. $\sin A = \frac{12}{13}$, $\tan A = \frac{12}{5}$
3. $\sin P = \frac{3}{5}$, $\cos P = \frac{4}{5}$
4. $\tan D = \frac{4}{3}$, $\sin D = \frac{4}{5}$
5. $\cos X = \frac{40}{41}$, $\tan X = \frac{9}{40}$
6. $\sin A = \frac{1}{\sqrt{2}}$, $\cos A = \frac{1}{\sqrt{2}}$
7. b) i) $\frac{\sqrt{3}}{2}$ ii) $\frac{1}{2}$ iii) $\sqrt{3}$
    c) i) $\frac{1}{2}$ ii) $\frac{\sqrt{3}}{2}$ iii) $\frac{1}{\sqrt{3}}$

8. b) i) $\frac{1}{\sqrt{2}}$ ii) $\frac{1}{\sqrt{2}}$ iii) 1
9. $\frac{120}{169}$, 0.7101, 67.4°, 0.7101;
    $\sin 2A = 2 \sin A \cos A$
10. $\frac{7}{25}$, 0.28, 36.87°, 0.2800,
    $\cos 2A = \cos^2 A - \sin^2 A$
11. 1
12. $\frac{1320}{3479}$

13. a) i) $\frac{4}{29}$ ii) $\frac{25}{29}$ iii) $\frac{29}{25}$ iv) $\frac{4}{29}$
    b) $\sin^2 A = 1 - \cos^2 A$
    c) $\dfrac{1}{\cos^2 A} = 1 + \tan^2 A$
    d) yes

Exercise 15f   Page 342

1. a) $\frac{\sqrt{3}}{2}$
    b) $\frac{1}{2}$

2. a) i) 1   ii) $\frac{1}{2}$
    b) 90°   c) 30°

Exercise 15g   Page 342

1. a) $-\frac{24}{25}$ b) $\frac{7}{25}$
2. 30°, 150°
3. -0.515
4. 108°
5. a) $\frac{4}{5}$ b) $\frac{3}{5}$
    c) $-\frac{3}{5}$

6.
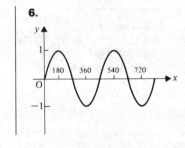

7.
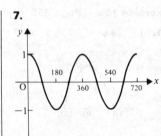

Exercise 15h   Page 345

1. 4.92 cm   **4.** 8.05 cm   **7.** 238 cm   **10.** 413 cm   **13.** 5.62 cm   **16.** 77.0 cm
2. 13.0 cm   **5.** 14.6 cm   **8.** 66.0 cm   **11.** 64.1 cm   **14.** 19.7 cm   **17.** 224 cm
3. 9.74 cm   **6.** 9.69 cm   **9.** 5.60 cm   **12.** 42.4 cm   **15.** 18.4 cm

18. QR = 7.57 cm, PQ = 7.84 cm
19. BC = 13.5 cm, AC = 9.08 cm
20. $p = 117$, $q = 175$
21. $a = 27$, $c = 35.4$

	AB	BC	AC	$\widehat{A}$	$\widehat{B}$	$\widehat{C}$
22.	23.7 cm	19 cm	19.5 cm	51°	53°	76°
23.	217 cm	221 cm	146 cm	72°	39°	69°
24.	81 cm	49.0 cm	69.8 cm	37°	59°	84°
25.	114 cm	123 cm	97 cm	71°	48°	61°
26.	12 cm	23.9 cm	28.9 cm	54°	102°	24°
27.	7.97 cm	15.6 cm	9.9 cm	26°	33°	121°
28. a) 11.8 cm	b) 5.85 cm					

Exercise 15i   Page 351

1. 5.73
2. 7.95
3. 7.68 cm
4. 18.4 cm
5. 7.03
6. 14.2
7. 13.7
8. 11.1 cm
9. 8.30 cm
10. 15.9 cm

11. 21.6 cm
12. 43.0 cm
13. 28.9
14. 4.75
15. 16.9
16. 96.4 cm
17. 9.05 cm
18. 24.1°
19. 108.2°
20. 92.9°

21. 29.0°
22. 95.7°
23. 48.2°
24. a) 13.1 cm   b) 72.3°
25. a) 0.9502
    b) If $\hat{C} = 71.8°$, $\hat{B} = 76.2°$
       and AC = 5.31 cm
       If $\hat{C} = 108.2°$, $\hat{B} = 39.8°$
       and AC = 3.51 cm

Exercise 15j   Page 355

1. 20.8 cm or 5.37 cm

2. The shortest possible distance from C
   to AB is 12 sin 48° cm, i.e. 8.92 cm which
   is larger than the given length of BC,
   or if the sine formula is used this gives
   sin B > 1 and there is no value of B for
   which this is true.

3. Yes, B = 90° since sin 30° = 0.5

   and $\dfrac{8.4(BC)}{16.8(AC)} = 0.5$

4. yes, see diagram

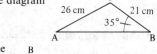

5. one, see
   diagram

It is impossible for $\hat{C}$ to be
acute since this would put B
on the opposite side of A,
and $\hat{A}$ would then be 136°,
not 44°.

6. Either $\hat{B} = 59.7°$, $\hat{C} = 78.3°$ and c = 6.15 cm
   or $\hat{B} = 120.3°$, $\hat{C} = 17.7°$ and c = 1.91 cm.

Exercise 15k   Page 357

	a	b	c	$\hat{A}$	$\hat{B}$	$\hat{C}$
1.		17.0				
2.	117					
3.		77.9				
4.			23.3			
5.			346			
6.			12.4			45°
7.	29.7				38°	
8.	25.9					
9.		28.6				
10.	21.6		29.3	47°		

11. b = 10.2 cm, $\hat{C} = 54°$
    c = 8.62
12. $\hat{R} = 106.2°$, $\hat{P} = 47.9°$,
    $\hat{Q} = 25.9°$
13. l = 17.7 cm, $\hat{M} = 49.7°$,
    $\hat{N} = 66.3°$
14. $\hat{E} = 33.9°$, $\hat{F} = 93.7°$,
    $\hat{D} = 52.4°$

Exercise 15l   Page 360

1. 81.1 cm²
2. 18 900 sq units
3. 2610 cm²
4. 572 sq units
5. 126 sq units

6. 22 800 cm²
7. 35.5 sq units
8. 6.62 m²
9. 2030 cm²
10. 148 sq units

11. $\hat{C} = 83.3°$, 27.8 cm²
12. PR = 9.91 cm, 53.8 cm²
13. $\hat{M} = 48.9°$, LN = 14.7 cm
14. 4.46 cm

Exercise 15m   Page 362

1. 62.3 km

2. $\widehat{APB} = 18.1°$, 42.7 m

3. 88°

4. a) 42 cm²   b) 44.4°
    c) 8.52 cm

5. AC = 5.76 km,
    BC = 4.29 km, 69.1 km/h

6. a) 0.2588   b) 97.6 m

7. a) 4.26 cm   b) 75.2°
    c) 16.0 cm²

8. a) 39°, 9°   b) 1430 m
    c) 1080 m

9. a) 10.5 m   b) 6.42 m
    c) 81.0 m²   d) 8.96 m

10. a) i) 14.1 cm,   ii) 8.89 cm
    b) 81.3 cm²

11. a) 47.2°   b) 17.3°
    c) 10.7 cm   d) 51.5 cm²

12. a) 27.9 miles, 298.7°
    b) i) 13.4 miles
      ii) 24.5 miles

Exercise 15n   Page 367

1. $\frac{12}{13}, \frac{12}{5}$

2. 21.5°, 158.5°

3. −0.43

4. 196 cm

5. 10.9 cm

6. 38.0 cm²

7. 13.5 km

Exercise 15p   Page 368

1. 143°

2. $y = 180 - x$

3. a) $\cos(180° - A) = -\cos A$
    b) $\sin(180° - A) = \sin A$
    c) $-\cos A = \cos(180° - A)$

4. 16.7 cm

5. AB = 8.94 cm, BC = 6.90 cm

6. a) 42.6°   b) 82.9°

7. a) 70.9°   b) 29.65 m²
    c) 2.37 m²

CHAPTER 16

Exercise 16a   Page 369

1. a) f is the function 'double'
    b) f is the function 'add 2'
    c) f is the function 'invert'
    d) f is the function 'cube'

2. a)

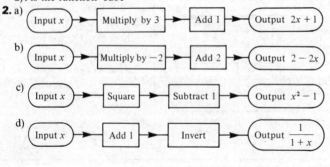

3. a) −1   b) 7
    c) −3   d) −11

4. a) 3   b) −1
    c) 7   d) 5

5. a) 0   b) 1
    c) 4   d) 9

6. a) 11   b) 3
    c) 6   d) 6

7. a) 1   b) −3
    c) 3   d) −1

8. a) 2   b) 7
    c) 2   d) $-15\frac{1}{2}$
    $\frac{4}{0}$ has no meaning.

9. $\frac{6}{5}$

10. $\frac{1}{5}$

11. 7

12. −5

13. 3 or −3

14. 1 or −1

15. −1 or 3

16. 1

17. −1 or 2

18. a) −4   b) −6

    c) 2 or −3

19. a) −15   b) −7

    c) i) 5, −3   ii) −4, 6

20. a) −8   b) −7

    c) 2   d) 2.08

21. a) $\frac{4}{3}$ b) 6

22. a) i) 13   ii) −3

    b) 1

23. a) −4, −2, 2   b) increasing

    c) 1.56 (approx.)

24. a) 8, 6, 2   b) decreasing

    c) 6   d) $x > 6$

25. a) 2, 6, 18, 102   b) increasing

    c) 2, 3, 11, 102   d) 2

Exercise 16b   **Page 373**

1.
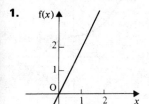

2.
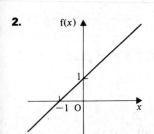

3.
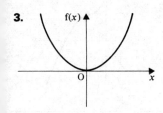

4.
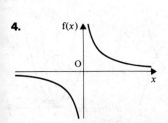

5.
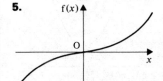

6.
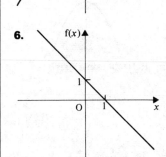

7.
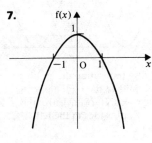

8.
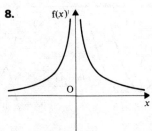

9.
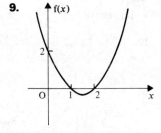

10.
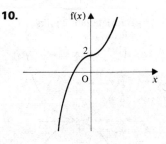

11.
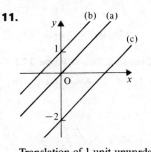

Translation of 1 unit upwards

i.e. defined by $\begin{pmatrix} 0 \\ 1 \end{pmatrix}$

12.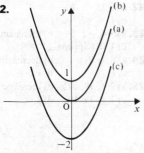

Translation of 2 units downwards

i.e. defined by $\begin{pmatrix} 0 \\ -2 \end{pmatrix}$

13.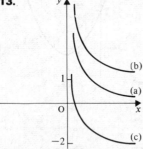

Translation of 2 units downwards

14.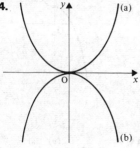

Reflection in x-axis

15.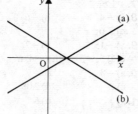

Reflection in x-axis

16.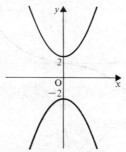

Reflection in x-axis

17.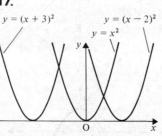

By translating the graph a units to the right along the x-axis. If a is negative the graph slides to the left.

18. a)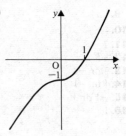

b)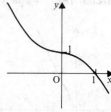

c)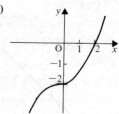

d)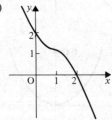

Exercise 16c   Page 378

1. a)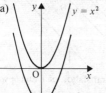

b)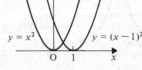

c)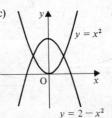

d)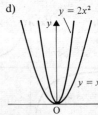

2. a)
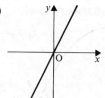

b)
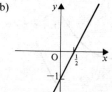

c)
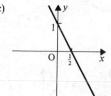

d)
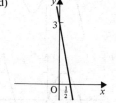

3. a)
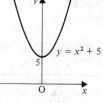

$y = x^2 + 5$

b)
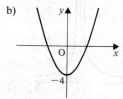

c)
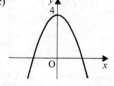

d)
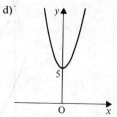

4. a)
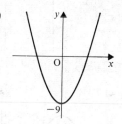

b)
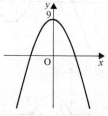

c)
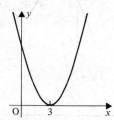

d)
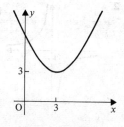

5. a)
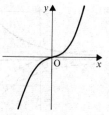

b)
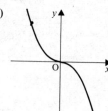

c)
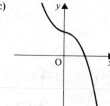

d)
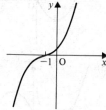

e)
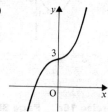

f)
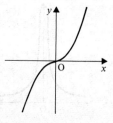

6.

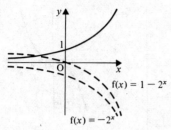

$f(x) = 1 - 2^x$

$f(x) = -2^x$

7.

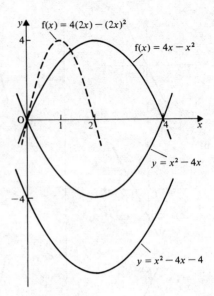

$f(x) = 4(2x) - (2x)^2$

$f(x) = 4x - x^2$

$y = x^2 - 4x$

$y = x^2 - 4x - 4$

8. a)

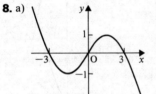

c)

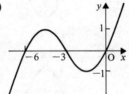

e)

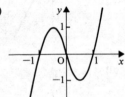

b)

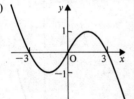

d)

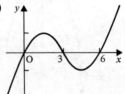

f)

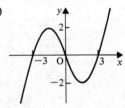

Exercise 16d   Page 381

1.

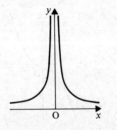

2.

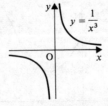

$y = \dfrac{1}{x^3}$

$y = \dfrac{1}{x^4}$

3.

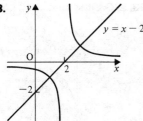

$y = x - 2$

4.

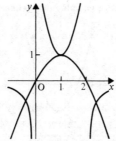

Exercise 16e   Page 383

1. The square of any real number is greater than or equal to 0.

2. The smallest value of $(x-1)^2$ is 0

3. a) The smallest value of $(2x-1)^2$ is 0
   b) $\frac{1}{2}$ c) 6

4. a) The smallest value of $(x+1)^2$ is 0
   b) -1 c) 5

5. a) greatest value
   b) 25 when $x = \frac{2}{3}$

6. a) Coefficient of x^2 is positive so parabola is $\bigvee$ and $\therefore$ has a least value
   b) $-25, 2$
   c)

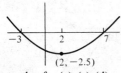

$(2, -2.5)$

7. least value for (a), (c), (d) and (e)
   greatest value for (b) and (f)

8. a) $(x-4)^2 - 9$ b) 4
   c) -9

9. a) $(2x+3)^2 - 14$
   b) -1.5 c) -14

10. a) $(x-\frac{3}{2})^2 + \frac{3}{4}$
   b) $(x+\frac{3}{2})^2 + \frac{3}{4}$
   c) $(x-\frac{3}{2})^2 - \frac{21}{4}$
   d) $2(x+1)^2 + 5$
   e) $2(x-1)^2 - 9$
   f) $-(x-\frac{1}{2})^2 + \frac{9}{4}$
   g) $-(x-1)^2 + 4$
   h) $-(x+1)^2 + 4$
   i) $-2(x-\frac{3}{2})^2 + \frac{29}{4}$

11. a)

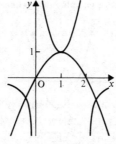

b)

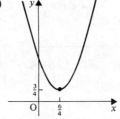

c)

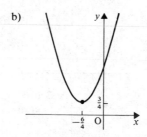

d)

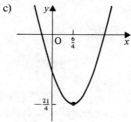

e)

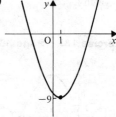

f)

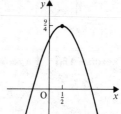

g)

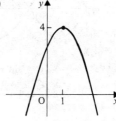

h)

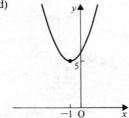

11. i)

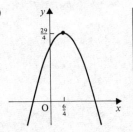

In each case the • marks the greatest/least value for f(x) and the value of x for which it occurs.

12. a) Least value of $\frac{11}{4}$ when $x = -\frac{5}{2}$

b)

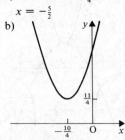

c) The graph does not cross the x-axis.

13. a) Greatest value is −2 when $x = 2$

b)

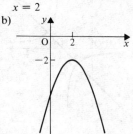

c) The graph does not cross the x-axis.

Exercise 16f   Page 385

2.

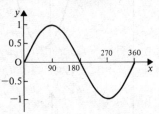

4.

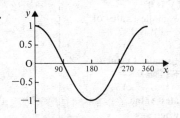

Exercise 16g   Page 387

1.

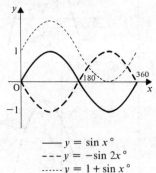

$$— \quad y = \sin x°$$
$$--- \quad y = -\sin 2x°$$
$$\cdots\cdots \quad y = 1 + \sin x°$$

2.

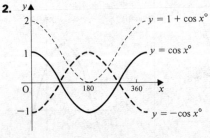

$$y = 1 + \cos x°$$
$$y = \cos x°$$
$$y = -\cos x°$$

3. b) 0, 180, 360

c) f(x)

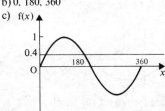

4. b) 90, 270

c) f(x)

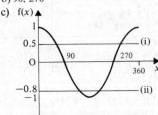

5. a) $-1 \leqslant \sin x° \leqslant 1$ **b)** $-1 \leqslant \cos x° \leqslant 1$

6.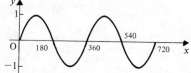

7.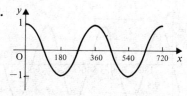

The cosine curve is the sine wave translated 90 to the left.

8.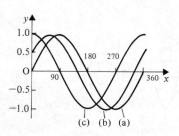

9.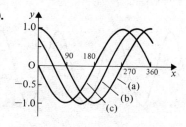

10. a)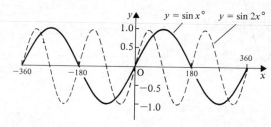

—— $y = \sin x°$
- - - $y = \sin 2x°$

b) The first curve is contracted horizontally to half its width.

c)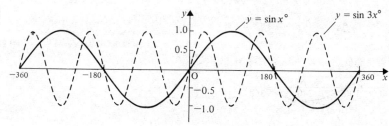

—— $y = \sin x°$
- - - $y = \sin 3x°$

d) The curve is stretched horizontally to double its width.

11. a)

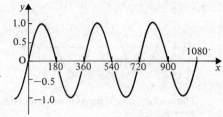

b) $-1 \leqslant \sin x° \leqslant 1$

c)

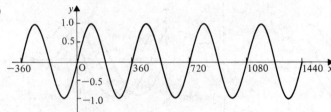

12. a)

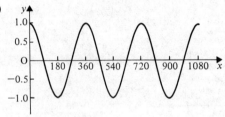

b) $-1 \leqslant \cos x° \leqslant 1$

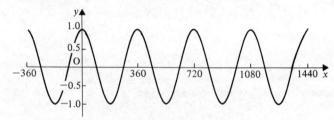

13.

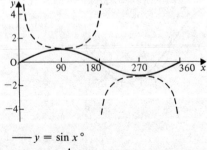

—— $y = \sin x°$

--- $y = \dfrac{1}{\sin x°}$

Exercise 16h   Page 389

1.

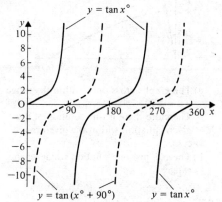

——— $y = \tan x°$
- - - $y = \tan(x° + 90°)$
a) $y = \tan(x + 90)°$
b) $y = \tan(x - 90)°$ is the same graph
as (a)
$y = \tan(x + 180)°$ is the same graph
as $y = \tan x°$

2.

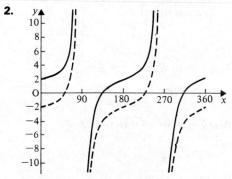

a) $y = \tan x° + 2$ (solid line)
b) $y = \tan x° - 2$ (broken line)

3.

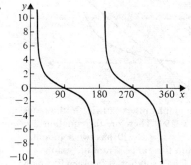

4.

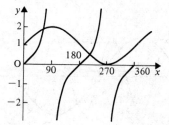

The graphs intersect twice at $x = 62$ and 208

5.

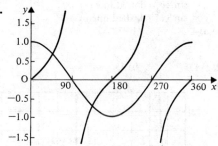

The graphs interesect twice at $x = 38$
and $x = 142$

6. A($0,2$), B($90, 1$), C($180, 0$), D($270, 1$),
E($360, 2$)

7. a) Reflection in the x-axis; $f(x) = -\sin x°$
b) Reflection in x-axis + translation of
1 unit ‖ to y-axis; $f(x) = 1 - \sin x°$
c) Reducing to $\frac{1}{2}$ its original width;
$f(x) = \sin 2x°$

8. a) Translation parallel to the y-axis through
2 units;
$f(x) = \cos x° - 2$
b) Reducing to $\frac{1}{3}$ of its original width;
$f(x) = \cos 3x°$
c) Reflection in the x-axis; $f(x) = -\cos x°$

9. a)

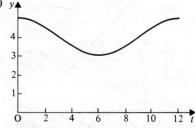

b) When $4 < t < 8$
c) 4.77 h, i.e. 4 hr. 46 min

10. a) 0, 180, 360   b) 90, 270

11.

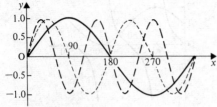

$y = \sin x°$ (solid line)
$y = \sin 2x°$ (dotted line)
$y = \sin 3x°$ (dashed line)
a) 4   b) 7

12. a) 135   b) 45

13.

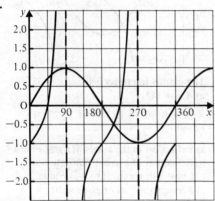

Between 0 and 180 the graphs cross once
at a value between $x = 60$ and $x = 70$.

14.

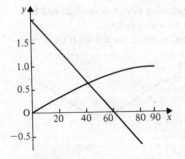

The graphs intersect between $x = 30$
and $x = 50$, showing that the equation
$60 - x = 30 \sin x°$ has one solution
within the range $0 \leqslant x \leqslant 90$

15.

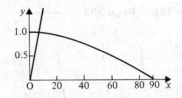

a) The graphs cross once within the range
$0 \leqslant x \leqslant 90$.
Therefore there is one solution of the
given equation within the given range.
5.97

b) There is just one solution whatever the
range.

16.

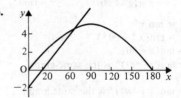

The graphs intersect for a value of x
between 60 and 70.
65

17. a) $y = \cos x°$ and $y = \dfrac{x}{50} - \dfrac{2}{5}$

b) $x + 50 \sin x° = 50$

18. a) $y = 30 \sin x°$ and $y = 20 - 2x$
b) $(x - 1)^2 = 14 \tan x°$

19.

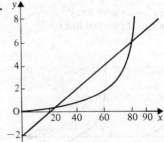

The graphs intersect twice in the range
$0 \leqslant x \leqslant 90$. Therefore the equation
$10 \tan x° = x - 20$ has two solutions
within this range. From the graph
the larger solution is between 75 and 85.

20.

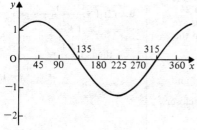

a) -1.41 b) 1.41

21. a) i) $\pi r^2 \times \dfrac{x}{360}$ ii) $\frac{1}{2}r^2 \sin x°$

iii) $\frac{1}{2}r^2\left(\dfrac{\pi x}{180} - \sin x°\right)$

d)

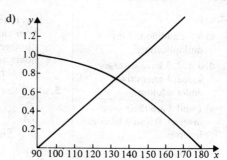

The graphs intersect for a value of x between 130 and 140.

e) 132

CHAPTER 17

Exercise 17a   Page 395

1. a) 3, 2, 2   b) 2
2. 26
3. a) 50   b) 0.009
4. Yes, e.g. $3 \times 2 \times 16$
5. 3.5×10^{-6}
6. a) 5   b) $\frac{1}{125}$ c) 2
7. $-\frac{1}{2}$

8. a) 0.2   b) 48
9. £60
10. b, c, d, e, f
11. a) $3\sqrt{2}$ b) 6   c) $\frac{1}{2}\sqrt{2}$
12. £20.70

13. If the weight of one coin is w grams, then $907.15 \leqslant 100w < 907.25$ so the weight of one coin is given by $9.0715 \leqslant w < 9.0725$ which the machine gives as 9.1 grams

Exercise 17b   Page 396

1. £19.66
2. 262.44 g
3. 8
4. a) $0.1\dot{4}285\dot{7}$ b) $\frac{3}{11}$
5. 19.2 cm² − 20.9 cm²
6. 0.336

7. 14
8. 11.4% to 3 s.f.
9. a) 28.3 km/h   b) 27.9 km/h
c) How the measured distance and times have been rounded.

10. 24.8 s to 3 s.f.
11. £49
12. Rounded down, because $0.043\,478\,2 \times 23 = 0.999\,998\,6$ which is less than 1.

Exercise 17c   Page 397

For many of the questions in this exercise there is no 'right' answer and for others, giving a full answer would destroy the purpose of the question. The answers that are given are intended as pointers to what may be possible.

1. a) e.g. $3 + 3 + 2 + 2$
c) Not true; e.g. the largest possible number that can be made is $3 \times 3 \times 3 \times 3$, i.e. 81.

2. a) True, e.g. three consecutive numbers must contain at least one even number so their product is even.

b) Not true, e.g. $2 + 3 + 4$ is not divisible by 2.
c) True, proof by contradiction similar to that given for $\sqrt{2}$ on p. **299**.

4. a) 0, 1, 2, 3

  c) 0 for addition, 1 for multiplication

  d) 0, 1, 2, 3 have inverses 0, 3, 2, 1 respectively under addition

  e) 1 and 3 are their own inverses, 0 and 2 have no inverses

g) e.g. time given by a 24 hour clock: minutes are $\text{numbers}_{\text{modulo } 60}$ and the hours and $\text{numbers}_{\text{modulo } 24}$.

5. d) $\sqrt{2}$ lies between 1.4 and $\dfrac{2}{1.4}$ so the mean is closer to $\sqrt{2}$ than either.

6. c) If $1 + \cfrac{1}{1 + \cfrac{1}{1 + \dots}} = x$,

then $1 + \dfrac{1}{x} = x$

$\Rightarrow x^2 - x - 1 = 0$

$\Rightarrow x = \dfrac{1 + \sqrt{5}}{2}$

Exercise 17d   Page 399

1. a) 0.6   b) 0.65

  c) $\sqrt{7} - 2$

2. a) 7   b) 3   c) 1

3. a) $3ab(a - 2b)$

  b) $(2x - 5)(3x + 7)$

4. a) $\dfrac{x}{2(x-2)}$ b) $\dfrac{x}{y}$ c) a^2

  d) $\dfrac{x - 18}{x - 5}$

  e) $\dfrac{5(x+1)}{(2x+1)(2-x)}$

5. a) $\dfrac{2^n - 1}{2^n}$ b) 1

6. a) $t = \pm \sqrt{\dfrac{2v}{g}}$

  b) $A = \dfrac{C^2}{4\pi}$

7. $(-14, -11)$

8. a) 8 days

  b) 14 men take a little under 3 days

9. a) i) 5

    ii) Printout is 9 which is wrong; the first value must be less than the cube root for the flow chart to work.

  b) $x^2 + x =$ (a value between 0.9 and 1.1), one decimal place

10. a) $13x^5$ b) -4

11. a) $a = \dfrac{5.12}{t^2}$

  b) 8 m/s²

  c) 0: the block floats

12. a) $\dfrac{3600}{x}$ b) $\dfrac{3600}{x - 24}$

  c) $\dfrac{3600}{x - 24} - \dfrac{3600}{x} = 5;\ 144$

13. a) $(x - \frac{7}{2})^2 - \frac{41}{4}$

  b) $-\frac{41}{4}$

  c)

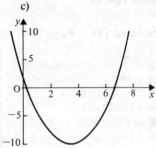

Exercise 17e   Page 402

1. a) $y = 4x - 6$

  c) $\frac{1}{2}$

  d) $\left(\frac{13}{7}, \frac{10}{7}\right)$

2. (required region is shaded)

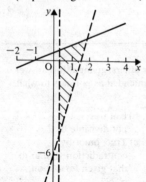

3.

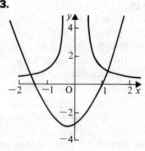

  c) 1.15, -1.58;

    $x^2(x - 1)(2x + 3) = 1$

4. a) 3.5 mins

  b) 10 km/h/min

  c) 7.5 km

5. a)

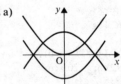

  b)

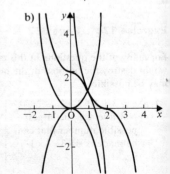

6. a) 6

   b) 2 cm

   c) $V = 4x(6-x)(8-x)$

   d) 194 cm^3

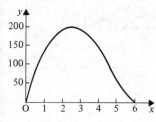

7. a) $v \propto \dfrac{1}{p}$ **b)** 1.7

8. b) 2.12 p.m.

   d) 1.50 p.m.

9.

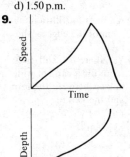

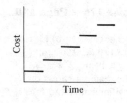

10. b) 8 %   **c)** 8 % p.a.

Exercise 17f   Page 404

For many of the questions in this exercise there is no 'right' answer and for others, giving a full answer would destroy the purpose of the question. The answers that are given are intended as pointers to what may be possible.

2. a) 3, 5, 8, 13, 21

   b) 0.5, 0.6667, 0.6, 0.625,
      0.6154, 0.6190, 0.6176,
      0.6182

   c) they all approach the
      same limit

3. A number with $2n$ digits, the first $n-1$ of which are 9, the next is 8, the next $n-1$ are zero and the last is 1.

4. c) If the three original numbers are a, b, c, then $x = 222(a+b+c)$.

6. a) 14   **b)** -5.4

   c) $4p + 4q + 2r = 2p + 4q + 4r$ only if $p = r$

   d) $r = 1$ or $p = 0$

7. a) 5   **b)** 18, 221

   c) because
      $(a \bullet b) \bullet c \neq a \bullet (b \bullet c)$

8. a) i) yes   **ii)** no

   b) i) yes   **ii)** yes

   c) i) yes   **ii)** yes

   iii) no   **iv)** no

   d) all except division

9. a) i) 5, -2.25, $-1.69\ldots$,
      $-1.628\ldots$, $-1.619\ldots$

   ii) u_2 cannot be found because it is not possible to divide by zero

   b) The answer is (i)

   c) $x^2 + x - 1 = 0$; the solutions are $x = 0.618$ and $x = -1.618$ to 3 s.f.

The iteration formula will not give the positive root however close the first approximation, e.g. even with $u_1 = 0.618$, the sequence diverges. A graphical interpretation, plotting $y = x$ and $y = \dfrac{2x-1}{1-x}$ shows the divergence.

10. c) $a = 4, b = 11$

Exercise 17g   Page 406

1. a) no, corresponding angles are not known to be equal

   b) yes, angles equal and sides proportional

   c) yes, angles equal and sides proportional

   d) yes, angles equal

2. a) 134 cm^3 **b)** 13.4 cm

   c) D

3. a) 16″   **b)** 53.1 °

   c) 26.6″

4. a) $(-2, 4, 0)$, $(-2, 0, 3)$, $(-2, 4, 3)$, $(2, 0, 3)$

   b) 6.40 units

5. a) prism with triangular cross-section

   b) 108 cm^2 **c)** 48 cm^3

   d) 10.6 cm, 9.43 cm

   e) 8.54 cm

6. 2.74 km

7. 90, 450

8. a) $\begin{pmatrix} 0 & -2 \\ 2 & 0 \end{pmatrix}$

   b) $n = 4, m = -4$

9. a) 3.5 m   **b)** 2.55 m^2

   c) 10 400 cm^3

10. a) 60 °   **b)** 30 °

   c) 60 °

11. a) 11.5 cm   **b)** 60.5 °

   c) 68.2 °

14. 5.57 cm

Exercise 17h   Page 410

1. a) 3.46 cm   b) 158 cm²

2. b) 3.19 p.m., 9.06 a.m.
c) 3 h 19 m

3. The diagram shows the positions of A and P as the lorry turns.

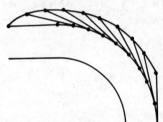

b) A comes to within about 1.7 m of the edge of the road.

c) Yes, there is insufficient room for a car 2 m wide to pass between the lorry and the kerb.

4. b) $\begin{pmatrix} 0 & -\frac{1}{3} \\ \frac{1}{3} & 0 \end{pmatrix}$

5. a) $\frac{8}{5}$ b) 8 cm
c) 53°   e) $\frac{4}{5}$

6. c) 2.8 cm

7. a)

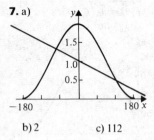

b) 2   c) 112

Exercise 17i   Page 413

For many of the questions in this exercise there is no 'right' answer and for others, giving a full answer would destroy the purpose of the question. The answers that are given are intended as pointers to what may be possible.

1. a) 2.83 m   b) 4.12 m

2. a)

b) e.g.

4. a) i) $(2n-1)^2 = 4n^2 - 4n + 1$
$= (2n^2 - 2n)$
$+ (2n^2 - 2n + 1)$
ii) e.g. $4 + 5 = 3^2$,
$12 + 13 = 5^2$ where
3, 4, 5 and 5, 12, 13 are
sides of right-angled
triangles.
b) $2n^2 = (n^2 + 1) + (n^2 - 1)$;
$(n^2 + 1)^2 = (n^2 - 1)^2 + 4n^2$
so $(n^2 + 1)$, $(n^2 - 1)$,
$2n$ are the sides of a
right-angled triangle.

6. a) 91 in the main diagonal, 67 elsewhere

7. The area of any shape drawn on the hypotenuse is equal to the sum of the areas of similar shapes drawn on the other two sides.

Exercise 17j   Page 415

1. a) 600   b) i) $\frac{77}{600}$ ii) $\frac{1}{2}$

2. a) 80 %   b) 33.6 %

3. a) $\frac{1}{216}$, i.e. 0.005
b) i) $\frac{5}{18}$, i.e. 0.278
ii) $\frac{1}{6}$, i.e. 0.167

c) 500

4. a) $\frac{1}{4}$ b) $\frac{1}{17}$ c) $\frac{1}{5525}$

5. a) $\frac{1}{2}$ b) $\frac{4}{27}$ c) $\frac{25}{216}$
d) $\frac{16}{25}$
e) about 60

6. a) 13 minutes
b) 17 minutes

7. a) $x + y \leqslant 200, y \geqslant 50,$
  $x \geqslant 10, y \geqslant 2x$

b)

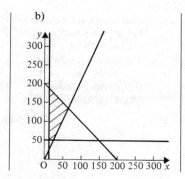

c) $P = 300x + 200y,$
  134 eaters, 66 cookers
8. a) 22 minutes

Exercise 17k   Page 417

1. a) 100
  b) e.g. the seeds did not
    germinate
  c)

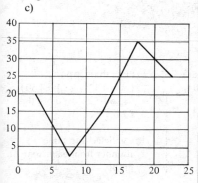

  d) The range of the second
    batch is greater and more
    of them germinated. The
    modes are the same.

2. The median for the first
  batch is about 1.5 cm higher
  than the median for the
  second batch. The
  interquartile range for the
  first batch is about 2 cm
  bigger than the interquartile
  range for the second batch.
  The values indicate greater
  variability in the heights of
  the first batch than the
  second batch and, on the
  whole, biggest tomatoes.

3. a)

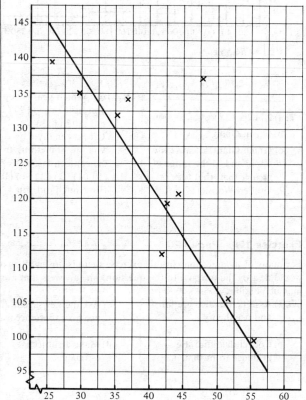

m.p.g.

  b) 137 m.p.h.
  c) 25 m.p.g. ± 5 m.p.g. approx.

4. a) £ 399, £ 108.50

c) £ 126, about £ 133

d) e.g. part-timers

e) Interquartile range as this discounts some of the part-time earnings and all of the small number of high wages. It also gives the impression of smaller differentials.

f) The median, as the large number of wages in the first group does not pull this down as much as the mean.

g) e.g. Assuming wages in the first group are for part-time work, leave these out of the calculation to give the mean of wages for full-time work.

5. b)

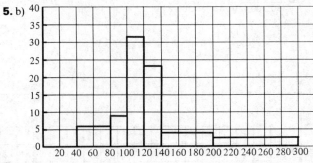

☐ = 5 apples

c) 130.8 g; because we assume that the halfway value is the average value in each group.

6. 289

7. a) 2.71 kg, 1.18 kg

b) Green Giant

c) Green Giant, because the upper end of the range is greater than that for Golden Wonder.

8. a) e.g. Which year group are you in? (7) (8) (9) (10) (11) (12) (13)
On how many days did you buy something from the canteen last week?
(5) (4) (3) (2) (1) (0)
How much did you

(less than 50 p)
(50 p–£1)   (£1–£1.50)
(£1.50–£2)   (more than £2)

b) e.g. Select the same number from each year group.

Exercise 17I   Page 420 ───

For many of the questions in this exercise there is no 'right' answer and for others, giving a full answer would destroy the purpose of the question. The answers that are given are intended as pointers to what may be possible.

3. a) Assume the dice are fair and use theory.

b) Collect data and use evidence from that.

c) Ask the newsagent and use his experience.

d) Make a subjective estimate.

5. a) e.g. Mean and standard deviation for number of letters per word, number of words per sentence, paragraph length.

$$\sin x = \sin(180 - x).$$
$$\cos x = -\cos(180 - x).$$

$$b^2 = a^2 + c^2 - 2ac \cos B$$

$$\frac{a}{\sin A} = \frac{b}{\sin B} = \frac{c}{\sin C}.$$

$$\frac{a}{\sin A} = \frac{b}{\sin B}.$$